FOR VALOUR
The Air VCs

FOR VALOUR

The Air VCs

by
CHAZ BOWYER

CAXTON EDITIONS

This edition published 2002 by
Caxton Editions an imprint of
The Caxton Publishing Group

Copyright © 1992 Grub Street, London
Text copyright © Chaz Bowyer

First published by William Kimber and Co Ltd

A catalogue record for this book is available from the British Library

ISBN 1 84067 2404

Typeset by Watford Typesetters

Printed and bound in Great Britain by
Creative Print & Design Wales (Ebbw Vale)

'Born of the sun they travelled a short while towards the sun,
And left the vivid air signed with their honour.'

STEPHEN SPENDER

'History (is) the legacy of heroes – the memory of a great name,
and the inheritance of a great example . . .'

BEACONSFIELD

Contents

PART ONE
1914 – 1918

PART TWO
1939 – 1945

Contents

Illustrations

PART ONE
1914 – 1918

PART TWO
1939 – 1945

Acknowledgements

During the many years of unhurried research into the lives of every air VC I have been most privileged to receive encouraging and generous help from, literally, hundreds of individuals, organisations, and institutions. To list here each and every one would, I feel, appear pretentious and, certainly, wearying for the reader. Nevertheless, I am highly conscious that without such selfless aid and splendid backing my self-imposed task must have been infinitely more difficult to resolve. To each therefore is owed a special debt of personal gratitude, heartfelt. I can only hope they will understand if, instead of compiling a somewhat mountainous tabulation here of names and titles, I simply refer in detail to those helpers directly related to the air VCs themselves.

Of the actual holders of the Victoria Cross my especial thanks go to the following who so very kindly responded to my many requests for information, confirmation, photographs and other material aid. Group Captain G. L. Cheshire VC DSO DFC; Air Commodore Sir Hughie I. Edwards VC KCMG CB DSO OBE DFC; the late Group Captain G. S. M. Insall VC MC; the late Flight Lieutenant A. Jerrard VC; Wing Commander R. A. B. Learoyd VC; Flight Lieutenant W. Reid VC; Group Captain L. H. Trent VC DFC; Air Commodore F. M. F. West VC CBE MC.

To the following close relatives of other air VCs I owe a particular debt for permitting a complete stranger to invade their privacy, and for unconditional direct help and constant encouragement; listed alphabetically. Dr A. L. Aaron; Mrs L. B. Anderson; Mrs P. Armstrong; the late Mrs M. E. Bazalgette; Captain L. Bell-Davies, RN; Mrs E. M. Gibson; Mrs S. Glenny; Flight Lieutenant R. M. Gray, RAF Retd; Mrs E. Gunn; the late A. J. Insall; Mrs K. Hair; Mrs J. L. Hannah; Lt-Colonel T. M. Hawker MC; P. J. Liddell, Esq; Wing Commander F. E. Lord AFC RAF Retd; Mrs C. Maidment; C. Manser, Esq; R. E. McNamara MA, Esq; R. Mottershead, Esq; Dr L. C. Newton; Air Commodore D. G. F. Palmer OBE RAF; the late Mrs L. Rhodes-Moorhouse; J. Thompson, Esq; Mrs N. Trigg; Mrs J. Voysey; W. H. Ward, Esq; J. D. Welby, Esq.

Whilst acknowledging the invaluable help received from all such sources, I would emphasise that any error of fact or omission within my text is solely my responsibility. Also, while extensive use of official documentation was made, and splendid help received from many official, sources, my text should not be misconstrued as necessarily reflecting official opinion or judgment. Indeed, I would welcome correction or additional relevant facts from any source, providing these derive from unquestionably authentic sources, with the ultimate objective of ensuring that posterity inherits a true and accurate account of each man described herein.

CHAZ BOWYER
Norwich, 1978

FOR VALOUR

The Air VCs

Introduction

Within the following pages the reader will find, chronicled briefly, the lives of fifty-one men. All have at least one achievement in common – the award of a Victoria Cross for supreme valour in aerial warfare. Should the reader seek a further facet in common, then surely it is contained in the much-abused military phrase 'Devotion to Duty'. The Serviceman's conception of his duty has changed very little in essence over the many centuries of man's attempts to commit genocide in war after war. Simply, he accepts a position of responsibility from his superiors in rank, and with that responsibility a code of duty, both written and unwritten. Implicit in this code is an unceasing need for sacrifice in many things, and, if necessary, the ultimate self-sacrifice; laying down his life in order to further the cause of his duty. Of the fifty-one men described herein, twenty-five gave their lives as a direct result of the action(s) which brought them the highest gallantry award. Six others were subsequently killed in action, still pursuing their duty as they understood and recognised it. Of the remainder – at the time of writing – only eight are still living.

Courage has no succinct class, race or creed; it is not the prerogative of any particular species of the human race. Thus, it should be well marked that sixteen of these men were not British-born, but came willingly from Commonwealth countries to fight for the British cause. Whatever their background, all fought for an ideal with no jingoistic overlays – freedom from oppression and dictatorial cruelties. It is a lamentable irony that today, only decades after their superb selflessness, many of their homelands are in direct contention with each other.

Another post-bellum aspect has been the peculiar form of Service bureaucracy which quibbles over 'correct' parent Service of certain air VCs when listing their names in official documents or records. I have no desire to delve into the merits or otherwise of such an argument, and for the purpose of this work I have considered only the prime factor; that each man described here received his award for an act or acts of the highest valour in aerial warfare. The 'right' to claim vicarious honours is of minute importance when set against such a backcloth of uncommon courage.

The purpose of my book is two-fold. Primarily I have set out to establish the truth; a term I personally interpret as meaning historical fact. The events described in the text are factual, cross-checked scrupulously with contemporary participants, first-hand witnesses, authentic documentation and records, and expanded by information and testimonies (where applicable) from former 'enemy' records and opponents. Discerning readers will quickly note many discrepancies between the actual events leading to the VC award as described here, and the official award citations in certain individual cases. If such contemporary 'evidence' is now in doubt, or even transparently incorrect, it has not been my intention simply to decry; merely to establish facts. It must be appreciated that nearly all original official citations were compiled virtually third- or fourth-hand by well-intentioned authors in officialdom, working solely from data supplied and known at the time. Such contemporary assessments were therefore necessarily limited in scope, notwithstanding the good faith and high intention which went into compilation. Other contemporary facets usually unconsidered by those with blind faith in the 'official' printed word include human failings, the near-unique comradeship and community spirit of all air crews, and not least individual attitudes to such matters at the times in question. The truth is a brutal taskmaster, but without it history and the recording of history for posterity are pointless.

Part of the intention of this book is to be a reference source for future historians requiring reliable information about the air VCs. With this uppermost in mind therefore, I have presented in each case a 'full' biography, rather than merely concentrated on the action(s) which led to each man's award. Inevitably perhaps this deliberate form of text description may contrast dully with many past, highly dramatic accounts published about certain individual VCs, but if I felt a need for a 'defence' in adopting a strictly 'non-journalistic' vein of description, it would be simply to quote a past historian, Thucydides; 'Very likely the strictly historical character of my narrative may be disappointing to the ear. But if he who desires to have before his eyes a true picture of the events which have happened . . . shall pronounce what I have written to be useful, then I shall be satisfied.'* Moreover, my researches, which have included interviews and private correspondence with surviving air VCs, relatives and close friends of other VCs, have convinced me that such would be their preference *if* their stories have to be told.

The blunt part-cynical Service cliché, 'Old men make wars, but young men have to fight them' is probably nowhere better illustrated than in the context of the air VCs. Of the fifty-one men so honoured, the oldest (at the date of the action/award) was thirty-four years of age;

* *Peloponnesian War*, Vol I. 400 BC.

the youngest barely eighteen. All but six were in their early twenties, the average overall age being little more than twenty-four. All received their awards in an era when any man below the age of twenty-one years was legally termed an 'Infant' . . . Yet, in the context of mortal combat, age has always been relative. Young men, hardly out of school, 'aged' quickly in wartime conditions where a few months, weeks, even days of constant witness to death in some of its more horrifying forms swiftly dispelled all youthful notions of glamour or glory, and compressed the normally more leisurely transit from adolescent to adult into a fraction of its expected time span. Perhaps only the boundless resiliency of youth enabled most to survive the mental and physical ordeal, but each had lost their 'innocence' of life in a cruel and often savage manner, never to regain it.

A final note of explanation is probably necessary for the chosen sequence of subjects. Each chapter is in chronological sequence of dates of VC actions, rather than by citation award dates, except in the few cases where the award was made for a period of consistent gallantry rather than any specific occasion. In the latter case the date of the *London Gazette* citation has been inserted in the overall sequence accordingly. Essentially these are fifty-one entirely separate stories and, be it remembered always, each is a description of an 'ordinary' human being. None were supermen, endowed with immortal god-like properties; but if the flesh was all too humanly weak, the spirit of each was truly magnificent.

Since the original publication of this volume in 1978, time has claimed three more air VCs – Hughie Edwards, Leonard Trent and Freddie West – leaving (at this moment of writing) merely five survivors of the 51 airmen ever awarded a Victoria Cross. It should also be remembered that these 51 airmen thus honoured are representatives of possibly many more airmen whose actions during their ultimate hours of life were unwitnessed in aircraft which 'failed to return' from operations. As with the nation's Unknown Warrior, their identities and fates are 'known only to God'.

Chaz Bowyer
Norwich, 1992

Prologue

'The most democratic and at the same time the most exclusive of all orders of chivalry – the most enviable order of the Victoria Cross.' Thus was the newly-introduced award described by the Prince of Wales, later HM King Edward VII. Instituted by a Royal Warrant dated 29 January 1856, the Victoria Cross was not, however, an Order, as its founder Queen Victoria was at pains to point out. Its recipients were to bear no special privileges of knighthood, Companionage, banners or robes. Instead it was intended simply as a decoration – the highest possible to attain, and taking precedence over all other awards and honours – which '. . . should be highly prized and eagerly sought after by the officers and men of our Naval and Military Services', as Queen Victoria herself expressed it. Styled and designated the 'Victoria Cross', it was to be a Cross Patee in bronze, bearing the Royal Crest in its centre, surmounting a scroll bearing the inscription 'For Valour'. Initially, the Cross was to be suspended on a royal blue ribbon for Naval personnel, and a red ribbon for Army recipients; but a further Royal Warrant, dated 22 May 1920, decreed that henceforth all Crosses would be hung from a plain red ribbon, irrespective of the recipient's parent Service.

Originally conceived as an award for all ranks of the Navy and Army who, in the presence of an enemy, should have 'performed some signal act of valour or devotion to their country'; in time the conditions of award and scope for receipt were extended to include virtually every possible citizen, including civilians and women. From its inception the actual Cross was deliberately intended to be intrinsically 'worthless', without rich gems or precious metals, but simply a scrap of bronze. Its true worth lay in its associations; an honour so rare that it was impossible to 'buy' or 'earn' in the manner of several other high awards. Though no specific comment on the Cross's intrinsic lack of value was made in its inauguration warrant, this was the theory behind its creation; exemplified in spirit by a clause which stated that 'neither rank, nor long service, nor wounds, nor any other circumstance or condition whatsoever, save the merit of conspicuous bravery' should 'establish a sufficient claim to the honour.' This condition thereby placed 'all persons on a perfectly equal footing in relation to eligibility for the decoration' – the nearest possible completely democratic award ever created within the British Empire.

The original warrant of 1856 has since been modified and extended considerably in its provisions. In 1902, for example, King Edward VII approved the principle of posthumous awards of the Cross; while the lengthy warrant of May 1920 included the keynote provision that the Cross '. . . shall only be awarded for most conspicuous bravery or some daring or pre-eminent act of valour or self-sacrifice or extreme devotion to duty in the presence of the enemy.' The Cross, in size little more than an inch square, was originally cast from metal of the cannons captured from the Russians at Sebastopol in the Crimean War, but in more recent years was made from gunmetal supplied by the Royal Mint; fashioned always by the London firm of Messrs Hancock, who had made the very first Victoria Cross.

Today the Victoria Cross remains the supreme British award, taking absolute precedence over all other awards and decorations. In the 122 years of its existence, 1,350 awards have been made by the British Sovereign. Of these, 633 were won in the 1914–18 war, and 182 in the 1939–45 war. These totals include three awards of a Bar to the VC – 'double VCs'. At the time of writing (1976), only some 200 holders of the Victoria Cross are still alive – an exclusive company of superlative courage, whose 'membership' has no barriers of race, rank, or creed. Privilege of birth or nation have no significance; all are perfectly equal of standing, having in common received the most coveted Victoria Cross – For Valour.

PART ONE

1914-1918

1. William Barnard Rhodes Moorhouse

Among the first Englishmen to settle in New Zealand was William Barnard Rhodes (1807–1878), who first set foot in the untamed country in July 1836, and returned three years later to take up permanent residence and set himself up in business. One of four brothers from the family of fourteen children of a Yorkshire tenant farmer, William Rhodes (1781–1869), William was soon joined by his three brothers, Robert Heaton, George, and Joseph Rhodes; the four pioneers later became known as the 'Shepherd Kings' of New Zealand, and established themselves (under William's driving energy and direction) as huge property owners of land and leading kings of commerce.

William Barnard, the eldest brother, was twice married, but his only family was a daughter, Mary Ann, by a Maori woman (reputedly a princess), who had been given to Rhodes by her father as a mark of respect and honour. William and his second wife, Sarah Moorhouse, adopted Mary Ann as their daughter-in-marriage, and she grew up in Wellington, idolised by her stern father and stepmother. On the death of her 'father', Mary Ann successfully contested his legal will and became sole heiress to 'upward of three-quarters of a million pounds'. Small in stature, and possessing the fragile beauty of petite appearance, Mary Ann was never lacking for eligible suitors to her hand; but she eventually married Edward Moorhouse, brother of her stepmother, in a sumptuous ceremony in Wellington Cathedral.

Edward and Mary Ann Moorhouse left New Zealand shortly after their marriage and moved to England, where they settled and raised four children; Anne, William Barnard, Mary, and Edward.

'Will' Moorhouse, the second child of the union, and destined to become the first-ever recipient of a Victoria Cross for aerial operations, was born in London on 26 September 1887; a robust, healthy boy with sandy-fair hair and unusually brilliant green eyes. Educated initially at the Golden Parsonage, Hertfordshire and Harrow, young Moorhouse soon gave ample evidence of a dynamic vitality in all things, coupled with an apparently inexhaustible well of physical energy. From his earliest years his one all-consuming passion was for speed and the relatively 'new' invention of the internal combustion engine, and he channelled most of

23

his energies into possessing and racing a succession of motor-cycles and motor cars.

From Harrow he went to Trinity, Cambridge, but always regarded his years at Cambridge as a waste of time, being uninterested in the classics and wholly absorbed in his many engineering projects and schemes. This attitude brought him into conflict with the more conservatively-minded dons on many occasions, but Moorhouse had few inhibitions and continued to follow his own inclinations.

Leaving Cambridge in 1909, he then devoted himself fully to the world of engines; participating in a variety of car races and cross-country rallies, and expanding his interests to include the latest application of the petrol engine – flying. Learning to fly at his own expense, Will began a series of experiments in designing monoplanes and, in 1911, joined forces with James Radley in designing the Radley-Moorhouse monoplane; an Anzani-engined derivant of the Bleriot XI aircraft. By then he had already established himself as a pilot of repute, and his many flights from the old Huntingdon airfield usually attracted several thousands of spectators from surrounding towns and villages; eager witnesses to the 'daring' pilot's skilful demonstrations of the new art of aviation. In 1911 Moorhouse travelled to America and there, piloting a 50hp Gnome-engined Bleriot monoplane, participated in most of the contemporary aerial speed and cross-country race meetings across the USA, and collected several thousand dollars in prize money for his successes. At a San Francisco meeting he not only won the Harbor Prize of roughly £1,000, but became the first man to fly through the archways of the Golden Gate bridge.

Selling the Bleriot to Earle Remington in Los Angeles, Moorhouse then returned to England, where he continued his quest for speed and adventure by taking part in most of the increasingly popular flying meetings in Britain, including the first Aerial Derby at Hendon in June 1912 in which he earned third placing. By then he had gained his Royal Aero Club Certificate, No 147, which was granted on 17 October 1911, after he completed all the necessary tests, flying a Bleriot monoplane.

The most notable event in 1912 for Moorhouse came with his marriage to Linda B. Morritt, a school-friend of his sister Anne. Their honeymoon was spent almost wholly on a typical Moorhouse project – preparation and achievement of a new record flight across the English Channel! After many days of sundry delays due to weather conditions and other minor frustrations, Moorhouse finally set off from Douai in a Breguet biplane on 28 July; carrying as passengers his wife Linda and a news reporter,

J. H. Ledeboer. After a 130-miles flight the Breguet eventually descended near Bethersden, Kent but crashed on landing, though without injury to its 'crew'. It was the first-ever cross-Channel flight by a pilot carrying two passengers.

Moorhouse's love of fast cars had, in the past, kept him in constant conflict with the police and legal authorities, but 1913 brought more serious consequences. He first suffered relatively serious injuries to the head in a car crash (in which, ironically, he had been merely a passenger in a friend's vehicle); but shortly after was brought into court, charged with the manslaughter of a man killed while leading a horse-drawn farm wagon. Moorhouse had driven safely past the wagon, but (it was alleged) the noise of his engine so disturbed the horse team that they had taken fright, and the man had fallen under the wagon's wheels, sustaining fatal injuries. Despite the patent bias of both judge and jury – motor cars then were generally regarded as playthings of the 'idle rich' – Moorhouse was eventually fined £20 and released.

In the same year, in order to become eligible to inherit his grandfather's considerable estate, Moorhouse legally adopted the additional surname of Rhodes; while later in the year he persuaded his mother to purchase a family home, Parnham House, a splendid example of Elizabethan architecture set in beautiful surroundings in Dorset.

At the turn of the year, while living temporarily in London, Linda Rhodes Moorhouse gave birth to their only son, William Henry, who – in the absence of a doctor – was assisted into the world by his father's own hands. His arrival also heralded the first overt rumblings of anarchy in Europe, where decades of relatively peaceful co-existence between nations were about to erode swiftly, bringing to an abrupt end the complacent and affluent Edwardian era in Britain.

With the outbreak of war between Britain and Germany in August 1914, 'Will' Rhodes Moorhouse volunteered to join the Royal Flying Corps, and was enlisted on 24 August as a Second Lieutenant. His first posting took him to the Aircraft Park at South Farnborough as officer commanding, but he soon agitated for a more active post on operations in France.

His wish was granted early in 1915, and eventually, on 20 March, he joined No 2 Squadron RFC, based at Merville, France. His new unit had been one of the original squadrons despatched to France after war was declared, and on his arrival at Merville was mainly equipped with early examples of the Farnborough-designed BE2 two-seat aircraft.

For the first four weeks on 2 Squadron, Rhodes Moorhouse flew a number of local 'familiarisation' sorties to accustom himself to his aircraft and the adjacent battle area; then joined his squadron comrades on various reconnaissance and bombing sorties across the German trenches.

The BE aircraft he flew, though undeniably safe and stable for pure flying purposes, were by no means ideal vehicles for war operations. Powered usually by a 70hp Renault engine, they could barely achieve a speed of 70 mph at ground level, even with a light loading of two crew men and no armament. When required to carry up to 100lb weight in bombs, it became the usual practice for a pilot to fly without his observer, in order to compensate for the extra war load.

In the late afternoon of 22 April 1915, troops of the French 45th Division, entrenched along the north-eastern sector of the Ypres Salient, saw a sudden bank of yellow-green cloud erupt from the opposing German trenches and, carried by the wind, begin to roll towards them. Within minutes the deadly cloud – poisonous gas – had enveloped the *poilus* and passed, leaving hundreds of dead Frenchmen behind; the first battle of Ypres had commenced. By the 24th German troops had exploited their advantage with a breakthrough of the Allied lines at St Julien, and began bringing up reserve formations to strengthen their advance. Reports from Allied agents indicated German reserves being concentrated around Ghent, and in an attempt to prevent these troops moving easily to the critical battle area, RFC units were called upon for a series of bombing raids against rail communications on the Staden-Cortemarck-Roulers line, and the rail stations at Thielt, Staden, Deynze and Ingelmunster.

Similar objectives were allocated to the First Wing RFC under whose aegis 2 Squadron operated, and four aircraft of the unit were despatched to attack Roubaix, Tourcoing and Courtrai. The latter rail junction was allotted to Rhodes Moorhouse. Leaving Merville airfield at 3.5 pm, piloting BE2b No 687, Rhodes Moorhouse flew without an observer, in deference to the single 100lb bomb suspended beneath his BE's fuselage. Given absolute discretion on what height to bomb his objective, Rhodes Moorhouse stayed at 300 feet as he approached the Courtrai rail junction.

Sweeping low over his target, he released his solitary bomb on the rail line west of Courtrai Station but immediately plunged into a barrage of small arms fire from hundreds of rifles and a machine gun situated in the belfry of the nearby Courtrai Church. One burst tore open Moorhouse's thigh and perforated the fuselage of his aircraft; while slivers of shrapnel from his own bomb pierced the BE's wings and tail in a dozen places.

Shocked and in great pain, Moorhouse could have landed immediately and thus receive medical treatment for his ghastly wound. He chose instead to try to regain the Allied lines, and turned the BE westwards. Descending to about 100 feet in order to gain a fractional increase in speed, Moorhouse ran the terrifying gauntlet of groundfire again, only to be wounded twice more. One bullet slashed open his abdomen, and another hit him in the hand. Losing blood steadily, and fighting increasing dizziness and weakness, Moorhouse continued his flight for some 35 minutes before eventually landing at his unit's airfield, at approximately 4.15 pm.

Lifted gently from his shattered cockpit by three mechanics. Moorhouse insisted on making his report before allowing himself to be moved to the Merville Casualty Clearing Station nearby for medical attention. His BE bore stark evidence of his ordeal, with a total of 95 holes from bullets and shrapnel, and the cockpit floor stained crimson with the pilot's blood.

Throughout that night the medical personnel did everything possible to save Rhodes Moorhouse, but by mid-day on 27 April his life was slowly ebbing away. Knowing instinctively that he had no hope, Moorhouse expressed his wish to be buried in England; then, with his Flight commander and friend Maurice Blake, and Padre C. N. Chavasse close by his hospital cot, Rhodes Moorhouse died just before 2.30 pm.

In accordance with his last wish, his body was taken to England, where his widow and her brother conveyed him to Parnham House. He was then buried in the grounds of his family home, in a small plot of land on the crest of a small hill overlooking the house – the plot on which had hoped at one time to build a cottage for himself, his wife and baby son. The RFC Casualty List dated 27 April 1915 announced his death 'from wounds'; while a posthumous announcement told of his promotion to Lieutenant, back-dated in seniority to 24 April. On 22 May 1915 came the *London Gazette* notification of the award of a posthumous Victoria Cross – the first-ever award of the little bronze cross to an airman.

A little over twenty-five years later there came a tragic 'footnote' to the Rhodes Moorhouse story. His son, William, after joining 601 Squadron, Auxiliary Air Force as a pilot in 1937, was mobilised with his unit on the outbreak of war in September 1939, and soon saw action as a fighter pilot. During the desperate fighting in France in May 1940, Flying Officer 'Willie' Rhodes Moorhouse was one of 601 Squadron's detachment sent to Merville – scene of his father's heroic sortie and death – and within a week had claimed three combat victories. Throughout July and August 1940, 'Willie' continued to fight daily during the legendary Battle of Britain, claiming a further nine possible victories and being awarded a Distinguished Flying Cross for his prowess.

Then, on 6 September 1940, his Hawker Hurricane was seen to dive vertically away from a furious dogfight and plunge straight into the earth, near Tonbridge Kent. His body was recovered and cremated, and the ashes were interred alongside the grave of his father at Parnham.

2. Reginald Alexander John Warneford

'He was one of the most astounding characters I have ever met and was sent to me from Eastchurch with a very indifferent "chit" to the effect that he lacked discipline and was as wild as a hawk . . . here was a case of a man who knew absolutely no fear, and my problem was to keep him alive as long as possible and use him to do the maximum damage to the Germans.' The speaker was the late Air Chief Marshal Sir Arthur Longmore*, while the 'wild hawk' he referred to was a newly-commissioned Flight Sub-lieutenant in the Royal Naval Air Service, Reginald Warneford. In a tragically brief fighting career spanning just five weeks, Warneford was to gain the highest military honours of Britain and France for an exploit which brought him international fame.

Born at Darjeeling, Bengal, on 15 October 1891, he was the son of R. H. W. Warneford, a civil engineer employed on the Cooch Behar railway in India. Brought to England as a small boy, Warneford's early education came from Stratford-upon-Avon Grammar school and, when his family returned to India, the English College at Simla. At the age of thirteen he was apprenticed to the Merchant Marine, eventually joining the India Steam Navigation Company, and on the outbreak of the European war in August 1914 was in Canada awaiting return passage to India. His immediate reaction to the news that Britain was at war with Germany was to sail to England, where he voluntarily enlisted in the 2nd Sportsmen's Battalion.

Within a month of donning Army uniform he applied for transfer to the RNAS as a potential pilot. Undergoing elementary flying instruction at Hendon under the tutelage of the renowned Warren Merriam, and advanced training at Upavon, Warneford was granted his Royal Aero Club Certificate No 1098 on 25 February 1915. His probationary commission as a Flight Sub-lieutenant, RNAS was then confirmed with effective seniority dating from 10 February. His first posting was to 2 Wing, RNAS at Eastchurch, Isle of Sheppey, where his unit commander, E. L. Gerrard, soon found him to be something of a 'problem child'. Unquestionably brave, Warneford possessed a firm streak of individualism which did not take readily to routine or mundane discipline. Nevertheless, Gerrard recognised Warneford's obvious potential as a fighting airman and arranged for him to join an operational unit in France.

* *From Sea to Sky*; Geoffrey Bles, 1946

Accordingly, on 7 May 1915, Warneford reported to 1 Wing, RNAS, at Furnes airfield, near Dunkirk; where his new commander, Arthur Longmore, warned him of his previous 'unsavoury' reputation but assured him that he would be judged solely on his record with 1 Wing. That same evening Warneford seriously damaged one of the squadron's few Talbot motor tenders by running it into a ditch! The patient Longmore gave him just one more chance to redeem himself or be sent back to England.

Next day, piloting a Voisin two-seater, Warneford flew a patrol of the Zeebrugge-Ostend area and spotted a German reconnaissance aircraft over Ostend. Characteristically, Warneford immediately set off in pursuit of the German machine, and continued to harass it until the German crew landed back at their own aerodrome.

During the following weeks Warneford's restless aggressiveness was exemplified in a series of sorties he undertook, bombing German troop and gun positions, and attacking any German aircraft encountered. Longmore instinctively felt that here was a man who must be killed in action sooner or later; a 'free spirit' who needed free rein. Accordingly, Longmore gave Warneford a roving commission, and obtained a Morane Saulnier monoplane fitted with a machine gun on its forward fuselage for the young pilot's exclusive use. This gun installation – unsynchronised, and firing through the propeller arc, with only steel deflector wedges on the propeller to prevent him destroying the blades – was one of the earliest examples to be used by British airmen.

On 17 May Warneford, piloting a Nieuport two-seater with Leading Mechanic G. E. Meddis as his observer, joined with Lieutenant Spenser D. A. Grey in an anti-Zeppelin patrol along the Belgian coastal strip. Both pilots soon sighted the German airship LZ39, one of three setting out to raid England. Grey and Warneford closed with the giant airship and raked it from below with machine gun fire, but the airship commander immediately jettisoned ballast and the LZ39 rose quickly out of range of its attackers. Further sorties over the German lines by Warneford soon produced a crop of minor damage to his 'exclusive' Morane aircraft, and Longmore allocated him a second, 'standby', Morane Saulnier Type L monoplane, No 3253 for use when the other machine was being repaired.

Operating from Belgian bases, the German rigid airships – collectively known as Zeppelins to the British public – were a priority target for RNAS units at that time. Late in the evening of 6 June 1915, Arthur Longmore received a direct message from the Admiralty in London, advising him of three German airships which had just raided England

and were now returning to base. Immediately Longmore detailed two
Henry Farman aircraft, piloted by John P. Wilson and John S. Mills,
to bomb the airship sheds at Evere; and Lieutenant Rose and Warneford,
in Moranes, to attempt an air interception. The latter pair, if unable to
find their giant targets in the air, were to bomb airship sheds at Berchem
St Agathe as a last resort.

Warneford had Morane Saulnier Type L 3253 loaded with six 20lb
Hales bombs, strapped under the fuselage, and eventually took off from
Furnes at 1 am on 7 June. As he flew over Dixmude only minutes later
he spotted one airship, apparently over Ostend, and set off in pursuit.
After some forty-five minutes flying he finally caught up with the airship
near Bruges and quickly came under fire from the airship's defensive
machine guns, whereupon Warneford banked away and attempted to
gain height for an attack. His prey was the LZ37, an Army airship
commanded by Oberleutnant von der Haegen, with a crew strength of
28 officers and men. With two companion ships, LZ38 and LZ39, von
der Haegen had set out to bomb England, but weather conditions finally
forced all three to abort their mission and return without crossing the
English coast. The Admiralty message to Longmore unwittingly referred
to the raid that night flown by a German naval airship; thus it was by
pure chance that 1 Wing RNAS's aircraft discovered the LZ37.

As Warneford's Morane wheeled away from his initial approach the
airship commander turned the nose of his vessel towards the attacker,
offering combat. For the next twenty minutes the 'contest' continued,
with the German gunners attempting to destroy the hovering Morane,
while Warneford tried to get above his target and use his bombs – his
only armament. Then, apparently losing interest in the tiny aeroplane,
von der Haegen resumed his previous flight path towards his base
airfield, Berchem St Agathe.

By then Warneford had reached a height of 11,000 feet and, switching
off his engine, he started a diving attack from above. Closing to within
150 feet over the airship, Warneford started to release his bombs one by
one, running in from the stern area and traversing the complete length of
the giant objective. At first no effect was seen, but as the sixth and last
bomb left the crude bomb 'rack' of the Morane, an explosion ripped
across the forward section of LZ37. Within seconds the leviathan broke
its back and a geyser-like eruption of red and yellow flames shot up from
the fracture. The rapidly expanding volume of released gas tossed the
tiny Morane over on its back and threw it upwards, inverted, for some
200 feet.

Disintegrating in an awesome cascade of blazing fabric and framework, the doomed LZ37 fell over 6,000 feet in seven seconds and crashed across a convent, Le Grand Beguinage de Sainte Elisabeth, in the Mont St Armand suburb of Ghent. Before the burning hulk reached the ground, its forward gondola car with the airship's coxswain, Alfred Mühler, inside fell away and crashed through the convent roof, discharging Mühler, the sole surviving crew member, onto a bed, virtually unharmed. As the shattered remains of the airship settled onto the convent it killed two nuns, a man and one child, apart from seriously injuring others.

High above Warneford was still struggling to regain control of his wildly pitching aircraft, but as the Morane fell into a nose dive he finally received response to the controls, though his engine had now stopped. With no alternative Warneford was forced to land in enemy-occupied territory, and accomplished this safely in a field adjoining a farmhouse. On inspection of the engine he discovered a separated joint in the petrol feed line to the pump from the rear fuel tank. Effecting a hasty repair after some 35 minutes' work, Warneford finally managed to restart the engine and took off, heading south-west through thick fog and mist. Unable to find his bearings, despite several descents through the fog to near-ground level, he eventually landed on the sands at Cap Gris Nez and awaited daylight. Obtaining fresh fuel from a nearby French unit, Warneford set off again and returned to Furnes, landing there at about 10.30 am.

It had been an eventful night for 1 Wing RNAS. Apart from Warneford's aerial victory, the two pilots sent to raid Evere, Wilson and Mills, had reached their objective and bombed separately. Their bombs found accurate marks, particularly Mills's, and set light to one airship shed containing the LZ38 which was destroyed. Warneford's feat – the first occasion of an airship being brought down by an aeroplane – resulted in a telegram from the Admiralty conveying to him the personal congratulations of King George V, and further informing him officially of his award of a Victoria Cross; the latter honour being confirmed in the *London Gazette* of 11 June 1915. On 9 June the French Secretary of War, General Joffre, recommended a further honour for Warneford, as Chevalier de Legion d'Honneur. Meanwhile a flood of congratulatory messages flowed into Furnes, and Warneford's name was headlined internationally in newspapers and journals.

Notification of the award of the Legion d'Honneur was sent to Warneford, and his commanding officer, Longmore, arranged for him to visit Paris for its presentation, utilising this visit as an opportunity to have Warneford and another 1 Wing pilot, Lieutenant Marsden, collect

William Barnard Rhodes Moorhouse   [33]

Reginald Alexander Warneford

some new aircraft from the Paris depot for the squadron; '. . . the first two single-seated Nieuports ready.' Accordingly, Warneford went to Paris where he received a telephone call from Longmore, instructing him to arrange to fly a new Henry Farman aircraft back to the squadron after his investiture ceremony.

On Thursday morning, 17 June, Warneford was duly presented with the Legion d'Honneur by General Joffre, and after a ceremonial luncheon, travelled to nearby Buc aerodrome to collect the new Henry Farman for delivery to Furnes. A short test flight, with a chance acquaintance Lieutenant-Commander R. F. Lee-Dillon as passenger, proved apparently satisfactory; then, after handing his uniform hat to Mrs Lee-Dillon to hold, Warneford climbed back into the aircraft for a second brief flight. His passenger was Henry Beach Needham, a freelance American journalist, taking this opportunity to have his first airborne experience. The still-warm engine roared into life again and Warneford took off at 4.30 pm.

After half a mile straight flight, the Henry Farman did a steeply banked lefthand turn, climbing, then minutes later, another lefthand turn with vertical bank. These violent manoeuvres in such a large, relatively lightly loaded machine caused it to switchback rather alarmingly, but Warneford seemed to be in complete control and shortly after appeared over the edge of the airfield, diving from 1,000 feet with engine full-on, and passing over the heads of the many spectators at a mere 60 feet height.

The Farman then shot up abruptly to about 200 feet, and at that height the righthand wings buckled. At the same moment the Farman's propeller hit the aircraft tail booms and disintegrated. Warneford and Needham were both ejected upwards, out of the nacelle, and plunged to earth. Horrified witnesses rushed towards the scene of the crash and found Warneford embedded in the ground in a nearby green cornfield; his Legion d'Honneur Cross part-driven into his chest. Still faintly breathing, Warneford was placed in a commandeered civilian car and rushed to Versailles Hospital, but died during the journey.

Warneford's body was brought home to England on 21 June and in the afternoon of Tuesday, 22 June 1915 he was buried in Brompton Cemetery, London with full naval honours; his mother Mrs A Corkery (by then the wife of Lieutenant-Colonel M. P. Corkery RAMC) and two sisters being the chief mourners.

Witnessing the impressive ceremony were thousands of spectators and, indeed, by the end of the day an estimated 50,000 people visited the cemetery to pay last respects to the dead VC. Three recruiting sergeants took the opportunity to station themselves outside the cemetery entrance

early in the morning, and later reported being 'well satisfied' with their
day's work. . . .

Warneford's Victoria Cross was sent by the Admiralty to his mother;
while shortly after she also received a replica in jewels of the Cross of
the Legion d'Honneur, subscribed in tribute by workers in the French
factories of Morane, Le Rhone, and Gnome. A year later, on 11 June
1916, Lord Derby, Under-Secretary of State for War, unveiled an
impressive memorial stone plaque in Brompton Cemetery, which had
been commissioned by the *Daily Express* newspaper.

3. Lanoe George Hawker

To single out one man as the prime example of the RFC's early pilots who – literally – formed the ground rules and tactics of aerial combat would be invidious. Yet if there could be chosen such an individual then undoubtedly one man who was responsible for a high proportion of the RFC's fighting efficiency in later years was Lanoe George Hawker. His outstanding contribution to formulating the future pattern of air fighting, and his personal creed of the offensive spirit alone would have earned him a distinguished niche in RFC annals. Add to this an instinctive genius for creating and fashioning a myriad of inventions and ideas – most of which became standard fitments and practices – allied with a character which evinced respect to the point of devotion in all with whom he came into contact; and it is understandable that the name of Lanoe Hawker has come to be regarded as the epitome of the RFC's first fighting pilots. His death robbed the RFC of a notable fighting leader and a potentially great future commander.

Born in Longparish, Hampshire on 30 December 1890, Lanoe Hawker was the son of Lieutenant H. C. Hawker RN, and a descendant of several generations of military ancestors. In July 1905, as the start of an intended naval career, Hawker entered the Britannia College at Dartmouth, but to his bitter disappointment he was forced to withdraw from training due to ill-health. Imbued with an inherited tradition of service to Sovereign and country, he next donned uniform as a Gentleman Cadet of the Royal Military Academy, Woolwich in February 1910. In June of the same year, along with his younger brother Tyrrel, he joined the Royal Aero Club, an indication of his growing interest in the new 'art' of flying. Commissioned eventually in the Royal Engineers on 20 July 1911, Hawker had already commenced flying instruction at Hendon, but a course at the Chatham School of Engineering occupied him fully for over a year, and it was not until 4 March 1913 that he finally passed his pilot's tests, on a Deperdussin, gaining RAeC Certificate No 435. Promoted to Lieutenant in October 1913, he was then posted to 33rd Fortress Company at Cork Harbour, but his request for attachment to the Royal Flying Corps resulted in a move to the Central Flying School at Upavon on 1 August 1914 where, in D Flight, he underwent Service flying training. Graduating from CFS on 3 October 1914, Hawker immediately joined 6 Squadron RFC at Farnborough, one of several pilots drafted to the squadron to replenish its officer establishment following dispersal of the unit's original pilots to other RFC units which moved to France on the outbreak of war.

On 6 October Hawker flew a Henry Farman, 653, to Dover, and the following day 6 Squadron collectively crossed the Channel to France for operations. Based initially on Ostend racecourse, the unit despatched its first war reconnaissance on 8 October when Captain A. C. E. Marsh, with Hawker his observer, flew BE2a 492, over the advancing German armies.

In the following months during several similar sorties, Hawker's instinctive fighting spirit was evidenced by his early attempts to carry a widely varying assortment of 20lb bombs, steel darts, grenades or other forms of armament calculated to discomfit enemy troops. Like most contemporary airmen he usually carried a Service revolver with him and on 31 October, during his first encounter with a German aircraft, he attacked instantly and fired all six shots from his side-arm. It was an example of his characteristic desire to come to grips with any opponent, without thought of personal safety – a trait he was to display throughout his fighting career.

Throughout the 1914–15 winter Hawker found little opportunity for air combat, enemy aircraft being seldom seen. By March 1915 his usual aircraft was BE2c 1780, in which he normally carried a Service rifle for 'offensive armament', and his main routine comprised reconnaissance and artillery 'spotting' sorties; during the course of which he was constantly subjected to increasingly accurate anti-aircraft fire. His attitude to such perils was one of disdain and, indeed, at one period of seeking out German gun and troop positions he flew low deliberately over suspected sites, inviting fire from enemy guns in order to pinpoint the batteries.

On 18 April 1915 Hawker set out alone in BE2c 1780, to find and bomb a reported Zeppelin airship shed at Gontrode. With only three 20lb Hales bombs as his normal load, Hawker supplemented these by carrying several hand grenades, and on locating his objective he spiralled down to attack, throwing his hand grenades at the crew of a captive balloon 'sentry' who maintained a machine gun barrage at him during the descent. Sweeping low over the huge hangar Hawker released his bombs and secured two hits on target. Unbeknown to Hawker the shed, which normally housed the airship LZ35, was empty; its 'resident' having crashed five days earlier.

His complete disregard for personal danger over many months of operations, culminating in this latest exploit brought Hawker a well-deserved award of the Distinguished Service Order (DSO) and promotion to Captain in command of 6 Squadron's 'A' Flight.

Six days later his luck ran out during a patrol over the Langemarck area. Flying low in customary style he was hit by a bullet in his left ankle. Despite his pain, he completed his patrol before landing for local medical treatment. Next day – such was the critical state of the land battle – he refused to be treated as an invalid and insisted on flying another sortie, having to be lifted into his cockpit; during the patrol he attacked a German two-seater with his rifle and drove it down. On 26 April, with Lieutenant Wyllie as observer, Hawker attacked and drove off two German aircraft, while a third which mounted a machine gun was eventually driven away by rifle fire at close range. As the ground battle eased from its critical stage, Hawker was granted two weeks' sick leave.

On his return to his unit in May he continued his previous routine of reconnaissance daily in BE2c's and (from early June) FE2b's; but on 3 June was delighted to receive a new aircraft, a single-seat Bristol Scout C, No 1609, for operations. With the practical help of Air Mechanic E. J. Elton (later Flight Sergeant DCM MM) Hawker devised a mounting for a Lewis machine gun for the tiny single-seater. With no practical synchronisation gun gear available at that time, the gun was affixed to the left side of the cockpit, with its barrel pointing forward and outside the propeller arc. It meant that in combat Hawker would need to attack 'crabwise' to an enemy, but on 7 June he made his first flight in the Lewis-equipped Bristol and promptly tackled the first German machine he met, forcing the two-seater to spin away to earth. 21 June saw him attack another two-seater which was last observed descending and trailing a plume of smoke; although Hawker made no claim for a 'victory', being unable to see the conclusion.

Next day, after three inconclusive engagements with German aircraft, Hawker's petrol ran out and in the subsequent forced landing his Bristol hit a wire fence and overturned. Escaping the crash with just minor bruising, Hawker was soon allotted a second Bristol Scout C, No 1611, in place of the damaged 1609. The new steed was immediately fitted with Hawker's 'crab' Lewis mounting – the backsight being clamped to the left rear centre-section strut – and Hawker could then continue his combat sorties in between normal reconnaissance patrols.

It was in Bristol Scout 1611 that Hawker set out on 25 July 1915 on an Offensive Patrol (OP) with the sole object of seeking out German aircraft. Spotting a two-seater near Passchendaele, he attacked and emptied a complete drum of bullets into his opponent, causing the

German to spin down. Sighting a second enemy machine over Houthulst, Hawker dived, fired, and then watched the German dive towards earth in .obvious difficulty; his opponent being from Flieger Abteilung Nr 3, and later confirmed by 20 AA Section as force-landing behind German lines.

Climbing to 11,000 feet, Hawker continued his hunt and at 7 pm noticed a German two-seater at 10,000 feet over Hooge being heavily shelled by anti-aircraft guns. Approaching from out of the lowering sun, Hawker closed to 100 yards' range and opened fire. The German, an Albatros, burst into flames, turned on its back throwing its observer, Hauptmann Roser, out of his cockpit, and finally crashed south-east of Zillebecke.

On his return from this sortie Hawker was recommended for a Victoria Cross – not only for his exploits of 25 July, but as fitting recognition of his continuous courage and splendid example during almost a year of constant operational flying and fighting. The award was approved, and officially gazetted on 24 August 1915. It was the first air VC awarded for consistent gallantry over a period of time, and, significantly, the first ever awarded for air *fighting*.

As always, Hawker continued to seek out hostile aircraft at every opportunity. On 2 August, flying FE2b 4227, he had three separate combats; his first adversary, a two-seat Aviatik, being forced down behind German lines at Wulverghem. Nine days later, with Lieutenant Noel Clifton as his observer-gunner in FE2b 4227, he dived on an Albatros two-seater and drove it off, only to then find himself the target for two single-seaters and another Albatros two-seater. Engaging all three for some twenty minutes Hawker and Clifton had the satisfaction of seeing each opponent retire from the fight. Sighting an Aviatik over Houthem, Hawker attacked, forcing the German crew to land east of St Yves.

With ammunition and fuel running low, the FE2b crew were completing their patrol at 9,000 feet over Lille when a German mono-plane scout dived and opened fire at them. Turning quickly to engage this latest opponent, Hawker skilfully manoeuvred the FE into a position where Clifton was able to slam a pointblank burst into the German, and the *Eindecker* spun down to crash on the outskirts of Lille.

Following a brief spell of leave in England, Hawker took up Bristol Scout 1611 on 2 September for a lone recce, during the course of which he tackled a German scout at 9,000 feet over Bixhoete and sent it down to crash. This particular victory exemplified his instinctive grasp of a basic essential in all fighting – the necessity of surprise. The German pilot had been completely unaware of Hawker's presence until the latter had come within 50 yards range and opened fire. It was the last action of note flown by Hawker with 6 Squadron, for on 20 September 1915 he was posted to Home Establishment, with a strong recommendation for promotion to Major and command of his own squadron.

Hawker's value as a commander was suitably recognised by an appointment to command the RFC's first single-seat scout unit to be created, 24 Squadron. Originally formed at Hounslow on 1 September 1915 from a nucleus supplied by No 17 Training Squadron, 24 Squadron came under the aegis of 5th Wing RFC, and on 28 September Hawker's appointment was made effective. Desperately fatigued from a full year of almost constant active service in France, Hawker found himself faced with a prodigious work task on his arrival at Hounslow. With no experienced officers to share the burden, he had to start literally from scratch to build a squadron fit for 'Fighting Duties' – terms of reference without precedent in the RFC. All proposed equipment, training, tactics were empirical, and very much matters of sheer trial and error. With his usual tremendous energy and meticulous attention to details, Hawker set about his task immediately.

On 5 October he attended an investiture at Buckingham Palace where he received his VC and DSO awards from the hands of King George V, but was quickly back at Hounslow working incredible hours in his attempt to get his squadron into fighting shape. On 10 January 1916 the first of the squadron's operational aircraft arrived at Hounslow, a De Havilland 2 'pusher' scout; and during the next three weeks aircraft and pilots arrived to complete the unit establishment of twelve of each. Finally, on 7 February 24 Squadron flew to France (St Omer). Hawker had preceded his men, crossing to France on 2 February, and his promotion to Major became effective from 3 February 1916.

For its first few days in France 24 Squadron provided air patrols for GHQ, St Omer, but on 12 February moved to Bertangles aerodrome, near Amiens. Eager to commence fighting, 24's pilots were soon beset by a series of engine faults in the as yet unproven DH2 aircraft. Applying his considerable engineering knowledge to these and other important details, Hawker began producing new aids for higher efficiency in both pilots and machines of his squadron. His fertile brain was responsible for 'inventing' the original fleece-lined, thigh-length flying boots later to become standard issue for RFC, RNAS and RAF crews. He devised a modification to the standard 47-round Lewis gun ammunition drum and virtually doubled its content; then introduced a ring sight which gave pilots an automatic deflection allowance; and a realistic 'rocking fuselage' ground trainer for practice in machine gun firing. These were merely a few of the many innovations and ideas which resulted from Hawker's restless brain – all of which were soon adopted by the remainder of Britain's flying services.

As squadron commander Hawker was officially forbidden to accompany his men across the trenches on patrols – indeed, the original RFC order expressly forbade unit commanders even to *fly* – but this was soon modified. Such non-participation was utterly foreign to Hawker's sense of honour and duty, and he circumvented the unimaginative dictum by simply omitting his name from the official daily flying orders – and then accompanying many patrols in a secondary position to the appointed patrol leader. He also made a habit of substituting himself for any pilot about to go home on leave by strolling to the aircraft concerned just prior to a patrol and quietly ordering the pilot to 'cut off on leave'; then climbing into the cockpit in the youngster's place.

In May 1916 the establishment of 24 Squadron (among others) was raised from twelve to eighteen pilots and aircraft in preparation for the forthcoming Battle of the Somme. As the newer men joined his unit, Hawker soon inculcated them into the 'Hawker Spirit' – a simple philosophy of the offensive creed which was epitomised by a tactical order which Hawker produced for the squadron notice board. Its executive command comprised just two words – 'Attack EVERYTHING'. During the next three months the unit's DH2's played a vital part in defeating the notorious 'Fokker Scourge', but by September 1916 the task of retaining their hardily-won air supremacy was becoming increasingly difficult. New German scout designs, such as the Albatros DI and DII and Halberstadt DIII were beginning to reach the freshly-formed *Jagdstaffeln* (literally, hunting squadrons) of the German air services. All carried twin, synchronised machine guns and possessed far superior performance ranges than 24's obsolescent DH2's. By that time Hawker had been notified of an imminent promotion to command of an RFC Wing, but the news in no way diminished his desire to fly and fight.

In the afternoon of 23 November 1916, a patrol of 24 Squadron's A Flight was due to take off, and Hawker decided to join it. With J. O. Andrews leading in DH2 5998, Lanoe Hawker to his left in 5964, R. H. M. S. Saundby to the right in 5925, and Lieutenant Crutch in the rear position, the patrol left Bertangles at 1 pm, and headed towards the lines. Crutch was forced to land almost immediately with a fractious engine, but the remaining trio continued to gain height to 11,000 feet over Bapaume.

Just before 2 pm Andrews sighted two German two-seaters below, north-east of Bapaume, and immediately led Hawker and Saundby down to attack. The Germans just as promptly dived away to the east and Andrews, suspecting a trap, searched the sky for possible German fighters. High above he saw two small formations of scouts and accordingly swung his DH2 into a turn towards the west in order to regain precious height, and was followed by Saundby. Hawker, with his usual complete concentration on any target, continued his original dive towards the fast receding German two-seaters. On seeing Hawker's intention, Andrews completed his turn full circle and tried to catch up with Hawker, still followed faithfully by Saundby. At that moment the German scouts came tumbling down in attack. These were Albatros DII's from Jagdstaffel 2, and the first three Germans to tackle the DH2's were Leutnants Manfred von Richthofen, Wortmann, and Collin. The leading Albatros lined himself for a tail shot at Hawker but Andrews fired a short burst and forced the German to break off his attack. Warned by the sound of Andrews' machine gun fire, Hawker promptly spun away from the enemy's line of fire.

Within seconds the remaining Albatri had joined the fight and Andrews had his engine and petrol tank shot out of action, forcing him to glide towards the trench lines and safety. Scenting an easy victim, his adversary continued to rake the crippled DH2 until Saundby, shaking off several determined onslaughts by other Albatri, hammered most of a drum of bullets into Andrews' tormentor. The German dived away steeply. Andrews eventually found sanctuary at a forward French airfield and Saundby, who had escorted him back, returned to the lines to finish his sortie. Neither pilot saw Hawker again, though Andrews during his flat glide to the west had momentarily spotted Hawker's DH2 below him at about 3,000 feet, circling in combat with an Albatros.

Hawker, after spinning out of the firing line of his first attacker, had recovered from his manoeuvre, only to find himself under attack from another Albatros DII. Its pilot was Manfred von Richthofen, at that date credited with ten confirmed victories and the leading living German fighter pilot. Banking into a circling turn, Hawker soon recognised that his opponent was no novice and he cheerfully accepted the challenge, waving briefly to von Richthofen during the continuing manoeuvring for a deadly firing position on each other's tail.

The odds against Hawker's survival were, however, tremendous. Apart from the all-round superiority of the Albatros over Hawker's DH2 in performance and armament, the fight took place well over the German side of the trenches, with the prevailing westerly wind gradually pushing both combatants further east.

After more than thirty minutes of wary circling and manoeuvring, Hawker knew the moment had come for him to break off the fight if he was ever to regain the Allied lines. With his petrol running precariously low, he elongated his circles, creeping ever nearer to the lines, despite the menacing Albatros slightly above and behind. Pulling his DH2 into a tight loop to distract the German, Hawker then pushed his control column forward and started a shallow dive towards the trenches, at the same time kicking his rudder from side to side. His zig-zag flight gave only a fleeting target to von Richthofen but the German started firing short bursts in the hope of making Hawker change direction. Hawker's brilliant flying gave no easy target and as von Richthofen's ammunition began to run low both of his guns jammed. By then both aircraft were within 1,000 yards of the trench lines and a mere 150 feet above the shell-pocked earth. Frantically rectifying one gun, von Richthofen managed to loose off one brief burst. Hawker's DH2 staggered slightly, stalled, and then flew straight into the mud some 250 yards east of Luisenhof Farm, a shell-shattered ruin just over two miles south of Bapaume, on the road to Flers. Lanoe Hawker's final crash had been witnessed by a group of German Grenadiers utilising the farm's cellars as their battalion headquarters, and next day their senior officer, Major von Schonberg, gave ready permission for one of his officers to bury Hawker's body beside the wreckage of his aircraft.

Examination showed that Hawker's only injury from his prolonged combat with Manfred von Richthofen, who had fired almost 900 bullets, was a single bullet through Hawker's head.

4. John Aidan Liddell

Born on 3 August 1888 at Benwell Hall, Newcastle-upon-Tyne, John Aidan Liddell was the son of Emily Catherine Liddell and John Liddell, KCSG JP for Northumberland, the eldest boy of three brothers and a sister born to these parents. Of somewhat delicate health, John Aidan showed early signs of natural talents and gifted insight to many scientific and mechanical subjects. Educated at Stonyhurst School, Lancashire, from September 1900 to 1908, he then entered Balliol College, Oxford. Already his many-faceted keen interests had included photography, chemistry, music and particularly astronomy, the latter leading to his election in February 1907 as a member of the British Astronomical Association. At Balliol he undertook the Honours course in zoology and was the only man of his year to secure a first class honours degree in this subject. In between studies his chief pastime was motoring, in which his mechanical aptitude was given full rein.

On going down from Oxford, Liddell stood poised on the threshold of a greatly promising future. To quote a contemporary of his at Oxford :

He was, in fact, one of those rarely gifted individuals whose natural ability and enthusiasm would have brought him distinction in any field of human activity he chose to enter. If he had not been sucked into the vortex of the Great War, I think his chosen field would have been the most adventurous kind of travel and exploration.

On leaving Oxford Liddell was offered a travelling scholarship in order to investigate the fauna of the isle of Krakatoa, in the Straits of Sunda (which had been devastated in the great volcanic eruption of 1883), but he was unable to accept. However, '. . . not wishing to be a slacker' (as he expressed it), he joined the special reserve of officers in the 3rd Battalion, The Argyll and Sutherland Highlanders on 1 June 1912. His deep interest in all things mechanical had already led him to consider aviation as a fresh avenue of experience, being fascinated with the potential of the new means of locomotion. There is some evidence that he gained air experience in 1913, but he eventually undertook private tuition at the Vickers Flying School at Brooklands, and gained his Royal Aero Club Certificate, No 781, on 14 May 1914.

Promoted to Lieutenant in July 1914, Liddell was further promoted to Captain on the outbreak of war; and on 28 August 1914 he sailed to France with his regiment, with overall responsibility for the machine gun sections of his battalion. From September 1914 to February 1915, Liddell saw continuous action in the primitive trench war; serving at one period for 43 consecutive days and nights in the frontline trenches without even a change of clothing.

His fortitude and courage were manifested on many occasions, and an inkling of the respect he unconsciously commanded among his subordinates can be judged by an extract from a letter written home by Private Alexander McCallum, 'We have a splendid officer in charge of the guns, one of those men who would give the faintest-hearted confidence.'

Liddell's courage and devotion to duty were officially recognised by being mentioned in despatches, and the award of a Military Cross on 14 January 1915, gazetted on 18 February. In February 1915 he returned to England on sick leave, his long ordeal having stretched his sensitive nervous system to its limits.

After an extended period of recuperation, Liddell decided to transfer to the Royal Flying Corps, and in May 1915 he was seconded from his regiment, on probation, to the flying service. A period of Service flying instruction followed at Shoreham, Dover, and Farnborough, until on 20 July he was officially transferred to the RFC. Three days later he returned to France and reported to 7 Squadron at St Omer, where he was allotted to A Flight of the unit.

On 29 July 1915 Liddell flew his first operational patrol – a reconnaissance over Ostend-Bruges-Ghent-Audenarde-Heesteert in RE5, 2458, with Second Lieutenant H. H. Watkins as his observer. It was an eventful 'introduction' to the new method of warfare, and Liddell had several running fights with enemy aircraft, though without apparent result. Two days later, on 31 July, Liddell undertook his second operational sortie, in RE5 2457, with Second Lieutenant R. H. Peck as observer. Ostensibly it was to be a routine reconnaissance patrol over the Ostend-Bruges-Ghent areas, but it was fated to be Liddell's last.

Taking off in the late morning of the 31st, Liddell arrived over Ostend at 5,000 feet and commenced his observation. Peck in the front cockpit had loaded both his Lewis machine gun and a spare Service rifle in case of any interference by enemy aircraft – having already noticed one German biplane hovering in the area when the RE5 first crossed the trenches. Leaving Ostend, Liddell headed towards Bruges, but as he reached it the RE5 was suddenly fired on from above. Manoeuvring quickly out of the line of fire, the RE crew caught a brief glimpse of a German tractor biplane above them, its gunner firing his machine gun.

Peck managed to retaliate with a full drum of Lewis gun ammunition, and was just replacing the empty drum with another full drum when the RE5 abruptly dropped its nose, fell onto its back, and began the long drop towards earth. Peck, who was not strapped in, managed to grip his machine gun mounting and stay in his cockpit, though everything loose fell away past his head. The RE5 continued to plunge towards the ground, with Peck unable to move from his desperate position, until the aircraft suddenly righted itself and he could resume his more normal stance.

In the rear cockpit Liddell was grievously wounded. A final burst of fire from the German adversary had slashed through the side of his cockpit and gouged away part of his right thigh; exposing the bone and ripping four inches of it completely out. The impact and shock rendered Liddell unconscious, and the aircraft control wheel slipped out of his hand, leaving the machine to its own devices. After falling about three thousand feet, Liddell revived partially, realised that the aircraft was not in a normal plane, and instinctively righted its flying attitude.

Damage to the RE5 was extensive. The control wheel was half shot away, the throttle control shattered, part of the undercarriage smashed, and the cockpit slashed and broken by bullet scars. Liddell faced a straight choice of either landing as best he could, in order to obtain medical succour – though this would automatically mean he and Peck would become prisoners of war – or attempting to regain the Allied lines. The prospect of surrendering to the Germans was repugnant to Liddell, and he scribbled a note to Peck, telling him he intended trying to fly the crippled RE5 to some sands, west of Nieuport and land there. Peck on reading this pointed to an Allied airfield near Furnes as being a better proposition, and Liddell nodded agreement.

The problem of actually controlling the RE5 was solved by Liddell holding the broken control wheel in one hand, and operating the rudder control cables with his other; and in this manner, with the agony of his gaping wound, Liddell guided his machine for almost half an hour before arriving over a Belgian airfield at La Panne, base for the 3rd Escadrille, Belgian Flying Corps. Unable to use the throttle control, Liddell put the aircraft down with full engine power and then switched off just as it was about to touch down.

The landing itself, with a damaged undercarriage, was described by one eyewitness as 'faultless'. Once the aircraft had ceased rolling, it was immediately surrounded by a host of Belgian airmen hoping to help, but

Liddell refused to be moved from his cockpit until a competent doctor was present, fearing further damage to his leg in unskilled hands. While waiting the arrival of a doctor, Liddell applied a splint to the broken leg, and then fashioned a tourniquet to staunch the flow of blood. When he was taken out of the aircraft and laid on a stretcher, Liddell remained cheerful and thanked his Belgian helpers, before being whisked away to La Panne hospital. Immediate surgical attention was given and the wounds cleaned and bandaged.

For the following four weeks Liddell remained in the hospital, but his condition showed no great signs of improvement. Then septic poisoning was discovered in the right leg, and it had to be amputated in the hope of preventing further spread. The surgery was in vain, and the end came almost suddenly on 31 August 1915 – the feast day of his patron, St Aidan. With him in his last hours was his mother, who had obtained permission from the military authorities to stay in the hospital, once it was known that Liddell could not survive long. His body was conveyed to London on 3 September, and on the following day he was interred in the Roman Catholic section of Basingstoke Old Cemetery, Hampshire.

The award of his Victoria Cross was notified to him personally on 18 August and officially gazetted on 23 August 1915. The actual cross was presented to Liddell's father by King George V at a Buckingham Palace investiture held on 16 November 1916. Lieutenant R. H. Peck, Liddell's companion on his final patrol, was fated to live little more than six months, being killed on active service in Mesopotamia (now, Iraq) on 10 March 1916.

5. Gilbert Stuart Martin Insall

Eldest son of G. J. Insall, a dental surgeon, Gilbert Insall was born on 14 May 1894 in Paris, and educated at L'Ecole Anglo-Saxon there. Entering Paris University, he intended studying to follow in his father's profession, but on the outbreak of war he volunteered to enlist in the army, and in September 1914 became a private in the UPS, Royal Fusiliers, 18 Service Battalion.

With his younger brother, Algernon, Insall showed an early interest in aeronautics, and both applied for transfer to the Royal Flying Corps. Algernon was officially accepted on 12 March 1915 and Gilbert obtained his transfer on 14 March. A period of pilot training at Brooklands early in March resulted in Gilbert obtaining Royal Aero Club Certificate No 1110 on 14 March 1915 – the date of his acceptance by the RFC for further Service training.

Gaining his pilot's 'wings', Gilbert Insall was posted to France on 16 July 1915, and later in the month joined 11 Squadron RFC at Vert Galand aerodrome, alongside the Amiens-Doullens road. 11 Squadron was equipped throughout with Vickers FB5 two-seat 'pusher' aircraft, and had originally been formed as the first homogeneously equipped RFC unit and intended for 'fighting duties' – a somewhat vague term at that period of the war, but one which virtually established the unit as the first-ever 'fighter' squadron in Britain flying services. The squadron arrived in France on 25 July 1915 and made its first base at Vert Galand, but by September had moved to Villers Bretonneux.

Although employed to a large extent in its intended 'fighter' role, usually as escort to bombing and reconnaissance aircraft from sister units, 11 Squadron was often tasked with photo-reconnaissance and bombing sorties too. The Vickers FB5, with its normal crew complement of pilot and observer-gunner, was normally fitted with a Lewis machine gun in the front cockpit, and could carry a few small bombs fitted on improvised racks. With full war load, the FB5's 100hp Gnome engine could provide a maximum speed of perhaps 60 mph.

Insall quickly settled in to the daily routine duties of the squadron, and from his earliest flights displayed a keen offensive spirit whenever he met any German aircraft. On 6 September 1915, for example, in FB5, 5455 with Second Lieutenant G. Manley in the front cockpit, Insall was detailed to undertake a photo reconnaissance of Albert. An LVG two-seater suddenly appeared about 200 feet above Insall, who promptly turned and engaged the German, eventually forcing it to dive to earth. A second LVG appeared and Insall now tackled this opponent, closing to within 50 yards before driving the German east. During the following weeks Insall engaged several other German aircraft without visible result, though on each occasion he emerged as the moral, if not physical, 'victor'.

On 7 November 1915, flying Vickers FB5, 5074, with Air Mechanic (later, Corporal) T. H. Donald as his observer-gunner, Insall set out on a fighting patrol across the German lines. Sighting a German Aviatik two-seater near Achiet, Insall set off in pursuit and attacked. The German pilot proceeded to lead his antagonist over a German ground rocket battery but Insall continued his chase by diving hard and getting to close range, whereupon Donald fired a full drum of bullets into the Aviatik, hitting its engine. Plunging into cloud, followed by Insall, the Aviatik emerged again and was once more attacked by Insall and Donald, causing the Aviatik pilot to descend hastily and make a rough landing in a ploughed field four miles south-east of Arras.

As he circled his opponent, Insall saw the two German crew members climb out and prepare to fire at him. Diving to 500 feet Insall gave Donald a chance to open heavy fire on the Germans, who then fled; one appearing to help the other who had – it seemed – been wounded by Donald's fire. By this time some German infantry in the region had begun firing at the Vickers but Insall ignored the barrage of small arms fire, and dived to drop a small incendiary bomb on the abandoned Aviatik. As he turned towards the lines to return, Insall saw that the grounded aircraft was wreathed in smoke.

Heading west, Insall reached the trenches, flying at 2,000 feet altitude, and dived across, with Donald taking the opportunity to rake the enemy trench system with his Lewis gun as he passed over. The answering barrage of rifle and machine gun fire found its mark when the Vickers' petrol tank was hit, but Insall coolly selected a suitable piece of flat land near a wood some 500 yards inside Allied lines on which to land his damaged machine. Remaining with their aircraft, Insall and Donald were then subjected to an accurate onslaught of about 150 shells as the frontline German gunners attempted to destroy their aircraft. As darkness fell, Insall arranged for a screen to be erected to shelter some torches and other lights, by which he and Donald repaired their damaged machine; and at dawn both men flew back to their base airfield at Bertangles, none the worse for their ordeal. Gilbert Insall was

Lanoe George Hawker

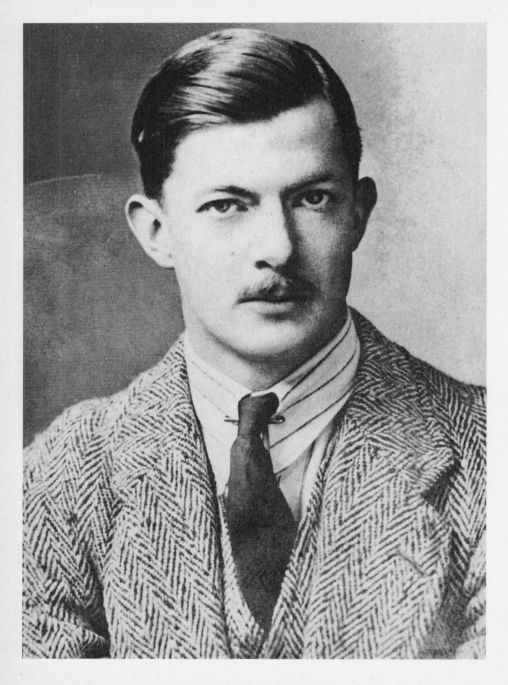

John Aidan Liddell

Gilbert Stuart Martin Insall

Richard Bell-Davies

awarded a Victoria Cross, while his Scottish companion, Donald, received a thoroughly deserved Distinguished Conduct Medal; Insall's award was later gazetted on 23 December 1915.

Donald was again in the front cockpit of FB5 5074 on 14 December 1915 when Insall set off on a routine patrol. Attacked by a German two-seater, Donald was wounded in the leg, while Insall was hit in the base of his spine by a sliver of shell as he attempted to regain the Allied lines. Forced to land in enemy-occupied territory, both men were taken prisoner and sent for medical attention; Insall was transferred almost immediately to Cologne hospital for surgery.

After a sojourn of several months in hospital, Insall was moved to the prisoner of war camp at Heidelburg. While still in hospital Insall had determined to escape imprisonment at the earliest opportunity, and at Heidelburg, in 1916, he succeeded, only to be recaptured five days later.

Sent to Crefeld Camp, Insall and several companions then proceeded to construct an escape tunnel extending outside the camp's wire barriers, and after several months' hard labour, Insall was among the inmates who used the tunnel to gain freedom to the nearby Black Forest. Again, he was unlucky and soon recaptured, being sentenced to a period of solitary confinement as punishment in the prisoner of war camp at Strohen.

Throughout these months of incarceration Gilbert had managed to establish a variety of methods of communicating with his brother and family in France, including many ingenious devices and means. Finally on 28 August 1917, Gilbert Insall, with two companions, managed to escape from Strohen, and for the following nine nights travelled, undetected, to the Dutch border and freedom. By coincidence, one of Insall's companions, Lieutenant Claude Templer, had been a former schoolfriend in Paris. Insall's unceasing efforts to escape imprisonment were recognised by the award of a Military Cross.

During the winter of 1917–18, Gilbert Insall, now a Captain, was attached to the training staff at Gosport; and in mid-1918 he was posted to 51 (Home Defence) Squadron at Bekesbourne, as commander of A Flight. By the armistice he was serving on the staff of 53 (Home Defence) Wing, Harrietsham.

Deciding to remain in the postwar RAF, Insall was granted a permanent commission in the rank of Flight Lieutenant, with seniority from 1 August 1919, and spent the next year serving in Germany with the British occupation forces. A spell at No 6 Flying Training School followed; then on 1 April 1922 he was posted to Uxbridge RAF Depot. In 1926 he married Olwen Scott, and in April 1927, with promotion

to Squadron Leader he moved overseas to Iraq, to command 70
Squadron.

Here his private interest in archaeology could be indulged, using the
unit's aircraft on occasion to seek ancient sites across the vast wastelands
from the advantageous position of an aircraft cockpit.

Two years later, with further promotion to Wing Commander, Insall
was appointed to command 35 Squadron in March 1929; and in 1932
he commenced a two-years' tour of duty as commander of RAF Station,
Upavon. His next appointment sent him to RAF Kenley as officer commanding the station headquarters staff, from May 1934. Promotion to
Group Captain on 1 July, 1935 meant another overseas tour of duty
in the Middle East; returning in 1940 to succeed in command of RAF
Uxbridge.

Serving in various capacities throughout the 1939–45 war, Gilbert
Insall eventually retired from the Service on 30 July 1945. In the same
year, on 22 November, his courageous companion of the 1915 VC
action, T. H. Donald died. Living in semi-retirement in Yorkshire for
many years, Insall nearly died of a heart attack in 1969 when his residence
was burgled, and – among many other items – his VC, MC and other
decorations were stolen. In the event, the medals were recovered in
1970. Two years later, on 17 February 1972, Gilbert Insall died, at
Bawtry.

6. Richard Bell-Davies

On 1 April 1918 the Royal Air Force was born; a 'child' of the amalgamation of the Royal Flying Corps and the Royal Naval Air Service. The compulsory change from their former services was not to the liking of many individuals within the RFC and RNAS, who much preferred to remain loyal to their original service and its traditions. Such a preference, though unexpressed officially while the war still continued, found outlet and release when the first peacetime establishment for the RAF came to be compiled. Many former naval and army men, despite proud war records in the flying services, opted to remain with their initial service. One such airman was Richard Bell-Davies VC CB DSO AFC. Stepped in naval tradition from his early years, Bell-Davies remained an advocate of air power throughout his life, but chose to remain loyal to the Senior Service as his career.

Born at Croxley Green, London on 19 May 1886, he was educated at Bradfield College before enlisting in the Royal Navy (HMS *Britannia*) on 20 April 1901. For the following ten years his career followed a normal pattern of service and promotion in various naval ships, being commissioned in 1905 and steadily gaining wide sea-going experience both in home waters and abroad. During the Fleet summer manoeuvres of 1910, Claude Grahame White, the dedicated British pioneer pilot, flew a Farman biplane over the assembled vessels at Mount's Bay, and the sight stirred Davies' imagination so much that when, months later, the press announced Mr Frank MacLean's offer to place two aeroplanes at the disposal of naval officers wishing to learn to fly, he applied for membership of the Royal Aero Club and, with the hope of eventually being selected officially for flying instruction, privately undertook initial instruction with the Grahame White school at Hendon, receiving his RAeC Certificate, British Empire No 90, on 19 May 1911. On rejoining his ship, Davies made formal application to the Admiralty for consideration as a flying officer, and then proceeded abroad to China on duty. His application was finally approved in November 1912, and Davies was brought back to England to commence Service flying at Eastchurch.

On completion of his course, he was appointed 1st Lieutenant to the Eastchurch commander, Charles Rumney Samson, and, on 10 July 1913, graded as Flight commander in the Royal Flying Corps, Naval

57

Wing. At the end of 1913 he received further upgrading to Squadron commander.

In May 1914 Davies was invited to accompany an expeditionary force to British Somaliland, where the 'Mad Mullah' continued to harass governmental forces, but soon returned to Eastchurch; and immediately after the outbreak of war Davies stayed with Charles Samson when the latter formed a mobile squadron and, on 27 August 1914, flew with the unit to Ostend. This unit, soon to be titled 3 Squadron, RNAS, under Samson's lively command, was initially tasked with air support of a force of Royal Marines occupying the town, and included a number of armoured cars and other vehicles.

Moving to Dunkirk three days later, Samson's squadron then undertook a number of widely varying fighting duties in the ensuing three months, both in the air and on the ground. Davies flew numerous sorties, varying from simple reconnaissance to specific bombing raids against airship sheds, ports and enemy depots.

On 23 January 1915, piloting a Farman 'pusher, No 1241, with an observer, Butler, he set out with a full load of 20lb Hales bombs to attack a submarine anchored in Zeebrugge harbour. Flying along the coast to Nieuport, Davies then headed inland, only to run into a particularly fierce and accurate barrage of anti-aircraft fire. His aircraft was hit several times, while Davies received a shrapnel bullet in his right leg. Turning out of the barrage, he took stock of the damage, then, despite the pain and loss of blood from his leg, he again crossed the coast line, arrived over Zeebrugge, and released his bombs in a perfect straddle across the submarine target. Returning to Dunkirk as night fell, Davies accomplished a safe landing, made his report, and was then sent to England after local medical attention to his wound. His many exploits during the previous three months, culminating in the Zeebrugge sortie, brought Bell-Davies the award of a DSO, which was promulgated in the *London Gazette* dated 9 April 1915.

While Davies recuperated from his injury, Samson's 3 Squadron, RNAS, was withdrawn from Dunkirk and based at Dover, where the unit began preparations for an imminent move abroad to the Mediterranean theatre of war, in support of the projected Allied landing in the Dardanelles. Davies rejoined the unit at Dover, and in April 1915 the squadron arrived at Tenedos. Here, with a motley mixture of aeroplanes, Samson's unit immediately undertook a prolonged offensive against the Turks, with tactical reconnaissance and a series of bombing sorties against enemy depots and communications, bridges, and aerodromes. Moving base to Imbros in August 1915, Davies and his fellow air crew provided air cover for the Anzac landings at Suvla, but by the end of October they became virtually a long range bombing unit, attempting to cut the Turkish supply routes from Germany which passed through Bulgaria, and therefore concentrating on destruction of road and rail systems. On 19 November 1915, Samson decided on a full strength attack on the railway system at two points, Burgess Bridge and Ferejik Junction, and therefore detailed every available crew for the dual sortie.

Davies, piloting Nieuport 12, No 3172 – a two-seater locally converted to single-seat by covering over the second cockpit – and carrying six 20lb Hales bombs under its fuselage, was detailed for the Ferejik target; the objective was just inside Bulgaria's border with Turkey, near the Maritza River. The objective lay in an area of marsh land which, in winter, became inundated with rains and river tributaries, turning the land into a quagmire, but leaving some channels as simply hard mud, well baked by the heat.

Davies completed his bombing attack and was turning back to Imbros when he noticed one of the unit's Henry Farmans, piloted by Flight Sub-Lieutenant G. F. Smylie (later Air Commodore, RAF), grounded in a dry water channel. Smylie had bombed the target from low level, only to run through a particularly accurate curtain of ground fire and have the Farman's engine hit and put out of action. Gliding back towards the river, Smylie finally accomplished a safe landing. He then saw a party of Bulgarian troops approaching in the distance, and promptly set fire to his aircraft; he had taken cover in a nearby hollow.

At that moment Davies spotted Smylie's dilemma and immediately decided to land and attempt to retrieve the stranded pilot. He was well aware that the ground was unsuitable for any safe landing, while the effect of an additional passenger's weight preventing his low-powered Nieuport from ever taking off again was, at least, problematical. As he approached for a landing Davies received a shock when the Henry Farman below him exploded – Smylie having seen Davies's apparent intention remembered that the Farman still had a bomb on board, and therefore detonated the bomb with a pistol shot. Davies climbed away hastily in case there were further explosions, then returned and landed as near as possible to the waving Smylie.

Even then Davies was not certain whether Smylie was alone, or whether there might be a second crew member with him, but to his immediate relief, only Smylie ran to the Nieuport as it rolled to a stop on the uneven mud strip. Turning the Nieuport by its wing tip, Smylie helped steady the machine as Davies taxied it back to get a full take-off run between the surrounding tall reeds and mud-flats; then Smylie

clambered into Davies's cockpit and wedged himself forward inside the
fuselage, crouching on all fours between the engine bearers and the
rudder bar, with his head bumping against the oil tank.

By now the approaching Bulgars were within rifle range and had
commenced firing to prevent the escape of the overloaded Nieuport.
Using full throttle Davies began his undulating take-off run and
eventually got airborne, then set course for Imbros, which he reached
some 45 minutes later and landed without mishap. His report afterwards
was a model of understatement, reflecting the genuine modesty of Davies;
'Returning saw H5 burning in marshes. Picked up pilot.'

His coolness under fire, and his decision to rescue Smylie despite the
obvious hazards, led Charles Samson to recommend Davies for the
supreme award. On 31 December 1915 the second supplement to the
London Gazette of that date announced the award of a Victoria Cross
to Bell-Davies; while his gallant companion of the venture, Gilbert
Smylie, received a Distinguished Service Cross for his courage.

The latter's coolness throughout the whole episode is probably well
illustrated by his final action before climbing aboard the Nieuport.
Removing his bulky jacket, Smylie left it beside the wreckage of his
Henry Farman, with a scribbled message in one pocket saying, 'Please
return my coat, which I have had to leave, to No 3 Wing RNAS. . . .'

By the end of the year Samson's unit was withdrawn from the scene
and returned to England, and on 1 January 1916, Bell-Davies was
promoted to Wing Commander, RNAS, and appointed in command of
the naval air stations in northern England – Killingholme, Redcar,
Scarborough, and Whitley Bay. Here he was concerned mainly with
administration of the various training duties of the stations under his
command, but continued to take every opportunity to fly when his ground
responsibilities permitted.

In early June 1916 Davies received notification from the Admiralty
that his former unit, 3 Wing RNAS, was to be re-formed, for service in
France as the nucleus of the first-ever British strategic bombing formation.
Formed at Manston aerodrome, Kent, the new 3 Wing was commanded
by Captain W. L. Elder RN, and Davies was appointed as chief of flying
operations. The majority of its air crews were Canadians, while
equipment was originally intended to be 20 Sopwith $1\frac{1}{2}$ Strutter two-
seaters and 15 Short bombers; an establishment which was scheduled to
be complete by 1 July 1916.

In the event, the shortage of aircraft within the RFC in France for air
support of the first battles of the Somme that summer led to large
diversion of aircraft from 3 Wing to the hard-pressed RFC units, and by

the end of August 3 Wing could only muster a total of 22 aircraft. Moving to Luxeuil at the end of June 1916, 3 Wing commenced operations on 30 July, and for the next five months Davies directed, and participated in, various bombing sorties against German industrial targets. In January 1917, Davies left 3 Wing and returned to England where, on 10 January, he received a new appointment as senior flying officer aboard HMS *Campania*. His subsequent service in 1917–18 was almost wholly concerned with proving the practicability of aircraft aboard sea-going naval vessels. In particular he became closely involved in a myriad of experiments in the techniques of landing and taking-off from the flush decks of the early aircraft carriers – such as *Campania* and, later, *Furious* and *Argus* – while, in July 1918, Davies was one of the organisers of the successful attack on the Tondern airship sheds by Sopwith Camels from HMS *Furious* which took place on 18 July. His invaluable contribution to progress in naval aviation, including the many individual experimental trials undertaken personally, led to the award of an Air Force Cross in 1918.

After the 1918 armistice Davies, though selected for a permanent commission in the RAF, was determined to remain with the Royal Navy, and on 7 May 1919 relinquished his RAF commission and took. up an appointment to HMS *Lion*. Promoted to Commander, RN on 31 December 1919, he married in September 1920, and commenced a lifetime association with naval air matters. A succession of normal postings and appointments over the succeeding years included promotion to Captain, RN, at the close of 1926; while in 1930–31 he became a naval 'air liaison officer' at the Air Ministry. At the outbreak of World War Two Davies had risen to the rank of Rear Admiral, in command of all UK Naval Air Stations, and on 29 May 1941 was further promoted to Vice-Admiral, RN.

Six months later he retired from regular service, but almost immediately returned to active war service in the RN Reserve as a Commodore on convoys. By March 1942 he was a Commander, captaining HMS *Dasher*, but finally retired in 1944.

On 26 February 1966, Richard Bell-Davies vc cb dso afc died in the Royal Naval Hospital at Haslar, Gosport. A pioneer of naval aviation who devoted his life to furthering the cause of the Fleet's air arm, Bell-Davies evinced total respect and admiration from all with whom he came into contact. As one colleague in 1918 said of him, 'We hero-worshipped him and would have done anything for him.'*

* *Early Bird* by Major G. W. Moore, DSC; Putnam, 1963.

7. Lionel Wilmot Brabazon Rees

The superb fighting traditions of the Celtic races over many centuries have produced a wealth of individuals whose prowess and natural gift of leadership are now legendary. Men – and women – born and raised in Scotland, Ireland and Wales, particularly, have always been prominent in war and in peace; warriors whose restless devotion to any worthy cause, blended with unquenchable courage, have marked them in the forefront of their peers. Just such a man was Lionel Wilmot Brabazon Rees – a Welshman who epitomised the inner fire and unfettered spirit of adventure characteristic of the Welsh from the days of the Brythons. In battle, Welshmen have seldom failed to live up to their national motto – *Chwell angau na chwilydd* – summed succinctly as 'Death before dishonour'.

Born on 31 July 1884, Lionel Rees was the son of a soldier, Colonel Charles H. Rees, VD and a gentle Welsh girl, Leonora Maria Davids, then resident in Caernarvon; and his early upbringing was at Plas Llanwnda, in Castle Street (now the site of education offices). Educated initially at Eastbourne College, Lionel followed in his father's footsteps by choosing the Army as his intended career, and enrolled as a Gentleman Cadet in the Royal Military Academy, Woolwich. On commissioning as a subaltern, Rees joined the Royal Garrison Artillery on 23 December 1903, and for the next ten years pursued the normal duties of his rank and position.

Promoted to Lieutenant on 23 December 1906, Rees spent two years (1913–14) with the West African Frontier Force on active duty, but had already shown great interest in the new military 'arm', aeronautics, and learned to fly at his own expense; obtaining Royal Aero Club Certificate No 392 on 7 January 1913. On return from his African detachment, Rees promptly applied for secondment to the Royal Flying Corps and was officially transferred on 10 August 1914. On 30 October in the same year his promotion to Captain was promulgated. His natural ability as a pilot brought him an immediate posting to Upavon as an instructor on the Central Flying School, but his stay was brief, and at the turn of the year he moved to join 11 Squadron RFC, then in the process of formation at Netheravon as the RFC's first 'fighting' squadron, and eventually equipped throughout with two-seat Vickers FB5's. Officially formed on

14 February 1915, 11 Squadron eventually moved to France on 25 July, and became based at Vert Galand aerodrome, near Amiens.

Once in France, Rees wasted little time in flying on war operations, and on 28 July, in the course of a reconnaissance patrol across the trench lines, tackled a German monoplane. In the ensuing combat, his Vickers FB5 had a main wing spar shot through and a rear spar shattered by German bullets, but he continued the fight and finally drove the *Eindecker* down behind German lines. Four days later, in FB5, 1649, he again engaged an enemy aircraft, but was only able to fire at long range before his opponent scuttled away east. On the last day of August, again in 1649, with Flight Sergeant J. M. Hargreaves as his observer-gunner in the front cockpit, Rees fought for some 45 minutes with a German LVG two-seater, using up all his ammunition. Returning for fresh supplies, Rees returned to the combat and attacked his adversary again, and sent it down to crash. Further combats brought moral, if not physical victories during September; and on 21 September Rees and Hargreaves, during a photo-reconnaissance of the Somme-Esteres zone, dived on an Ago two-seater and eventually brought it down in German lines, near Herbcourt.

On 30 September another positive victory came when Rees and Hargreaves attacked an Albatros two-seater over Gommecourt. The fury of gunfire from the Vickers FB5 riddled the Albatros, hitting its pilot in the head, and tearing off the German aircraft's right wings. The wreckage fluttered to earth and final destruction. Further combats throughout October added to Rees's combat record, and on 29 October 1915, the *London Gazette* announced the award of a Military Cross to Rees, and a Distinguished Conduct Medal to his erstwhile companion on so many of his sorties, Hargreaves. The citation for the MC particularly emphasised the fighting record of the two men in engaging hostile aircraft. In November Rees returned to England, with a posting to CFS, Upavon, and promotion to Major on 1 December.

After a spell of leave, Rees was notified of his new appointment, as commanding officer of a newly-forming fighter unit, 32 Squadron. The nucleus of the new squadron was formed at Netheravon on 12 January 1916, and Rees arrived on his unit on 1 February. The intention was to form a complete, single-seater fighter unit for service in France, and on 13 February the first example of the unit's equipment, a De Havilland 2 'pusher' scout was received at Netheravon. By 26 May the squadron's complement of machines and personnel was complete, and two days later the pilots flew their DH2's to Dover, and then across the Channel to St Omer. On 4 June the unit moved base to Auchel, and on the 7th to

Treizennes, Aire, with the Martinsyde G.100 'Elephants' of 27 Squadron, RFC moving out the same day and handing over its accommodation to 32 Squadron. Rees and his pilots were in action the following morning, and the squadron suffered its first war casualty.

Throughout June 32's DH2's flew a variety of purely offensive patrols over the lines, interspersed with escort duties for the RFC's bombing squadrons as the latter made increasing efforts in preparation for the imminent Allied land assault along the Somme. In these sorties, Rees took a fairly full part; refusing to consider himself as 'non-operational' merely because of his command duties.

On 1 July 1916, preceded by an artillery barrage of an intensity never before seen in France, the first battle of the Somme commenced. In common with every other air unit in the area, 32 Squadron was early astir. Though prepared to tackle any air opposition met on this critical morning, the DH2s' main concern was prevention of German air reconnaissance behind the Allied lines. At a little after 3.30 am six of 32 Squadron's pilots set off to escort bombers attacking Don railway station and generally scour the air above the battlefront for German aircraft.

A few minutes before 6 am, a second patrol left; two DH2's, piloted by J. C. Simpson, a Canadian officer, and Lionel Rees. Simpson, in DH2, 7856, soon became separated from Rees, and when flying alone between La Bassée and Souchez, ran head-on into a formation of eight German two-seaters. Without hesitation Simpson dived onto the enemy formation, but within seconds had become the nodal point of each aircraft's rear guns. With eight bullets through his head, Simpson fell 8,000 feet and crashed. Rees in DH2, 6015, meanwhile was patrolling over the Double Crassieurs zone, where, at 6.30 am, he saw what he took to be a formation of British bombers returning from a raid, and decided to formate on these as fighter escort for their homeward flight.

In fact this formation, according to an anti-aircraft gunner officer who witnessed Simpson's fight and the subsequent combat by Rees, was the same echelon of German machines. As Rees came within striking range he realised his error in identification and – as soon as the leading German was within comfortable gun range – fired. His bullets tore splinters and fabric away from the fuselage between pilot and observer, whereupon the machine turned and dived away to safety. Lining his sights on the next, Rees fired again, obtaining hits and causing the German gunner to frantically fire off some red signal flares, requesting help from the other aircraft of the formation. Three of these immediately dived at Rees, firing, but flashed past him without doing any harm.

Still concentrating on his second victim, Rees continued to fire and saw a cloud of blue haze erupt from its forward fuselage – a hit in the engine in all probability. The German two-seater veered erratically into a turn and dived towards the east, still under control but out of the fight. Looking around for a fresh target, Rees saw five enemy machines in close formation; their gunners firing at him at reasonably long range. Diving nose-on at these, Rees fired a complete drum of ammunition into the centre of the bunched aircraft, and all five broke formation hastily, flying in different directions.

Turning again, Rees spotted the enemy leader with two companions heading westwards and set off in pursuit. Overhauling these quickly, he tackled the lowest machine, which turned sharply, released a bomb, and began firing at Rees. Closing in for the kill, Rees was about to open fire when he felt a blow in the leg; a second enemy aircraft had come up from below him and its gunner had raked the DH2. With his leg out of action, and therefore unable to operate his rudder bar, Rees continued his attack; firing a full drum of bullets and switchbacking his aircraft by pumping his control column back and forth until he was within ten yards of his opponent. As Rees broke away, he noticed the German gunner sitting back, his head thrown back, and his gun still firing into the sky with a dying finger on the trigger.

Intent on finishing off this machine, Rees did not wait to change the empty drum on his Lewis gun, but instead drew his personal pistol from its holster with the intention of getting to close quarters to administer the *coup de grace*. In his haste he dropped the pistol onto the cockpit floor. Not waiting to recover this, he placed a fresh ammunition drum on the Lewis, then set off after the enemy formation leader, whom he spotted making towards the lines.

Getting within range Rees emptied the drum at the German just as he crossed the trenches, flying eastwards. A glance around the sky showed Rees that he had effectively cleared it of all enemy opposition and, with the numbness of his wounded leg wearing off, and the beginning of pain, Rees set course for his own aerodrome. Making a near-perfect landing at 6.50 am, Rees taxied his bullet-riven DH2 to its normal hangar, and was then lifted out of his cockpit; he sat on the grass nearby, coolly instructing mechanics to send for a vehicle to take him to the nearest hospital.

Medical examination showed that Rees had been fortunate in not having a leg artery severed, but the actual wound and consequent loss of blood during the continued combat and return flight was sufficiently serious to keep Rees in hospital for some weeks, and thereafter he had a slight but permanent limp. On 5 August 1916 came the news of his Victoria Cross award; which he received from the hands of his Sovereign at an investiture on 14 December 1916.

Once fit again for duty, Rees was promoted to Lieutenant-Colonel on 1 May 1917 and travelled to the USA as one of Harold Balfour's Mission entourage. On his return he was appointed, appropriately, as commander of No 1 School of Aerial Fighting, Turnberry in Ayrshire, where his experience, skill and example were to play a large part in inculcating many of the RFC and RAF's great fighting pilots in the tradition of constant offensive which had always been his personal creed. He remained at Turnberry for the remainder of the war, and was awarded an Air Force Cross on 2 November 1918, and decorated with the OBE.

Deciding to make the newly-constituted Royal Air Force his future career, Rees was granted a permanent commission in 1919 as a Wing Commander. Further honour was paid to Rees when, on 15 January 1920, he was given the Freedom of Caernarvon, his home town, and he was presented with an ornate Sword of Honour to mark the occasion. In 1923-24, Rees became Assistant Commandant to the newly-created RAF College, Cranwell; and in 1925 he commenced a two-years' stint in the Directorate of Training, at the Air Ministry, and appointed ADC to King George V. In April 1926 Rees was posted to the Middle East as a Group Captain, in command of Headquarters RAF, Transjordan and Palestine; and on his return to England three years later succeeded to command of the RAF Depot at Uxbridge. In 1930 he became commander of No 21 Group, but finally retired from regular service in 1931.

Two years later, in the autumn of 1933, alone and unpublicised, Lionel Rees set sail from Porth-y-Aur in a 34 feet ketch, *May*, and sailed across the Atlantic to Nassau in the Bahamas, arriving there in January 1934. This solo sailing feat was recognised by the Cruising Club of America's award of its 'Blue Water Medal' to Rees in 1934.

Recalled briefly for RAF service in 1941–42, Rees returned to the Bahamas; and it was there, at Andros, that the gallant Welshman died on 28 September 1955. McKinlay Hargreaves, who knew and flew with Rees in 1915–16, once described Lionel Rees as, '. . . a gentleman, a real gentleman, a rare species . . . the greatest, gifted individual national asset that ever donned the uniform of the Corps (RFC).'

Yet another, who served under Rees' command in 32 Squadron in 1916, was (now) Wing Commander Gwilym Lewis DFC, a fellow Welshman. In a letter home to his parents dated 2 July 1916, Lewis wrote of Rees, 'I told you he was the bravest man in the world.'* If such superlatives *are* superlative in the case of Lionel Wilmot Brabazon Rees, VC OBE MC AFC, then it cannot be denied that Rees had embellished superbly the inherited fighting courage of his ancestors.

---

* *Wings over the Somme*, by Wing Commander G. H. Lewis, DFC; Wm Kimber 1976.

8. William Leefe Robinson

Of all the Victoria Crosses ever awarded, six were won by men within United Kingdom territory; and the first of these went to an airman, William Robinson of the Royal Flying Corps. The deed which brought him the supreme honour was witnessed by many hundreds of people, and the official notification of his VC was promulgated within forty-eight hours of the deed – probably the quickest such award in the history of the little bronze cross.

Youngest of seven children of Horace Robinson, a coffee planter on the Kaima Betta Estate at South Coorg, India, William Leefe Robinson – his second Christian name, Leefe, being taken from his mother's maiden surname – was born at Tollideta, South Coorg on 14 July 1895. Brought to England as a baby, Robinson returned to India with his family at the age of seven where he received his elementary education at the Bishop Cotton School. At fourteen he returned once more to England and, with his brother Harold, entered St Bees in Cumberland in September 1909. At St Bees Robinson quickly became a popular figure, and in the course of his next five years' schooling became captain of Eaglesfield House, captain of the Rugby XV, a prefect and sergeant in the school's Officers Training Corps. Leaving St Bees, Robinson enrolled at the military academy at Sandhurst on 14 August 1914, and on 16 December 1914 was commissioned as Second Lieutenant in the 5th Battalion of the Worcester Regiment. Three months later on 29 March 1915, Robinson transferred to the Royal Flying Corps as an observer for flying duties.

Immediately following his transfer he was posted to France, where he soon joined No 4 Squadron RFC at the St Omer depot; a BE2c army co-operation unit commanded by Major C. A. H. Longcroft. His stay with 4 Squadron was brief, for on 9 May, during a routine reconnaissance over Lille, he was wounded in the right arm, and invalided home to England. Recovering quickly from this injury, Robinson applied for pilot training, was accepted, and reported to South Farnborough to commence training on 29 June 1915.

Making his first solo flight on 18 July, Robinson qualified for his Royal Aero Club Certificate, No 1475, on 28 July. A further course of 'advanced' instruction at the Upavon Central Flying School resulted in the award of his RFC 'wings' on 15 September 1915. On 2 February

1916 Robinson joined his first operational unit as a pilot when he travelled to Sutton's Farm airfield in Essex, base for 39 (Home Defence) Squadron.

Sutton's Farm aerodrome (later retitled Hornchurch to become one of RAF Fighter Command's vital fighter bases in the 1940 Battle of Britain) was one of a chain of air defence stations in south-east England tasked with the aerial protection of (mainly) London against marauding German airships and, later, long range bombers. 39 Squadron was not fully formed as an individual squadron until 15 April 1916, but its nucleus comprised detachments of six BE2c aircraft stationed at various makeshift airfields in Essex; and it was to one such detachment at Sutton's Farm that Robinson first reported.

The BE2c's used were makeshift 'night fighters'; standard designs slightly modified locally for their purpose. The normal front observer's cockpit was faired over, and a locally-devised fixture was attached to the rear of the upper wing centre-section, on which a single Lewis machine gun was mounted, slanted upwards. Spare ammunition drums were carried in the rear (pilot's) cockpit; also a Very Light signal pistol, and – eventually – Holt flares affixed at the under extremities of the lower wings to aid night landings. Further improvement towards efficiency at night was the marking of essential instruments on the pilot's dashboard with luminous paint. Night 'runways' consisted simply of petrol-soaked rags in tin barrels, spaced along either side of appropriate clearways across the grass airfield. Without benefit of wireless communication, oxygen equipment, cockpit heating – or parachute – the RFC's 1916 'night fighter' pilots were expected to locate and destroy any enemy raider penetrating English skies by night. Their aircraft seldom had a performance range adequate to even approach the high-flying Zeppelins; while 'interception' was difficult in a BE2c, which took nearly an hour in favourable conditions to climb to 10,000 feet.

Notwithstanding the high odds against success, RFC Home Defence crews persevered nightly; gaining valuable experience and never daunted by the inherent risks they undertook so willingly. Robinson was soon inculcated into the nightly routine of flying and searching, and on the night of 25/26 April 1916 was fortunate enough to sight and close with a Zeppelin. The airship was the LZ97, flying at about 10,000 feet. Only able to climb to 8,000 feet, Robinson caught up with the LZ97 over Seven Kings and opened fire from below at extreme range. The airship merely released part of its ballast, rose swiftly, and was almost immediately lost to Robinson's sight.

The following four months were frustrating for Robinson and his

Lionel Wilmot Brabazon Rees

William Leefe Robinson

Thomas Mottershead

Frank Hubert McNamara

fellow 39 Squadron pilots, with many attempts to intercept raiding airships but without tangible success. Individual pilots now became detailed to patrol specific 'lanes' athwart the probable incoming flight paths of the Zeppelins, and slowly an overall co-ordinated defence organisation of aircraft and anti-aircraft ground defences began to evolve.

On the night of 2/3 September 1916, a total of 16 German airships set out with one common objective – London. It proved to be the greatest single airship raid of the war. Of these, 12 were naval airships, and four army vessels; one of the latter being the Schutte Lanz SL11, commanded by Hauptmann Wilhelm Emil Ludwig Schramm, on only its second operational sortie. Schramm, ironically, had been born in London, the son of a German representative of the Siemens firm; and this night he was fated to die within a few miles of his birthplace.

Crossing the English coast at Foulness Point at 10.40 pm, Schramm made a wide sweep to approach London from the north, and began dropping bombs as he reached London Colney, Hertfordshire. Scattering more bombs at North Mimms, Littleheath, Cockfosters and Hadley Wood, Schramm's giant airship was suddenly lit up by searchlights over Tottenham, and became the target for several anti-aircraft guns. Turning north-eastwards, then north, Schramm continued spasmodic bombing of Edmonton, Ponders End, and Turkey Street; but at that moment came the first stuttering sounds of a machine gun – the airship was under attack from an aeroplane; a BE2c from 39 Squadron, piloted by William Robinson.

The ground defences had received little pre-warning of the approaching Zeppelin force, and at Sutton's Farm Robinson and his friend Fred Sowrey set out in their BE2c's just after 11 pm to carry out normal night patrols. Robinson, in BE 2092, left the ground at 11.08 pm with orders to reconnoitre the Sutton's Farm to Joyce Green area, and climbed steadily to 10,000 feet, taking 53 minutes to reach this patrol height. The night was beautifully clear, with few clouds, and Robinson spent the next hour dutifully patrolling his designated air 'lane' without incident.

Then, at 1.10 am his attention was drawn to an airship illuminated by two searchlights south-east of Woolwich. By this time Robinson had increased his height to a little under 13,000 feet, and he immediately turned towards the airship, hoping to cut it off on its homeward flight. Slowly gaining on the Zeppelin, Robinson cut his speed in order to remain some 200 feet above the airship, but before he could get into an attacking position, the airship (LZ98, commanded by Oberleutnant

Ernst Lehmann*) slid into cloud and was lost to sight. For 15 minutes Robinson searched desperately for his lost quarry, but then resigned himself to his bad luck and returned to his patrol duties.

Hardly had he regained patrol height, however, than he noticed a red glow on the ground north-east of London, and, taking this to be due to an airship's depredations, set off in that direction with all speed. A few minutes after 2 pm Robinson saw an airship illuminated by search-lights ahead of him and, remembering how he had sacrificed speed for height in his earlier encounter, thereby losing his prey, he began a downhill race from 12,000 feet to gain speed. His target was the focal point for anti-aircraft shells and night tracers – most of which either fell short or were wide of the mark – but Robinson continued his diving approach until he came within 800 feet below the silver leviathan.

Flying steadily along its length, he fired a complete drum of Brock and Pomeroy ball and incendiary bullets; raking the massive hull from bow to stern, but apparently without effect. Banking steeply, Robinson made a second run along the airship's flanks, and fired a second full drum of bullets – again, without visible result. With only one drum of ammunition left, Robinson closed to within 500 feet of the Zeppelin's belly, and concentrated his fire on one small section of the hull. Before he had emptied the drum, he saw the target area begin to glow; then, within seconds, the rear part of the hull erupted in flames. The SL11 staggered and turned broadside on, out of steering control; the blazing tail sections dipped; huge engulfing flames ran like quicksilver along the vessel's entire length towards the blunt nose; and then fell towards earth in a near-perpendicular stance.

As the awsome pillar of blazing wreckage began to descend, Robinson was forced hastily to manoeuvre quickly out of its path; then, his whole being surging with the excitement of the moment, he fired off several red Very Lights and released a parachute flare. A glance at his instruments showed that the BE2c was by now low on fuel, so Robinson planed down and returned to Sutton's Farm; landing there at 2.45 am. Examination of his aircraft showed that his Lewis gun mounting had worked loose during the engagement, and Robinson had unknowingly shot away the gun's wire guard, torn away the rear part of the wing centre-section, and pierced the main wing spar in several places. Luckily for the pilot, he had attempted no violent manoeuvres after destroying the airship; any such moves might easily have caused a complete break-up in mid-air. His victim, SL11, trailing a comet's tail of flaming fabric and wood structure

* Died 21 years later in the *Hindenburg* disaster.

members, finally fell in a field near Cuffley. None of its 16-member crew survived the holocaust.

The whole engagement had been witnessed from the ground by countless hundreds of civilians, whose subsequent reaction to Robinson's triumph was overwhelming. After many months of suffering under the onslaught of apparently unassailable airship bombing raids, the British population's feelings exploded in a national wave of near-hysterical relief at the fiery proof of the Zeppelins' vulnerability; and expressed that relief in showering William Robinson with adulation, gifts and congratulatory headlines.

Epitomising the nation's feelings came the announcement, on 5 September, of the immediate award to Robinson of the Victoria Cross; while from many quarters came individual gifts, and cheques of 'prize money' contributed by a score of private citizens. In all, Robinson received some £4,200 in 'prize' contributions, and used some of this cash to purchase a new Vauxhall 'Prince Henry' automobile. On 8 September 1916, Robinson attended a special investiture at Windsor Castle, where he received his VC from the hands of King George V; and afterwards was literally mobbed in Windsor High Street by the many thousands of spectators who had gathered to catch a glimpse of their national hero.

The constant public attention was an embarrassment to Robinson, a modest man, who pleaded with RFC higher authorities for duties in a less public area. His request resulted in a posting to 48 Squadron at Rendcombe, with the rank of Captain. The new unit was in the process of forming for operational service in France, and was the first to equip with a new design; the Bristol F2A fighter two-seater. On 8 March 1917, the squadron finally moved to France and took up quarters at Bertangles.

After a few weeks of preparation, 48 Squadron despatched its first operational sortie on 5 April – and met near-disaster. Led by Robinson in Bristol F2A, A3337, with Lieutenant E. D. Warburton as his observer, six F2A's crossed the trench lines and were almost immediately set upon by five Albatros DIII's from Jagdstaffel 11, led by Germany's leading fighter pilot, Rittmeister Manfred von Richthofen. Unused to their new machines, the F2A crews stood little chance against such battle-hardened veterans. Of the six F2A's, four were shot down within minutes; Robinson being brought down intact by Vizefeldwebel Sebastian Festner near Mericourt, for the German's fourth accredited combat victory. Robinson and Warburton, both uninjured, were taken to Douai; there to await transportation to a regular prisoner of war camp.

For the remainder of the war Robinson suffered imprisonment in a series of camps. Going initially to Freiburg-in-Breisgau, he became one of a four-man team attempting to dig an escape tunnel under the outer defences – despite a lifetime sufferance of claustrophobia. The tunnel attempt came to nothing. but on 18 September 1917, Robinson and a companion managed to escape in broad daylight, and set off towards the border. Four days later, within four kilometres of their objective at Stuhlingen they were recaptured by an alert sentry and returned to Freiburg. The escape attempt led to a court-martial for Robinson, who was sentenced to one month's solitary confinement in the fortress at Zorndorf.

From here, after his punishment period, Robinson was again moved; to Clausthal on 2 May 1918. An attempt to jump from the train taking him to Clausthal was frustrated, and at the new camp Robinson found himself under the command of Camp Officer Niemeyer – one of twin brothers whose harsh treatment of Allied prisoners became notorious. In July 1918, Robinson was moved from Clausthal to Holzminden, where he became singled out for harsh treatment by the other Niemeyer Camp Officer, Karl.

A fellow prisoner at Holzminden has publicly testified to Karl Niemeyer's vendetta against Robinson;*

. . . and here also lay Leefe Robinson, VC, whose gallant spirit Niemeyer, with subtle cruelty, had endeavoured for months past to break. That Robinson's untimely death on his return from captivity was assisted indirectly by the treatment he received at the hands of Niemeyer no one will deny who was in a position to witness that treatment.

The general indignation of fellow prisoners at Robinson's severe treatment led to a full report being smuggled out of the camp, concealed in the hollow of a tennis racket handle, and despatched to the War Office in London. When the armistice of November 1918 was eventually declared, Robinson was a sick man, and he was finally repatriated to England on 14 December 1918.

Desperately ill, Robinson became a bed patient in the home of a colleague, Captain Noel Clifton, in Stanmore, Middlesex; and further complication set in when Robinson contracted the influenza virus then sweeping a deadly swathe across Europe. With his fiancée, Joan Whipple, and one sister (Baroness Heyking) at his bedside, William Leefe

* *The Tunnellers of Holzminden* by H. G. Durnford; 1920.

Robinson vc died on 31 December 1918, due to heart failure, brought on by virulent influenza. On 3 January 1919, with full military honours, Robinson was buried in a quiet corner of All Saints Church cemetery in Harrow-Weald, Middlesex.

9. Thomas Mottershead

With the distinction of being the only non-commissioned officer to be awarded a Victoria Cross during aerial operations of 1914–18, Thomas Mottershead was a native of Lancashire; born at 6 Vine Street, Widnes, on 17 January 1892. His early education came from the Simms Cross Council School in Widnes, where his obvious intelligence gained him entry to Widnes Technical School in 1907. For the next three years Mottershead studied engineering both in school and in private, obtaining several certificates of skilled competence in engineering theory and practice; and on leaving school he was apprenticed as a fitter and turner to Widnes Alkali works. Continued spare-time study brought him membership of the Amalgamated Society of Engineers, and he took up employment with Cammell Lairds in Birkenhead. Of robust health, he played football as a junior for St Mary's Recreation team and, later, the Widnes Wesley Guild; while his deep Christian faith led him to become a Bible reader at St Paul's Sunday School. A popular figure, Mottershead's instinctive honesty gave him a reputation of a man whose word was his bond. On 10 February 1914 he married Lilian Bree, a childhood sweetheart, and in the following year she bore him a son, Sydney Thomas.

Seeking to better his position in view of his increased domestic responsibilities, Mottershead travelled south and took a temporary job as a garage motor mechanic in Andover, Hampshire in the summer of 1914. Then, with a friend also from Widnes, he made his way to Portsmouth with the intention of securing a permanent position in the Portsmouth naval dockyard. Their arrival in Portsmouth coincided with the outbreak of war and both Mottershead and his friend, Frank Moore, enlisted in the Royal Flying Corps on 10 August 1914. Now No 1396 Air Mechanic 2nd Class, Mottershead's first posting was to the Central Flying School, Upavon, and in September he arranged for his wife and son to join him there. For the next eighteen months he continued to serve on the school's maintenance staff, gaining promotion to Corporal on 15 September 1915; acting Sergeant on 1 January 1916; and substantive rank of Sergeant from 1 April 1916. Meanwhile his growing ambition to become a pilot culminated in his being accepted for training, and in May 1916 he commenced pilot instruction. He proved to be an excellent pilot, due in no small measure to his expert technical knowledge and experience, and obtained a 2nd Class Pilot's Certificate at Upavon in the same month; followed quickly by a 1st Class Certificate on 9 June 1916. A month of duties as a flying instructor followed but on 4 July, in company with three other NCO pilots – Flight Sergeant J. T. B. McCudden MM, Sergeants Pateman, and Haxton* – he was posted to France and the RFC Pilot's Pool at St Omer; arriving there on 5 July. Next day he reported to 25 Squadron at Auchel for operational duties.

Equipped with FE2b and FE2d two-seat 'pusher' aircraft, 25 Squadron was regarded officially as a fighter/reconnaissance unit, though the squadron's varied duties included a high proportion of bombing sorties. With the first battle of the Somme only a week old, the squadron was in action daily when Mottershead joined it, and little time was available to initiate fresh pilots into operational conditions. Allotted an experienced observer-gunner, Lieutenant W. E. Harper, Mottershead made only two brief local flights to familiarise himself with the terrain, before being detailed for an operational sortie. His fighting spirit was evident from the start, and on his initial war sortie he carried out a low-level bombing attack on a particularly troublesome German anti-aircraft battery and destroyed it from a height of 1,000 feet.

For the following two months he continued to add to a growing reputation for cool courage, and on 22 September his bravery earned him his first gallantry award. Flying FE2b, 6998, with Second Lieutenant C. Street as observer, Mottershead was detailed to bomb the railway station at Samain. Diving to 1,500 feet over the objective, Mottershead bombed an ammunition train and destroyed it; then he flew very low over a second train and raked it with machine gun fire along its entire length. As he climbed away from this target, his FE was attacked from behind by a Fokker scout, but by skilful manoeuvring he outfought the German monoplane and Street finally shot it down. For this, and his previous record of sustained courage, Mottershead was awarded a Distinguished Conduct Medal (DCM); the announcement and citation appearing in the *London Gazette* dated 14 November 1916.

Shortly after, with the acting rank of Flight Sergeant, Mottershead was posted from 25 Squadron to another FE unit, 20 Squadron at Clairmarais. By then, after five months' almost continuous operational service, he was permitted two weeks' leave in England, and spent Christmas 1916 with his family; taking time out to visit his old school where he was persuaded to give the pupils a brief account of the work

---

* All later killed on active service. McCudden rose to Major, VC, DSO, MC, MM before his death—see Chapter 15.

of the RFC in France. He then returned to 20 Squadron at the beginning of 1917.

On Sunday, 7 January 1917, Mottershead was detailed along with another FE crew for a fighting patrol over the Ploegsteert Wood area. The second FE took off just before noon but Mottershead's aircraft was found to be unserviceable, and with his observer, Lieutenant W. E. Gower, he was forced to transfer to a reserve FE2d, A39. Leaving Clairmarais in great haste, he soon caught up with his companion FE, and both eventually reached their designated patrol area at a height of some 10,000 feet. Almost before the FE crews had begun to systematically search the sky for hostile aircraft, they were attacked by two Albatros scouts and became separated. Gower managed to fire an accurate burst at one Albatros which immediately spun down, seemingly out of control; but only seconds later the second Albatros, piloted by Vizefeldwebel Göttsch of Jagdstaffel 8, closed under the tail of Mottershead's FE and fired at point-blank range. His bullets ruptured the aircraft's petrol tank and the FE burst into flames.

With the engine and rear nacelle a holocaust of fire, the FE dropped towards earth. Gower could plainly see how quickly the fire was consuming the plywood fuselage, and snatched a hand extinguisher from its clip in his cockpit and began playing the jet over Mottershead in an attempt to keep the flames away from the pilot, whose flying clothing was already smouldering on its back. As the burning bomber came closer to earth infantry in front-line trenches could see clearly Gower's attempts to smother the roaring furnace threatening to engulf the pilot.

The stricken aircraft passed closely over the first line of Allied trenches heading for safer ground in the rear. It would have been possible for Mottershead to have crashlanded at any time then, but he was obviously determined to bring his machine down as safely as possible in order to give his observer every possible chance of survival. In the rear reserve trenches other infantry watched Mottershead deliberately circle a reasonably flat field and head the FE into wind for a normal landing approach. Trailing flames and smoke, with pieces of burning fabric and ply whirling in its fiery slipstream, the cumbersome FE finally settled in its landing run, but as soon as the undercarriage touched earth it collapsed. The FE toppled forward in a slithering crash, digging its fragile nose into the mud and throwing Gower clear, but at the same time pinning Mottershead in his cockpit; surrounded by blazing petrol and wreckage, with the engine poised to crush him.

Gower, who had sustained cuts, shock and extensive bruising only from his tumble, joined nearby troops in extricating the pilot from the blazing wreckage, and, despite horrific burns to his back, hands and legs, Mottershead was still able to converse readily and rationally to his rescuers, and remained cheerful, even talkative, as he was rushed to the nearest medical centre for emergency treatment. For the next four days and nights army surgeons fought to save the pilot's life, but his burns were too great to be treated effectively with the scanty facilities immediately available. Remaining cheerful and uncomplaining to the end, Mottershead finally succumbed to his extensive injuries on 12 January 1916.

On the 13th he was buried with full military honours in Bailleul cemetery, with every available man from his squadron present to pay final respects to their comrade. As the unit's temporary commander, Captain G. J. Mahoney-Jones, wrote to Lilian Mottershead on 14 January, '. . . at the funeral, as we lifted the wreath and Union Jack from the coffin and laid it on the ground, we sorrowfully knew that we had laid to rest one of the bravest men who had ever fallen in war.'

On 12 February 1917 came the announcement of the posthumous award of the Victoria Cross to Mottershead; while Gower was awarded a Military Cross (MC) for his part in the heroic exploit. The bronze cross was later presented personally to Mrs Lilian Mottershead by King George V at an open air investiture in Hyde Park, London on 2 June 1917. When the VC award was first made public Mottershead's native town, Widnes, opened an appeal fund with the declared objective of providing materially for the pilot's widow and small son. Among other methods of raising the fund was a concert held on 11 April 1917 in the Premier Picture House in aid of 'Mayor of Widnes Memorial Fund to Thomas Mottershead'. Part of the official programme's appeal message read, '. . . and Widnes, for its honour and good name's sake, cannot forget the wife and little son who, in life, were the Sergeant's special affection.'

In all a sum of nearly £1,000 was soon raised – yet neither widow or son ever received a penny of the money collected. Indeed, it was to be nearly 50 years before an alert civil servant 'unearthed' the records of the fund and 'discovered' the outstanding money; which was then used to endow the Mottershead Scholarship at Widnes Technical College – in tribute to the supreme courage and sacrifice of its most gallant ex-pupil.

10. Frank Hubert McNamara

The only Australian to be awarded a Victoria Cross for aerial operations in 1914–18, Frank Hubert McNamara was born on 4 April 1894 at Waranga, near Rushworth, in Victoria, Australia. His early education in Rushworth led him to a teachers' training college and Melbourne University, with the intention of a career in academic teaching; and on graduation from the university he took up posts as a teacher at Shepparton and, later, Melbourne. Though comparatively young, McNamara's patent ability soon led to appointments as Head Teacher at Red Bluff, Mordialloc and North Koo-wee-rup schools. In 1912, however, he joined the Brighton Rifles, 46th Infantry Battalion, and in July 1913 was commissioned as a Second Lieutenant.

Mobilised at the outbreak of war, he saw service with the home defences, and by early 1915 was an instructor at the Broadmeadows Training Depot. Already he had developed an interest in aviation, and in July 1915 was selected to attend the third course in military aeronautics at Point Cook flying school, where his baptism of the air came in the exposed pilot's seat of a Bristol Boxkite. Further training eventually led to McNamara being granted Royal Aero Club Certificate No 2254 on 20 October 1915. A further brief course of instruction followed, and in January 1916 he was posted as adjutant to No 1 Squadron, Australian Flying Corps (AFC).

The first complete Australian Flying Corps unit to be formed, No 1 Squadron AFC left Melbourne on 16 March 1916 for service in Egypt; where all aircraft and operational equipment was to be supplied by the Royal Flying Corps, under a previous arrangement with British authorities. However, it was six weeks after 1 Squadron AFC arrived before the first aircraft were received, and in the interim many of the air crews were sent to England for further training in operational flying, including McNamara.

Arriving in England on 16 May, he underwent advanced tuition at Filton, Reading and Netheravon, and eventually returned to Egypt on 24 August 1916. Further refresher training in desert conditions at Aboukir followed, before McNamara finally rejoined his squadron. By then (December 1916) 1 Squadron's equipment comprised mainly obsolescent BE2c's, BE2e's and a few Martinsyde G100 Scouts; and it was in a BE2c, 4475, that Frank McNamara made his first operational sortie on 22 December – as one of 13 aircraft detailed to bomb Turkish positions at Magdhaba, prior to an infantry assault on these at daybreak of the following morning.

Such close tactical support for the ground forces was to be the prime duty of the squadron throughout the remaining years of the war; including bombing, aerial photography, general reconnaissance, and – occasionally – air combat, over an area of bald wasteland which offered no succour to any man forced to land therein. Apart from the trackless desert wastes, baking under a constant sun, a stranded airman also faced the unwelcome attentions of hostile Arab tribesmen and the possibility of cruel captivity in Turkish hands. In these circumstances the normal close-knit comradeship of the unit's air crews was heightened, and whenever possible attempts were always made to rescue any crew forced down in hostile territory.

Throughout January and February 1917, McNamara flew in most of the squadron's bombing and reconnaissance operations; usually as pilot of a BE, but occasionally in a single-seat Martinsyde as fighting escort for the unit's bombers. Such operations usually entailed flying low over heavily-guarded enemy positions, with the consequence of having to run a gauntlet of intensive gun fire; but such dangerous missions were inter-spersed with bombing raids from relatively safe heights against German air strips. Even in the grim conditions of constant war, an occasional light relief was introduced; as on 18 February 1917 when McNamara, in BE2e 7133, bombed the German aerodrome at Ramleh – and then dropped a note suggesting that the Germans move their dummy airfield outside Ramleh to a more concealed location!

On 20 March 1917, two BE2c's, piloted by Captain D. W. Rutherford and Lieutenant Drummond, were detailed to bomb a section of railway across Wadi Hesse, at Tel el Hesi; and in part-escort two Martinsyde G100's, piloted by McNamara and Lieutenant L. Ellis; each aircraft loaded with six 4.5 howitzer shells hastily 'modified' as bombs, with a delay action of 40 seconds. On arrival over the target, the BE's bombed, followed by Ellis, and then McNamara. As Ellis completed his bombing he spotted a German aircraft and set off in pursuit.

McNamara, in Martinsyde 7486, following in behind Ellis, swept low over a train and released three of his makeshift 'shell-bombs' onto it; then dropped two more on the railway lines. The last shell-bomb exploded almost as it left the Martinsyde's rack, and slivers of shell casing ripped through the aircraft's lower wings and fuselage, one jagged chunk tearing McNamara's right buttock. Dropping two smoke bombs as markers for the other aircraft, he turned for home. Then, glancing down at the curving railway track, he noticed a BE2c on the ground – Rutherford's No 4479 – with a formation of Turkish cavalry galloping towards the stranded Rutherford.

Disregarding his painful wound, and the obvious dangers, McNamara switched off his engine and glided down to land. Taxying across the rough ground towards Rutherford, he saw the BE pilot attempting to set fire to his machine, so yelled at him to hurry. Rutherford abandoned his attempt to destroy his BE, sprinted to McNamara's Martinsyde, and hauled himself up onto its engine cowling in between the centre-section struts. Opening up his Beardmore engine to full power, McNamara started his take-off, with Rutherford clinging precariously above the fuselage's forward section. McNamara's right leg had by now become numb with loss of blood from his wound and as the Martinsyde reached a speed of 35 mph the aircraft began swinging to the left. Unable to counter the swing due to his useless right leg, McNamara could only hope to get airborne before the swing became too pronounced, but his luck was out. Continuing its veering flight, the Martinsyde dipped its nose as the undercarriage collapsed, and crashed on its left side; shattering the propeller, breaking both left wings, and wiping off its undercarriage.

Climbing painfully out of the wreck, McNamara remained remarkably cool-headed, and immediately set about destroying the remains of his aircraft by firing a bullet into the Martinsyde's main petrol tank, and then igniting the escaping petrol with a Very cartridge. By now the approaching Turkish cavalrymen were within rifle range, and as McNamara and Rutherford scrambled towards the latter's stranded BE2c, bullets started whipping the sand up around them. As they ran McNamara's Martinsyde erupted in an explosion – the one remaining shell-bomb on board had detonated.

Reaching the BE2c, McNamara took a swift inventory of its damage. In landing Rutherford had ripped off a wheel tyre, broken several centre-section wires, cracked a longeron, and dropped some spare Lewis gun drums of ammunition in the cockpit which were jammed under the rudder bar. Climbing into the rear cockpit, McNamara managed to extricate the ammunition drums, yelled to Rutherford to swing the propeller, and as the BE's engine roared into life, started to taxi. Rutherford jumped into the observer's seat after a wild scramble onto the lower wing, as McNamara turned the BE round for a take-off run. Opening the throttle wide, McNamara started his run across the soggy sand. Behind him were the enemy cavalry, still firing and racing to overtake the aircraft.

Three times the BE began to bog down in soft patches but McNamara continued to urge the BE on, and finally the overladen machine achieved flight and climbed away. Once at 1,500 feet McNamara wasted no time in setting course for the nearest Allied airfield, Kilo 143, about 70 miles away. The after-effects of his wound and exhausting activity on the ground brought McNamara near to fainting at one point, but by keeping his head outside the cockpit and thereby reviving himself from the rushing slipstream, he managed to reach his goal without further mishap one hour and twenty minutes later. It was only after he had landed safely at Kilo 143 that he discovered the BE still had three of its bombs on the under-rack. Weak from blood-loss and exhaustion, McNamara was quickly transferred to a hospital train and evacuated for medical attention.

For the following five months McNamara remained in hospital and on convalescence, but in the same period his promotion to Captain was promulgated on 10 April 1917; while on 8 June came the *London Gazette* announcement of the award of a Victoria Cross for his selfless action of 20 March. In September 1917 he was invalided home to Australia, and officially discharged from the Australian Flying Corps on 31 January 1918. On 9 September 1918, however, he was reinstated, with Captain rank and former seniority, and became an instructor. On 27 April 1920 he was formally presented with his Victoria Cross by HRH The Prince of Wales at a ceremony in Federal Government House in Melbourne; and when the Royal Australian Air Force was inaugurated in March 1921, McNamara was given a permanent commission in the rank of Flight Lieutenant.

After a short spell as a staff officer at RAAF Headquarters, he returned to Point Cook as commander of No 1 FTS, and in March 1924 was promoted to Squadron Leader. In the same year he married Helene Marcelle Bluntschli; and in June 1925 came to England for a two-years' exchange tour of duty with the RAF, at No 5 FTS and at the Air Ministry in London. Returning to Australia in November 1927, he resumed his former duties at Point Cook, remaining there until 1933, and becoming the station commander after his promotion to Wing Commander in October 1931.

In February 1933 he was appointed in command of No 1 Aircraft Depot and RAAF Laverton Station, and in the same year completed his studies for a Bachelor of Arts degree at Melbourne University. Promotion to Group Captain followed in 1936, and in the following year he attended the Imperial Defence College in England. A post as Air Liaison Officer at the Air Ministry, London brought him a CBE in the 1938 New Year's

Honours List, and in 1939 he reached air rank with promotion to Air Commodore.

Throughout the 1939–45 war McNamara remained with the RAF; appointed as Air Officer Commanding RAAF Headquarters in London until the close of 1942, and then being appointed as AOC British Forces in Aden until the end of the war – duties which brought him a CB award in 1945 and promotion to Air Vice-Marshal. In July 1946, and in a sense bringing him full circle to his original career intentions of his youth, he was appointed Director of Education at the headquarters of the British Occupation Forces Administration in Westphalia, Germany. Retiring from Service life in 1947, he next became a member of the National Coal Board, with his permanent home in Buckinghamshire. On 2 November 1961 Frank McNamara died at his home, as the result of a fall when working in his garden.

11. William Avery Bishop

Canada's vast and invaluable contribution in men, material and effort to the British cause in both world wars is seldom given the prominence it deserves in official histories and accounts. From a population spread thinly over a massive geographical area came many thousands of young men, eager and willing to join the 'Mother Country's' struggle against Britain's foes; men whose fighting prowess became near-legendary, and whose sacrifices were proportionately higher than most countries involved in the global conflicts. As with most Dominion youth, Canada's sons were always highly individual in their approach to their fighting duties; exemplified particularly by the many Canadian airmen in the Allied air services of 1914-18. For merely one example, of the twenty top-scoring fighter 'aces' of the RFC, RNAS and RAF, seven were from Canada. Heading the list of Canada's fighter pilots, in terms of numbers of enemy aircraft conquered, was William Avery Bishop, with an officially accredited tally of 72 victories in aerial combat.

The son of W. A. Bishop, Registrar of Grey County, Ontario, William Avery Bishop was born at Owen Sound, Ontario on 8 February 1894; the third son of the marriage. From his earliest years young 'Billy' Bishop – his universal nickname – was a rebel against authority in any shape or form, who seldom lost any opportunity to break imposed rules of conduct. Ungifted in the academic field, Bishop preferred to develop his natural talents for the 'outdoor' life; excelling as a rifle shot and equestrian, and quickly achieving a high local reputation for his ability to use his fists whenever an occasion demanded it. In contrast with his elder brothers' brilliant academic achievements, young Billy's school record was an abysmal series of bad reports and the despair of his tutors; a scholastic career succinctly summed up by his head teacher as, 'The only thing your son is good at is fighting.'

On his seventeenth birthday in 1911, Bishop decided to follow in his brother's footsteps and applied for entry to Canada's Royal Military College (the equivalent of America's West Point or England's Sandhurst). Accepted in August, Bishop spent the following three years as a cadet, despite failing his first year examinations and constantly transgressing the strict disciplinary code of behaviour on numerous occasions.

At the close of the 1914 summer term Bishop's many escapades culminated in the threat of expulsion from the college; the college staff officers
having reached the common opinion that young Bishop was, 'the worst
cadet RMC ever had.' During the summer vacation of 1914, and before
Bishop could return to the college and learn the staff's final decision, the
European War commenced, and despite Bishop's incomplete military
instruction, he was hastily commissioned on 30 September in a Toronto
militia regiment, the Mississauga Horse, then mobilising for service
overseas.

When his regiment finally embarked for England on 1 October 1914,
Bishop was in hospital, suffering from pneumonia, but soon after his
recovery he was transferred to the 14th Battalion of the 7th Canadian
Mounted Rifles, stationed in London, Ontario, and with this unit left
Canada on 9 June 1915 in a cattleship, *Caledonia*, bound for England
and the war.

Three weeks later, stationed at Shorncliffe, Kent, Bishop was
thoroughly depressed with his lot – living in primitive conditions of mud
and mire amongst the morass created by hundreds of horses in the dank
winter conditions. It was then he saw an RFC aeroplane land in a nearby
field briefly, then take off again, and the sight stirred his determination
to get away from the earthbound cavalry and transfer to the air service;
in his own words, 'the only way to fight a war; up there above the mud
and the mist in the everlasting sunshine.'

In July 1915 Bishop applied for transfer to the RFC as an observer,
rather than wait for possible acceptance as a pilot, and on 1 September
reported to 21 (Training) Squadron at Netheravon for elementary air
instruction. By Christmas the squadron was under orders for a move to
France, and on 1 January, 1916 arrived at Boisdinghem airfield, near
St Omer. By mid-January the unit had received its full complement of
new RE7 two-seat aircraft; lumbering reconnaissance machines with low
performance range.

Operations started almost immediately, with Bishop taking a large part
in the unit's activities and gaining his baptism of enemy fire. His progress
was punctuated with a number of accidents and injuries – Bishop always
seemed accident-prone throughout his life – including an injured knee
sustained when his regular pilot, Roger Neville, made a crashlanding.
Though in severe pain, Bishop refused medical attention which might
have meant his withdrawal from flying duties. Bishop's last operational
sortie as an observer came on 2 May, 1916 – a trial of air co-operation
with frontline infantry – and that same day he returned to England on
leave. His injured knee still gave trouble and on the last day of leave he

William Avery Bishop

Albert Ball

sought medical help. As a result he was admitted to hospital and remained unfit for operational flying until September, when he was sent home to Canada for convalescent leave. On his return to England, Bishop applied for pilot training, was accepted, and reported to Brasenose College, Oxford on 1 October 1916 for initial ground training.

In November he moved to the Central Flying School at Upavon to begin pilot instruction but quickly proved to be a bad pupil, despite the patience and skill of his instructor, Captain Trygve Gran. The pure 'art' of flying was always a difficult one to achieve for Bishop, while his many crashlandings throughout his war career became notorious. He persevered and, with Gran's help, finally received his pilot's 'wings', and was posted to Northolt for advanced nightflying training; followed by an attachment to 37 (Home Defence) Squadron at Sutton's Farm, Essex. It seemed highly illogical that a pilot seemingly unable to produce competent landings in broad daylight should be promptly employed on night flying duties, but Bishop was content to be accepted as a pilot in any form of operational unit, and overcame his admitted terror of flying by night.

Luckily for him, his request for transfer to France was soon approved, and on 9 March, 1917 he arrived at Filescamp, base of 60 Squadron RFC, where the unit commander Major A. J. Scott, had him allotted to B Flight. 60 Squadron at this period was equipped with single-seat Nieuport Scouts – tiny little biplanes powered by a rotary engine, and armed with a single Lewis machine gun mounted above the top wing, firing above the propeller arc. Highly manoeuvrable, though not particularly speedy, the Nieuport was an excellent combat aeroplane for the period. Its lightness in weight and response to controls soon proved too delicate for Bishop's heavy-handed method of flying, and after several damaging landings, he finally crashed during landing on 24 March – virtually at the feet of several visiting staff officers including his brigade commander. Later that day he was told that he was being posted back to England for further flying instruction, but was permitted to remain with 60 Squadron until a replacement pilot was found.

Next day Bishop was one of four Nieuport pilots from 60 Squadron who engaged a trio of Albatros DIII Scouts near St Leger. As one Albatros attempted to get under the tail of the leading Nieuport it came into Bishop's sights, and the Canadian promptly fired, splashing bullets around the German's cockpit. The Albatros dived away steeply with Bishop in pursuit, still firing, and after a headlong dive of nearly 9,000 feet the German plunged into the ground.

Pulling out of his dive, Bishop was elated – and then his engine cut completely. Managing to land undamaged on a stretch of shell-cratered mud, some 300 yards beyond the German frontline trenches – one of the very few good landings Bishop had ever made, ironically – he spent the night by his Nieuport and then returned to Filescamp. His victory, confirmed by several independent witnesses, saved Bishop from the pending ignominy of being posted back to England, and he now began a remarkable run of victories.

Where routine piloting was concerned Bishop's ham-handed flying technique never improved; yet once joined in combat with enemy machines, Bishop's superb marksmanship combined with an entirely unconscious talent for precise handling of his aircraft to produce a truly formidable fighter. On 8 April, Easter Sunday, Bishop claimed his fifth victim, but returned with his windscreen perforated by a bullet which had narrowly missed killing him. To 'celebrate', Bishop had the nose engine cowling and interplane Vee-struts of his Nieuport doped in bright blue colour – reminiscent of the red spinner which had marked the Nieuports flown by Bishop's idol, Albert Ball vc dso mc. On 25 April Bishop was promoted to Captain and given command of C Flight, and by the end of the month was credited with a total of at least 12 victories and awarded a Military Cross (gazetted 26 May, 1917).

Though usually leading men from his Flight, Bishop was by then beginning to fly solitary patrols, hunting for German targets. Like Albert Ball, Bishop was never entirely happy with the responsibility of other men's lives depending on him and much preferred a lone role in combat. Unlike Ball, however, Bishop could and did participate in formation patrols throughout his fighting career, without any great impediment to his skill and aggression. Four more victories during the first week of May were credited to Bishop, before his return to England on 7 May for a leave spell.

Returning to Filescamp on 22 May, Bishop quickly resumed his daily fighting, but had already given thought to the possibility of a particularly hazardous venture – a lone, surprise attack, preferably at sunrise, on a German aerodrome. He discussed the thought briefly with 60's commander, Jack Scott, who simply told him to 'go ahead'. In the tradition of an unceasing offensive, the RFC's pilots constantly fought their opponents miles deep into enemy territory, thus Bishop was no stranger to the German hinterland; yet the idea of a cold-blooded, planned, solo attack on an enemy airfield presented obvious hazards. Nevertheless, on 1 June, after several patrols without result, Bishop prepared for the venture by checking his Lewis gun and ammunition drums meticulously, while his mechanic Corporal Walter Bourne gave Bishop's Nieuport a thorough overhaul. That night Bishop was in bed early, shunning his normal late night revels in the squadron Mess.

June 2 1917 commenced in a depressing drizzle of rain and low mist clouds, and when Bishop was called at 3 am, he simply pulled his flying suit on over his pyjamas, sipped a cup of tea, and then made his way out to the squadron hangars. Walter Bourne, the only other man on the areodrome at that hour, had already wheeled out Bishop's blue-nosed Nieuport, B1566, and had its engine run up and ticking over. Bishop climbed into the snug cockpit and wasted little time in taking off. Climbing hard into driving rain which smothered his windscreen, Bishop headed towards Arras, then turned and followed the dimly visible Cambrai road below. After an hour's flying in the cloud and mists Bishop was lost and miles inside German territory, and on emerging from cloud found himself over an apparently deserted airfield.

Disappointed, Bishop continued to grope his way through the low cloud and soon found himself above a second aerodrome – Estourmel, on the outskirts of Cambrai. On the airfield he could see much dawn activity as the mechanics and pilots of a Jagdstaffel busied themselves preparing for the day's work ahead. Six Albatros Scouts and a two-seat machine were already out of their hangars, their engines being run up and tested, with pilots standing nearby ready to climb in.

Dropping to 200 feet, Bishop started his first running attack along the line of aircraft, spraying bullets as he streaked across the field through a barrage of small arms' fire from the alert ground defences. Lifting over the edge of the airfield, the Nieuport executed a tight banked turn for its reverse run, and Bishop saw that one Albatros pilot had already started to taxi for take-off. Concentrating on this machine, Bishop fired just 15 rounds as the Albatros rose to ten feet height. The shark-tailed Albatros dipped a wing, hit the grass and disintegrated, spewing wreckage in a long slide along the field.

As the first German crashed, a second Albatros started its take-off run and Bishop frantically fired at this but missed. His fire caused the German pilot to swerve away from his onslaught and the Albatros hit a tree on the perimeter, tearing away its right wings. Firing another brief burst into the wreckage, Bishop pulled hard on his control column and climbed fast. Intent now on returning, Bishop saw below him two aircraft taking off in opposite directions – he had little alternative but to remain and fight.

One Albatros climbed to Bishop's height but waited at a distance, while the other made straight for the silver Nieuport. As this opponent closed behind him, Bishop turned and fired, then began to circle, seeking a killing position. With its greater agility the Nieuport soon came up under the tail of the Albatros and Bishop emptied his Lewis drum into the forward fuselage of his adversary, who dropped away and crashed about 400 feet from the edge of his own airfield.

Still intent on escaping, Bishop completely forgot the hovering Albatros behind him, which now dived, flying at 300 yards' range and closing fast. Hastily replacing the empty drum on his Lewis gun, Bishop turned his Nieuport's nose towards the latest antagonist, pressed his gun trip, and fired the whole fresh drum of ammunition in one long smoking burst. Apparently unnerved by such a prolonged burst, the German dived towards the aerodrome and safety.

Bishop did not wait to see the fate of his fourth attacker, but fled at full throttle west. To assist his headlong flight, Bishop then dismounted his Lewis gun and threw it overboard – without more ammunition available, the machine gun was simply dead weight. The whole episode had lasted 37 minutes.

As he headed westwards Bishop spotted a formation of four enemy aircraft some 2,000 feet above him near Cambrai. Unarmed and alone, Bishop did his utmost to avoid being seen and after following the enemy's manoeuvres for a few minutes, dived at full power for the trench lines; crossing these near Bapaume amidst a flurry of anti-aircraft fire which added further damage to his already bullet-riven aircraft.

Once across the lines into Allied territory and comparative safety, Bishop immediately suffered reaction to the past hour's high-key tension, feeling sick and dazed.

Finally arriving over Filescamp aerodrome at 5.30 am, Bishop circled the sleeping squadron's huts and hangars and fired off a succession of Very Light signal flares; then rumbled in for landing and greeted his 'welcoming committee' of mechanics by extending three fingers of one hand excitedly to indicate his three victories. The Nieuport bore silent testimony to its ordeal of fire, with torn and slashed fabric hanging raggedly from wings and fuselage. As soon as Bishop had made his report of the morning's foray, Major Scott reported it to Wing headquarters and within hours the news had spread along the Western Front RFC units. A host of congratulatory messages flooded into Filescamp, including one from the GOC, Hugh Trenchard who termed Bishop's solo sortie as, 'the greatest single show of the war'.

Throughout July and early August Bishop continued his daily sorties within 60 Squadron, his victory tally continuing to mount but on 28 July he underwent an experience which stayed in his memory for many years after. Flying one of the squadron's newly issued SE5 scouts, Bishop

attacked a pair of German two-seaters over Monchy-le-Preux but was hit
in the engine by anti-aircraft fire.

Turning out of the fight, Bishop coaxed the badly-running engine as
long as possible but, when only two miles from Filescamp, it burst into
flames and, as Bishop side-slipped to keep the flames from him, the fire
spread to one wing. He eventually crashed, still burning, in some poplar
trees, and was left hanging upside down in his cockpit, with the flames
still threatening to consume both aeroplane and pilot.

Bishop fainted, and recovered consciousness later, after being rescued
by some passing infantrymen. This, his closest brush with death, remained
in his memory for many years, recurring as a constant nightmare.

On 9 August Bishop was informed personally by Trenchard that he
was to receive the Victoria Cross for his one-man raid of 2 June, and
two days later the *London Gazette* announced the award. He was also
informed by Trenchard that he would soon be leaving 60 Squadron for
an instructor's post in England. This news dismayed Bishop who by then
had become slightly obsessed with bringing his victory tally to a total
higher than any contemporary Allied fighter pilot.In the event he finally
left 60 Squadron on 1 September 1917 with an officially accredited
score of 47 victories. By that date he had received the VC, DSO (gazetted
18 June), and MC; and on 25 September a further award of a Bar to his
DSO was promulgated. All had been gained in five months of intensive
fighting serving with 60 Squadron.

Returning to Canada for extended leave, Bishop married his fiancée,
Margaret Burden, sister of a fellow Canadian fighter pilot serving with
the RFC, 'Hank' Burden; whom he had first met prior to enlisting in the
Royal Military College. The wedding ceremony at Timothy Eaton
Memorial Church in Toronto took place on 17 October 1917, and
thousands of local citizens lined the roads adjacent to the church to catch
a glimpse of Canada's national air hero, 'Billy' Bishop and his bride. On
his return to England Bishop expected to be appointed to the proposed
school of aerial fighting at Loch Doon, Scotland, but was instead promoted to Major on 13 March 1918 and given command of a freshly-
forming fighter squadron, No 85, at Hounslow, Middlesex.

Given a reasonably free hand in selecting his own pilots, Bishop
gathered together a hybrid collection of British, Canadian, New Zealand
and American individuals; the latter including the now legendary trio of
'Warbirds', Elliot Springs, Larry Callaghan and John McGavock Grider.
Equipped initially with Sopwith Dolphin scouts, 85 Squadron was re-
equipped with the latest versions of the SE5A, and eventually left Hounslow for France led by Bishop on 22 May 1918, and became based at

Petite Synthe, near Dunkirk. Bishop wasted little time in resuming his personal war in the air, and on 27 May shot a German two-seater to pieces in mid-air east of Passchendaele for his 48th victory. Next day he destroyed two Albatros scouts east of Ypres to bring his tally to a round 50.

By June he had added five more victims to his count; while four more victories were recorded by 4 June. On 8 June he received orders to move his squadron south to St Omer, and the move 'interrupted' Bishop's fighting activities for eleven days; but on the 15th he destroyed a Pfalz D III east of Estaires, and the following day destroyed two more Pfalz scouts near Armentières. A triple victory came on 17 June, followed by a double claim on the 18th. The rising pace of destruction reflected Bishop's anxiety that he would soon be withdrawn from operational flying; a fear confirmed on 17 June when he was officially informed that he was to return to England, to assist in the long-proposed formation of a Canadian Flying Corps. The actual movement order came through to St Omer on 18 June, ordering Bishop to leave France by noon the following day.

Mid-morning on the 19th Bishop decided to have 'one last look at the war', and took off alone for the German lines. In just 15 minutes of furious combat Bishop accounted for five enemy aircraft – four Pfalz D III scouts and a two-seater; bringing his officially accredited victory tally to 72. On 3 August 1918 the *London Gazette* announced the award of a Distinguished Flying Cross to Bishop, in recognition of his 25 victories in 12 days of actual combat while serving with 85 Squadron; and shortly after the French government decorated Bishop with its Croix de Guerre avec Palmes, and made Bishop a Chevalier de Legion d'Honneur.

On his return to England, Bishop was promoted to Lieutenant-Colonel on 5 August and posted to the Canadian Forces headquarters as the first Officer Commanding-designate for the proposed Canadian Air Corps. Intended, initially, as a two-squadrons' fighting force for service in France, the Canadian Corps Wing was still not fit for operations by October 1918, and Bishop was sent to Canada to report to the Prime Minister on progress. He was in mid-Atlantic aboard a ship bringing him back to England when news of the 11 November armistice with Germany was received. On 31 December Bishop was demobilised from the Royal Air Force and returned to Canada.

Re-adjustment to civilian life was not easy for Bishop, who spent several months touring the USA on a lecture tour, but in the summer of 1919 he went into partnership with another Canadian air VC, George Barker, to form one of Canada's first air charter lines. Still embued with the carefree attitudes of their war days, the pair of celebrated pilots soon ran into legal and financial problems and, shortly after Bishop had had a serious crash, the partnership was dissolved. At the end of 1921 Bishop brought his family to live in England, where he built up a highly success-ful business, but the Wall Street crash of November 1929 wiped out his amassed fortune, and he returned to Canada.

Shortly after his return he was offered a vice-presidency of the McColl-Frontenac Oil Company, and in 1931 was appointed an honorary Group Captain in the Royal Canadian Air Force. In 1936, with the growing menace of Nazi Germany's ambitions, Bishop was made an honorary Air Vice-Marshal, RCAF, whose main task for the Canadian government was to campaign extensively for vast enlargement of the RCAF. On 10 August, 1938 Bishop was further promoted, to the honorary rank of Air Marshal, and became head of the Air Advisory Committee. Convinced of the European war to come, and therefore Canada's immediate in-volvement, Bishop concentrated on expanding the RCAF as fast as possible, including a scheme for recruiting American pilots. A new appointment as Director of Recruiting, RCAF became effective from 23 January 1940, and for the following four years Bishop was tireless in his myriad of duties.

Due to ill-health and mounting exhaustion, Bishop requested that he be relieved of his post in 1944, and fitting recognition of his many years of devotion to the cause of the RCAF in particular, and aviation gener-ally, was made with the award of a CB in the King's Birthday Honours List of 1 June 1944. Returning to the oil business in 1945, Bishop even-tually retired in 1952, and in the early hours of 11 September 1956 Bishop died peacefully in his sleep at his Palm Springs, Florida home.

Bishop's award of a Victoria Cross was unique in that it was the only occasion of an air VC being granted solely on the uncorroborated (by Allied or German) evidence of the recipient's personal testimony.

12. Albert Ball

Of the 19 airmen awarded a Victoria Cross during the 1914–18 war, it is doubtful if any one received more publicity and public adulation than Albert Ball. At a period when officialdom frowned upon any form of publicity for individual deeds within the air services, Ball's name became virtually a household property. His youth and prowess captured the layman's imagination, and his highly individual fighting record became almost a symbol of hope to a British population dazed and weary of Allied losses and setbacks in the European struggle.

Born in Nottingham on 14 August, 1896, Albert Ball was the son of a master plumber who, in later years, became Mayor of the city and was knighted. Educated variously in Nottingham, Grantham, and finally Trent College, Ball's natural aptitude for anything of a mechanical nature was put to good practice when he left college and started in business with a small electrical engineering and brass-founding firm in his home town. At the outbreak of war Ball volunteered for service in the army and enlisted in the 2/7th Battalion of the Notts and Derby Regiment as a private on 21 September 1914. Promoted almost immediately to Sergeant, he was soon commissioned as a Second Lieutenant on 29 October 1914. With no apparent hope of being sent to the fighting zone in France, Ball transferred to the North Midlands Divisional Cyclist Company, but continued to be stationed in England throughout 1915.

Still determined to see active service, Ball turned to flying as a possible means of achieving his aim, and in June 1915 commenced private tuition as a pilot at Hendon with the Ruffy-Baumann School.

Due to his routine duties Ball's flying progress was relatively slow, but on 15 October 1915 he finally gained his Royal Aero Club Certificate, No 1898, and applied for transfer to the Royal Flying Corps. Further flying instruction was undertaken at Norwich and Upavon, and on 22 January 1916 he was awarded his RFC 'wings' brevet.

Transferred officially to the RFC on 29 January, Ball was sent to Gosport for a brief period as an instructor with 22 Squadron, but on 18 February he was in France, reporting to his first operational unit, 13 Squadron RFC at Marieux. His squadron was equipped with two-seat BE2c's – slow, stable machines, intended and used for general reconnaissance and bombing roles – and, after a series of moves, became based at Savy Aubigny airfield by mid-March 1916.

Ball was soon in action over the fighting area and on 20 March had his first close brush with death when his BE2c, 4352, crashed on the aerodrome due to engine failure. In the following weeks Ball was flying almost daily; bombing and observing for the artillery, and ever alert to any opportunity to get to grips with German aircraft, despite the unsuitability of his aircraft for any form of air combat. He also became increasingly unhappy with the responsibility of flying with an observer; preferring to fight alone unfettered by the thought of another man's life depending on him. An occasional flight in one of the squadron's two single-seat Bristol Scouts gave Ball the individual 'freedom' he longed for, and on 7 May 1916 he was posted to 11 Squadron RFC and given a single-seat Nieuport Scout in view of his obvious fighting potential.

During his first month as a fighter pilot Ball flew on every possible occasion and had a series of combats with German aircraft without positive success. His urge to be in constant action was exemplified by the small wooden hut he personally erected next to his Nieuport's hangar on the airfield, in which he lived and ate; always 'on the spot' for any chance of combat. On 1 June, flying Nieuport 5173, he deliberately circled above the German airfield at Douai, inviting combat, and then forced two aircraft which took up this impudent challenge to hastily land again. After a brief spell of home leave, Ball returned eagerly to the fighting scene, and on 26 June destroyed an observation balloon with phosphor bombs. This action added to his constant good work during the preceding months led to his first gallantry award, a Military Cross, gazetted on 27 July 1916. By mid-July however the effect of almost continuous fighting and flying began to tell on Ball's highly sensitive nervous system, and he approached his commanding officer to request a 'brief rest' from flying.

Two days later, to his dismay, he was taken away from his beloved Nieuport and posted to 8 Squadron, RFC at Bellevue – flying the obsolete BE2c's again! This 'retrograde' step (as Ball regarded it) had been authorised by his Brigade commander, and Ball later admitted ruefully that his original request had been due, perhaps, to a certain amount of youthful 'swell-headedness' (sic). Determined to regain his Nieuport, Ball flew the normal routine sorties expected of him but also badgered his new squadron commander with numerous requests to volunteer for any unusual or dangerous jobs. These voluntary missions included spy-dropping flights behind German lines; while on 9 August he attacked a German observation balloon in his cumbersome BE2d and forced its crew to take to their parachutes. His desperate attempts to 'prove' himself paid off, and on 14 August – his 20th birthday – he was posted back to 11 Squadron, where a newly-issued Nieuport Scout was already allotted for his personal use.

During the remaining weeks of August Ball began a run of combats and victories. On the 16th he tackled five Roland two-seaters single-handed and shot one down to force-land. Within minutes of this engagement he attacked a second batch of five Rolands, forcing one of these to land. Six days later he dived onto a gaggle of seven Rolands; his deadly accurate fire sent one down to destruction. He then attacked a formation of five Rolands and the fury of his onslaught sent one down pluming smoke, while a second spun down and crashed onto a house, with an already mortally wounded observer in its rear cockpit.

On 23 August Ball and a 11 Squadron companion, Leslie Foot, ferried two Nieuports to 60 Squadron RFC at Filescamp airfield; and Ball was allotted to A Flight of 60 Squadron, with a roving commission to fly and fight as he pleased. Ball's response to this latter 'honour' was to increase the intensity of his fighting, and in the next two weeks his Nieuport scout, distinguished by a large red-painted spinner cone fixed to its propeller boss, was an ever-present sight above the Somme battlefields. As always, numerical odds meant little to Ball, who employed one basic tactic to all his fighting – attack on sight. Such a ploy meant that his aircraft usually returned shredded with bullet and battle damage, but Ball's victory tally increased almost daily.

On 1 September 1916, 60 Squadron moved base to Savy Aubigny, and Ball returned with delight to the wooden hut which had been his 'home' there. On the same date his brigade commander, Brigadier-General Higgins, wrote of Ball, '. . . he has forced 20 German machines to land, of which eight have been destroyed. During this period he has (also) forced down two hostile balloons and destroyed one.'

On this fitting note, Ball returned to England for two weeks' leave, with the added distinction of an award of the Distinguished Service Order (DSO). On his return to 60 Squadron he was greeted with the news that he had been promoted to command of his Flight, while on the 13th came the award of a Bar to his DSO.* Only two days later he was notified that Russia had awarded him her Order of St George, 4th Class.†

Although now a Flight commander, Ball seldom led his men into action; preferring as always to hunt and fight alone; thereby leaving his mind wholly concentrated on his task of fighting. Even on the ground the Nottingham boy was something of a 'lone wolf' – polite, usually

* Both DSO and Bar were gazetted on 26 September 1916.
† Gazetted 15 February 1917.

smiling, but seldom interested in the social aspects of the squadron and Mess life. To Ball he was in France for one purpose – to fight his country's enemies. Nothing which might interfere with that purpose was worthy of his attention.

Yet to label Albert Ball as a 'killer' would be to do him grave injustice. Deeply religious in faith, Ball's sensitive nature suffered in immediate retrospect whenever he succeeded in combat. His private attitude to the war was best summed in a letter he wrote to his father, dated 10 July 1916:

> You ask me to 'let the devils have it' when I fight. Yes, I always let them have all I can, but really I don't think them devils. I only scrap because it is my duty, but I do not think anything bad about the Hun. Nothing makes me feel more rotten than to see them go down, but you see it is either them or me, so I must do my duty best to make it a case of *them*.

Of the boy himself, one who knew him well* described Ball as:

> Of striking appearance, medium height, sturdily built, with a mass of black hair, a fresh complexion, with deep-set, piercing dark eyes – rather a Red Indian type of countenance. He never wore goggles of any sort when flying. He always wanted to be in the air; during flying weather he was up and out by five o'clock in the morning and – completely exhausted by his efforts – would be in bed and asleep by six o'clock in the evening.

Another contemporary† said of Ball, 'He never flew for amusement, only the minimum requisite to test guns and engine apart from war sorties. Ball never boasted or criticised, but the example he set us all was tremendous.'

In September 1916 Ball had a total of at least 23 individual combats, from which he claimed six enemy aircraft destroyed, eight more forced down, and one out of control. A final day of fighting on 1 October brought him three more claims – bringing his overall 1916 tally to at least 30 officially recognised victories. On 4 October Ball was sent home to England, for leave and a 'rest' posting on instructor duties. His return to Nottingham was heralded with nationwide publicity, and he was feted wherever he appeared. On 18 November Ball and his family attended

* Wing Commander T. B. Marson in his *Scarlet and Khaki*; J. Cape, 1930.
† *Sagittarius Rising* by Cecil Lewis; P. Davies, 1936.

an investiture at Buckingham Palace, where he received the medals of his DSO and Bar, and MC. On 25 November the *London Gazette* cited the further award of a second Bar to his DSO – thereby making Ball the first 'triple DSO' in the British Army.

Civic pride in his prowess culminated on 19 February 1917 when he was made an Honorary Freeman of the city of Nottingham – a rare privilege for one so young. Such adulation and publicity, though flattering, was never to Ball's liking, and he began to agitate higher authorities for a posting back to France and the operational zone. His persistence eventually succeeded, bringing him a posting to London Colney airfield where he joined 56 Squadron RFC; a newly-forming fighter unit soon to be sent to France for operations. His arrival on 56 Squadron on 25 February 1917 coincided with his appointment as commander of the unit's A Flight. Soon 56 Squadron began to receive its war equipment – SE5 single-seaters, which 56's men were to 'introduce' to operational service. Ball selected SE5, A4850 as his personal machine, and immediately proceeded to have it extensively modified to meet his personal requirements. On 7 April 1917, 56 Squadron's SE5's left London Colney to fly to France, and finally arrived at its war station, Vert Galand airfield, a few miles north of Amiens.

For its first two weeks in France, 56 Squadron was forbidden to operate across the trench lines, and spent much of its time improving and modifying the SE5's; while Ball, who had taken a positive dislike to the design, had requested a Nieuport Scout for alternative use, and been given Nieuport B1522 for that purpose. On 22 April, Ball led 56 Squadron's first operational patrol, and on the following day, flying his Nieuport, scored the unit's first war victory by crashing an Albatros two-seater. In the afternoon, this time flying SE5, A4850, he destroyed another Albatros and forced a third to land. On the 26th Ball claimed a double victory, and another pair on the 28th. May 1 and 2 brought him four more victims; another victory on 4 May; and further claims on 5 May. From these combats Ball usually returned with damaged aircraft, but was never deterred from returning to the fray. On 6 May, flying Nieuport B1522, Ball claimed his last victim; an Albatros Scout of Jagdstaffel 20, which he surprised and sent down to crash near Sancourt.

On 7 May 1917 Ball participated in a routine fighter escort patrol for some Sopwith bombers of 70 Squadron RFC in the morning; but at 6 pm that evening Ball, in SE5 A4850, spearheaded an eleven-strong fighting patrol hunting for German aircraft.

Within the hour 56 Squadron's SE5's were split up and engaged in a sprawling series of furious combats with Albatros D.III's of the notorious

Jagdstaffel 11, commanded by Germany's 'ace of aces' Rittmeister Manfred von Richthofen, but led on this occasion by the 'Red Baron's' younger brother, Lothar.

During the confused fighting which spread across many miles of sky, 56 Squadron suffered heavily; having two pilots killed, two wounded, and two others forced to land. One of the missing pilots was Ball. Possibly the last pilot to see Ball alive was Captain Cyril Crowe of B Flight, who joined him at about 8 pm in attacking a lone red Albatros DIII piloted by Lothar von Richthofen. After both SE5's had made their initial diving attacks, Crowe watched Ball and the red Albatros disappear into a heavy bank of cloud, but on skirting the cloud failed to find either machine again.

The only witnesses to Ball's death were three German army officers who saw von Richthofen's Albatros crash with a dead engine near Annoeullin village; then a few minutes later, Ball's SE5 emerge from low cloud, inverted and shallow-diving, emitting a thin plume of black smoke. The SE5 continued its dive into the ground, near Seclin. Examination of the wreckage revealed no evidence of it having been brought down by any form of gun fire; while Ball's body had no combat wounds, and his several injuries were all sustained in the crash.

On 9 May, the Germans gave Albert Ball a military funeral with full honours; while on 8 June 1917 the *London Gazette* announced the posthumous award of a Victoria Cross to the Nottingham boy, and the French government announced its decision to enrol Ball as a Chevalier de Legion d'Honneur. Recipient of two country's highest awards for courage, Albert Ball died before attaining his 21st birthday, but left behind a tradition of utter devotion to duty for later generations to inherit and embellish. Today he lies where he fell – the only Englishman among hundreds of his former foes, in the Annoeullin Cemetery in France.

13. Alan Arnett McLeod

A grandson of Scottish immigrants, Alan Arnett McLeod was born on 20 April 1899 in the small town of Stonewall, Winnipeg in Manitoba, Canada. Educated locally, he evinced a deep interest in all matters connected with the military from his earliest years, and on 24 June 1913 he lied about his age and volunteered to join the local territorial force, the Fort Garry Horse, for their annual training at Fort Sewell. Once his true age was discovered, however, young McLeod was promptly returned to his school studies. Undismayed, McLeod waited impatiently until attaining the minimum age decreed for military service, and then promptly applied for pilot training with the Royal Flying Corps. He was accepted and enlisted on 23 April 1917.

His flying training commenced at Long Branch, Toronto, where he made his first flight on 4 June, and after almost three hours dual instruction, flew his first solo flight on 9 June. A week later he reported to Camp Borden for advanced instruction, and was eventually awarded his RFC 'wings' brevet on 31 July 1917. On 20 August McLeod was among a large draft of Canadians which sailed in the SS *Metagama* to England, and on arrival he was posted to Winchester to complete his Service training.

His first operational assignment was to Lincolnshire, where he joined 82 Squadron RFC at Waddington; a new unit then in the process of forming for service in France, equipped with Armstrong Whitworth FK8 two-seat bombers. In spite of some disappointment at being allotted to a bomber unit instead of the more glamorous single-seat scouts, McLeod consoled himself with the thought that at least he was going on active service in France. Nevertheless, when 82 Squadron moved to the fighting zone in November, McLeod had been reposted; joining 51 Home Defence Squadron.

In the event the young Canadian's ambition to fly in France was realised when he was sent to the RFC Pilots' Pool at St Omer in late November 1917, and reported to 2 Squadron RFC at Hesdigneul on 29 November. One of the RFC's original pioneer units, 2 Squadron was equipped with Armstrong Whitworth FK8's in an army co-operation role, and McLeod was allocated to B Flight. The AWFK8 – known colloquially by the crews as the 'Big-Ack' – was a lumbering general purpose two-seater, with a maximum operational speed in the region of 90 mph; a stable platform for the various bombing, photographic and general reconnaissance duties which were its normal functions.

Alan McLeod, who by then had acquired the nickname 'Babe' in spite of his healthy six feet two inches' height, performed all the routine duties conscientiously; but his urgent desire for more direct offensive action often led him to complete sorties by ground-strafing German troop concentrations, trenches, and gun sites. Sweeping low over such targets McLeod handled the cumbersome Big-Ack as if it were an agile fighter, and his reputation as 'a young fire-eater' (his commander's description) was enhanced on 19 December when, in FK8 B5782, with Lieutenant Comber as his observer-gunner, McLeod calmly *attacked* a formation of eight yellow and green-striped Albatros scouts. Completely surprised by the sheer audacity of the FK8 crew, the Germans broke formation immediately, but not before Comber had shot down the nearest Albatros, which spun erratically into the mists below.

With Lieutenant Reginald Key as observer, McLeod set out on 14 January 1918 to destroy a German observation kite balloon at Bauvin, south-east of Lille – a task considered dangerous enough for a well-escorted fast scout, but tantamount to near-suicide for a slow bomber, which would need to run a gauntlet of well-sited anti-aircraft guns deployed around the balloon site, apart from the ever-present German scouts available for air protection.

On arrival over the objective, McLeod started his dive towards the balloon, only to notice three Albatros scouts emerge from some nearby clouds and dive in his direction. Continuing his dive, McLeod destroyed the balloon in flames and banked sharply to avoid the flaming wreckage. One Albatros tried to get under the tail of the FK8 but Key responded by shattering the German aircraft's upper wing centre-section with a crisply accurate burst from his Lewis gun, and the Albatros tore itself apart in mid-air. Fighting off the two remaining Germans, McLeod and Key returned to base, and were subsequently mentioned in despatches for this action. Two days later the same pair completed a routine artillery co-operation sortie by strafing an anti-aircraft battery, and then dispersing a column of German infantry, before returning to their own airfield. Ten days later McLeod returned to England for two weeks' leave and a brief rest from action.

At the time McLeod was relaxing in England, preparations on a massive scale were being made behind the German lines for a spring land offensive, intended to finally break the deadlock of static trench warfare and force the Allied armies back to the English Channel coast. Men, guns, ammunition and a myriad of other essentials were being stockpiled in reserve areas, and the Allied air services were on constant alert; seeking information, bombing, and generally attempting to weaken the potential of the expected onslaught.

On 21 March 1918 the German offensive was set in motion with widespread initial success, and 2 Squadron was one of several units which were hastily moved southwards to the Amiens area and the Bapaume battle zone to help stem the flood of German infantry pouring through many breaches in the Allies' defences. Reinforcements for local German air units were also flown in, and notable amongst these was the notorious Jagdgeschwader Nr 1, comprised of four elite fighting *Jagdstaffeln* banded together and known to Allied fliers as the 'Richthofen Circus'. Led by Germany's supreme fighting pilot of World War One, Rittmeister Manfred von Richthofen, the Circus moved into Lechelle airfield on 26 March – directly opposing 2 Squadron RFC.

On 27 March, the seventh day of the raging land struggle, seven AWFK8's of 2 Squadron took óff with full bomb racks to attack infantry concentrations in the Bray-sur-Somme area which (it was reported) were massing for an assault on Allied trenches at Albert. The day was grey and misty and shortly after take-off the bombers became split up, each FK8 proceeding independently.

Alan McLeod, flying FK8 B5773, with Lieutenant A. W. Hammond MC as his observer, groped his way through fog and mist for almost two hours before deciding to land, refuel and continue the vital sortie. He chose Avesnes-le-Comte airfield, home of 43 Squadron, near Arras, but in landing his full-loaded aircraft at this strange (to him) airfield the FK8's tail skid was cracked. While waiting for fuel and the damaged skid to be repaired, McLeod and Hammond took lunch with 43 Squadron's pilots; then, at 1 pm they took off again to complete their original mission, heading towards Albert.

Weather conditions had not improved noticeably since the morning, and after a further two hours of fruitless reconnaissance McLeod was about to abandon the sortie when he spotted a German observation balloon below. Determined that his effort would not be entirely wasted, McLeod promptly dived to attack.

Before he could come within firing range, however, McLeod's attention was diverted by Hammond pointing upwards to a lone Fokker Triplane cruising at about 3,000 feet.

Immediately the Canadian pulled the FK8 into a climb towards the German, and with his first burst of fire Hammond damaged the triplane,

Alan Arnett McLeod

Alan Jerrard

which fell away in an uncontrolled spin and crashed on the outskirts of Albert.

The action had already been seen by a loose formation of eight other Fokker Triplanes which had just emerged from cloud, and all eight piled down on the FK8 to avenge their lost comrade. All were from Jagdstaffel 10 of the Richthofen Circus, and included a future 'ace', Leutnant Hans Kirchstein.

As the first triplanes bore in Hammond hit one with a steady burst and the German scout burst into flames and fell away. The remaining Fokkers attacked in succession, but Hans Kirchstein dived past the FK8 then pulled up under its fuselage; raking the bomber from nose to rudder and wounding Hammond twice. A simultaneous attack by another triplane from the beam resulted in a third wound for Hammond, while McLeod received a bullet through one leg.

Steadying himself against the triple shock and pain of his wounds, Hammond levelled his gunsights at the nearest German and his bullets must have found the triplane's petrol tank because seconds later the German scout exploded. Banking in steeply towards the FK8 for his second attack, Kirschstein again raked the bomber from stem to stern; his bullets rupturing the Big Ack's petrol tank. The bomber erupted in sudden flames and the fury of the fire burned away the fragile flooring between McLeod and Hammond's cockpits; at the same time burning out the floor of the pilot's cockpit. The wind-driven flames burned away McLeod's knee-length flying boots and the lower skirt of his leather flying coat, while his instrument board and control column started smouldering.

Unable to support himself on the charred remains of his cockpit flooring, Hammond climbed painfully onto the top of the fuselage, clinging precariously to his Scarff Ring gun mounting. McLeod meanwhile had climbed out of his burning wicker seat onto the left lower wing root and, holding the smouldering control column with one hand, guided the crippled bomber into a crablike sideslip in an attempt to keep the raging flames away from Hammond. Satisfied that his victims were doomed, Hans Kirchstein withdrew from the unequal fight, making a mental note of the time of his second air combat victory as 3.20 pm in a position three kilometres south-west of Albert. Only five minutes later he was to claim a Sopwith Camel as his third *Luftsieg*. One Fokker followed the burning FK8 down to see its finish, and paid for his morbid curiosity with his life. In spite of their wounds and the terrifying flames, the 'doomed' crew were far from giving up the fight for survival, and Hammond managed one final burst from his Lewis gun as the German nosed towards him. The triple-winged scout heeled over and fell into a German reserve trench.*

The blazing FK8 eventually crashed in the No Man's Land between the opposing front-line trenches and slithered into a crater – a burning mass. Although wounded in five places, badly burned, and shocked, McLeod fought his way clear of the wreckage and started to pull the now-unconscious Hammond from the flames. He knew that the original bomb load was still intact when the bomber crashed, and the bombs were liable to explode at any second.

Finally dragging Hammond free, the boy started crawling towards the British trenches, bearing the inert Hammond on his back through the shell-pocked mud. As he stumbled and crawled he was again wounded by a sliver of shell shrapnel, but reached an outpost of a section of the line held by some South African Scottish troops, where McLeod now collapsed from loss of blood and utter exhaustion. For the next five hours they were unable to be moved to a dressing station owing to a German artillery barrage in progress, but when the two airmen were eventually handed over to a medical team and examined, Hammond was found to have sustained six wounds, including a shattered leg.

Their journey to expert medical facilities and safety was a long one. Having been carried through the reserve trenches for three miles to the nearest dressing station, McLeod and Hammond were stretcher-borne until an ambulance was found to transport them to Amiens, and then Etaples Hospital.

On the following day McLeod was sent via Boulogne and Dover to the Prince of Wales' Hospital, London, where for several weeks his young life hung precariously in the balance. Notified of his son's critical condition, McLeod's father travelled from Canada to spend two months of almost constant vigil by his boy's hospital bed.

On 1 May 1918 the *London Gazette* announced the award of a Victoria Cross to McLeod, and on 4 September, wearing the newly-introduced Royal Air Force uniform, the young Canuck, in company with his father, hobbled on two walking sticks into Buckingham Palace where he received his cross from King George V. Immediately afterwards he was sent home to Canada to convalesce, arriving in Winnipeg on 30 September en route to his home town of Stonewall.

In the peace and surrounding kindness of his birthplace the boy's health

* The Fokker Triplanes claimed as destroyed in this epic fight were officially confirmed as such by Allied authorities – apparently based on eyewitness confirmation. German records, however, give no clue to identities of any such casualties, while the diary of Jagdgeschwader 1 admits no casualties for this date. It is, therefore, highly probable that there were Fokkers from other units involved alongside Jagdstaffel 10.

steadily improved, but in November 1918 an epidemic of virulent influenza swept through Canada and Alan McLeod, still terribly weak from his ordeal, fell victim to the killer virus and, on 6 November, he died. At 19 years of age he was the youngest recipient of a VC for aerial operations during the 1914–18 war, and only the second youngest air VC of both world conflicts. On 9 November 1918 – just two days before the Armistice in Europe – they buried Alan Arnett McLeod vc in Kildonan Cemetery, Winnipeg.

His courageous companion Hammond also recovered from his wounds and was awarded a Bar to his Military Cross, but he had to suffer amputation of his smashed leg. He later emigrated to Canada and settled in Winnipeg, where he continued to live until his death in recent years. Leutnant Hans Kirchstein, the German pilot officially responsible for shooting them down, continued on active service for several months; being finally credited with a tally of 27 confirmed combat victories and awarded Germany's highest military honour, the Ordre Pour Le Merite – the so-termed 'Blue Max' – before being killed in a flying accident on 16 July 1918.

14. Alan Jerrard

Nearly one third of the nineteen men awarded a Victoria Cross for aerial operations during 1914–18 received it for the destruction of relatively large numbers of enemy aircraft in combat over extended periods of operational flying. Paradoxically, of the many high-scoring pilots who flew the Sopwith Camel – an aircraft which accounted for nearly 3,000 opponents, thus becoming the most successful fighter of any participating air service, and a name virtually synonomous with World War One air fighting – only one was a recipient of the little bronze cross.

His name was Alan Jerrard, and he held the double distinction of being the only air-VC winner during the prolonged and bloody war in Italy. The circumstances which resulted in Jerrard's award remain un-resolved completely, though – as will be seen – Jerrard himself played no part in the various steps which were taken in recommending and even-tually awarding him the VC.

Born at Lewisham on 3 December 1897, Alan Jerrard was initially educated at Bishop Vesey's Grammar School, Sutton Coldfield, where his father held the headmastership. He later attended Oundle and, in 1915, Birmingham University; but at the close of 1915 he volunteered to join the Army, and was commissioned as a Second Lieutenant in the South Staffordshire Regiment on 2 January 1916.

After a few months as an infantry subaltern, Jerrard applied for transfer to the Royal Flying Corps, and on 16 August 1916 began ground instruc-tion at the School of Military Aeronautics, Oxford. On 23 September he reported to No 25 (Reserve) Squadron at Thetford for initial flying in-struction, and on 20 November 1916 moved to No 9(R) Squadron at Mousehold Heath, Norwich for further training. His next move, on 5 December, took Jerrard to 59 Squadron at Narborough, a unit then in the process of formation for operations in France, but a bout of illness pre-vented him staying with the squadron, and he was attached temporarily to another Narborough unit, 50 (Reserve) Squadron, pending his return to full flying fitness. His next move was to the Upavon Central Flying School, from which he graduated as an RFC pilot on 14 June 1917; was officially transferred to the RFC from this date, and briefly attached to No 40 Training Squadron at Croydon.

Still intended (by officialdom) to become a two-seater pilot, Jerrard was sent to 20 Training Squadron at Spittlegate (now spelt Spitalgate), near Grantham for further experience in handling RE8 two-seaters, but his above-average abilities as a pilot led to a spell of training at London Colney, from 4 July as a single-seat scout pilot. From here he received his first operational posting, to 19 Squadron based at Liettres, .France, equipped with Spad S7 single-seaters. Two days before his course at London Colney, on 2 July, Jerrard received notification of his promotion to Lieutenant.

Arriving on 19 Squadron on 24 July, Jerrard soon adapted himself to the Spad scout, and flew his first operational patrol on 29 July; only to lose his formation and eventually land at St Omer having seen nothing of the enemy. His second war patrol came on 5 August, when he became one of six Spads led by the veteran Captain John Leacroft searching for German aircraft. Due to the grey evening mists Jerrard, still inexperienced in war flying, lost contact with his formation, and flew low in the hope of finding his bearings. Coming upon a long road convoy of German transport vehicles, Jerrard proceeded to rake the convoy with his machine guns, leaving several vehicles in flames, before climbing through the fog and low clouds to 10,000 feet, where his unreliable engine cut out completely. Gliding down again, with virtually no visibility, his Spad, A8830, crashed head-on into a railway embankment, near St Marie Cappel.

Nearby infantry literally dug Jerrard out of the impacted wreckage; his nose and jaw broken in several places, plus other minor injuries, necessitating his immediate removal to hospital and surgical attention.

Invalided back to England, Jerrard spent several months recuperating from his injuries, and, after a brief flying 'refresher' course, was declared fit for operational flying again and posted overseas to 66 Squadron in Italy; arriving at his new unit on 22 February 1918. 66 Squadron, commanded then by Major J. T. Whittaker MC, was one of three Sopwith Camel units which had been transferred from France to Italy only weeks before to bolster the Italian military campaign against Austro-Hungarian forces.

Jerrard wasted little time in joining his squadron's operations, and on 27 February claimed a Berg single-seat scout as shot down out of control. On 7 March he attacked and destroyed an enemy observation balloon in flames; and on 11 March claimed a pair of Berg scouts, one of which crashed, while the second was driven down, damaged. On 21 March he tackled an Albatros scout, and sent it down to crash. By this date 66 Squadron had moved from its former aerodrome at Treorso, and was now based at San Pietro-in-Gu, just north of Grossa.

On 30 March 1918 the morning weather was unsuitable for flying, being clouded and offering little visibility. By late morning, however, it was decided to attempt a fighting patrol, and three pilots were detailed for the sortie; Captain Peter Carpenter, Lieutenant H. R. Eycott-Martin, and Alan Jerrard. Carpenter was an experienced veteran of air fighting, both in France and Italy, with a credited victory tally of seven, and a Military Cross, and eventually ended the war with DSO and Bar, MC and a total score of 21 combat victories. Martin was a relatively new war pilot. Due to the previous evening's late revels in the squadron Mess, Jerrard was sleeping late on the morning of 30 March and, when called for the offensive patrol, merely donned his flying overall over his pyjamas before trudging out to the hangars and aircraft.

The three Camels left the aerodrome together, with Carpenter flying Sopwith Camel B7387; Martin in Camel B7283, and Jerrard at the controls of Camel B5648, 'E'. Climbing for precious fighting height to 13,000 feet the trio flew steadily due eastwards towards enemy-held territory. At 11.35 am the Camels spotted four Albatros Scouts apparently escorting a 'Rumpler two-seater' (sic) some 1,000 feet higher, and immediately attacked.

The sequence of events which then ensued differs widely according to whether one reads the British account, or the Austrian version. When Carpenter and Eycott-Martin eventually returned to their squadron airfield, both reported straightaway to the squadron commander, Whittaker, and after they left the squadron office a combat report was issued covering the events of the patrol; unsigned by either pilot, but 'countersigned' by Whittaker. Giving the time of total combat as from 1135 to 1200 hours, and the location as Mansue aerodrome, the narrative section of the report read :

'Owing to bad visibility and under instructions from the squadron commander, the WOP (Western Offensive Patrol) went on patrol and then went on to the old Eastern Patrol. At 11.35 am a formation of four Albatros D.III's and one Rumpler 2-seater were observed about 14,000 feet over Fontane crossing our lines. Patrol immediately attacked them from about 13,000 feet but were unable to get within range so held off in the sun. Patrol observed that EA* were obviously making for their own aerodrome and Capt Carpenter shot down and crashed one D.III at about three miles south of Mansue. Lt Jerrard attacked another D.III and followed it down to about 100 feet from the ground, where it burst into flames at the same place. Lt Martin confirms Capt Carpenter's crash and Lt Martin and Capt Carpenter confirm Lt Jerrard's. Capt Carpenter

* EA = Enemy Aircraft; the common RFC abbreviation used.

and Lt Martin, who were now at about 6,000 feet saw Lt Jerrard attacking the other machines. The leader on looking round saw Lt Jerrard at about 50 feet over the aerodrome shooting it up and attacking machines one after another who were trying to take off. At this time there were about 19 EA in the air. Lt Jerrard was attacking six D.III's. Lt Martin went to Lt Jerrard's assistance and crashed a D.III which was on Lt Jerrard's tail, in a field next to the aerodrome. This was confirmed by Capt Carpenter. Just after Lt Jerrard crashed his second EA into the same field and this is confirmed by Capt Carpenter. Lt Jerrard continued to shoot up the aerodrome and at this moment all the machines, with the exception of those shot down, were in the air. Capt Carpenter, who was attacking three D.III's, lost sight of the other two Camels for the moment. A D.III climbed on to Lt Martin's tail and was shot and crashed by Lt Jerrard two fields north of the aerodrome; confirmed by Capt Carpenter and Lt Martin. Meanwhile Lt Martin attacked another D.III and drove it into the ground without firing a shot. The machine was seen to crash by Capt Carpenter and Lt Martin. At this moment Lt Jerrard was attacking vigorously [sic] six D.III's. Capt Carpenter and Lt Martin went to his assistance but were driven off by other EA. Capt Carpenter and Lt Martin drew away to break off the flight [sic] owing to superior numbers but Lt Jerrard remained attacking with great vigour every EA who came within range of him. Lt Jerrard then joined the formation but was flying very weakly as though wounded. Ten D.III's were following Lt Jerrard. Capt Carpenter and Lt Martin were unable to go to his assistance owing to other EA and observed Lt Jerrard, who although apparently wounded, repeatedly attack these EA until he crashed four miles West of Mansue Aerodrome.'

Though this account is disjointed in sequence and offers several minor(?) anomalies to the scrupulous historian, in summary it claimed a total of six Albatros scouts actually destroyed in combat (three by Jerrard; two by Eycott-Martin; and one by Carpenter). It also claimed that at least 19 enemy aircraft were in the air; and gave witness to an aerodrome being thoroughly attacked by Jerrard in between individual air combats. The actual combat report (as already stated) was not signed by either Carpenter or Eycott-Martin; only by the squadron commander Tudor Whittaker; but such was not an uncommon occurrence on many RFC squadrons at that period. What is not known is whether Martin or Carpenter ever actually saw this report in written form; their immediate testimony after landing was verbally given in the squadron office.

What must be certain is that this combat report narrative provided the basis for Jerrard to be recommended for the award of the Victoria Cross, and when the award was announced in the *London Gazette* on 1 May 1918, its citation was simply a condensed version of the combat report narrative.

The official Austro-Hungarian Air Corps' documents covering the day's operations and casualties for 30 March 1918 give a very different account of the day's events. Part of the official interrogation report of Alan Jerrard reads :

> On March 30 I (*Jerrard*) was flying in formation with two other Camel fighters near the Front when we met an Austrian fighter squadron near Mansue. I attacked an Albatros D fighter successfully (as he believed), then having lost height during the dogfight, my engine started to misfire and run rough. I was pursued by other Austrian fighters and eventually shot down.

Even allowing for a natural reluctance on any captured pilot's part to claim too much for himself, it is remarkable that nowhere in the interrogation was the subject of an attack on an aerodrome mentioned. Indeed, a careful check of the relevant records of all Austrian units* based at various airfields north of the river Livenza at that period reveal no mention of any form of air attack on their aerodromes. On this date Mansue was the base field for Flik 32D, and the only Albatros fighter unit involved with Camels was Flik 51J, based at Ghirano, commanded by Oberleutnant Benno Fiala von Fernbrugg.

Amalgamating von Fernbrugg's personal account with the known Austrian casualties for 30 March 1918 produces a simpler but entirely different picture of the sequence of events that day. Just before noon four Oeffag-built Albatros D Scouts of Flik 51J, led by Fiala von Fernbrugg in Albatros D, 152-155, were returning from an escort mission for a photo-reconnaissance two-seater aircraft of FLIK 32D, and watched their 'charge' descend for a safe landing at its base airfield at Mansue. Turning north towards their own base at Ghirano, the four Albatros were attacked by three Camels diving out of the sun from a 'great height' (sic). The first Camel (Jerrard) was soon dog-fighting with one of the Albatros scouts; the second Camel attacked von Fernbrugg from above, but the Austrian pulled the nose of his aircraft up and fired into the belly of the Camel. The second Camel was then engaged by Offizierstellvertreter Stefan Fejes and was forced to turn south towards the Piave River. Resuming his

* Fliegerkompagnies (Fliks) 4, 5, 12, 19, 22, 28, 32, 34, 35, 37, 41, 44, 49, 50, 51, 58, 61, 62, 63, 67, 69, 71.

original flight-path, von Fernbrugg headed south-west and saw the first Camel (Jerrard) flying in the opposite direction.

At 1,000 metres von Fernbrugg commenced firing, pouring 100 rounds into the engine and forward fuselage of Jerrard's Camel, and the Camel dropped its nose, while the Austrian pulled his Albatros up into a 180-degrees turn. Seeing the Camel heading towards the Italian lines, on a southerly course below, von Fernbrugg pursued and fired another 100 rounds from behind Jerrard's tail. At that moment the Austrian leader was joined by Stabsfeldwebel Bönsch who started firing at Jerrard's Camel but ceased to do so when he realised his commander was already attacking the Englishman, and saw that the Camel's engine had stopped.

The Camel made a crash-landing in a meadow surrounded by willow trees and trenches, north of Gorgo di Molino at Gorgo al Montico, two miles due south of Mansue airfield. It hit a tree, ripping off the left wings, tipped on its nose and finally slithered to a stop, still perched on the engine cowling, with the tail section breaking away as it ploughed across the meadow.

Luckily for Jerrard there was no fire, and he was extricated from the wreck by nearby Austrian infantrymen, and – still suffering from shock – sat nearby to recover his senses. His conqueror, von Fernbrugg, landed almost immediately at Ghirano (about four kilometres from the crash location) and rushed to the site by car, where he took charge of the still-dazed Jerrard and took him by car to the nearest Army command centre at Oderzo.

Investigation of the wreckage of Camel B5648 revealed excellent marksmanship on the part of Fiala von Fernbrugg; with a total of 163 bullet holes or marks, including 27 bullet holes in the petrol tank. The latter air damage, which released the remaining fuel, accounted for Jerrard's engine stopping in the air, and probably saved him from a fiery end when he crashed later. In the engine itself were 16 bullet strikes.

Of the four Albatros pilots involved in the combat, Stefan Fejes was lightly wounded in one foot; while a second Albatros had been obliged to land at Ghirano with a bullet through the engine's coolant pipe, with consequential overheating of the engine. Fejes (mistakenly) claimed a Sopwith Camel as shot down across the lines in the Oderzo Front region. Von Fernbrugg's victory over Jerrard was witnessed by the remaining pilots of FLIK 51J, and he was later credited officially with the Camel as his 14th victory.

On the day following the fight, the Italian command headquarters issued a claim – patently based on the 66 Squadron combat report – that six Austrian fighters had been shot down; an assertion immediately denied in the Austrian Daily Summary dated 3 April 1918, with the suggestion that the Italian claim was 'over-exuberant'.

Regrettably at the time of writing it is no longer possible to establish unequivocally the full facts of the events of 30 March 1918; Benno Fiala von Fernbrugg died on 29 October 1964, and Jerrard is no longer living. Interviewed in the early 1960's, Alan Jerrard admitted to only hazy memories of the actual events, and had no documentary evidence to consult for prompting his recollections. On the afternoon of that eventful day Jerrard was in no state to worry about academics, being concerned only with his near-miraculous escape from death, and the weary prospect of many months of imprisonment facing him.

His first concern was in the matter of clothing, being clad only in pyjamas under his bulky flying overall. His chivalrous Austrian captors sympathised with this state, and arranged for a note to be dropped behind the Allied lines, requesting various items to be air-dropped for Jerrard. When this was received by 66 Squadron, two bundles of personal items – uniform and Sam Browne belt, shoes, socks, cigarettes *et al* – were eventually flown across the lines and dropped on an Austrian airfield, addressed to Jerrard. Once his routine interrogation had been completed, Jerrard was whisked away to a regular prisoner of war camp at Salzburg.

After the war, and repatriation to England, Jerrard opted to remain in the RAF as a career, and after investiture with his Victoria Cross at Buckingham Palace on 5 April 1919, joined the RAF Murmansk detachment in Russia. Serving in various minor capacities at Henlow, Sealand, Grantham and Halton during the next fourteen years, Jerrard rose to Flight Lieutenant rank, but in 1933, due to continuing ill-health, he retired from the Service. Eventually, on 14 May 1968, Allan Jerrard died in the Buckfield Nursing Home, and was buried with full military honours at Lyme Regis on 17 May.

15. James Thomas Byford McCudden

Even without the ultimate award of a Victoria Cross, the career of James ('Jimmy') McCudden was a remarkable one by any standards of Service history. In an era of Service aviation overlain with social class distinctions and, in particular, a period in which few other than commissioned officers were considered suitable candidates as pilots, McCudden, starting from the lowest possible status in Army circles, rose steadily through the ranks to become the leading contemporary fighting pilot of the British air services, and received seven awards for gallantry, including the supreme honour, the VC. His Victoria Cross was awarded for no individual act of outstanding courage, but in fitting recognition of a long operational fighting career in the RFC in which his consistent prowess and clear devotion to his duties placed him at the apex of his contemporaries. But for his tragic death in a trivial flying accident, James McCudden might well have become an influential figure in the post-1918 infant Royal Air Force.

Descendant of a long line of soldiers in regular Army service, James Thomas Byford McCudden was born at Gillingham, Kent on 28 March 1895; one of four sons of Corporal (later, Sergeant-Major) W. H. McCudden RE, all of whom joined the Royal Flying Corps at various times, and three of whom eventually died while flying for their country. Educated in the army garrison schools, McCudden's first close acquaintance with the world of aeronautics came in 1909, when his father retired from the army, and the family moved to Sheerness; close to the original Eastchurch airfield.

Joining the Royal Engineers as a boy soldier on 26 April 1910, McCudden was regraded as a bugler six months later, and on 24 February 1911, sailed to Gibraltar. Returning to England in September 1912, he was attached to No 6 Company, RE stationed at Weymouth, Dorset, and whilst there applied for transfer to the newly-created Royal Flying Corps. Though lacking formal training in engineering, McCudden's constant interest and curiosity about all things mechanical had given him a sound knowledge of internal combustion engines, and he was accepted into the RFC as No 892, Air Mechanic, 2nd Class on 28 April 1913, and mustered as an engine fitter.

On 9 May he was posted to Farnborough, but within his first week

there was almost returned to his original army regimental corps for causing extensive damage to two aircraft. In the event he was sentenced to a
spell in detention (the notorious 'glasshouse' punishment centre), and
remained in the RFC; he was posted on 15 June 1913 to 3 Squadron RFC
at Larkhill, and moved with the unit to Netheravon the following day.

In the following year McCudden's meticulous attention to his work
received favourable comment from his various officers, and whenever
the opportunity presented itself he gained airborne experience as a
passenger in the squadron's multi-varied types of aircraft; his ambition
now was to become a pilot. With promotion to Air Mechanic, 1st Class,
McCudden moved to France with 3 Squadron on 13 August 1914, and
on 20 November was promoted to Corporal. On 1 April 1915, his abilities
were further recognised with a promotion to Sergeant, in charge of all
engine maintenance on the unit; a senior position which accorded
quaintly with his bare twenty years' age.

Only four weeks later he was notified of the death, in a flying accident,
of his eldest brother Flight Sergeant William McCudden, who had
qualified as a pilot in August 1912; only the fourth NCO in the RFC to
gain his pilot's certificate. The news, though heart-breaking to Jimmy,
did not divert him from his determination to become a pilot, and he
again applied for pilot training; only to be refused by virtue of his valuable work as a maintenance NCO.

When 3 Squadron moved base to Auchel on 1 June 1915, McCudden
managed to get a few 'private' hours of instruction in piloting from a
fellow SNCO, Sergeant J. Watts; but decided meanwhile to gain air
experience as an observer in the squadron's Morane Saulnier 'parasol'
two-seat monoplanes. Flying his first qualifying sortie as such on 8 June,
McCudden soon began to accumulate many hours of operational experience, in between his normal ground duties, and on 19 December was
involved in his first aerial combat when his aircraft was attacked by a
German monoplane scout.

On 1 January 1916 he was officially remustered to observer, and continued to be involved in various aerial clashes with enemy aircraft. His
exploits led to his first award, a French Croix de Guerre, with which he
was presented on 21 January at a field investiture. Only three days later
he was delighted to be told that his last application for pilot training had
been approved, and on 31 January he left 3 Squadron, bound for
England, with promotion to Flight Sergeant becoming effective from the
next day.

Reporting to the Reserve Aircraft Park at Farnborough to commence
training, McCudden managed to get a few hours' private instruction from

a friend, Sergeant Frank Courtney, before starting his official course of instruction on 22 February under the aegis of Sergeant-Major W. S. Power. A further spell of flying instruction with 41 Squadron at Gosport followed, and on 16 April 1916 Jimmy McCudden qualified for his Royal Aero Club Certificate No 2745 in a Maurice Farman machine Two weeks later he started Service flying training at CFS, Upavon, gaining his 2nd Class Pilot's Certificate on 3 May, and his 1st Class Certificate, and therefore RFC 'wings' on 30 May 1916.

Once officially qualified as a pilot, McCudden was sent back to France, and joined 20 Squadron at Clairmarais on 7 July. 20 Squadron at this time was equipped with the ungainly (though curiously efficient) FE2b and FE2d two-seat 'pusher' bombers and McCudden flew his first operational sortie as a pilot on 10 July. His stay with the FE squadron was brief, and on 7 August he achieved his ultimate ambition by joining 29 Squadron at Abeele, a scout squadron equipped with De Havilland 2 single-seat 'pusher' machines, whose role was fighting. Allotted to C Flight, McCudden commenced operational flying with 29 Squadron next day, and for the following month participated in various uneventful, routine fighting and bomber escort patrols. Then on 6 September he scored his first aerial victory, a white two-seat Albatros which he attacked and sent down to crash. Typically modest, his combat report afterwards made no claim for any victory, but confirmation of the German machine's fate came from ground witnesses.

In the following weeks he had several indecisive engagements, and on two occasions attempted to destroy German observation balloons; a continuing record which brought him the award of a Military Medal on 1 October. In November McCudden applied to be considered for a commission, but was fortunate to survive several close dogfights with the new Albatros fighters of Jagdstaffel 2, led by experienced fighters, stationed in opposition on 29 Squadron's sector of the Western Front.

His commission was granted with effect from 1 January 1917, and after a brief 'kitting' leave, Second Lieutenant 'Jimmy' McCudden rejoined 29 Squadron on 21 January. Five days later he claimed his second official victory, a two-seater out of control, and by 15 February had brought his score up to five accredited victories. Next day he was personally notified of his third gallantry award, a Military Cross (gazetted 12 March 1917), after flying his final war patrol with 29 Squadron. On 23 February he returned to England, earmarked for a 'rest' period on instructional duties.

Except for brief spells of leave, Jimmy McCudden had now been on active service in France for eight months as a pilot; apart from his many previous months of service as an observer and, previously, maintenance

NCO. In this extended period of operational service, McCudden had accumulated an unusually large amount of insight into the business of aerial fighting. This knowledge, combined with his long technical experience, was the foundation for McCudden's growing analytical approach to all facets of aerial combat.

Ever-critical privately of his own combat techniques, he soon developed a cool, near-scientific appraisal of every combat situation, and was never complacent about the unceasing necessity of learning and re-learning lessons in the arena of the sky. Equally, his tactical approach to any individual engagement was strictly in terms of military advantage; though never hesitating to tackle an enemy aircraft on any occasion, McCudden also never baulked from withdrawing from a fight if the circumstances were tactically disadvantageous.

He lived by the simple precept that his job – and that of any pilot – was to wreak the utmost destruction upon the enemy, without sustaining proportionate damage to himself and his men. This dispassionate attitude to his 'job', added to a keen, enquiring mind, and a detailed mechanical knowledge, made McCudden one of the first fighting leaders of the RFC to apply logic and science to the air war.

In England McCudden was posted as a fighter instructor to the 6th Training Wing, RFC, Maidstone, and attached to the advanced pupils' course at Joyce Green airfield, near Dartford. Here he put his experience to good practice, preparing novitiate scout pilots for their future role in France; one of whom was a slim, rangy Irish pilot, Edward Mannock, destined to become the RAF's leading fighter pilot a little more than a year later. For several weeks McCudden imparted by word and example his skill to the embryo fighters, and then began a touring series of lectures and demonstrations around East Anglian training airfields.

On 1 June 1917 he was gazetted to the rank of Captain, and six weeks later returned to France for a three-weeks' 'refresher' attachment; joining 66 Squadron RFC at Estrées Blanche, flying Sopwith Pups on operations. Though mainly uneventful, his brief spell on operations included joining a sortie of SE5's of 56 Squadron, at the unit commander's invitation, before returning to England on 4 August.

Just ten days later he rejoined 56 Squadron, as the new commander of its B Flight. Equipped throughout with the new SE5A fighters, 56 Squadron had, since its arrival on operations in April 1917, built up something of a reputation as an 'élite' unit; numbering many pilots in its ranks who quickly established huge fighting reputations. None had longer operational experience than McCudden, though a few had already been credited with more than McCudden's victory tally at that date.

Determined from the very beginning that his new command would be the best in the squadron, McCudden immediately imposed his own meticulous standards for aircraft and engine maintenance on his ground crews, and began to inculcate his pilots with the maxim that the highest proficiency in combat came from a team effort, not the more glamorous exploits of individuals. If any of the pilots had any reservations about their new, ex-ranker commander, these were swiftly dispelled.

On 18 August McCudden, after indecisive fights with some two-seaters, fastened onto an Albatros scout and fired both guns into it at close range, sending the Albatros down spinning hopelessly out of control. Within the following two days three more German aircraft fell to his deadly marksmanship – all being single-seat Albatros machines.

For several weeks McCudden, in common with many other 56 Squadron pilots, suffered a series of frustrations with his aircraft machine guns, which repeatedly jammed at crucial moments in combat. McCudden spent many hours with his ground crew, dissembling and servicing his guns, engine and airframe, but the stoppages continued. Eventually the problem was cured and on 14 September McCudden led his Flight down onto seven Albatros D V's of Jagdstaffel 10 of the notorious 'Richthofen Circus' over Roulers. Closing behind one Albatros to 75 yards range, McCudden fired just 20 rounds, and Leutnant Weigand, wounded, spiralled down to a forced landing.

Five days later McCudden spotted a Rumpler C V two-seater west of Armentières, and patiently stalked it. Coming out of the sun's glare, he fired about 60 rounds into the Rumpler, killing or wounding the observer; then followed the falling machine down, firing short bursts into it, until the German crashed behind enemy lines.

A further victory came on the 21st, while on the 23rd he made a swift 'kill' when he shot down a DFW two-seater. That same evening McCudden led his Flight, in company with C Flight, on a roving patrol which eventually became involved in one of the classic dogfights of the war. Their opponents were three German single-seat scouts; one of which was a new Fokker Triplane, flown by Werner Voss, a leading fighter 'ace' of 48 victories. In the subsequent melée Voss, after a magnificent single-handed fight with 56's SE5A's, was shot down and killed. McCudden afterwards recorded in his diary,' He was the bravest and most skilful Hun I have ever seen' – an honest, objective tribute to a brave man, which typified McCudden's habitual refusal to denigrate his enemies.

Four days after Voss's death, McCudden claimed his fourteenth confirmed victory when he shot down a Rumpler CV of Schusta 27; the aircraft and its pilot falling behind British lines, while its observer was thrown out in mid-air and fell inside German lines. Next day McCudden again witnessed an enemy airman fall clear of his machine and plunge to death, when he shot the wings off an Albatros scout over Houthulst. October 1 saw him shoot down another Rumpler, and on the following day he was officially notified of the award of a Bar to his Military Cross. For the rest of the month, McCudden claimed just two more victims – both reconnaissance two-seaters – when a combination of bad weather conditions and a spell of home leave precluded operational flying.

Returning to France on 9 November, McCudden moved with his squadron to a new base, Lavieville airfield, north-east of Amiens in preparation for the Battle of Cambrai. Once settled in to the new fighting zone, McCudden continued to add to his mounting tally of enemy aircraft; with victories on the 18th, 23rd, 29th, and 30th. The last was an LVG C V two-seater of Flieger Abteilung 19, which McCudden forced down inside British lines, and McCudden took the German machine's red propeller spinner as a 'souvenir' and had it fitted to his own SE5A.

At the start of December 1917, McCudden's officially accredited score stood at 23; by the end of the month he was to add at least 14 more victims. By now his combat flying and marksmanship were at the height of efficiency, and he sought constantly to enhance his chances of success by lavishing many hours of labour on his aircraft, engine, and guns; improving and modifying to his own ideas and thereby gaining more speed, height and all-round performance from his machine. No detail was too small for his attention, and the result was a truly formidable fighting combination of man and machine. His victories during December – 13 two-seater reconnaissance machines and an Albatros Scout – were all brought down by application of skill, patience and superb marksmanship, and on the 15th he was awarded the Distinguished Service Order; not simply for his individual prowess but also for the excellent qualities of leadership he had shown in command of his Flight in action. McCudden's disciplined control of his men in combat undoubtedly contributed to the Flight's well below average casualty figures, as well as its successes. Emphasis on McCudden's reputation as a fighting leader was given on 3 January 1918 when a Bar to his DSO was promulgated. Of the 18 enemy aircraft claimed during December by the whole of 56 Squadron, 14 had been obtained by McCudden's guns. Nine of these he had scored while flying lone high patrols between routine sorties, but the rest had fallen while leading his men.

January 1918 started slowly in terms of air combat for 56 Squadron, but on the 9th McCudden sent an LVG two-seater down to crash at

James Thomas Byford McCudden

Ferdinand Maurice Felix West

Rumilly for the squadron's 250th claimed 'kill' of the war. By the end of the month he added eight more German machines to his tally; including a triple victory on the 13th. His next victory came on 2 February, an LVG C V, but the following two weeks brought little activity, during which period McCudden continued his custom of studying German tactics, working out new methods of attack, and spending many hours with his maintenance crew on servicing his SE. With improved weather conditions, McCudden set out on 16 February, destroyed three two-seaters in the morning patrol, and added a fourth for the day's 'bag' on his second sortie – his 50th accredited victory.

In the following ten days he added seven certain and two possible claims to his tally; his 57th confirmed victory coming on 26 February when he closed to pointblank range under the tail of a Hannover CL III two-seater, poured 200 rounds into it, and watched it fall apart in mid-air, ejecting its observer through the shattered floor of the machine's rear cockpit. He then flew two more solo, but indecisive patrols on 28 February and 1 March – his final combat sorties of the war. Since joining 56 Squadron Jimmy McCudden had personally destroyed 52 German aircraft for certain – almost 40 per cent of the total squadron tally for the same period of just over five months – and in that same period his Flight had lost only four pilots; in itself a unique tribute to McCudden's fighting leadership. On 5 March 1918, McCudden left the squadron on posting to England, where he spent part of his leave with his younger brother, Anthony, who was by then a fighter pilot with 84 Squadron, and had already gained eight combat victories and the award of an MC. On 17 March Anthony returned to France, but was killed in a sprawling dogfight the following day.

On 29 March the *London Gazette* announced the award of a Victoria Cross to Jimmy McCudden, and the citation details (published on 2 April) laid emphasis not only on his personal record of combat successes, but equally on the careful leadership he had given to the pilots under his direct command. His investiture took place on 6 April, and four days later he reported to No 1 School of Aerial Fighting at Ayr, Scotland for a tour of duty as an instructor. This school, commanded by another air VC, Lieutenant-Colonel Lionel W. B. Rees, was literally an advanced course of training for prospective fighter pilots in combat tactics, both in theory and, mainly, in practice.

On 11 May the school moved south to Turnberry, and McCudden continued to be pleasantly occupied with his task of converting freshly-arrived pilots into well-trained combat fliers. His VC award had naturally brought McCudden into the national limelight, though to his instinctive modesty and reticence, much of the acclaim was not at all welcome. One honour bestowed upon him did please him privately however, when his birthplace, Gillingham decided to offer him the Freedom of the Borough; an unusual honour for one so young in years. The ceremony, set for 13 June, never took place, because two days previously McCudden flew a Sopwith Snipe to France for viewing by operational staff in France. During his three days in France, McCudden flew two fighting sorties with his old unit, 56 Squadron, but though engaging several enemy aircraft, he had no success, and returned to England. On 25 June McCudden left Turnberry, having been notified that he was about to be appointed as commander of a new unit, 91 Squadron, then forming at Tangmere and due to be equipped with the new Sopwith Dolphin scouts.

On learning that it would be several months before 91 could proceed to France for operational duties, McCudden forcefully pleaded for a more immediate return to war flying, and was duly instructed to take over command of 60 Squadron, already in France, with the rank of Major, from the effective date of 9 July 1918.

McCudden's last few days in England were busy. During his period at the fighting school, he had (at the persuasion of a friend) written a complete manuscript for a possible book, describing in unemotional and objective terms, his complete service from Air Mechanic to Captain in the Royal Flying Corps; and on 7 July delivered the bulky screed to C. G. Grey, editor of the weekly aviation journal, *Aeroplane*, for Grey's perusal and comments.*

Saying good-bye to his sister Mary on the morning of 9 July, he suddenly thrust an envelope containing all his medals into her hands – possibly a hint of a premonition that he might not return from France; then travelled to Hounslow aerodrome, where he prepared a newly-issued SE5A, C1126, for his flight to France to take up his appointment as commander of 60 Squadron. Leaving Hounslow shortly after 1 pm, he crossed to France, landed briefly at Hesdin, then set off again for 60 Squadron's base airfield at Boffles. At approximately 5.30 pm he sighted what he thought might be his destination and landed. In fact he was at Auxi-le-Chateau, home of Nos 8 and 52 Squadrons. Rolling to a stop, with his engine still running, McCudden asked two duty air mechanics where he was, and the direction to take for Boffles (five miles north-east of Auxi-le-Chateau). They answered his query and watched him taxi back to the end of the small, tree-lined airfield for take-off.

Turning into wind, McCudden quickly took off again, rose to about

* Published 1918 by Aeroplane Publishing Co, titled *Five Years in the Royal Flying Corps*.

100 feet, started to turn – then rolled on the side and plunged into some trees bordering the south-eastern perimeter of the aerodrome. McCudden was found by the wreckage, unconscious, having suffered a fractured skull. Taken immediately to the nearby No 21 Casualty Clearing Station, McCudden did not regain consciousness, and died about 8 pm.

James Thomas Byford McCudden vc dso mc mm, Croix de Guerre, was buried on 10 July 1918 in the little British war cemetery at Wavans, just north of Auxi-le-Chateau, where his grave can be seen today.

16. Ferdinand Maurice Felix West

The award of a Victoria Cross to a Serviceman might logically be regarded as the peak of his endeavours, and in the context of pure courage will always be regarded as such. Yet the action which led to the award may have occupied but minutes of a man's life; a brilliant moment in an otherwise unspectacular career. Occasionally however such a brief glimpse of a man's hidden resources of inner strength epitomises a sustaining courage which is manifested by later events. One such man is Air Commodore 'Freddie' West VC CBE MC. In a lifetime crowded with incident, he seldom failed to display an instinctive courage and nobility of spirit in the face of odds which could have daunted men of lesser valiancy. Add to these qualities a deep and genuine modesty, and an unfailing sense of good humour in every circumstance of fate, and one begins – but only begins – to know the man.

Born in Paddington, London on 29 January 1896, he was the only son of Lieutenant Francis West, East Lancashire Regiment, and his French wife, Comtesse Clemence de la Garde de Saignes; and the grandson (on his father's side) of Admiral of the Fleet, Sir John West. When his father's regiment was ordered overseas, he resigned his commission in order to remain with his young bride, but at the outbreak of the Boer War, Francis West immediately volunteered for service again and in 1902 was killed in action. His widow left England to take up residence in Milan, Italy, where young Freddie commenced his education in a private school.

His upbringing soon resulted in West becoming trilingual – English, French and Italian – and on graduation in 1912, he chose to study international law at Genoa University, and was on vacation in Switzerland in August 1914 when the news came of England's declaration of war with Germany. Making a circuitous route to England almost immediately, West had no sooner arrived in London when he was enlisted, as a private, in the Royal Army Medical Corps (to his utter dismay, in view of his urgent wish to see fighting service in France). Several months of frustration in his attempts to transfer to an infantry unit finally resulted in West being accepted for a commission in the Royal Munster Fusiliers – half-French, half-English, he was now to become an 'Irish' officer. . . .

Commissioned on 15 May 1915, West eventually arrived in France on 8 November, and within forty-eight hours was ensconced in the front-line trenches After four months of the primeval conditions of trench warfare, West chanced to have his first flight, in an aeroplane of 3 Squadron RFC, and he resolved to transfer to the air service. Accepted for training in March 1916, West returned to England for a few weeks elementary training at Brooklands as an observer, and at the end of April he returned to France on posting to 3 Squadron.

Flying operational sorties in the unit's Morane 'Parasol' two-seaters, West became obsessed with an ambition to become a pilot, and therefore volunteered at every possible opportunity for sorties in order to accumulate an impressive total of flying hours as an observer, before applying for pilot training. By July 1917 he had flown more than 100 hours on operations, and duly requested a course of pilot instruction, and in October (with an overall total of 225 hours as an observer) he again returned to England to commence his training. Making his first solo flight on 15 November, West accomplished a total of 60 hours solo flying by Christmas 1917 and was awarded his RFC 'wings', and on 4 January 1918 was posted to 8 Squadron, based near Amiens in France.

Commanded by Major Trafford Leigh-Mallory, 8 Squadron was equipped with Armstrong Whitworth FK8 two-seaters; the unit's role was mainly one of tactical co-operation with the artillery and the few tank formations. The FK8 – known more familiarly to its crews as the 'Big Ack' – was a robust, slab-sided machine, powered by a reliable 160 hp Beardmore engine which gave it a maximum (loaded) speed of almost 90 mph. Armament comprised a fixed Vickers machine gun forward for the pilot, while in the rear cockpit the observer had one or, on occasion, two Lewis machine guns mounted on a movable Scarff Ring. Though decidedly inferior in performance to the swift Albatros and Fokker scouts opposing, the Big Ack was well liked by its crews and gave sterling service throughout 1918.

West soon settled in to the unit's work, and gradually gained wide experience in low-level co-operation with the earthbound infantry and gunners, usually having to endure a constant barrage of enemy ground-fire as he and his fellow pilots kept faith with their ground formations. In March West became regularly crewed with Lieutenant John A. G. Haslam, an ex-Cambridge student, and the two men shared a variety of hazardous sorties during the German offensive which commenced on 21 March.

A particularly dangerous low-level sortie for West and Haslam came on 23 April, when they sat out to bomb a concentration of German transport well behind the enemy lines. Reaching their objective, the FK8 crew made an accurate bombing run and then strafed the target from near-zero height before turning for home. As they reached the front line again their aircraft was hit repeatedly by an intense barrage of groundfire, suffering hits in its engine and having an aileron shot away. By skill and good judgment West scraped across the Allied front lines and accomplished a safe landing only 100 yards west of the trenches. This sortie typified many of West's patrols during the fierce air activity of April 1918, and it became almost a common sight for 8 Squadron's FK8's to return from the battle scarred and tattered, victims of the unceasing ground barrage through which they were constantly required to operate. On 1 May, West and Haslam were each awarded a Military Cross for their own parts in the struggle.

The ground opposition was not the only hazard for the Big Ack crews; the cumbersome two-seaters were all too often the targets for roaming German fighters scouring the battle skies, and on 18 June, with Lieutenant D. R. Sharman in the rear cockpit, West had his designated bombing sortie abruptly interrupted by four Pfalz scouts which piled down in attack. Turning quickly, West shot the leading Pfalz into the ground, while Sharman's Lewis gun sent a second Pfalz spinning down out of control. More Pfalz joined in the attack but West managed to evade and shake these off.

Next day, again crewed with Sharman, West set out to bomb a suspected arms dump at Mericourt, only to be jumped by a formation of Fokkers as he reached the objective. Dropping down to 200 feet to protect himself from attack from below, West found himself in the middle of a balloon barrage, and was forced to manoeuvre wildly to avoid the several steel suspension cables. Above him the waiting Fokkers were then set upon by some Allied fighters, and West seized the opportunity to complete his original intention, and bombed his target successfully. His return to base brought news of his promotion to Captain and command of a flight.

On 1 July, 8 Squadron was attached to the Tank Corps for specific co-operation duties; part of the immense preparation then in hand for the forthcoming Allied offensive along the Amiens front. Though experiments were immediately made with the possibilities of direct wireless communication between aeroplane and tank, such an obvious tactic could only be used in ideal conditions, and in the event, the most practical role for 8 Squadron's FK8's proved to be visual reconnaissance at very low heights in 'contact' sorties.

When on 8 August 1918 the first waves of Allied infantry swept forward through the morning mists and completely surprised the German defences, West and his companions flew through the fog and managed to obtain much useful intelligence on the progress of the ground forces, though he only located his aerodrome again with the assistance of rocket flares fired from the airfield through the blinding mist, and subsequently crashed on landing, sustaining minor cuts and bruises.

Next day West and Haslam were out again, attacking German troops from tree-height, when their engine was shot out of action and West was lucky to reach the Allied lines and effect a safe landing. On the morning of 10 August, West and Haslam climbed into AWFK8 C8594 and set out from their unit base at Vignacourt (north of Amiens) tasked with co-operation with tanks advancing towards Roye. Breaking through the persistent low mists into blue sky, West headed south-east, skirting the top layer of fog, hoping to find breaks in the cloud to help him locate his charges.

Suddenly a clear gap revealed a large wood, along the edge of which was a huge concentration of German troops and transport. Diving low to verify his whereabouts – he was then in the Ham and Hombleux area, north-east of Roye – West made a tally of the strength of the enemy formation; he then flew through a curtain of machine gun fire to concealment in the low clouds again.

Still unsatisfied that he had pinpointed the German troop concentration accurately, West dived through the mists again, but was attacked from behind by several German scouts, one of which put a burst through West's cockpit, smashing his wireless transmitter and wounding him in the right foot. Despite his pain, West finally rediscovered the clear gap in the clouds and flew low over the enemy concentration, marking its position precisely in his mind.

Turning for home in order to get his information back quickly, he ran straight into the path of at least five more German scouts which dived in attack. With his front gun in action, and Haslam's Lewis adding to the exchange, West then received five bullets in succession in his left leg; slashing through the flesh and bone, and severing an artery. The shock misted West's mind and vision, and it was several seconds before he vaguely realised that his machine was diving out of control. Hauling back weakly on his control column, he levelled out just above the trees and headed west, still under attack from one persistent German scout. His shattered left leg was losing blood copiously and West twisted the khaki shorts' leg into a makeshift tourniquet with his left hand.

It became obvious to him that he could never reach Vignacourt in such a rapidly weakening state; his senses reeled under bouts of pain and lapsed into semi-consciousness between bouts. Deciding to land as soon as a safe area was seen, West lifted his useless left leg from the rudder bar, and then manoeuvred into a flat glide to earth, still under fire from the relentless scout still pursuing.

Rolling to a shaky halt on a patch of rough ground, West became only distantly aware of the subsequent events, as some nearby Canadian troops rushed to assist the FK8 crew. Ripping away the fabric from the side of the cockpit, the soldiers lifted West out, bound his near-severed leg, and carried him across the field to the nearest roadway, where he was placed in an ambulance and taken to a nearby casualty station. Though now lapsing into recurring waves of unconsciousness due to the massive pain from his wounds, West insisted, in a lucid moment, on having an officer sent over from 8 Squadron, in order to tell him of the enemy troop concentration he had discovered. This was done when the squadron recording officer came to the casualty station and jotted down West's information after which West fainted.

When Freddie West finally woke up again, the pain in his legs had disappeared, to be replaced by a violent itch in both feet and toes. Throwing back the blankets to reach the irritation, West was completely shocked to see that his left leg had gone – amputated – despite the still irritating itch he could distinctly feel in the missing leg.

After a short spell in Rouen hospital, West was sent home to the London hospital in Whitechapel; where on 8 November 1918 he was told of the *Gazette* notice that day of his award of a Victoria Cross. In December he was finally discharged from hospital, wearing a clumsy wooden left leg, with the official compensation award of £250 from the Air Ministry for the loss of his leg. On 1 March 1919, West attended an investiture at Buckingham Palace to receive his decorations; but now faced a very uncertain future in civilian life. Deciding to resume his interrupted career in law, West then met the Swiss tool manufacturer, Desoutter, who had also lost a leg but had designed an ingenious false leg which permitted almost normal operation without the aid of crutches or walking sticks. West quickly adapted himself to a Desoutter leg, and began to seek readmission to the air service hoping eventually to fly again.

Backed by the influence of Hugh Trenchard, he was temporarily recommissioned and posted to the Foreign Office in April 1919 as an RAF 'Liaison officer'; while in August his name appeared in the relatively short list of officers granted permanent commissions in the peacetime Royal Air Force. Two other names on the same list were his previous commander, Leigh-Mallory, and his observer, John Haslam MC DFC.

In February 1921 West was posted to RAF Uxbridge, and soon began flying again at nearby Northolt; though his piloting was entirely unofficially sponsored. He soon found that despite the discomfort and pain of using an artificial leg, he had lost none of his skill, and thereafter continued to fly at every possible opportunity. A staff college course in 1923 was followed by a posting to 17 Squadron at Hawkinge in 1924; and three years later a spell at CFS, Upavon. A tour of duty at Kalafrana seaplane base, Malta in 1928–29, was followed by an administrative post at the Old Sarum school of army co-operation; while from 1933 to 1936 he commanded No 4 Squadron at Farnborough.

There then followed West's first significant spell as an RAF 'diplomat' when he was appointed Air Attaché to Finland, Estonia and Latvia; and the outbreak of World War Two saw West as a Group Captain, commanding RAF Odiham in Hampshire. In 1940 West was promoted to Air Commodore and sent to Rome as Air Attaché in the British Embassy there, but in June he moved to Switzerland and joined the British Legation at Berne.

Here he remained for the rest of the war – and despite confirmed rumours of the Nazi Gestapo placing a 'price' on his head, Freddie West commenced his second war; a secret war of counter-intelligence and 'underground' activity which, even now, cannot be fully detailed publicly. Neutral Switzerland became a honeycomb of spy and counterspy activity by both Allied and Axis powers; yet West succeeded in inaugurating an increasingly fruitful 'escape' route for Allied servicemen who would normally have remained interned in Switzerland throughout the war. West's unfailing humour and undiminished dedication to his self-imposed task was eventually recognised after hostilities ceased by the award of a CBE.

Retiring from the RAF in March 1946, West then joined the world-wide Rank Organisation, and later became managing director of Eagle-Lion Distributors. In January 1976, Freddie West, by then the sole surviving air VC of the 1914–18 conflict celebrated his 80th birthday; still astonishingly busy with his many social and charitable activities, chairmanship of the local RAF Association, and work on the Victoria Cross and George Cross Society committees.

The last surviving air VC of 1914–18, West died in the Princess Margaret Hospital, Windsor on 7 July, 1988.

17. William George Barker

The third Canadian airman to be awarded a Victoria Cross during 1914–18, William George Barker, typified to some extent the highly individual approach to fighting which characterised so many of the thousands of Commonwealth youths who bore arms in Britain's armed Services. Dedicated primarily to the task of fighting, and often in trouble with pedantic authority for their scant observance of the more mundane aspects of regular Service discipline and custom the 'Colonials', as they were affectionately dubbed by their British comrades, established war records second to none.

Highly publicised individuals, such as 'Billy' Bishop vc, were no outstanding exceptions from the overall fighting prowess displayed by the men of the overseas contingents. Born and raised in countries relatively thinly populated over their vast areas of mountains and plains, such men brought with them a spirit of high adventure reminiscent of the early pioneers of exploration, and an outlook on life and death as broad-minded as that of the ancestors who first established civilisation in their respective homelands.

Born in Dauphin, Manitoba on 3 November 1894, George Barker's upbringing soon gave him wide experience in various outdoor activities, and he quickly became an accomplished horseman and an excellent marksman with rifle and pistol. Educated mainly at Dauphin College, Barker was living with his family in Winnipeg just prior to the outbreak of the European war in 1914, and wasted little time in volunteering for military service. On 1 November 1914 he enlisted in the 1st Battalion, Canadian Mounted Rifles as No 106074 Private Barker, W. G. and because of his wide knowledge of firearms, was attached to his battalion's machine gun section. In the spring of 1915 the Canadian Mounted Rifles sailed to England, and were based initially at Shorncliffe, Kent, and Barker received promotion to Corporal before his battalion finally crossed the English Channel on 22 September 1915 to join the fighting. Barker, who had already had one application for transfer to the Royal Flying Corps rejected, soon re-applied for the RFC and was accepted, and attached to 9 Squadron, RFC as a Corporal observer in December 1915.

For the next three months he flew many sorties in the cramped front cockpit of the unit's BE2c's, and early in 1916 claimed a Fokker mono-

plane as shot down after a close combat. Commissioned as Second
Lieutenant on 2 April 1916, though still not officially qualified to wear the
observer's half-wing brevet, Barker was posted to 4 Squadron on 7 April,
and continued his probationary 'experience' period of operational flying.

On 18 July Barker joined 15 Squadron at Marieux, still flying the
cumbersome BE2c's and three days later claimed a Roland two-seater as
shot down near Miraumont. Shortly after, on 15 August, he claimed
a second Roland, which spun down and crashed at Achiet-le-Grand. His
nine months of operational flying finally brought him official qualification
as an observer on 27 August, and he immediately applied for training as
a pilot. His various exploits and accredited victories as an observer had
been noted well by higher authority, and brought him the award of a
Military Cross (gazetted 10 January 1917); while his bid to become a
pilot was successful and on 16 November 1916 he returned to England
and reported to Narborough, Norfolk to commence instruction. His long
air experience, including many unofficial lessons in handling aircraft
controls, paid off in training school, and after only 55 minutes' dual
instruction, Barker was sent off for his first solo flight. Completing his
training at Netheravon, Barker returned to France on 24 February 1917,
as a Captain, and was posted back to his old unit, 15 Squadron, based at
Lealvillers, where he succeeded to the command of the unit's C Flight.

Still flying the outdated BE2's, Barker was in action within 24 hours
of rejoining his unit, flying a dangerously low contact patrol over the
frontline trenches and bringing back valuable information on the infantry
positions and movements. 15 Squadron at this time was mainly engaged
in close co-operation with the ground troops, and during the following
months Barker was seldom out of the air; flying constant low-level sorties,
usually through a constant barrage of groundfire and, like the rest of his
squadron's crews, ever inviting attack from fleet German single-seat scouts
roving the battlefields.

On 23 March Barker was the intended victim of a Fokker scout, but
by adroit manoeuvring and expert marksmanship, Barker shot the Fokker
down to crash near Cambrai. Particularly quick thinking on 9 April
resulted in Barker managing to range an artillery barrage onto a
developing German assault against some Australian positions, and for
this and his previous splendid example of unceasing air operations soon
brought him a Bar to his MC (gazetted 18 July). On 7 August, during
a particularly hazardous low-level contact patrol, his BE received severe
damage from the intense groundfire, and a shard of shrapnel almost
blinded him by slashing a furrow alongside his right eye. In the custom
of the period, having completed some six months of operational flying in

France, Barker, much to his personal disgust, was then posted to England for a 'rest' as an instructor.

The prospect of a 'tame' occupation, teaching raw youngsters to fly, held no attractions for Barker who immediately began agitating for an operational posting back to the fighting, and on this being refused, commenced to make a thorough nuisance of himself with higher authority by disobeying flying regulations and continually 'stunting' in the various school aircraft. In the event his insubordinate exploits led to a choice between being posted to 56 Squadron (SE5A's) in France, or to a newly-forming Sopwith Camel unit, 28 Squadron, at Yatesbury, soon to go to France.

Preferring the more agile Camel as a fighting vehicle, Barker chose 28 Squadron, and on 2 October was posted in to Yatesbury, and took over command of the squadron's A Flight. Six days later 28 Squadron flew to France and settled in at Droglandt aerodrome.

That same evening Barker led three of his Flight on a 'familiarisation' sortie along the trench lines. Despite orders to the contrary, he then led his men across the lines into enemy-occupied territory and, by chance, found himself over a formation of German aircraft. Unable to resist the temptation Barker dived headlong onto the enemy formation and his first burst sent one scout down to crash between Dixmude and Ypres. Pulling out of his dive, and now mindful of his responsibility to the three inexperienced men faithfully following him, he led the Camels back into Allied territory and to base. On landing, he submitted no combat report or claim for a victory; perhaps because of his disobedience of squadron orders.

His first (and the squadron's first) official victories came on 20 October, when, in the midst of a wheeling dogfight, Barker shot the wings off one Albatros Scout, and then riddled a second which fell to pieces in mid-air high over Roulers. Within the following week two more certain victims fell to his guns, while two others were claimed as damaged, possibly shot down. By this time events on the Italian front, culminating in a disastrous defeat of the Italians at Caporetto, resulted in hasty removal of a large British contingent from France to bolster the failing Allied front in Italy. On 28 October, 28 Squadron was warned of its imminent move to the new fighting zone, and commenced the transfer the following day. By 14 November the squadron had reassembled in Milan, and by the 28th become based for operations at Grossa airfield, north-west of Camisano. No time was wasted in resuming operational sorties, and on 29 November the squadron despatched several patrols.

Just before mid-day Barker led three of his Flight down on a formation of five Austrian scouts, and shot the wings off one. The victory was achieved in Barker's personal Sopwith Camel, B6313; a machine he had taken over shortly after joining 28 Squadron in England, and in which he scored all his victories throughout the Italian campaign. Ever an individual, Barker continually modified this Camel to his own ideas; including removing the standard Aldis gun sight and substituting two steel strips across the front and rear of his gun barrels, each cut to give him a plain rifle-type sight-line.

Typical of Barker's restless aggression was a sortie on 3 December, when he led seven other Camels on an ostensibly 'routine' escort patrol for 34 Squadron's RE8 two-seaters. Once his protection duties were complete, Barker led his men across the enemy lines again intending to destroy an observation kite balloon north-east of Conegliano. As he attacked the balloon a brightly-hued Albatros scout attempted to attack one of Barker's men. He immediately left the balloon, dived on the Austrian interloper, and shot it down in flames. Returning to the balloon, Barker's fire set this alight, and Barker then proceeded to strafe its ground crew. On his return flight he attacked a car, causing it to overturn into a ditch; then rounded off his patrol by machine-gunning several concentrations of Austrian infantry.

Even on Christmas Day, 1917, when little activity was planned by either side in the struggle, Barker was not content to stay on the ground. Accompanied by one other Camel, he flew to the Austrian aerodrome at Motta, dropped a note wishing the Austrian fliers a merry Christmas – then dived and strafed everything which came into his view. Barker remained with 28 Squadron until early April 1918; claiming at least 15 victories over the Italian front, and being awarded a DSO. Then, due to a disagreement with higher authority, he 'exchanged' posts with 66 Squadron Flight commander on 10 April, taking his 'personal' Camel B6313 with him to the new unit.

During his service with 66 Squadron, Barker claimed a further 16 combat victories, and received several more gallantry awards. On 24 April came a second Bar to his MC (gazetted 16 September 1918); on 19 May the French commander presented Barker with his country's Croix de Guerre; and he was mentioned in despatches. On 3 July a new squadron was formed in Italy, 139, equipped with two-seat Bristol F2b Fighters, and on 14 July, with promotion to Major, Barker took up his appointment as commander of the squadron; bringing with him his Camel, B6313. A week later came the award of a Bar to his DSO, and its citation officially credited Barker with a victory tally of 33 enemy aircraft and nine kite balloons.

Despite his increased ground duties as squadron commander, Barker refused to be bound to a desk, and continued to fly his Camel; and between 18 July and 18 September 1918 made claims for a further six victories. He was further decorated when the Italians awarded him their Silver Medal for Military Valour. On 30 September, having flown on operations continually for nearly a full year without a rest, Barker left Italy and returned to England, where he was posted to Hounslow's school of aerial fighting tactics.

Almost as soon as his leave was finished, and he had reported to Hounslow, Barker began agitating authority for a more active post in France, and eventually persuaded his superiors to permit him a brief attachment to an operational squadron, 201, as a form of 'refresher' course in operational conditions over the Western Front. Accordingly, on 17 October he flew a new fighter, Sopwith Snipe, E8102, across the Channel to 201 Squadron at La Targette airfield; ostensibly to 'evaluate' the new rotary-engined design under fighting conditions. His attachment was for two weeks only, and by 27 October, the day he had to return to England, Barker had tried his utmost to gain further victories, but without success.

Packing his small kit into the Snipe, Barker left La Targette airfield early on the morning of 27 October 1918, en route to Hounslow, but could not resist one last look at the fighting zone and therefore climbed high across enemy lines. At 0825 hours he spotted an all-white German two-seater at 21,000 feet over the northern edge of the Foret de Mormal, and joyfully climbed to attack. His first bursts killed the German observer and then the enemy machine broke up, ejecting its pilot who, uncommonly, parachuted to earth.

Intent on his victim, Barker failed to notice a German Fokker D VII scout which came from underneath, and its first fire ripped through Barker's cockpit, wounding him in the right thigh. Incensed at being caught unawares, Barker dived on his assailant and closed to pointblank range. His opening fire found its mark and the Fokker fell away trailing flames. Following it down, Barker suddenly found himself plunging into the centre of a German formation of some 15 Fokker D VII's, which reacted swiftly to his arrival and promptly bore in from every angle to attack. Firing crisp bursts at any Fokker which came into his sights, Barker drove two down in succession, but was hit badly in his left thigh by a particularly murderous burst from close quarters. The shock and added pain caused Barker to faint, and his Snipe fell away out of control.

Recovering consciousness, Barker realised he was still under attack by a host of Fokkers – though whether these were the same opponents or a fresh batch he could not ascertain. He then realised that his engine was trailing a plume of smoke and, under the impression his Snipe was on fire, decided that if he must die he would take at least one more opponent with him.

Charging one Fokker head-on, with both guns firing steadily, Barker deliberately sought to ram the German, but his opponent erupted in flames and dropped its nose for a death plunge before Barker could close with it. At that moment another Fokker put a burst through the side of the Snipe, shattering Barker's left elbow, and Barker lapsed into unconsciousness again. Recovering his senses, Barker found a Fokker only five yards in front of him and instinctively pressed his gun trips. The German flicked sideways with a jerk and burst into flames.

The Snipe now commenced a dive and Barker, with both thighs seriously wounded and his left arm useless, could only retain minimal control of the machine. A last onslaught by one Fokker ripped bullets through the Snipe's petrol tank, but then left the obviously defeated Snipe to crash. As Barker neared the ground he felt himself beginning to faint again and in a last despairing movement he flattened out for a landing near an Allied observation balloon site.

As the battered Snipe touched earth, it bounced, overturned onto its back, and slithered to a halt; at the same time throwing the now unconscious Barker violently forward and breaking his nose on the cockpit rim.

Nearby troops lifted the shattered, unconscious Barker from his bloody cockpit and transported him to No 8 General Hospital, Rouen, where he remained unconscious for several days. Surgeons managed to save his left arm, rather than amputate, and Barker revived eventually, to be given the news shortly after that his epic fight on 27 October had brought him the supreme honour – the Victoria Cross.

In a short note to the commander of 201 Squadron on 9 November, Barker wrote, 'By Jove, I was a foolish boy, but anyhow I taught them a lesson. . . .'

His VC was officially gazetted on 30 November 1918, and on 1 March 1919 Barker, his left arm still in a sling, and hobbling on a walking stick, was invested with his many decorations at Buckingham Palace. The idea of a peacetime career in the RAF did not appeal to him, so on 29 April 1919 he resigned his commission and returned to Canada; there to seek suitable business employment. Unable at first to settle into the hum-drum routine of civilian life, Barker partnered another Canadian air VC, 'Billy' Bishop, in a charter aircraft scheme, but the airborne antics of

William George Barker

[145]

[146]   Andrew Frederick Weatherby Beauchamp Proctor

the two wild Canadians soon caused the business to fail.

In 1920, Barker joined the Canadian Air Force as a Wing Commander and was sent to England as Liaison Officer at the Air Ministry; and in the following year married Jean Kilbourn Smith. Two years later he was appointed aide-de-camp to HM King George V, but had already decided that peacetime Service life was not his vocation. Leaving the CAF in 1924, he started in a tobacco business, until a bout of pneumonia in 1929 prostrated him for several months, and he was forced to relinquish his interests in the business.

An opportunity to return to his main delight, aviation, came when in January 1930 he was appointed Vice-President of the new Fairchild Aviation Corporation of Canada, with the company headquarters at Montreal. Not content to simply regard his position as a desk-bound executive post, Barker preferred to personally test the firm's new designs, and on 12 March 1930 he took off from Rockcliffe, Ottawa in a new Fairchild two-seater aircraft to give an air demonstration of its capabilities. He had hardly become airborne when the machine stalled viciously and crashed at full power into the river. Rescuers who rushed to the scene found Barker dead in the cockpit. Three days later they buried George Barker in the Mount Pleasant cemetery in Toronto, and a witness to the funeral has stated that there was a queue five miles long of people anxious to pay their last respects to the lion-hearted Canadian.

18. Andrew Frederick Weatherby Beauchamp Proctor

When war between Britain and Germany was declared in August 1914, amongst the many embryo pilots under training at the RFC's Central Flying School were six officers of the South African Aviation Corps. By November 1914, five of these officers were serving with the RFC in France – the first of many thousands of young South Africans who eagerly volunteered to fly with Britain's flying services; despite the still-fresh memories of the Anglo-Boer war of only a dozen years previously. Such became the high reputation of these men and their successors that in October 1916 one South African veteran pilot who had already seen wide operational service in France, Captain Allister M. Miller DSO, was – at the request of the British government – sent home to South Africa to recruit volunteers for pilot training and service with the RFC. Tasked with recruiting a total of 30 volunteers, Miller actually enrolled 450.

Returning to London in June 1917, Miller was again sent to South Africa for a further RFC recruiting tour. From some 8,000 applications, Miller personally selected 2,000 young South Africans for training in England. One of these emerged as the most decorated South African pilot of World War One – Andrew Proctor VC DSO MC DFC.

Born on 4 September 1894 at Mossel Bay, a minor port on the east coast of the Cape Province, and baptised as Andrew Frederick Weatherby Proctor, he was the son of John James Proctor, a teacher and ex-Army officer. Educated at his father's schools at George and, later, Mafeking, Proctor became a boarding pupil in the old South African College (predecessor to Cape Town's University) in 1911. Matriculating in 1912, Proctor commenced studies in 1913 for an engineering diploma, and in 1914 was granted a Second Year Pass. His studies were then interrupted by the war, and on 1 October 1914, he voluntarily enlisted in the Duke of Edinburgh's Own Rifles ('The Dukes') as No 6348 Signaller Proctor, A. W. for active service in the German South-West Africa campaign; despite his full-grown height of only five feet two inches. The subsequent arduous campaign meant battling more against scorching heat, waterless desert sands, rugged mountains, and the ever-present flies, than the German forces.

148

Though small in stature, Proctor played his full part in the campaign, and at its end was transferred to the South African Field Telegraph and Postal Corps for a further three months' service, before being demobilised in August 1915, and returning to his college to continue his engineering studies. A year later he successfully passed his Third Year examinations, but by then his thoughts were turning more to the war, and the possibilities of joining his many friends who had already left for England to enlist and fight.

His opportunity came with the Miller recruiting drive, and on 12 March 1917, Proctor was officially enlisted as an Air Mechanic, 3rd Class in the RFC, and sailed to England for training as a pilot. Though no specific date can be found for the change, it was about this time that Proctor, mainly at the bidding of his father, 'adopted' the name Beauchamp before his surname – a tenuous link with distant relatives of Irish and English extraction in the early 19th century; and at the same time 'dropped' the German-sounding Christian name Frederick.*

Reporting to No 6 Officers' Cadet Battalion at South Farnborough on 26 March 1917, Proctor was sent to the Oxford School of Military Aeronautics on 13 April for a month's ground training, and in May commenced his flying instruction with 5 (Reserve) Squadron, Castle Bromwich. Further instruction with 24 (Reserve) Squadron at Netheravon, led to an advanced Service flying course at CFS, Upavon in July 1917; and on 29 July he was awarded his RFC 'wings', and posted to Beaulieu, Hampshire to join 84 Squadron RFC.

No 84 Squadron, commanded by the veteran Major Sholto Douglas, MC (later to achieve distinguished rank in the RAF in World War 2), had originally formed in January 1917, and when Proctor joined the unit, was in the process of working up for operations in France. Equipped throughout eventually with SE5A Scouts, 84 Squadron moved to the war zone on 21 September 1917 and became based at Flez for the remaining winter months. After several weeks of routine patrols to accustom themselves to their fighting area and conditions, 84's pilots, led by Sholto Douglas, began offensive patrols seeking German aircraft.

Proctor's short stature had meant much modification and adjustment to the cockpit seat and controls of his SE5A to enable him to fly safely, but once in the air he quickly proved himself to be a 'natural' pilot. His first 'blooding' came on 22 November when he and a companion shared in the destruction of a German observation kite balloon. Flying SE5A

* Proctor's British passport gave the names Andrew Weatherby Beauchamp Proctor; while RFC and RAF documents usually hyphenated Beauchamp-Proctor. He signed his personal letters 'A. Beauchamp Proctor', without a hyphen.

B597, Proctor plunged through the usual intense barrage of anti-aircraft gun fire, sent one kite balloon down to a hasty landing, and then joined another SE in flaming a second balloon. It was an appropriate opening to his fighting career, because later in the year he was to partly 'specialise' in the destruction of these lighter-than-air 'eyes' for the German artillery guns. On 29 November he tackled a German two-seater and forced it to dive to earth; and sent another two-seater down in a near-vertical dive on 5 December.

Proctor's first confirmed destruction of an enemy aircraft came on 3 January 1918 when, in SE5A B539, he attacked a two-seater over St Quentin and sent it down to crash in mid-afternoon. Next day yet another victim spun down completely out of control after Proctor's attack, but he was unable to see its eventual fate and could not claim a positive victory. By mid-February Proctor's patent ability in combat led Sholto Douglas to detail the South African to lead fighting patrols, despite his junior rank as a Second Lieutenant. The first patrol as leader was flown on 15 February, and Proctor engaged one German aircraft which he proceeded to harry until it dived to earth and safety. Later in the day Proctor tackled an observation balloon, forcing its ground crew to haul it down. Two days later Proctor, in SE5A B539, attacked an Albatros Scout and sent it spinning down utterly out of control, and then concentrated on a two-seater which eventually escaped across the trench lines. On the 19th, however Proctor claimed a certain victory when he closed with an Albatros Scout south-east of La Fère, and so riddled the German with close-range fire that it crashed. His combat and the fate of his opponent was later confirmed by an eye-witness, Captain 'Jimmy' McCudden (later VC) of 56 Squadron. Two more possible victories for Proctor that month were a kite balloon 'driven down', and a single-seat scout sent down out of control on the 28th.

March 1918 brought Proctor a total of eight victories. Commencing on the 1st by sending one German down out of control, he destroyed a kite balloon on the 10th; but next day nearly killed himself whilst landing in SE5A B539 when a wheel hit some unnoticed obstacle and the SE crashed. Unshaken, Proctor was again in action the following day, flying a new SE, D259, and shared with Captain Leask in the destruction of a German two-seater. On the 15th, in the early morning Proctor had a rare victory; trapping a DFW C.V of Flieger Abteilung (A) 207 behind British lines, and shooting it down near Villeret. 17 March proved to be his best combat day to date, with a triple victory. In SE5A D259, Proctor led a fighting patrol down onto a formation of Pfalz D III scouts, and in the ensuing, milling dogfight, shot the wings off one and sent two others down gyrating wildly and quite apparently out of control. His own SE was badly damaged by enemy fire and the SE's engine eventually seized up, but Proctor managed to land without injury. A further, though indecisive, fight on 21 March resulted in an Albatros Scout being 'driven down' near Marcelcave in the early afternoon, and closed Proctor's 'account' for the month.

1 April 1918 ushered in the newly-formed Royal Air Force, by amalgamation of the former RFC and RNAS into a third Service; and on the same date Andrew Proctor was promoted to Lieutenant. On the 8th he was further promoted to Captain and given command of C Flight, 84 Squadron – recognition of his prowess and leadership qualities. His new responsibilities curtailed his fighting activities to some extent; though on 12 April Proctor claimed a pair of German single-seaters as out of control; and on the 20th drove a two-seater down behind the German lines. His next positive victory came on 21 April when, in SE5A C1772, he closed with an Albatros Scout and killed its pilot. In the late afternoon of 23 April, Proctor led his Flight down on an enemy formation of ten single-seaters; singling out the leader's Fokker Triplane as his own target, and shooting this down to crash at Framerville with a total of 200 rounds fired. May 1918 proved to be Proctor's most successful month of his fighting career, being credited with 14 victories. The first of these, an Albatros Scout, was sent down out of control on 9 May; and next day, while leading a squadron patrol Proctor spotted a Rumpler two-seater climbing for height. Patiently stalking the German in the hope that it would cross into Allied territory, Proctor saw the Rumpler begin to dive away east, obviously having seen the SE5A patrol.

Diving after the two-seater, Proctor fired 50 rounds into it and saw the observer crumple into his cockpit. Closing in, Proctor fired again and the Rumpler veered erratically; only to fall into a vertical nose dive as the South African poured in a third burst of fire. Plunging through the low-lying mists, still vertically diving, the Rumpler crashed near the river Somme, south-east of Bray.

At this period German night bombing activity had increased along the Western Front, with almost nightly raids being undertaken against premier Allied towns and centres; and in the pre-dawn hours of 15 May Proctor decided on a lone sortie to attempt an interception of the night raiders. Flying directly east he located one of the aerodromes used by the night bombers and then waited at 3,000 feet a few miles west of the airfield for homecoming German aircraft. Just before 4 am he saw a twin-engined AEG bomber flying overhead and fastened under its tail. The German rear gunner was alert and commenced firing at Proctor, who returned his fire and apparently wounded the gunner. The AEG started a dive with Proctor following, but as he was about to fire Proctor's gun jammed. Rectifying the stoppage, Proctor fired 150 rounds into the AEG, whose pilot immediately fired a red signal flare; the signal for an immediate barrage from ground defences which surrounded the SE. Continuing to harass the bomber, Proctor chased it well beyond its airfield before finally breaking off the combat, by which time the AEG, apparently much damaged, was last seen still diving.

Crashing an Albatros Scout on 17 May, and a two-seater on the 18th; Proctor had a field day of combat on 19 May. On the early morning patrol he engaged a two-seater over Vauvillers and watched it spin away out of control into the ground mists, then, an hour later, sank 100 rounds into an Albatros Scout which flicked into an uncontrolled spin and also disappeared towards the ground. That evening, leading three other SE's of his Flight, Proctor tackled five Albatros Scouts. Proctor's first burst caught one Albatros amidships and it fell to earth, crashing near Cachy; while one of the other SE pilots, Lieutenant H. O. MacDonald, shot down a second Albatros.

Of the remaining trio of Germans, two collided in mid-air and dissolved into a tumbling pyre of burning wreckage. During the last week in May Proctor claimed six more victims – four aircraft and two kite balloons – and on 28 May was awarded a Military Cross 'In the Field' (Gazetted 22 June 1918). By the end of May Proctor's officially-accredited victory tally stood at 11 'Hostile Aircraft' (including kite balloons) destroyed and 13 more Out of Control. Flying SE5A D333 now, Proctor continued his reign of destruction during the first two weeks of June by claiming eight more victims – five balloons and three aircraft – and then left for England for a spell of leave. On 3 August came the announcement of his second decoration; the newly-instituted Distinguished Flying Cross.

Returning from leave in early August, refreshed and eager to return to the fighting, Proctor took over a new SE5A, D6856, and quickly showed that he was now at his peak. On the 8th he destroyed a kite balloon in flames, and next day sent two aircraft down; one in flames and the other wildly out of control. On the 11th he scored his first victory over one of the new, deadly Fokker D VII scouts, and three days later sent two more D VIII scouts down to their last 'landing'.

Just after 10 am on the morning of 16 August, Proctor spotted a DFW C.V two-seater well below him, and dived headlong for some 10,000 feet to attack it. Firing both guns, he closed with the DFW and it burst into flames. As he watched, Proctor was horrified to see the German observer climb out of his cockpit and, rather than face death by burning, jump clear into space, despite his lack of a parachute. If the sight bothered Proctor, it had no apparent effect on his nerves, and on the 21st he tackled an Albatros two-seater and shot it down to crash at Estrées-Fay.

Next morning Proctor set out to attack the German balloon lines in an attempt to 'blind' the enemy artillery guns. Destroying two balloons in quick succession, he then proceeded to attack five others, one after the other, causing each one's observers to take to his parachute. On the same date officialdom confirmed Proctor's score as standing at 33 enemy aircraft and seven kite balloons conquered. He was recommended for a third gallantry award – a Bar to his MC – which was later gazetted on 16 September 1918.

A pair of Fokker D VII's were his next victims, on 24 August; followed on the 25th by another double victory; a Fokker D VII which crashed at Tempeux, and a Rumpler two-seater, which Proctor shared in destroying with other members of 84 Squadron. Two days later, with his patrol, he attacked an observation balloon heavily guarded by eight German scouts and shot the *Drachen* down in flames. Chased back to the lines by the vengeful German fighters, Proctor led these away from their 'charges', then slipped into cloud, steered by compass back to the balloon line, and destroyed a second *Drachen*. As he jinked his way out of the furious ground fire his aircraft was hit in the engine and Proctor only scraped across the trench lines to safety at 500 feet. His final August victim was a Fokker D VII; the destruction of which he shared with Captain C. F. Falkenberg in the early evening.

Throughout September 84 Squadron concentrated on low-level fighting in support of the advancing Allied armies; strafing and bombing a myriad of ground targets daily; and Proctor's specific contribution in terms of 'victories' was the destruction of four kite balloons. On 1 October, however, the German airmen once more became prime prey, and Proctor sent two Fokker D VII's down to crash in a prolonged combat in the late afternoon. Two more kite balloons fell to his guns on 2 and 3 October, and on the latter date he added yet another Fokker D VII to his tally. On the 5th he shared the destruction of a kite balloon with Second Lieutenant A. E. Hill.

Andrew Proctor's final war sortie came on 8 October when, just before noon, he sent a Rumpler two-seater down to crash near Maretz; but as he turned for home he was set upon by eight German fighters. In the ensuing combat Proctor was hit badly in the arm, and barely managed to escape death and eventually return to his own aerodrome. Receiving immediate medical attention, Proctor was then invalided back to

England, where he was sent to the Northumberland Hospital, near Newcastle-upon-Tyne to recuperate.

Already in the RAF administration 'channels' was a recommendation that he be awarded a Distinguished Service Order, and this award was officially promulgated on 2 November 1918. Added to this was a recommendation from Sholto Douglas that the diminutive South African pilot – in Douglas's own words, 'that little man who had the guts of a lion' – be awarded the supreme decoration, the Victoria Cross.

Almost three weeks after the armistice the *London Gazette* of 30 November 1918 confirmed the award of the VC to Proctor, its citation crediting him with destroying 22 enemy aircraft and 16 kite balloons, and driving a further 16 enemy aircraft down completely out of control. This total of 54 'victories' represented almost exactly one-third of 84 Squadron's total war tally of combat victories.

Discharged from hospital in March 1919, Proctor joined a mission to America, where he toured various United States cities lecturing to help raise funds for the US 'Liberty Loan'; and then on his return to England in July 1919, he was posted to Lee-on-Solent, Hampshire for a course in piloting seaplanes. His next posting was to Cranwell, where on 1 November 1919 he was granted a permanent commission, with Flight Lieutenant rank, in the RAF. On 27 November 1919 he attended an investiture at Buckingham Palace, where he received his VC DSO and DFC from King George V. Longing to see his family again, and to resume his much-interrupted engineering studies, Proctor persuaded the Air Ministry to allow him one year's leave in South Africa, and on arriving at Cape Town in the *Armadale Castle* on 23 February 1920, Proctor was given a hero's welcome by the city.

Returning to his old college, he was given a Webb scholarship and completed his studies for the degree of Bachelor of Science in Mechanical Engineering, University of Cape Town; and at Christmas 1920 sailed back to England to commence a promising RAF career. On arrival he was posted to 24 Squadron, and then attended an engineering course at Henlow.

In June 1921 Andrew Proctor was detached temporarily to RAF Upavon as one of a small number of selected pilots detailed to participate in the imminent Royal Air Force Pageant – forerunner of the annual RAF Displays of the inter-war years. Proctor's particular role was appropriate to his war record, in that he was to demonstrate destroying a 'hostile' kite balloon. On 21 June, flying Sopwith Snipe E8220, Proctor was practising for his display item, and began a loop.

As the Snipe inverted at the top of its arc, it fell away viciously into an inverted spin and the horrified spectators on the ground watched the Snipe continue to spin right into the earth, crashing just near Enford. Andrew Proctor, survivor of a hundred dogfights, had died in a simple flying accident in a peaceful Wiltshire meadow.

Several theories were advanced as to the cause of the accident, and the general consensus seemed to point to Proctor being thrown onto his webbing shoulder harness straps while at the top of the loop and his usual seat cushions – necessary to permit his short arms to reach the aircraft controls – working loose and either jamming the controls or falling loose soon after. Unable to regain his normal piloting position, Proctor was thus helpless to prevent a crash.

His body was returned to South Africa, arriving at Cape Town aboard the *Balmoral Castle* on 8 August 1921. As the cortege passed through the city it was given the full ceremonial of a State Funeral, before being put aboard a train bound for Mafeking. Here Andrew Frederick Weatherby Beauchamp Proctor VC DSO MC DFC was laid to his final rest – the first but not the last South African airman to be awarded the Victoria Cross 'for valour'.

19. Edward Mannock

In an era when genuine modesty and studied understatement were desirable national characteristics of the normal British citizen, both official policy and individual grass-roots' opinion in the ranks of Britain's flying services favoured non-publicity for individual deeds and exploits. The 'ace' cult for high-scoring scout pilots, fostered originally by both France and Germany, and later adopted by the American air services, was mainly derided by the RFC, RNAS and RAF. The consequence was that although occasionally individuals, such as William Robinson vc and Albert Ball vc, received international acclaim for their prowess; the vast bulk of air crews in the British air services remained virtually unknown to the public at large – and, indeed, remained so until fairly recent years.

No better example exists of the result of such deliberate anonymity than the career of Major Edward Mannock vc dso mc who, despite *official* recognition as Britain's highest-scoring fighter pilot of the 1914-18 conflict, was not considered for an award of a Victoria Cross until after the war, and was not awarded the honour until almost exactly a year after his death in action; the culmination of several depositions and much agitation by former flying colleagues of Mannock.

The full career of Edward Mannock was not simply a story of a skilled fighting pilot who eventually became recognised as the RAF's leading name in his field; it was equally a life in which a man privately overcame many obstacles of social deprivation, physical disability, and – not least – a natural, instinctive fear of death. Though born in England, Edward Mannock came from Irish parentage, the son of Julia Mannock, née O'Sullivan, and her husband Corporal Edward Mannock, a regular service soldier of the 2nd Dragoons, Royal Scots Greys. It was while his father was stationed at Preston Cavalry Barracks, Brighton that Edward was born on 24 May 1887. Of slight build and indifferent health, the boy soon developed severe astigmatism in his left eye and was virtually blind in this eye for the remainder of his life.

After his father's service in the Boer War, the family moved to the cavalry depot at Canterbury, and Edward received a scant education at St Thomas's School until his thirteenth year, after which he undertook a variety of menial jobs simply to supplement the family income. The cessation of his academic education was not of his choosing, but a necessity; no sooner had the family moved to Canterbury than Mannock's father simply deserted his parental responsibilities, leaving his wife penniless and with four young children to feed, clothe and raise.

Struggling against the poverty, Mannock soon joined his brother Patrick in the employ of the National Telephone Company, first as a clerk and later as a maintenance man; while what little spare time was left to him was usually devoted to an insatiable hunger for book-reading, leavened by participation in local sports activities. He also joined a local army territorial unit of the Royal Army Medical Corps – his tall (nearly six feet), slender figure looking well in uniform.

In January 1914 Mannock left England, having volunteered for a post with the telephone company in Turkey, and became based in Constantinople in a field supervisory capacity. Mannock was still in Turkey on 5 November 1914 when Britain and France made their joint declaration of war against Turkey, and within days he was one of the many British nationals 'interned' by the Turkish Government. The 'internment' was in fact primitive imprisonment in conditions which soon reduced Mannock and his companions to a parlous physical condition, due to malnutrition, fever, disease and utter lack of medical facilities. Only the intervention of the American Consular Agent saved Mannock from possible permanent ill-health, and, still feeble and racked with fever, Mannock was repatriated to England on 1 April 1915 as 'Unfit for military duties'.

By the time Mannock finally set foot on English soil again, he had become obsessed with one idea – to join the fighting services and start 'destroying Germans'. He immediately rejoined the RAMC, being promoted to Sergeant and, later, Sergeant-major in the mounted transport section; then applied for a commission in the Royal Engineers.

After three months cadet training at Fenny Stratford, Mannock was commissioned as a Second Lieutenant, RE on 1 April 1916; only to apply for transfer to the Royal Flying Corps for training as a pilot. His restless urge to get to grips with his country's enemies was frustrated by the (to him) lengthy training considered necessary before despatching him to France, and at this period the name of Albert Ball, a 19-years old Nottingham boy, was being publicised nationally because of his lone prowess as a fighting pilot. Ball became Mannock's succinct inspiration to transfer to the flying service.

In August 1916 Mannock's application was approved and, after a brief ground school course of instruction at the Reading School of Military Aeronautics, he reported to Hendon for initial flying instruction, followed by advanced instruction at Upavon. Granted Royal Aero Club Certificate

No 3895 on 28 November 1916, he was next posted to 19 (Training) Squadron at Hounslow in early December; then attached briefly to the Hythe gunnery school. His final training came at Joyce Green aerodrome with No 10 (Reserve) Squadron, where amongst his instructors was 'Jimmy' McCudden (later VC). Since his first application to join the RFC Mannock had managed to conceal his defective sight in his left eye and, though at a disadvantage when in the process of landing an aircraft, his flying standard was high, and he was selected to become a single-seat scout pilot.

His orders to proceed to France came through on 1 April 1917 and next day he arrived at St Omer depot. Four days later he reported to his first operational unit, 40 Squadron based at Aire, equipped with the tiny Nieuport Scout and commanded by Major Leonard Tilney. Allotted to C Flight, Mannock made his first solo in a Nieuport Scout the following day, and on the 8th flew to the lines, got lost, and overturned when landing.

On 19 April he had a narrow brush with death when flying his Nieuport above the aerodrome. A lower wing became loose and flew off, but by skilful piloting Mannock managed to land without injury.

During his first month with 40 Squadron Mannock took part in several patrols and had inconclusive engagements with various German aircraft, but it was not until May 7th that he could claim his first confirmed victory – a kite balloon destroyed in flames; one of several attacked by six Nieuports from the squadron. On 25 May and 1 June he drove down a two-seat reconnaissance machine, neither of which did he claim as a victory, but on 7 June, while part of a fighting escort for some FE2b bombers, he attacked an Albatros D III Scout, fired just 30 rounds into it, and saw his opponent tumble 14,000 feet towards the earth completely out of control. Two days later he became involved with five German two-seaters north of Douai and afterwards claimed two as 'Driven down'.

After a period of leave in England, he returned to 40 Squadron, and on 12 July, in Nieuport B1682, he shot down a DFW CV two-seater from Schusta 12, killing its pilot and wounding the observer. Next day he attacked another DFW CV near Billy-Montigny and sent it down hopelessly out of control. Though a 'slow starter', Mannock's consistent good work since his arrival in France had been noted, and on 22 July he was awarded a Military Cross, and promoted to Captain in command of a Flight.

Having spent several weeks in action, and gained much first-hand experience of the business of air fighting, Mannock, as commander of a Flight, now began to implement his private ideas on how air combat tactics should be utilised. Primarily, he considered that the day of the 'lone' fighter was over; in future it would be necessary to fight in 'teams' – co-ordinated formations of fighters who could inflict the maximum damage upon the German air service with the minimum Allied losses. Within such a 'team' – remembering his own first, tentative sorties over the fighting zone – he paid particular attention to nurturing the fresh, inexperienced pilots during their initial war sorties; the most dangerous period of any fighting pilot's career.

His constant concern for his men did not prevent him adding to his personal tally however, and between 28 July and 15 August he claimed five German single-seaters; one being a six-victory pilot of Jagdstaffel 30, Leutnant Joachim von Bertrab, whom Mannock wounded and forced to land inside Allied lines in 12 August. Within the following seven days he added five more victories – all DFW two-seaters; then on 4 September 1917 Mannock claimed a triple victory by bringing down three DFW's – one in flames, one out of control, and a third which he merely claimed as 'Driven down'.

Throughout the remaining weeks of September Mannock claimed a further seven victims, all two-seat reconnaissance machines. The last of these, a Hannover CL3 from Flieger Abteilung (A) 288, was destroyed on 1 January 1918, his final day of combat in 40 Squadron because on the next day Mannock returned to England for a month's leave and a home posting. Meantime, on 18 October 1917 came the announcement of the award of a Bar to his Military Cross. When the day came for Mannock to leave 40 Squadron, the car transporting him to Boulogne was 'loudly cheered by the officers outside the Mess, and we found the road lined with cheering mechanics'*; while the squadron commander recorded Mannock's service as a Flight commander in the words, 'His leadership and general ability will never be forgotten by those who had the good fortune to serve under him.'

On completion of his leave, Mannock was first attached to the Wireless Experimental Establishment at Biggin Hill, then in mid-February 1918 ordered to join 74 (Training) Squadron at London Colney aerodrome. 74, a new unit forming up for operations in France, was equipped with SE5a single-seat scouts, and commanded by Major Keith Caldwell MC, a veteran New Zealand pilot. Mannock was appointed A Flight commander, and immediately began inculcating his pilots with his personal creed of 'teamwork' in fighting.

On 1 March the unit officially ceased to be regarded as a training squadron, and on the last day of the month flew to France to join the

* *Fighter Pilot* by W. MacLanachan; Published 1936 by Newnes.

war; becoming based initially at Teteghem, near Dunkirk for a week's armament practice, and then on 9 April moving to La Lovie airfield, near Poperinghe.

Just three days later Mannock scored the squadron's first victory by crashing an Albatros Scout east of Carvin, and then sharing in the destruction of a second shortly after. Before April was out he added six more German aircraft to his personal tally. May 1918 proved to be his most successful month of operations, in the course of which he claimed no less than 24 victories – almost all of these while leading his Flight into combat, though he was now tending to fly additional lone sorties in his mounting lust to seek and kill.

Few leading air fighters of 1914-18 possessed any form of personal hatred for their opponents, but Mannock was always an exception to the general attitude held by most pilots. To him (like Albert Ball, in certain respects) he was in France to destroy the 'enemy'; sporting or chivalrous attitudes to any adversary held no meaning for Mannock. But whereas Ball was genuinely upset when he had killed an opponent, Mannock simply exulted in the destruction of another enemy. On 19 May came the award of a Distinguished Service Order (DSO), and a week later, in a letter to a friend in England, Mannock showed that he was now taking interest in the actual figure of his victory tally, saying, 'Now have 41 victories. . . .')

Awarded a Bar to his DSO at the end of May, Mannock started his June tally with a triple victory on 1 June. During a late afternoon patrol over Estaires, his formation encountered a batch of Pfalz D III scouts from Jagdstaffel 52. Mannock attacked one Pfalz which immediately burst into flames and fell, its wings tearing away from its fuselage at 13,000 feet. Tackling a second Pfalz immediately, Mannock's fire reached its petrol tank and it too plunged to earth, spewing flames and smoke. His third victim was hit and spun helplessly down, but being unable to verify its eventual fate Mannock merely claimed it as out of control. By 18 June – the date he finally left 74 Squadron to return to England – Mannock added at least eight more German aircraft to his personal score. By then his reputation as a superb fighting leader had spread along the Western Front in RAF units, yet he was still virtually unknown outside the Service circles.

Promoted to Major on 21 June, he was chosen to succeed Major 'Billy' Bishop, vc dso mc dfc in command of another SE5a fighter unit in France, 85 Squadron, when Bishop was withdrawn from operations to assist in formation of the Canadian Flying Corps. Mannock took up his appointment on 3 July, and wasted little time in resuming his fighting career. Having briefed his new unit on his own methods of fighting as a whole fighting team, instead of a gaggle of individuals, he then proceeded to exemplify his methods in action.

On 7 July he led his men down on a formation of Fokker D VII's and personally destroyed one, sent a second down completely out of control, and caused two others to collide in mid-air (though he made no personal claim for the latter pair). Another victory followed on the 8th; a scout in flames on the 10th; and two victories on the 14th; an Albatros C XII two-seater in flames on 19 July; two victims on the 20th; and, on 22 July, a Fokker Dr 1 triplane.

By now the pilots of 85 Squadron, who included men from South Africa, New Zealand and the USA, had come to have utter faith in Mannock's leadership, feeling that he was invincible. Whereas under Bishop's command they had been simply a collection of brilliant individuals, they now formed integral sections of a complete fighting 'whole' – a destruction *unit*.

26 July 1918 dawned clear and bright, and shortly after 5 am, two SE5a's took off from 85 Squadron's base at St Omer and headed at low level towards the trench lines. Leading was Edward Mannock, flying SE5a E1295, while close behind came a young New Zealander, Donald C. Inglis, in SE5a E1294. Though Inglis had been with 85 Squadron for several weeks, he had yet to register a confirmed combat victory, and Mannock, fully aware of the psychological uplift in morale that a young pilot experienced after his first combat victory, had suggested that Inglis should accompany him on a dawn sortie in the hope of flushing a German aircraft.

Remaining below 50 feet height on their flight to the lines, Inglis suddenly noticed Mannock jerk the nose of his aircraft upwards, and realised Mannock had spotted an enemy machine. Mannock's prey was a DFW CV from Flieger Abteilung (A) 292* out on an early reconnaissance mission, and Mannock bore straight in firing both guns. Inglis followed suit and fired into the body of the DFW, which fell in flames and crashed near Lestrem.

Then, completely in contrast to his own strict ruling, Mannock flew down to deck level again over the trenches. As his SE5a flew over the trenches occupied by Germans of the 100th Regiment, a barrage of rifle and machine gun fire greeted him, and Inglis, still faithfully obeying Mannock's original instructions to 'stick to my tail', noticed a small bluish flame appear on the right side panel of Mannock's engine cowling.

---

* DFW CV, 2216/18, Ltn Schopf/Vzfw Heim both killed.

As the flame spread, Mannock's SE5a banked gently to the right, then turned slowly left and crashed into German-occupied territory, erupting in a gushing column of flames and oily smoke.

Inglis, horrified by the sight, flew low over the burning wreck, hoping for a sign of life, but was then hit in his own engine by the continuing small arms' barrage. With his petrol tank riven by bullets, Inglis turned towards the Allied lines, and when his engine seized up scraped down for a forced landing near Floris. A subsequent report from German Intelligence stated that Mannock's remains were, 'Buried at a point 300 metres north-west of La Pierre-au-Beure, in the vicinity of Pacaut, east of Lillers'. This report was never officially confirmed.

After the Armistice of November 1918, when the final awards and honours for wartime service had been promulgated, many former colleagues of Mannock began to express dismay that he had not been recognised by the award of a Victoria Cross. Investigation into his war record at Air Ministry resulted in an *official* accreditation to Mannock for a total of 73 air combat victories; a fact which was published ir. the *Weekly Dispatch* dated 18 May 1919, with an added comment that Mannock, '. . . should be awarded the VC.'

The growing agitation for Mannock to be honoured with a post-humous award reached the newly-appointed Air Minister, Winston Churchill, who was sympathetic. Finally, on 18 July 1919 the *London Gazette* announced the award; its citation quoting only a total of 50 victories, but ending with the words :

> This highly distinguished officer, during the whole of his career in the Royal Air Force (sic), was an outstanding example of fearless courage, remarkable skill, devotion to duty, and self-sacrifice, which has never been surpassed.

2. Warneford

1914-1918

1. Rhodes Moorhouse

1 W. B. Rhodes-Moorhouse, 1913.

2 Standing beside an early Bleriot monoplane.
3 In the cockpit of a pre-war monoplane.
4 W. B. Rhodes-Moorhouse, VC (at wheel).
5 Lt W. B. Rhodes-Moorhouse, VC at Farnborough, 1914.

2. Warneford

6 Warneford, in flying gear, beside one of 1 Wing's Morane-Saulnier 'parasol' monoplanes.
7 Zepp-strafers. L–R: J. S. Mills; A. Bigsworth DSO; J. P. Wilson; R. A. J. Warneford VC – all pilots of 1 Wing, RNAS who successfully attacked German airships in early 1915.

8 Morane-Saulnier Type L, No 3253, in which Warneford destroyed the LZ37.
9 Warneford seated in the cockpit of Morane-Saulnier Type L, No 3253.
10 Another view of Warneford's aircraft, autographed on 7 June 1915.

11 Only hours to live. Warneford, wearing his *Legion D'Honneur*, on 17 June 1915. He died that same day.

12 Warneford (far left figure) talking to Queen Elisabeth of the Belgians and Princess Alice of Teck. At right are Prince Alexander of Teck (hidden) talking to Flight Commander S. V. Sippe. June 1915.

3. Hawker

13 Hawker at the controls of an early BE2 aircraft at CFS, Upavon in 1914.
14 Lanoe George Hawker on commissioning in the RE, 1911.
15 Henry Farmans of 6 Squadron RFC at Ostend, late 1914.

16 Hawker in his goatskin, self-made 'flying clothing' at Bailleul, winter 1914, while serving with 6 Squadron, RFC.

17 Hawker on 5 October 1915 after a Palace investiture.

18 De Havilland 2 Scouts of 24 Squadron at Bertangles aerodrome in mid-1916.

19 Bristol Scout D, No 1611 in which Hawker fought on 25 July 1915, and was subsequently awarded his VC. Note stripped machine gun affixed to port side of cockpit, with sight fixed separately to centre-section strut.

20 The wreckage of Hawker's DH2, 5964, at Luisenhof Farm. Just beyond (left) is the crude grave dug by the Germans for Lanoe Hawker.

4. Liddell

[174] 21 Liddell in the Argyll & Sutherlands' uniform, whilst on leave in England, 1915.
22 Liddell (nearest camera) in the front-line trenches at Houplines, near Armentieres, early 1915.

23 Liddell at the controls of a 'Boxkite', while learning to fly at the Vickers School, Brooklands, [175] early 1914.

24 Second Lieutenant R. H. Peck, who was Liddell's observer on 31 July 1915. He was later killed in Mesopotamia, in action, on 10 March 1916.

25 Liddell in his cockpit (RE5, 2457) at Furnes aerodrome after his fateful sortie on 31 July 1915. His observer, Peck, is handing up a glass of water.

26 Liddell (in cockpit) attending to his gaping leg wounds, Furnes, 31 July 1915

27 Liddell is finally lifted from his shattered cockpit. On ground third from left (holding water jug) is Second Lieutenant R. H. Peck.

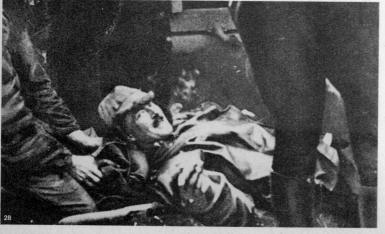

28 About to be borne by stretcher to hospital, Liddell still manages a wave and a smile for the camera, 31 July 1915.

5. Insall

29 Insall, in overalls, in a Brooklands hangar.
30 Second Lieutenant G. S. M. Insall RFC in April 1915.
31 Gilbert Insall (left, civilian clothes) and Sergeant Watts RFC at Brooklands, 1915. Behind are two Bleriot trainers.

32 Insall posing in the civilian disguise he used to escape from prisoners-of-war camp, Germany, in 1917.

33 Vickers FB5 'Gunbus' of 11 Squadron, RFC during the winter, 1915–16 – the type of machine on which Insall 'earned' his VC.

34 Insall in cockpit of an SE5a of 50 (Home Defence) Squadron, 1918.
35 Investiture. Gilbert Insall receives his Victoria Cross from the hands of HM King George V at Buckingham Palace, 26 September 1917.

6. Bell-Davies

36 Richard Bell-Davies.

37 Sopwith No 104 – one of the aircraft often piloted by Davies at Eastchurch Naval Air Station, 1914.

38 Air crews of 3 Wing, RNAS in October 1916. Seated are Captain W. L. Elder (OC Wing) and Squadron Commander R. Bell-Davies VC DSO. At far left is the noted Canadian fighter 'ace', Ray Collishaw.

39 Nieuport 10 two-seater, No 3172 – the aircraft in which Bell-Davies rescued Lieutenant Smylie on 19 November 1915. Seen here in earlier colour markings.

40 Lieutenant Gilbert Smylie 'demonstrates' how he was brought back (tailplane of Nieuport 10, 3172) – for the amusement of his fellow pilots.

41 Rear Admiral R. Bell-Davies VC CB DSO AFC at Lee-on-Solent 1940.

7. Rees

42 Major L. W. B. Rees wearing the ribbons of his VC and MC, 1917

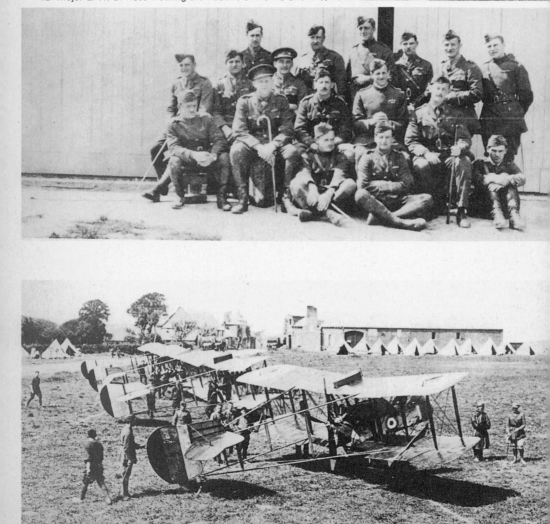

43 The original complement of pilots of 32 Squadron, RFC, at Netheravon, May 1916. Major [183]
W. B. Rees MC is seated second from right, centre row.

44 De Havilland 2 Scouts of 32 Squadron at Vert Galand Farm, France, July 1916.

45 Instructional staff of No 1 School of Air Fighting, Turnberry with Lieutenant Colonel L. W. B.
ees VC MC seated fifth from right, front.

46 Wing Commander L. W. B. Rees VC OBE MC AFC seated in a Sopwith Snipe at Cranwell, 1923.

47 Rees, when Assistant Commandant, Cranwell, 1924.

8. Robinson

48 With his sister, Irene, at St Bees School, Cumberland, aged 14.
49 Zepp-killers of 39 Squadron, RFC. L–R : W. L. Robinson VC ; V. Stammers AFC ; W. Sowrey DSO.
50 Robinson in the cockpit of BE2c 2092, in which he destroyed the German airship, SL.11. In foreground, mechanics hold the shattered upper wing centre-section damaged during that action.
51 German Army airship, Schutte-Lanz (SL).11 – destroyed by Robinson on the night of 2/3 September 1916.

52 Robinson leaving Windsor Castle on 8 September 1916 after his investiture with the VC.

53 William Robinson VC (at wheel) with Major L. G. Hawker VC DSO as a rear-seat passenger, 1916.

54 In durance vile. W. L. Robinson VC (at right), 1917, while a prisoner of war in Germany.

9. Mottershead

[186]   55 Flight Sergeant T. Mottershead in December 1916, wearing the ribbon of his Distinguished Conduct Medal.
56 Thomas Mottershead VC DCM as an Air Mechanic, RFC in 1914 shortly after enlistment.
57 Second Lieutenant W. E. Gower MC, Mottershead's observer on 7 January 1917.

58 Offizier-Stellvertreter Göttsch of Jagdstaffel 8, who was credited with shooting down Flight [187]
Sergeant Mottershead.
  59 FE2b two-seater. Mottershead's aircraft was similar in general design, but had a more powerful engine.

10. McNamara

60 F. H. McNamara wearing the ribbon of his VC.
61 McNamara shortly after gaining his RFC 'wings'.
62 An immediate post-war shot of McNamara.

63 Martinsyde G100 'Elephant' Scout, No 7486 in which McNamara flew initially on the sortie of [189]
20 March 1917, but crashed on take-off behind enemy lines.
64 BE2c 4479, in which McNamara eventually flew himself and Rutherford to safety.

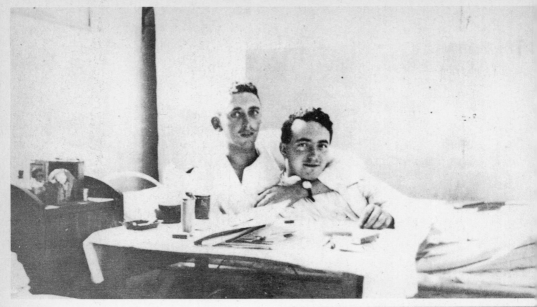

65 F. H. McNamara VC (right) and Lieutenant R. F. Baillieu in an Egyptian hospital shortly after both men's individual 'pick-up' air exploits. Baillieu had successfully rescued an RFC pilot forced down in hostile territory on 19 March 1917.
66 McNamara as a Group Captain RAAF prior to World War Two.
67 Air Vice-Marshal F. H. McNamara VC CB CBE RAAF.

68 William Avery Bishop as an observer in the RFC, 1916.
69 Bishop in front of Nieuport Scout B1566 of 60 Squadron, RFC in which he 'earned' his VC on 2 June 1917. Note blue-painted engine cowling/interplane struts and tiny propeller boss 'spinner'.
70 Bishop in the pilot's seat of Bristol Scout D, A1742 at Hounslow, mid-1918.

11. Bishop

"BISH"

71 At St Omer on 20 June 1918, about to leave for England — his last day in France. At left is Larry Callaghan, one of the legendary American *Warbirds* immortalised by the late E. W. Springs' book of that title.

72 A Lieutenant-Colonel, RAF, Bishop shows off his 'fighting row' (his term) of VC, DSO, MC and DFC ribbons, late 1918.

73 On leave in Canada, 1918 with his wife Margaret (nee Burden) at right of picture.

74 Bishop and W .G. Barker VC DSO MC at Leaside aerodrome, Canada in August 1919, on the occasion of the New York—Toronto Air Race. Behind them is a captured Fokker D VII fighter.

75 Albert Ball in 1911, standing before the Armoury door at Trent College, Long Eaton, Notting- [*193*]
hamshire. The motto above the door was strangely prophetic . . .
76 Albert Ball DSO MC, November 1916
77 Nieuport Scout, A126 – one of several such fighting aircraft of 11 and 60 Squadrons, RFC in
which Ball achieved lasting fame.

78 At Buckingham Palace, November 1916 for investiture of his DSO and MC awards ; with (from left) his father, sister Lois, and far right, mother.

79 Ball with the famous red spinner (from Nieuport 5173 of 60 Squadron, RFC), Nottingham, November 1916.

80 Ball in his personally-modified SE5, A4850 at London Colney airfield, March 1917, with 56 Squadron. It was in this machine, further modified, that he died on 7 May 1917.

81 About to leave London Colney for France, 7 April 1917; seated in SE5, A4850. As always, Ball flew without flying helmet or goggles.

82 Another view of Ball seated in SE5, A4850 at London Colney, March 1917. Note upper Lewis gun lowered on its Foster rail mounting to fire upwards.

13. McLeod

83 Young Alan McLeod as a proud member of the Fort Garry Horse in Canada, 1913.

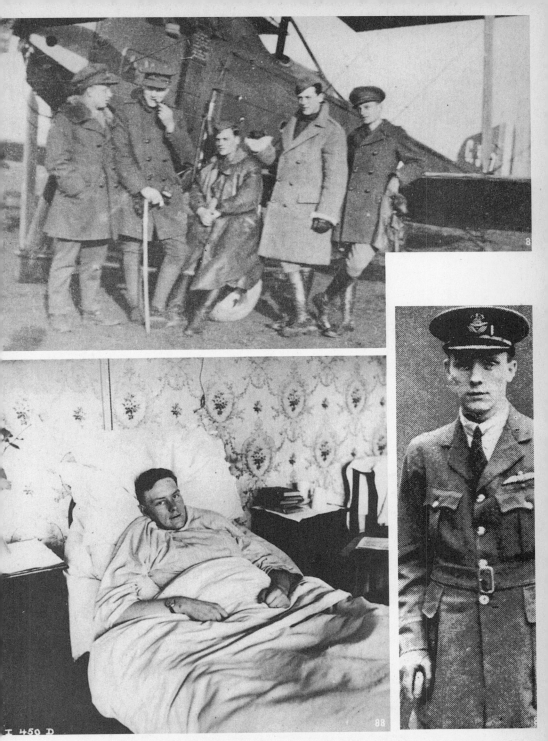

84 Lieutenant A. W. Hammond мс (left) and A. A. McLeod of 2 Squadron in France.

85 Lieutenant A. W. Hammond мс, observer to Alan McLeod on 27 March 1918.

86 Armstrong Whitworth FK8 – the type of machine in which both Alan McLeod and 'Freddie' West 'won' their respective VC's.

87 Second Lieutenant Alan McLeod (2nd from left) and other pilots of 2 Squadron RFC in France. Behind, an Armstrong Whitworth FK8 two-seater.

88 Alan McLeod recovering in hospital from his multiple wounds received on 27 March 1918.

89 Wearing the first RAF uniform style, Alan McLeod hobbled into Buckingham Palace on 4 September 1918 for his VC investiture.

14. Jerrard

90 Oberleutnant Benno Fiala, Ritter von Fernbrugg, the noted Austrian fighter leader, who shot Alan Jerrard down.

15. McCudden

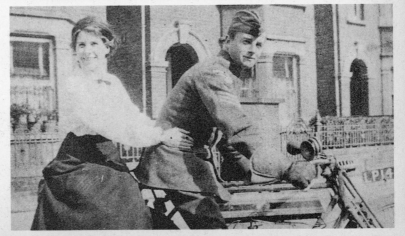

91 Alan Jerrard, the only
opwith Camel pilot to be
varded a VC.
92 The wreck of Jerrard's
amel, B5648, 'E' of 66
quadron on 30 March 1918.
93 Still dazed with shock,
an Jerrard sits by the remains
his Camel. Note his leather
ce mask-helmet on ground at
ht.
94 Victor and 'vanquished'.
berleutnant von Fernbrugg (in
ying helmet) and his 'victim'
lan Jerrard walking away from
e scene of Jerrard's crash,
0 March 1918.

95 Air Mechanic, RFC, 1913.
96 J. T. B. McCudden (right)
s a Sergeant Observer, with his
ther, and younger brother
nthony, early 1916. Lieutenant
nthony McCudden MC was
lled in action on 18 March
918, as an SE5a pilot with 84
quadron, RFC.
97 Flight Sergeant J. T. B.
1cCudden MM with his sister
1ary.

98

99

100

98 First award. McCudden receiving a Croix de Guerre from General Joffre at Lillers, 21 January 1916.

99 Flight Commander. Captain J. T. B. McCudden with his SE5a, B4891, with 56 Squadron. Note the red spinner for the propeller – a trophy from one of McCudden's victims.

100 McCudden with the ground staff of his Flight in 56 Squadron.

101 McCudden seated in his SE5a, wearing the silk cloth copy of a German pilot's hat which he had specially made.

102 McCudden, wearing his full decorations' ribbons, and a black mourning arm-band for his late brother, Anthony, mid-1918.

103 McCudden in an informal pose, when instructing potential fighter pilots, 1918.

104 McCudden with his pet bulldog, 'Bruiser', at Turnberry, 1918.

16. West

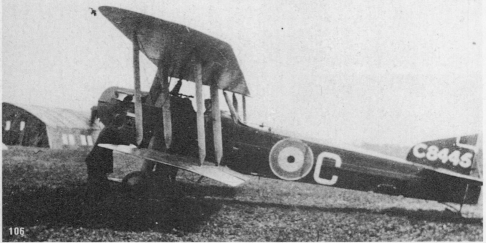

[202]   105 'Freddie' West on leave in Paris, 1917.
       106 West in the pilot's seat of Armstrong Whitworth FK8, C8455 of 8 Squadron, RAF, 1918. The
FK8 two-seater was universally nicknamed the 'Big-Ack' in flying circles.
       107 Armstrong Whitworth FK8, C8594, in which West flew his ultimate sortie on 10 August 1918 —
for which he was awarded his VC.

108 'Freddie' West (right) as an observer with 3 Squadron, RFC in 1917 ; with his pilot, Lieutenant   [203]
Golding.
109 West (leaning against propeller) and unidentified captain. The 'Big-Ack' is C8594, in which
West 'won' his Victoria Cross.

17. Barker

111

112

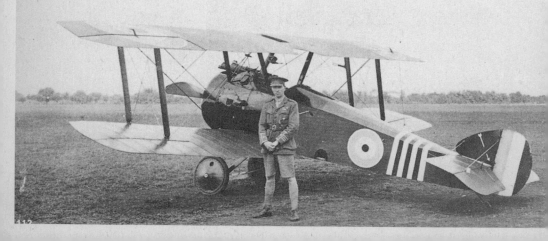

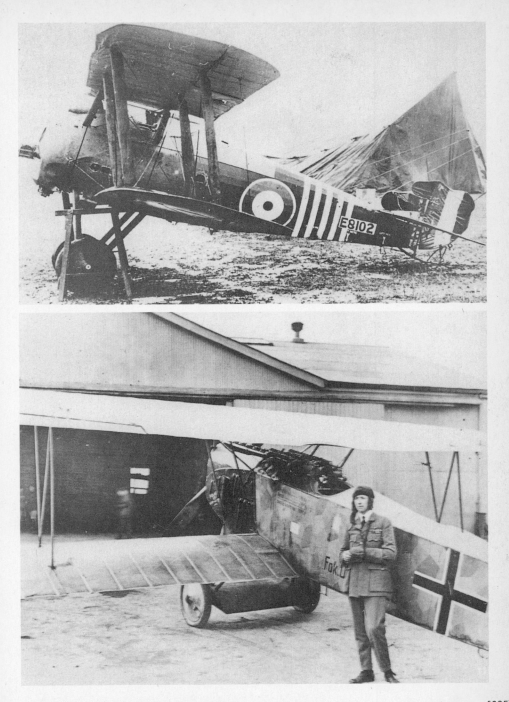

110 W. G. Barker in front of an RE8 of 15 Squadron.
111 Barker (right) and Matthew Frew (45 Squadron) at Istrana airfield, Italy, early 1918.
112 George Barker DSO MC with a trophy from an Austrian victim in February 1918.
113 Major W. G. Barker, OC 139 Squadron at Villaverla, Italy in July 1918; with Sopwith F1 Camel, B6313, his personal fighter, in which he scored the bulk of his victories.
114 Sopwith 7F1 Snipe, E8102, in which Barker fought vastly superior odds on 27 October 1918 — a feat which led to his VC award. Note damage to tail and wings, due to Barker overturning on crashing after the combat.
115 Barker, with left arm still in a sling, poses beside a Fokker D VII; the main type of opponent he fought in his epic fight.

117

18. Proctor

116 Barker in the Fokker D I he flew in the New York–oronto Air Race in August 919.

117 Wing Commander W. G. arker VC DSO MC in full dress AF regalia – a photo taken at ttawa, Canada on 20 March 930.

118 Reunion. W. G. Barker C DSO MC; Mrs A. U. McLeod other of Second Lieutenant . A. McLeod VC); and W. A. ishop VC DSO MC DFC; at a union for VC's and their next--kin, held at Government ouse, Toronto on 1 September 920.

119 Senior officers of the anadian Air Force at Camp orden, 4 April 1923. From left: quadron Leader G. M. Croil; Ving Commander W. G. Barker C DSO MC; Squadron Leader . E. Godfrey MC.

120 A. W. F. B. Proctor (far right) s aviation officer cadet, 1917.

121 Proctor (centre) during is probationary period as a upil pilot in the RFC, 1917.

122 In the cockpit of his E5a, 84 Squadron in France, 918. His small stature required arious blocks and cushions dded to controls and seat in rder that he could fly and fight.

123 84 Squadron group, including Nel, Matt, 'Tiddler', and Proctor (second from left).
124 Lieutenant Simpson; Captain Highwood; Captain A. F. W. B. Proctor; Lieutenant Boudwin,
USAS – all of 84 Squadron RAF, late summer, 1918.

125 Promoted Captain, and wearing the ribbon of his MC, Proctor in June 1918.

126 Informal pose, taken post-1918, in South Africa while completing his university degree studies.

127 Taken during a Liberty Loan mission to the USA in 1919, this photo of Proctor illustrates his small stature compared with the average-height US officer by his side.

128 Proctor as a Flight Lieutenant in the post-1918 RAF, wearing his full medal ribbons. (Note original horizontal striping of his DFC ribbon).

19. Mannock

129 Edward Mannock when under initial pilot instruction at Hendon in August 1916.
    130 Mannock (left, at telescope) and Pettigrew of 40 Squadron, Bruay 1917, 'spotting' hostile aircraft.
    131 Mannock at Bruay in April 1917, when serving with 40 Squadron.
    132 Mannock seated in an SE5 of 74 Squadron, about to leave for France on 31 March 1918.
    133 Off-duty view of 85 Squadron pilots at St Omer, June 1918. From left: Dymond; Major Edward Mannock (OC Squadron); unknown; Callaghan; and Longton.

134 Mannock relaxing in a deckchair, St Omer, June 1918.

135 Major Edward Mannock VC DSO MC – the highest-scoring Allied fighter pilot of the 1914–18 conflict.

136 Mannock (left) with D. C. Inglis (lighting pipe), the New Zealander who accompanied Mannock on his last, fated sortie on 26 July, 1918.

PART TWO

1939-1945

20. Donald Edward Garland

The histories of Britain's military, naval, and aerial services proliferate with examples of multiple sacrifices by individual families. The brothers McCudden; brothers MacRobert; Rhodes Moorhouse, father and son; the Beamish brothers – the list is long, noble, and tragic. Such a family was that of Doctor P. J. Garland CMG and his wife Renée, who raised four boys and a girl; only to have all four boys killed or die in service with the RAF in the second world war.

Patrick James Garland, rejected for flying duties with the RAF as being 'too old', enlisted in the Irish Guards, was commissioned in the Green Howards, and then transferred to the RAF for pilot training, in late 1942. Graduating as a fighter pilot, he eventually flew many operations with 168 Squadron of Nos 39 and 143 Wings in France, 1944, but lost his life in a flying accident in January 1945. Desmond Garland gained his 'wings' with the RAF at the outbreak of war, but was then invalided out of the service on medical grounds. Enlisting in the RASC as a private, Desmond eventually transferred back to the RAF as a pilot again, and died during a bomber-mining sortie off the Dutch coast in September 1942. A third brother, John, rejected for flying duties as medically unfit, was then – somewhat ironically – commissioned in the RAF as a medical officer. Ill-health eventually caused John to be invalided out of the service, and he died in March 1943.

The fourth brother, and the first to lose his life, was Donald Edward Garland, who was born on 28 June 1918 at Ballincor, County Wicklow, Eire. Educated at the Cardinal Vaughan School, Kensington, Donald then became a clerk in the office of an insurance company briefly, while awaiting the result of his application to join the RAF. Accepted for a short service commission on 12 July 1937, he undertook elementary flying training at Hamble and was confirmed in rank as a Pilot Officer on 5 September before starting his Service training at No 2 Flying Training School. On graduation on 7 May 1938, he was posted to his first unit, No 12 Squadron, based then at Andover, and still in the process of complete conversion from biplane Hawker Hind bombers to the new monoplane Fairey Battle light bomber aircraft. Promoted to Flying Officer in 1939, Garland was serving in B Flight when 12 Squadron was alerted for an imminent move to France at the end of August 1939.

The Munich crisis of September 1938 had shown the more astute higher authorities in the Air Ministry a need for preparatory planning for an apparently inevitable war with Nazi Germany; and as a first measure No 1 Group, RAF Bomber Command – a total of 10 Fairey Battle squadrons – was earmarked to form an Advanced Air Striking Force (AASF) of short-range bombers to be sent to France in the event of any German threat to Britain's ally. With the German invasion of Poland on 1 September 1939, orders were immediately sent out to commence Operation Panther – the code name for the immediate transfer of the Battle squadrons to the Continent – and next day all ten units, a total of 160 Battles, flew across the Channel and arrived in the Reims area. Within twenty-four hours Britain formally declared war against Hitler's Germany.

No 12 Squadron's 17 Fairey Battles flew into a small cornfield at Barry-au-Bac, and settled in quickly, and on 17 September flew the unit's first operational sorties; a simple reconnaissance of the border zone with Germany. As the bitterly icy winter weather set in, the squadron moved base in December to Amifontaine, a satellite airfield to Barry-au-Bac, but operational sorties remained few due to the wintry conditions. For its first six months in France, 12 Squadron – in common with most RAF units – flew relatively few operations; a period dubbed the 'Phoney War' by headline-hungry journalists of the British press. Activity stepped up in March with the beginning of the spring thaw, and on 24 March the squadron began a series of reconnaissance sorties over German-held territory.

Then, early in the morning of 10 May 1940 the 'Phoney War' evaporated abruptly as German forces commenced their *Blitzkrieg* advance through the Low Countries. Word of the enemy advance did not reach 12 Squadron until late afternoon, whereupon five Battle crews set out immediately for a bombing mission – and only one returned to Amifontaine. Next day the unit airfield was bombed by the Luftwaffe, though ineffectively, and 12 Squadron flew no bombing sorties.

On 12 May, however, the squadron was selected for a vital mission. On the first day of their assault German infantry had captured several vital bridges spanning the Albert canal, and although several attempts had been made by other RAF bombers to destroy these transit pathways into Allied territory, all had failed due to massive air and ground opposition. Accordingly, early on the morning of 12 May, 12 Squadron's crews were called to an emergency briefing, and told that the unit was specifically tasked to destroy two bridges, at Vroenhoven and Veldwezelt. Volunteers were called for and, as the whole squadron stepped forward, it was decided that the six crews already detailed on the 'readiness' roster should undertake the mission.

The six Battle crews were divided into two sections – each section to attack one bridge – and the section leaders chosen were Flying Officer Norman Thomas, whose three Battles would tackle the concrete bridge at Vroenhoven; and Donald Garland who would lead his section to the metal bridge at Veldwezelt. Before take-off Thomas indicated that he intended making a high-level, diving attack on his target, while Garland decided to take his section in low to bomb his objective.

Just before 9 am all six Battles prepared to take off but one of Thomas's section found his Battle to be unserviceable and had to abandon the sortie. Garland, at the controls of Battle P2204, 'K', had with him as crew Sergeant Thomas Gray, observer, and Leading Aircraftman (LAC) L. R. Reynolds, rear gunner.

Sent on ahead of the bombers were eight Hawker Hurricane fighters from No 1 Squadron, led by Squadron Leader 'Bull' Halahan, intended to engage any Luftwaffe opposition to the bombers; but on arrival over the target area Halahan's men were promptly swamped by a host of Messerschmitt fighters from the crack Jagdgeschwader JG27 and in the ensuing fierce dogfighting were helpless to protect the following bomber sections.

Norman Thomas (Battle, P2332) and Pilot Officer T. D. H. Davy (L5241) reached their objective at Vroenhoven but had to run a terrifying gauntlet of flak and fighters; and Thomas was quickly shot down and captured, while Davy, his Battle pluming smoke and flames, ordered his two crew men to bale out and then managed to nurse his crippled Battle back to a forced landing in French territory. Both had carried out their plan of a diving attack from some 6,000 feet, and their bombs caused some damage to the concrete bridge.

Donald Garland, leading the second section, stayed below cloud base at 1,000 feet and on reaching the Veldwezelt area started a shallow bombing run through a veritable inferno of anti-aircraft fire – from an estimated 300 guns firmly entrenched in a defensive ring around the approaches to the bridge – only to be blasted into the ground. Behind him came Pilot Officer I. A. McIntosh (Battle L5439) who, before he could start his bombing run, had his main petrol tank hit by flak and the aircraft erupt in flames. Jettisoning his bomb load, McIntosh scraped a forced landing and survived, though as a prisoner of war. The third Battle, L5227, piloted by Sergeant Fred Marland, plunged through the curtain of shellfire and released its bomb load but was then seen to head upwards in a wild, semi-controlled climb, wing over, and dive into the ground. When the smoke cleared it could be seen that some bombs had achieved the object of the mission, with the western end of the Veldwezelt bridge part-shattered and broken; and the fragmentary evidence suggested that this damage had possibly been caused by Garland's cool attack.

On 11 June 1940 the *London Gazette* announced the posthumous awards of a Victoria Cross to Donald Edward Garland and his navigator, Thomas Gray; though no award was mentioned for the third member of Garland's crew, LAC Reynolds. Almost exactly a year later Garland's mother, accompanied by her son Patrick, attended the investiture ceremony at Buckingham Palace, to receive the little bronze cross awarded to Donald – first of her four sons to die during the war.

21. Thomas Gray

When Hugh Trenchard made his first proposals for the 'foundation' of the future Royal Air Force in 1919, he made particular provision for its eventual 'permanent' personnel by creating an embryo-officer college at Cranwell, and, equally important in his eyes, a technical apprenticeship scheme for the Service's future technical ground tradesmen. The latter he based at Halton, an ex-Army camp on Rothschild land, nestling closely in the ring of the Chiltern Hills in Buckinghamshire. Here, boys of initial entry age of fifteen to seventeen would undergo a three-years' technical training course, and then pass into the lower ranks of the RAF to complete a 12-years' regular engagement of service.

Commencing in 1920, the scheme has since provided the RAF with many thousands of 'Trenchard's Brats', as they came to be dubbed; a literal backbone for the service in both peace and war. Yet it is doubtful if even Trenchard's huge vision imagined just how important an impact his 'boys' would eventually make on the service to which he devoted so much of his life. Ex-Halton apprentices made their mark in virtually every sphere of RAF activity, especially during the 1939-45 conflict; and the list of honours and awards made to ex-Brats is a long and impressive tribute to their prowess and achievements. Heading that list is 563627 Sergeant Thomas Gray, winner of a posthumous Victoria Cross.

Born in Urchfont, Wiltshire on 17 May 1914, 'Tom' Gray, like Donald Garland, his pilot, was from a large family. Fourth-born of seven brothers, he was one of five Gray boys who eventually joined the Royal Air Force; three of these as aircraft apprentices at Halton. By 1946 three of these Gray brothers had died while flying with the RAF. Educated at Warminster Secondary School, Thomas Gray enlisted as an apprentice of the 20th (Halton) Entry on 27 August 1929, and for the next three years trained to become an aero engine Fitter II(E).

On leaving Halton in August 1932, Gray's first posting was to 40 Squadron, servicing the unit's Fairey Gordon bombers. Whilst with 40 Squadron Gray volunteered eagerly for 'part-time' flying duties as an air gunner – an air crew category usually filled at that period by ground tradesmen on a voluntary basis additional to their normal duties, and which carried with it the attraction of extra 'flying' pay for those who eventually qualified as regular gunners.*

He soon caught the 'flying bug' and became almost wholly absorbed with the hope of becoming full-time air crew one day, regarding his more mundane servicing chores as of secondary personal importance. His keenness soon brought him the qualified air gunner's sleeve badge, a brass 'winged' bullet.

In 1933 Gray passed his qualifying trade tests for upgrading to Leading Aircraftman (LAC), and in June was posted to 15 Squadron, equipped then with Hawker Hind day bombers. Here he continued to fly whenever circumstances permitted, but soon returned to Halton for a lengthy conversion trade course to Fitter I; completing his training at Henlow and, in May 1936, joining 58 Squadron at Driffield, a heavy bomber unit equipped with obsolescent Vickers Virginias. In February 1938 came another move, this time to 12 Squadron at Andover, and shortly after joining his new unit Gray received promotion to Corporal.

A short course of instruction at No 1 Air Observers School that year saw Gray finally achieve his ambition and he was remustered as an air observer; equivalent of the later category navigator. His skill as an aerial gunner was exemplified in the 1938 annual firing competition held by the RAF, and resulted in Gray receiving the Silver .303 Bullet prize. This and his skill in air navigation led to promotion to Sergeant in January 1939. On 2 September 1939, when 12 Squadron received its final movement order to fly to France as a unit of the AASF, Gray was a member of B Flight; and his experiences between then and the fateful mission of 12 May 1940 were much in common with the other air crew members of 12 Squadron. When he climbed into Fairey Battle P2204 for the specially-mounted raid on Veldwezelt bridge, it was in fact Tom Gray's first bombing sortie.

After the raid local civilians recovered the bodies of Donald Garland, Tom Gray and LAC Reynolds and buried all three quickly in a secret location to prevent the Germans claiming them; a secret which remained as such until near the end of the war when the Allied authorities were notified of the grave and all three bodies were re-interred in Lanaken cemetery. Subsequently, the three were buried in the Imperial War Graves Commission cemetery at Haverlee. The citation for Garland and Gray's VCs, which appeared in the *London Gazette* dated 11 June 1940 read in part :

* A princely sum of ten shillings and sixpence per week; roughly equivalent to 52½ pence today. . . .

Much of the success of this vital operation must be attributed to . . . the coolness and resource of Sergeant Gray who navigated Flying Officer Garland's aircraft under most difficult conditions in such a manner that the whole formation was able to successfully attack the target in spite of subsequent heavy losses.

The little cross was given to Gray's parents at an investiture in Buckingham Palace held on 24 June 1941.

22. Roderick Alastair Brook Learoyd

Of the 32 VCs awarded during 1939-45, 19 went to air crew members of RAF Bomber Command, and the first of these to Flight Lieutenant (later Wing Commander) Roderick Alastair Brook Learoyd of 49 Squadron. The son of Major R. B. Learoyd of Littlestone, Kent, Roderick Learoyd was born at Folkestone on 5 February 1913. Educated at Hydreye House Preparatory School, Baldstow, Sussex, and Wellington College, Berkshire, Learoyd then attended the Chelsea College of Aeronautical and Automobile Engineering.

There followed a two years spell in Argentina as a fruit farmer, and a brief period as a motor engineer, before Learoyd decided to join the RAF to learn to fly. Accepted in March 1936 for a short service commission, he received his elementary training at Hamble AST, and his Service training at Wittering; graduating in December 1936 and being posted to 49 Squadron, equipped with Hawker Hinds at Worthy Down aerodrome.

In March 1938, 49 Squadron moved base to Scampton where it became the first RAF squadron to re-equip with the new monoplane Handley Page Hampden bombers. Sharing the grass airfield and accommodation at Scampton was 83 Squadron, which began conversion from its Hawker Hinds to Hampdens in October 1938, and was completely re-equipped with the type by early January 1939. The change from biplanes to all-metal monoplane bombers gave both units many months of necessary practice flying though, strangely, virtually no night-flying was undertaken – indeed, it was only on the outbreak of war that the Hampden crews had their first experience in flying Hampdens with full bomb loads.

As the European political scene rapidly deteriorated in the high summer of 1939, Bomber Command began to implement its plans for possible war, and on 26 August the bomber squadrons were brought to a state of two hours' 'Readiness' for dispersal under the command's 'Scatter' scheme. On 1 September, as German forces swept into Poland, the Scampton Hampden squadrons were ordered to bomb up a flight of aircraft each, and at midnight general mobilisation orders were issued throughout the RAF in Britain.

By dawn of 3 September the war-loaded Hampdens were still at standby and, at 6.15 pm, six Hampdens from 83 Squadron and three from 49 Squadron left Scampton on an 'armed reconnaissance' over the North Sea, seeking German naval ships to bomb. The trio of 49's bombers, led by Flight Lieutenant George Lerwill, included Roderick Learoyd. In the event the sortie flew as far as the Horns Reef lightship, found no targets to bomb, and returned to Scampton without incident.

During the next ten months Learoyd participated in 23 more bombing sorties, apart from various other types of operations, proving himself to be a cool-headed pilot, seemingly imperturbable in the most dangerous situations. One target he attacked was a vital waterway, the Dortmund – Ems canal – a heavily-defended objective which received considerable attention from RAF bombers in mid-1940. And it was this canal that was to be Learoyd's target on the night of 12 August 1940.

Eleven Hampdens – six from 49 Squadron, five from 83 Squadron – were detailed for the whole sortie, and the specific objective was to destroy the old aqueduct carrying the canal over the river Ems, north of Munster (a second, new, aqueduct had already been destroyed in a previous RAF raid). The 6 pm briefing of the crews was thorough, explaining that four Hampdens were to bomb diversionary targets, and that timing over the target was crucial in view of the special 'canister' bombs being used, each of which was fitted with ten-minute delayed action fuses. Learoyd was detailed as captain of Hampden P4403, EA-M, and his crew comprised Pilot Officer John Lewis (navigator and bomb aimer), Sergeant J Ellis (wireless operator and dorsal air gunner) and LAC Rich as ventral air gunner. Each captain was given a precise time to arrive over the target and a specific sequence in which to bomb.

At exactly 8 pm Learoyd got airborne from Scampton, lifting 'Pinocchio' (the Walt Disney character painted just below the left side of the Hampden's cockpit) into the clear night air and setting course south-east. He was due to be over the aqueduct at precisely 11.15 pm, the last of the five Hampdens detailed to carry out the actual bombing attack, and John Lewis's skilled navigation brought Learoyd to a point just north of the target at ten minutes before their designated ETA.

The moon was half-full, reflecting clearly the canal water, and Learoyd circled leisurely, awaiting his turn to bomb. Elsewhere, unseen by Learoyd, four Hampdens were making their diversion raids, as per the pre-arranged plan, while two other Hampdens, having failed to locate their primary targets, bombed Texel Island instead. As Learoyd waited calmly he saw the first Hampden begin its run over the canal; Squadron Leader 'Jamie' Pitcairn-Hill DFC of 83 Squadron in Hampden P4402.

Alongside each bank of the canal were rows of deadly accurate mobile flak guns, well-sited, and presenting any potential attacker with no choice but to run the narrow gauntlet of anti-aircraft fire during his actual bombing attack. Knowing these odds against survival, Pitcairn-Hill led the way in – threading his way through a curtain of shells and tracer bullets, and in the face of blinding searchlights focussed directly on the approach lane. Levelling out at 100 feet above the silver water canal, he suffered numerous hits but refused to evade the punishment, maintaining a rock-steady bombing run and releasing his bomb canisters with precision, before banking away from the danger zone and limping home to England.

The second Hampden, P4410 piloted by an Australian, Pilot Officer E. H. Ross, received a direct hit as he nosed into the flak lane and crashed in a holocaust of flames alongside the canal.

Third to run the gauntlet was another Australian from 83 Squadron, Flying Officer A R. Mulligan DFC in Hampden P4340. Before Mulligan had reached his bomb-release point however his aircraft was hit in its port engine, which erupted in flames. Jettisoning his bomb load quickly Mulligan climbed swiftly to 2,000 feet and then ordered his crew to abandon the aircraft. Once the three crew members were out, Mulligan took to his parachute and watched his machine plunge into the earth and explode. All four men survived their hasty exit and were soon taken prisoner by the Germans.

Fourth in line came Pilot Officer Matthews who bombed successfully and then struggled back to England with one engine reduced to junk by flak damage. It was now Learoyd's turn to bomb. Just six minutes had elapsed since Pitcairn-Hill's initial attack.

Due to bomb at exactly 11.23 pm, Learoyd let down to 300 feet, some three miles north of the target, then started a shallow diving attack run straight along the canal. By now the German gunners and searchlight operators had fixed the height of the raiders, and were waiting impatiently for the next aircraft. Levelling out at 150 feet, Learoyd reached a point where the canal forked just before the two aqueducts, and then handed over final 'control' of the bomber to his bomb-aimer, John Lewis.

At that moment all hell broke loose as the flak barrage opened up and several searchlights coned the approaching bomber. Blinded by the lights, Learoyd ducked his head below the windscreen to fly solely on instruments at the bidding of Lewis; while both gunners began raking the searchlight sites as these flashed by on either side.

A sudden thump as a shell blasted through the starboard wing almost threw the Hampden off course, and was immediately followed by a second shell which tore through the same wing between the engine and

Learoyd's cockpit. Machine gun bullets splashed the underside of the bomber continually, but Learoyd held firm, waiting for Lewis to release the bomb load.

Then he heard Lewis yell, 'OK Finish', and immediately pulled the battered Hampden into a steep banking turn out of the flak fury, climbing as fast as possible towards a safer area of sky.

Once clear of the danger zone Learoyd and his crew took stock of the damage. Most serious was a ruptured hydraulic system which leaked oil almost everywhere, resulting in drooping wing flaps and a useless undercarriage indicator. The wing damage, though serious, had fortunately missed the wing petrol tanks. One moment of relief from the tension was provided when Ellis calmly reported over the intercom that one of his carrier pigeons had laid an egg at the height of the attack !

Carefully nursing the shell-shattered Hampden home, Learoyd crossed the English coast line just after 2 am, and soon reached Scampton, where in the pre-dawn blackness he considered it best not to attempt a night landing in a machine with unknown damage, and continued to circle the area until first light, and finally made a safe landing minutes before 5 am.

Post-raid intelligence showed that the raid had been entirely successful, and 'Jamie' Pitcairn-Hill was awarded a DSO for his leadership, while the imprisoned Mulligan received a Bar to his DFC.

Learoyd, whose final deliberate run into the well-alerted defences had been possibly the most dangerous attack of all, was awarded a Victoria Cross, gazetted on 20 August 1940. Part of the citation read : 'The high courage, skill and determination, which this officer had invariably displayed on many occasions in the face of the enemy sets an example which is unsurpassed.'

The award was a popular one to the men of Scampton who held 'Babe' Learoyd (his universal nickname, due to his impressive physical size) in the highest regard for his quiet modesty and cool 'unflappability'.

The cross was awarded at an investiture on 9 September 1940, by which time Learoyd had been taken off operations, promoted to Squadron Leader, and was acting temporarily as personal assistant to Air Chief Marshal Sir Robert Brooke-Popham. In November 1940 Learoyd was further honoured by receiving the Freedom of the Borough of New Romney, Kent.

On 28 February 1941 Learoyd rejoined the operational scene when he was appointed Officer Commanding 83 Squadron at Scampton, but in June he left 83 to take up a new post as Wing Commander Flying at 14 OTU, Cottesmore. In December, after six months on instructing, he succeeded to the command of 44 Squadron at Waddington; the first operational Avro Lancaster unit. He was still commander of 44 when one of his flight commanders, John Nettleton, led the epic Lancaster daylight raid on Augsburg in April 1942, which brought Nettleton his award of a VC; but in the following month Learoyd was posted to 25 OTU, Finningley on further instructional duties.

From 1943 until the end of hostilities in Europe, Learoyd remained non-operational, with postings to Air Ministry in January 1943 – an attachment to the PRO Branch, giving various talks and lectures about the RAF in what was termed the 'Line-Shoot Squadron'; and further postings to 109 OTU in December 1944, and 107 OTU at the end of March 1945.

In May 1945 Learoyd returned to flying when he joined 48 (Dakota) Squadron, and a month later moved overseas to West Africa to fly with No 1314 Flight's Dakotas at Accra. A year later he returned to England, and was finally demobilised on 14 October 1946 when he was transferred to the RAF Reserve as a Wing Commander.

For his first three years as a civilian 'Babe' joined the Malayan Civil Aviation Department, becoming personal pilot to succeeding governors of Malaya; and on expiry of his contract in 1950 he returned to England and accepted a position in a tractor and road construction company. In January 1953 he became the export sales manager to the Austin Motor Company – a reflection of his pre-RAF interests and training – and has remained in the motor engineering sales business until the present day.

23. Eric James Brindley Nicolson

With the lion's share of publicity about the deeds and exploits of the Royal Air Force in 1939-45 going to pilots in fighter aircraft, it is perhaps surprising that of the 32 VCs awarded to airmen during the Second World War just one went to a fighter pilot. Though this distinction was made to one of the 3,080 pilots whose raw courage achieved victory in the now legendary Battle of Britain, the sole 'fighter' VC award was not to a pilot who had accrued any high tally of air combat victories – a criterion for several such awards during the 1914-18 war – but for a specific act of individual courage displayed by a pilot during his first-ever experience of aerial combat.

The psychological effects of receiving the supreme honour at the very outset of a fighting career might well have had unfortunate, even disastrous impact on a young man's future outlook. Yet, although there is evidence that James Nicolson felt an inward compulsion to 'prove' himself 'worthy' of such an honour in his remaining years; his constant determination to overcome his physical pain and disabilities and return to operational flying, and the splendid example he set when he finally led a squadron in combat under difficult conditions, were in themselves ample 'proof' of his 'worthiness' to wear the ribbon of his award.

Born in Hampstead on 29 April 1917, and educated in Tonbridge, Kent, Nicolson commenced in business in 1935 as an experimental engineer in Shoreham. In the following year, however, he decided to make a career in the Royal Air Force, and began training as a pilot at the White Waltham civil flying school on 12 October 1936. Enlisted officially in the RAF on 21 December, he then completed his Service training at the Ternhill FTS, and on 7 August 1937 joined his first Service squadron, No 72, based at Church Fenton, flying Gloster Gladiator fighters.

'Nick' Nicolson quickly proved himself to be a 'natural' pilot, handling the Gladiator with ease and expertise and revelling in the contemporary mode of set aerobatics. A natural extrovert by nature, ebullient, talkative, gregarious; 'Nick' was usually the centre of any party, and was a gifted raconteur. As a pilot he was above average and a first-class shot in air-to-air firing; displaying at all times the characteristics which epitomised the RAF's esoterically-termed 'press-on' type of pilot.

When, in April 1939, 72 Squadron began receiving Spitfires to replace their biplane Gladiators, Nicolson soon adapted himself to the sleek monoplanes, and remained with the squadron until the outbreak of war. In October 1939 the squadron moved base to Leconfield, from where it flew its first operational sorties, though saw no combat action.

Further moves to Drem, Church Fenton, and Acklington took place between October 1939 and March 1940; but Nicolson had still not seen combat action when, on 15 May 1940, he was posted to a newly-formed fighter squadron, 249, as an acting Flight commander. Moving to Leconfield five days later, 249 Squadron exchanged its Spitfires for Hawker Hurricanes in mid-June, and was at Church Fenton, working up on their aircraft prior to being declared fully operational from 3 July. On 14 August 1940 the squadron was sent south to Boscombe Down, Wiltshire to join in the desperate defence of the southern counties against the onslaught of the Luftwaffe's daily armadas.

On Friday, 16 August, Nicolson took off from Boscombe Down in Hurricane P3576, GN-A, as leader of three Hurricanes comprising Red Section, with orders to patrol the Poole-Ringwood-Salisbury air space. His two companions were Pilot Officer M. A. King in Hurricane P3616, 'F', and Squadron Leader E B. King, a supernumerary officer attached to the squadron for combat experience. For all three pilots this was to be their baptism of fire in aerial combat.

In a cloudless sky, the trio climbed quickly to 15,000 feet and headed towards Southampton, when Nicolson spotted three Junkers 88 bombers crossing his flight path about four miles away at a slightly higher level. Leading his section towards the Junkers, he closed to within a mile when he saw his intended prey tackled by a formation of Spitfires.

Reluctantly abandoning the chase, Nicolson began climbing again to 18,000 feet over Southampton's suburbs, intending to rejoin the main 249 Squadron formation, when his Hurricane suddenly shuddered under the impact of a burst of cannon shells. Unseen by Nicolson, he and his companions had been 'bounced' by some marauding Messerschmitt Bf 109 fighters. Behind Nicolson, Pilot Officer King's Hurricane almost immediately erupted in flames, and its pilot took to his parachute when he realised that he could do nothing further. As he descended, an over-zealous Royal Artillery officer ordered his men on the ground to fire at the presumed 'enemy' flier; King's parachute canopy was shredded, and the hapless pilot plunged to his death. Squadron Leader King, his aircraft severely damaged, spun down and eventually managed to make a forced landing at Boscombe Down.

Nicolson meanwhile was in deadly peril. Of the four cannon shells

Donald Edward Garland

Thomas Gray

Roderick Alastair Brook Learoyd

Eric James Brindley Nicolson

which had scored direct hits on his Hurricane, one tore through the cockpit canopy and drove a shard of perspex through Nicolson's left eyelid; a second hit his fuselage petrol tank, setting it afire; a third smashed through the cockpit side tearing the pilot's right trouser leg to shreds; while the fourth hit the heel of Nicolson's left shoe and wounded him in the foot.

With blood obscuring vision from his left eye, the pain of his left leg, and a veritable furnace of petrol flames erupting in front of him, Nicolson instinctively put the Hurricane into a right-hand diving turn to escape further punishment. As the flames began licking around his instrument panel, Nicolson prepared painfully to take to his parachute, when in his undamaged windscreen there appeared another German, a Messerschmitt Bf 110 two-seat fighter.

Nicolson's reflector gunsight was still switched on from his initial pursuit of the Junkers bombers, and on seeing this Bf 110 Nicolson saw red. Dropping back into his bucket seat, he pressed his gun firing button and watched his tracers riddle the slim fuselage of his target. The German pilot jinked wildly from left to right, trying to evade the Hurricane's fire, but Nicolson, oblivious of all else, was totally determined to destroy his victim.

As Nicolson continued firing he glanced down at his left hand holding the throttle lever and saw the flesh peeling off in the stifling heat, but as yet felt no pain. The flames were now akin to a blowtorch, beating back from the instrument panel into his face, and he realised that he could not hold on much longer. Giving the Messerschmitt one final burst from all eight wing guns, Nicolson pushed himself up from his seat, only to bang his head on the shattered cockpit frame, still closed above him.

Pulling back the hood cover, he tried again to get out of his blazing cockpit, forgetting that he was still strapped to his seat. Unbuckling one restraint strap, and snapping the other, burnt strap, Nicolson finally managed to evacuate the cockpit and dropped into space. Somersaulting downwards from 12,000 feet, Nicolson was partly revived by the rushing air, realised he was now diving head-first for the ground, and pulled the ripcord of his parachute.

As the canopy deployed, a Messerschmitt fighter roared past him and turned to come back again. Fearing that the German might try to machine-gun him, Nicolson let himself hang limply, simulating death, and the German roared by him without further trouble.

As he descended to lower height, Nicolson took stock of his condition. Now for the first time he realised he was wounded in the foot, and could see blood oozing from his boot. Both hands were badly burned; the left already contracted by the heat into a curved claw with the finger bones exposed, while the right had strips of charred flesh hanging loosely. Across his face was still strapped his leather face mask, but above the nose piece his eyelids and brow were burnt, and he was still blind in his left eye from the near-severed eyelid. His uniform hung in tatters; one trouser leg completely torn away and the other shredded in rags. Only now did the conscious pain all over his body commence, his leg and hands particularly beginning to ache and jar his nervous system.

Still fully conscious of his surroundings, Nicolson guided his parachute to take him clear of the nearby English Channel – a descent into the sea would have meant certain drowning in his parlous physical condition – and then managed to avoid a high tension cable, before realising that his ordeal by fire was by no means over. As he swung helplessly in his harness he too became a victim of the trigger-happy volunteer 'soldiers' below, and was hit in the buttock by a blast of 12-bore shot. Finally, and thankfully, he came to earth in an open field, where he lay, unable to release himself from his parachute due to his crippled hands. From his original take-off from Boscombe Down at 1.5 pm his epic battle 'initiation' had lasted exactly 47 minutes to the moment when he finally baled out of his doomed aircraft.

Immediately rushed to Southampton Hospital, Nicolson's life hung in the balance for several days and nights – indeed, the first doctor to examine him gave him only twenty-four hours to live. Far away in Yorkshire, his wife Muriel, only weeks away from the imminent birth of Nick's son, was unable to travel to be with him; his battle for life was solely a matter of his will to live and the surgeons' skill.

Three weeks later Nicolson had recovered sufficiently to be moved to the RAF hospital at Halton, which specialised in burns treatment, and by November he was a convalescent patient in the Palace Hotel 'hospital' at Torquay. His foot wound had healed, as had much of his facial burns and injuries; but his left hand was still virtually unusable, while his right hand had only begun to retrieve some of its former tractability of movement.

On 15 November 1940 the award of his Victoria Cross was promulgated. Nicolson's personal notification of the award came in a telegram from King George VI, addressed to him at Torquay; and Nicolson's immediate reaction was one of disbelief. Showing the message to another patient, F. 'Hiram' Smith DFC, Nicolson's first words were, 'Now I'll have to earn it'. . . . Ten days after the announcement Nicolson received his cross from the King at Buckingham Palace.

Though still not medically fit for full flying duties, Nicolson soon began agitating for a flying post, and on 24 February 1941 he joined the instructional staff of 54 OTU. His burnt hands were slow to heal – he was to suffer alternate bouts of pain from these until his death – but on 22 September 1941 he finally became 'operational' again by being appointed in command of No 1459 Flight, Hibaldstow; a night fighter experimental unit equipped with twin-engined Douglas Havoc 'Turbinlite' fighters (later retitled as 538 Squadron).

After six months he received an overseas posting and on 17 March 1942 became a staff officer at Headquarters 293 Wing, Alipore in India; moving to another desk job at Air Headquarters, Bengal in mid-December. Continuing to plead for a more active operational post, Nicolson got his wish on 4 August 1943 when he succeeded to the command of 27 Squadron at Agartala, Burma. 27, known from its squadron badge as 'The Flying Elephants', had been the first unit to operate Bristol Beaufighters in the Far East theatre of war, and had just introduced the all-wood De Havilland Mosquito fighter-bomber to the jungle campaign. Tasked mainly with what is now termed interdiction operations – attacking logistic ground targets – the 'Elephants' had already achieved a high reputation for its operational results, and when Nicolson joined the squadron he immediately set to work to raise that reputation to the highest possible peak of efficiency.

For almost exactly a year, 'Nick' led the 'Elephants' to war; refusing to allow his physical disabilities to deter him from flying in any circumstances, and when he finally left the unit on 11 August 1944 with a posting as Wing Commander Training at the 3rd Tactical Air Force HQ at Comilla, Bengal, he was recommended for a decoration, and was later awarded a Distinguished Flying Cross.

By April 1945, Nicolson had joined the staff of RAF Burma Headquarters, but still itched for operational flying as the end of the war approached.

On 2 May 1945 he managed to persuade higher authority to allow him to accompany a bomber crew on a bombing sortie, as an 'observer'; joining the crew of Liberator KH210 of 355 Squadron, based at Salbani, Bengal.

Leaving Salbani minutes before 1 pm, the Liberator had reached a point about 130 miles south of Calcutta en route to the target when one engine erupted in flames, and the bomber eventually crashed in the open sea.

Sixteen hours later rescue Catalina flying boats located the scene but found only two senior NCO survivors. The rest of the crew, including Wing Commander E. J. B. Nicolson VC DFC had perished with their aircraft.

24. John Hannah

During the Second World War members of 83 Squadron RAF won an impressive total of 429 decorations for gallantry. The name at the apex of the unit's long list of honours is that of a young Scot, John Hannah. Not only was he the squadron's highest award-winner, but he also had the distinction of being the youngest-ever recipient of a Victoria Cross for aerial operations.

Born in Paisley on 27 November 1921, John came from a hard-working family background. His father was an employee of the Clyde Trust and, after receiving an education at the Bankhead Public School, Victoria Drive and Glasgow Secondary School, young John Hannah started earning a living, as a shoe salesman, in order to contribute to the family purse. On 15 August 1939, however he decided to join the RAF for a six years' regular engagement, and after initial indoctrination and attestation at RAF Cardington that month, was posted to No 2 Electrical and Wireless Training School on 14 September 1939 to train as a wireless operator.

On qualifying in this basic trade he was sent to No 4 Bombing and Gunnery School at West Freugh for a brief course in air gunnery, and on 18 May 1940 was sent to 16 OTU, Upper Heyford to complete his aircrew instruction as a Wireless Operator Air Gunner (WOP/AG). Promoted to Sergeant on 27 May 1940 – he was then only eighteen years old – he joined 106 Squadron on 1 July, based then at Thornaby, Yorkshire and operating Handley Page Hampden bombers. His stay with 106 was brief, and on 11 August he arrived at Scampton to join 83 Squadron's Hampden crews for operations.

When Hannah joined 83 Squadron the unit, in common with most UK-based bomber squadrons, was undertaking an intensive series of day and night operations raiding German-occupied ports and installations bordering France and Belgium along the English Channel – potential jumping-off points for a threatened sea-borne invasion of Britain. The legendary Battle of Britain was reaching its peak of desperate activity and, with RAF Fighter Command fully extended in the daily defence of British skies, only Bomber Command could provide any form of purely offensive operations against Germany's military might.

It was on one such mission on the night of 15/16 September 1940 that 83 Squadron put up a force of 15 Hampdens – the unit's biggest effort to date – with the intention of bombing a reported concentration of German invasion barges gathered in the port of Antwerp.

For this sortie Hannah was crewed with Pilot Officer C. A. Connor, a Canadian pilot, Sergeant D. A. E. Hayhurst, navigator and bomb-aimer, and another gunner, Sergeant George James. All three were already variously experienced on operations – James had flown nine sorties; while for Hayhurst this was to be his 39th operation over Germany. Their aircraft was Hampden P1355, named 'Betty' by its former 'owner' Squadron Leader J. Collier who had flown it as one of the diversion aircraft on 12 August 1940, when Flight Lieutenant R. A. B. Learoyd of 49 Squadron had won a VC over the Dortmund-Ems Canal.

Just before 10.30 pm on the evening of 15 September, Connor began his take-off run across the grass airfield at Scampton and slowly gained height, heading directly towards the coast.

Inside a Hampden the four-man crew had little space in which to move around; the maximum internal width of the slender fuselage being just three feet. The navigator in his perspex nose cupola, and the pilot sat high and central, were both virtually cut off from the rear crew members by an aluminium-alloy door amidships which could be opened rearwards and had a central 'window' for observation. Immediately behind the pilot's seat was a well in which the crew's collapsible dinghy and two hand-operated fire extinguishers were normally stowed. Behind this well came the door, spanning the full width of the fuselage. Behind the door was the upper compartment for the wireless operator/gunner with its hinged perspex cupola. Just beneath the wireless operator's cabin sat the under-gunner. Hannah, in the upper position sat facing the tail with his wireless set and a basket containing two carrier pigeons at hand, behind a pair of .303 Vickers Gas Operated (VGO) machine guns, with spare ammunition pans racked alongside the cabin. Below him came a step down of some two feet depth into the 'Tin', or under-gunner's compartment. The vertical step was cushioned as a back rest for the ventral gunner (James), who sàt facing aft with his legs stretched out behind his own twin VGO's and surrounded by spare pans of ammunition. All four crew members, encased in bulky flying clothing, were virtually confined to their respective positions throughout the flight, restricting movement within the narrow fuselage to the necessary minimum.

The outward trip was uneventful until the Hampden began to approach Antwerp where it was greeted by a fierce barrage of anti-aircraft fire (flak) and probing searchlights. Connor commenced his bombing run over the massed landing barges which were clearly visible below in the light of a full moon; holding the Hampden rock-steady as it ran in, despite the fury of bursting shells all around him. He quickly realised that his flight path was slightly out of alignment and, rather than waste his bombs, swung the bomber out of its run and circled for a second attempt. Dropping to 2,000 feet for more accuracy, Connor plunged through the flak barrage again and the Hampden shuddered repeatedly as it was hit by shrapnel and bullets.

Finally Connor heard Hayhurst yell that the bombs were away, but before he could swing the aircraft out of the flak zone it was hit in the bomb bay by a shell and ricocheting shrapnel ripped chunks out of the left mid-wing section, perforated the tail boom, and pierced the wing petrol tanks.

Almost instantly the rear of the fuselage exploded into an inferno of flames, and Hannah and James were enveloped in the first rush of flame heat. The blowlamp effect of the slipstream-driven flames literally burned George James out of his seat, melting the fuselage flooring around him, and leaving him no alternative but to take to his parachute through the rapidly enlarging hole beside him.

Just above James, John Hannah saw the alloy flooring under his feet dissolved into molten metal and blown backwards, plating in great ugly smears against the rear bulkhead. Around him electrical wiring was aflame, and the boiling heat started exploding the spare ammunition drums in their racks.

Hannah's first reaction was to inform Connor over the intercommunication microphone, 'The aircraft is on fire.'

'Is it very bad?', queried Connor.

'Bad, but not too bad', replied Hannah calmly.

Connor then yelled for Hayhurst to come back from the nose, and then told him to see how James and Hannah were. Hayhurst wriggled under Connor's seat to the midships door but couldn't open it. Looking through the door window, he could see no sign of James; while Hannah appeared to be literally alight from head to toe. Hayhurst concluded that both men had 'bought it', and made his way forward, then baled out of the aircraft quickly in order to give Connor time to get out too. At that moment Hannah was attempting to open the door at his back in order to reach the fire extinguishers in the well. The door had already buckled in the fierce heat and it took all of the young Scot's strength to finally pull it open. Having done so, he noticed his parachute pack, in its door stowage, beginning to smoulder but ignored this and grabbed the nearest extinguisher and set about quelling the raging fire.

In the ultra-confined space, with the added restriction of his bulky flying clothing hampering his every movement, Hannah soon found himself being slowly suffocated by fumes and heat. He tried sucking pure oxygen through his face mask but soon was forced to remove the mask for fear of fainting in the sweltering cocoon of heat inside the fuselage. Worming his way back into his upper compartment he flipped open the hinged perspex cupola cover and leaned out into the slipstream, gulping fresh air into his lungs.

Revived, he next returned to the fire and emptied a second extinguisher. When this became exhausted Hannah resorted to using his flying log book and finally his hands to beat out the flames. All this time spare ammunition pans were detonating around him in all directions and, turning to this added menace, Hannah started heaving the red-hot loose pans out of the Hampden.

In the pilot's seat Connor had his hands full trying to evade the deadly flak. The blazing bomber provided the German gunners with a first class target for every gun they could bring to bear – in the words of another 83 Squadron Hampden captain, Guy Gibson (later VC) flying nearby, '. . . flames and sparks came out like the wrong end of a rocket hanging in the air.'

On the windscreen in front of him Connor could see the red-yellow reflection of the flames in the rear fuselage, and he could feel his back seat armour plating being struck spasmodically by detonating bullets. After the first few minutes he could also begin to feel the heat increasing at the back of his neck. Nevertheless he was determined to fly the Hampden out of range of the flak in order (as he thought then) to give his crew a chance to bale out safely.

Then Hannah's voice came through his earphones saying, 'The fire is out, sir.' The time had seemed like an eternity to Connor, although the whole episode had lasted less than ten minutes.

Having satisfied himself that the last glowing remnants of flame were subdued, Hannah crawled forward to the pilot's seat to report the extent of the damage to his skipper. On his first sight of the boy Connor was shocked. Those parts of Hannah's face not protected by his flying helmet were burned black, his eyes badly swollen, eyebrows singed off, and both hands severely burned; while the major part of Hannah's flying suit was charred and tattered. Asked by Connor to check on the other two crew members, Hannah was surprised to find no sign of either James or Hayhurst.

'We're all alone' he reported to Connor, then crawled back to his wireless compartment in the hope of signalling base for a position fix. He found his radio completely gutted, while the two carrier pigeons had been roasted alive in their wicker basket. Going forward again, Hannah retrieved the navigator's maps, positioned himself behind Connor's seat, and helped the pilot to navigate the scarred bomber home.

Just after 3 am on 16 September Connor brought the Hampden down for a safe landing at Scampton, and on climbing out saw for the first time the true extent of the damage. The upper wireless compartment was a charred ruin, and the under-gunner's 'Tin' was completely burnt out, with a jagged hole running along its length big enough for a man to climb through. The tail was shredded with flak holes, but it was only when Connor inspected the damage to the wings that the full significance of their escape from near-certain death became apparent. Both wing petrol tanks had been torn wide open by flak, and it seemed little short of miraculous that the remaining fuel had not ignited. Had it done so there could have been no hope for the aircraft.

As Hannah climbed out of the Hampden a thoughtless airfield guard shone a torch directly into his scarred face and in the boy's own words, 'I went blind.' Connor could now see the full extent of Hannah's injuries and immediately arranged for the boy to be transported to a nearby Service hospital for emergency treatment.

On 1 October 1940 came the officially promulgated awards of a Victoria Cross to John Hannah; a Distinguished Flying Medal to Hayhurst, then a prisoner of war; and a Distinguished Flying Cross to Connor. Tragically, Connor was not destined to wear his DFC for long. Returning from a bombing sortie to Norway in Hampden L4093 on the night of 3/4 November 1940, he crashed into the sea just off the east coast, and his body was later found in a dinghy. He was brought back to Scampton and then buried in nearby Brattleby village cemetery.

Hannah was informed of his award while still a patient in Rauceby hospital, Lincolnshire, but after his discharge from hospital on 7 October accompanied his skipper, Connor, to Buckingham Palace on 10 October for the investiture of their awards.

He did not return to operational flying and on 4 November reported to 14 OTU, Cottesmore for instructional duties. Here, in January 1941, he first met his future wife Janet, and on 1 April 1941 Hannah was promoted to Flight Sergeant. A further posting on 4 September 1941 took him to No 2 Signals School, Yatesbury for further instructional duties, but now his health began to deteriorate and he soon contracted tubercolosis; resulting eventually in his being discharged from the RAF on 10 December 1942 with a full disability pension. Unable to take up full-time employment, Hannah was hard put to support his young family for the next few years, and soon his health failed completely. Finally, on

9 June 1947, John Hannah, the youngest airman ever to be awarded a Victoria Cross, died in Markfield Sanatorium, Leicester, leaving a widow and three very young daughters.

Twenty years later, on 6 May 1967, a short ceremony took place inside one of the huge aircraft hangars at RAF Scampton. Present were members of 83 Squadron's Vulcan bomber crews and their guests Mrs Janet Hannah and her three daughters. She had come to present her husband's bronze cross to his old unit on permanent loan – in her own phrase, 'This is where it belongs'. When 83 Squadron was disbanded later, the cross was re-presented to Hannah's former station, Scampton on 19 July 1969, where it remains today.

25. Kenneth Campbell

By the spring of 1941 German and Italian occupation and mastery of most of Europe had left Britain virtually alone in continuing the fight against Hitler's and Mussolini's vainglorious dreams of world conquest and domination. The attempt in the summer of 1940 by Hitler to prepare the way for invasion of the United Kingdom by a devastating air assault had been broken by RAF Fighter Command in the now-legendary Battle of Britain. Yet as an island, fully dependent on her sea lanes for import of food and vital war materials, Britain remained highly vulnerable. The Atlantic became the prime battleground. A largely ineffective Bomber Command continued to wage its offensive against the German homeland; while Fighter Command, hardly recovered from the crippling casualties and depletions of the long defence of 1940, was only just beginning to extend its activities across occupied Europe in probing offensive sweeps.

Defence of Britain's seas and trans-ocean lifelines now depended primarily on the Royal Navy and RAF Coastal Command. Acutely aware of the importance to Britain of these lifelines, Hitler gave priority to the struggle at sea. Apart from the expanding U-boat fleet, the German navy had three major 'weapons' to hand; two so-termed battle-cruisers, *Scharnhorst* and *Gneisenau*, each displacing 32,000 tons and each armed with nine 11-inch guns, and capable of a speed of 31 knots – outpacing and/or out-arming any British capital ship afloat. The third was the *Bismarck* – the largest warship in the world at that time. By March 1941 the *Scharnhorst* and *Gneisenau* had already been responsible for sinking well over one million tons of Allied shipping between them, including the aircraft carrier HMS *Glorious*. And now the *Bismarck* was poised to join them to form a trio of destructive power which, Hitler firmly believed, would then starve Britain into submission within two months.

Such a distinct possibility had long been recognised by Winston Churchill, the British Prime Minister, and his Service chiefs; resulting in a sustained 'campaign' by RAF Bomber Command to destroy these capital ships whenever they were in harbour. Such attempts merely produced high casualties among the bombers, and had little or no effect on the ships. Churchill's reaction to these 'failures' was typically volatile, and his strictures against the RAF's inability to neutralise the German surface raiders culminated in a direction, on 22 March 1941 :

If the presence of the enemy battle-cruisers in a Biscayan port is confirmed, every effort by the Navy and the Air Force should be made to destroy them, and for this purpose serious risks and sacrifices *must* be made.

On the very same day, by coincidence, the *Scharnhorst* put into Brest harbour to re-tube her boilers, accompanied by the *Gneisenau*. This news was communicated almost immediately to England by French Resistance workers, and an RAF reconnaissance flight on 28 March confirmed their presence in Brest.

Bomber Command immediately instigated a week of bombing attacks on Brest, to no avail, but left a legacy, unwittingly, which was to initiate a train of events which nullified the power of Hitler's bid to subjugate Britain by isolation. One bomb dropped near the *Gneisenau* failed to explode, and the huge ship was moved out of dry dock into the open harbour to allow bomb disposal teams to deal with the bomb. Its sister raider was already tied up to the harbour's north quay, protected by torpedo nets. Such protection was not available for the *Gneisenau*, but anticipating that the bomb disposal team would complete its work quickly, the ship was left in open harbour waters, ready to be run back into dry dock as soon as the unexploded bomb was cleared. That day 5 April, a photographic reconnaissance Spitfire photographed the harbour, revealing the vulnerable position of the *Gneisenau*, totally exposed to an aerial torpedo attack, in Brest's inner harbour. Such an attack was quickly ordered, and the task was delegated to 22 Squadron, a veteran Coastal Command unit equipped with Bristol Beauforts; to take place at first light the following day, 6 April.

Twenty-two Squadron at this time was nominally based at North Coates but had moved nine of its Beauforts south-west to the Cornish airfield at St Eval, just north of Newquay, to be within striking range of the ports and harbours along the coastline of the Bay of Biscay. When the squadron commander received the order for the sortie, he had already sent three Beauforts off on another mission; leaving him with merely six aircraft available. He decided to despatch these in two formations of three Beauforts; one trio to bomb any torpedo nets surrounding the *Gneisenau* first, and the other three to carry torpedoes for the vital attack.

Such intelligence as was available about the defences at Brest presented a chilling prospect; the harbour was literally ringed by hills in which hundreds of anti-aircraft guns were located to provide a virtually impenetrable cross-fire, while in the harbour three flak ships added their weight of fire to the massive guns of the two ships which would be the targets for any aerial onslaught. In all, perhaps 1,000 guns, of which about a quarter were of heavy calibre; all with sights set to predictable and relatively short range. Any aircraft daring to pierce such a curtain of fire would have only the remotest chance of survival. If any attack could be classified as suicidal, this was certainly one.

Chosen for the torpedo attack were Flying Officer J. Hyde DFC, Sergeant Camp, and Flying Officer Kenneth Campbell. All three were experienced men in their role, and for Campbell this was to be his twentieth operational sortie. These were detailed to leave St Eval first, then wait on the outskirts of Brest for the bombing trio to make the first attack against any torpedo nets; after which the torpedo trio would go in individually to make their runs.

Even on initial take-off the whole sortie seemed fated to fail, when two of the bomber Beauforts became bogged down in the slush and mud of a water-soaked airfield, leaving just Sergeant Henry Menary, a Belfast-born Irishman, to actually get airborne. Unknowing of this mishap, the three torpedo Beauforts had already left at intervals of a few minutes, between 4.30 am and 5 am on 6 April.

Leading off was Campbell, piloting Beaufort N1016, OA-X, whose three-men crew comprised Sergeant James Philip Scott, a blond Canadian as navigator, Sergeant William Cecil Mullins, an ex-Somerset farmer as wireless operator, and Sergeant Ralph Walter Hillman, an ex-chauffeur from Edmonton, London as air gunner.

The hasty plan for the raid allowed each man to fly independently to Brest, where the three torpedo men were to rendezvous and circuit until the bombers had gone in; the bomb explosions being the agreed signal for the torpedo attacks immediately following.

Groping his way through the darkness and atrocious weather conditions of rain, fog and mists, Menary – the only bombing pilot to eventually get away safely from St Eval – soon lost his way. When daylight came he realised he was many miles away from Brest, too late for his appointed task, and accordingly he dropped his bombs on a ship near Ile de Batz and turned for home. The torpedo Beauforts were now on their own.

Even had they known that the second formation was unavailable for the operation, it is very doubtful if this would have prevented Hyde, Camp or Campbell continuing the sortie. Hyde and Camp had many months of experience behind them, while Campbell already had a reputation for quiet determination and unwavering courage in the face of odds on operations.

'Ken' Campbell was born on 21 April 1917 at Saltcoats, Ayrshire, the youngest in a family of six children, and had attended Sedbergh School

before gaining entrance to Clare College, Cambridge, to study for a
degree in chemistry. Joining the Cambridge University Air Squadron, he
had been commissioned as a Pilot Officer in the RAF Volunteer Reserve
on 23 August 1938, and eventually mobilised for RAF service on 25
September 1939.

A brief course of Service training at Cranwell commencing 21 October
was followed by a move to Abbotsinch on 20 April 1940; by which time
Campbell had been promoted to Flying Officer. On 8 June he completed
his training with a posting to No 1 OTU; and on 28 September 1940
joined 22 Squadron to start his operational career. The non-stop Battle
of the Atlantic then being waged saw him quickly introduced to the
role of 22 Squadron; attacking enemy shipping at every opportunity.

Now, in his seventh month of war flying with the unit, Campbell was
becoming a veteran; thoroughly versed in individual and independent
action so necessary for a torpedo bomber pilot. Thus, when Campbell
finally reached his objective minutes after 6 am, he was not perturbed to
find himself alone. Following his orders, he then circuited the area, waiting for the bomb explosions he had been briefed to expect as his signal to
commence his own attack.

The pre-dawn mists and drizzle obviated any clear view of his surroundings, but he was aware that it could only be a matter of minutes
until daylight would expose the harbour – and himself – to plain view,
but he still waited patiently. Then, perhaps assuming he must be the last –
or only – aircraft to arrive, Campbell began his attack. As he swept in
towards the harbour on a descending flight path, he was seen from above
by Hyde in the second Beaufort to reach the target; disappearing lower
into the mist and greyness of sea fog, heading towards the harbour. Hyde
continued to circle, having seen no bomb explosions, and momentarily
undecided whether he was supposed to follow Campbell yet.

What followed over Brest harbour can only be pieced together from
the few eye-witnesses and fragmentary evidence still available after 1945.
Campbell made his initial approach at approximately 300 feet across the
outer harbour approaches, then dived to less than 50 feet height as the
protective stone mole of the inner harbour, behind which the *Gneisenau*
was anchored, came into view. The distance from the mole to the ship
was at most 500 yards, entailing a torpedo drop immediately inside the
mole wall if it was to have an effective run to its target. Racing between
the flak ships' masts in the outer harbour, the Beaufort was as yet un-
molested, having the slim advantage of complete surprise for the moment.

As the mole came under his aircraft nose, Campbell released his 'fish'
accurately, then pulled the Beaufort in a port climbing turn, heading for

cloud cover above the rapidly-approaching hills behind Brest. At that precise second the whole defence system erupted and a withering wall of flak shells focussed on the Beaufort. Nothing could have survived such a barrage, and Campbell's aircraft, out of control, crashed straight ahead into the harbour.

It is virtually certain that Campbell, having released his torpedo, was almost immediately killed or wounded by the first predicted flak. When the aircraft was later salvaged the Germans found the body of 'Jimmy' Scott, the fair-haired Canadian, in the pilot's seat usually occupied by Campbell. All four crew members were buried by the Germans in the grave of honour in Brest cemetery. Campbell's torpedo ran true to its mark, crippling the *Gneisenau*, and forcing the Germans to hurriedly utilise every available ship in the harbour to support the battle-cruiser as they rushed it into dry dock. Eight months later the *Gneisenau* was still high and dry, its starboard propeller shaft still undergoing repair.

Reports of Kenneth Campbell's unswerving devotion to his designated task, and the sublime courage he displayed in completing his attack in the face of unnerving odds, filtered through to England from local French patriots; and on 13 March 1942 Campbell was awarded a posthumous Victoria Cross, which his parents received from King George VI at an investiture on 23 June 1943. And in Sedbergh, where Kenneth Campbell had spent his schooldays, they erected a memorial to perpetuate the name and deeds of the truly gallant Scot.

26. Hughie Idwal Edwards

First of three Australian-born airmen to be awarded a Victoria Cross in World War Two, Hughie Idwal Edwards was the son of a Welsh emigrant couple who settled in Fremantle, Western Australia in 1910. Born on 1 August 1914 at Fremantle, Edwards was educated at White Gum Valley School and, later, Fremantle High School, before taking up employment in a shipping agent's office. In 1934 he enlisted as a private in the local garrison artillery, but in July 1935 transferred to the RAAF and commenced flying instruction at Point Cook; receiving his pilot's 'wings' in June 1936.

He next applied for transfer to the RAF and was commissioned in the RAF on 21 August 1936 and posted initially to 15 Squadron at Abingdon, flying Hawker Hind bombers. In March of the following year he moved to Bicester, posted to 90 Squadron as unit adjutant, and flying the new twin-engine metal monoplane Bristol Blenheim I bombers, with which the squadron began to re-equip in May, tasked with Service development and trials of the new design. The squadron crews soon adapted to the Blenheims, albeit with distinct reservations on the ability of any pilot to abandon the design safely in the event of any emergency.

This particular aspect of flying a Blenheim I was forcibly demonstrated in August 1938 when Edwards was forced to take to his parachute. As he baled out his parachute became entangled with the radio mast pylon, and in the subsequent crash he suffered extensive injury to his right leg; severing the main nerve and, later, becoming paralysed below the knee. He spent the following nine months in hospital, and was eventually declared fit for flying again in April 1940.

After completing an armament specialist course of instruction he returned to flying duties, and in February 1941 joined 139 Squadron, based at Horsham St Faith aerodrome (now, Norwich Airport) to fly Blenheim IV 'long-nosed' bombers. His stay with 139 was brief and on 11 May he was appointed as commander of 105 Squadron, another Blenheim IV bomber unit, based on the grass airfield at Swanton Morley, east of Norwich. On 15 June he led six of the squadron's Blenheims on a low-level search for enemy merchant shipping and came upon a small convoy of eight vessels near the Hague. Dropping to a mere 50 feet above the waves, Edwards led his men in, selecting a 4,000-tonner for his own

Hughie Idwal Edwards

John Hannah

Kenneth Campbell

James Allen Ward

victim and raking its decks with machine gun fire before releasing his bombs from mast height; in the face of a hail of cannon and machine gun fire. His bombs found their mark, leaving the vessel seriously damaged, and on 1 July he was awarded a Distinguished Flying Cross (DFC) for this and many previous operations.

In late June 1941, 105 Squadron, along with the other units of 2 Group, Bomber Command, participated in various daylight raids against vital communications targets in Germany; the intention being to strike swiftly and often while the bulk of Hitler's military forces were engaged in the east against Russia. One such operation was Wreckage – a daylight bombing assault on Bremen on 30 June which did not prove particularly successful. It was decided to repeat Wreckage on 4 July.

Fifteen Blenheims (nine from 105 Squadron and six from 107 Squadron, Great Massingham) were to be led by Hughie Edwards, flying Blenheim IV, V6028, GB-D, with his crew of two, Pilot Officer Ramsay (navigator) and the veteran air gunner, Sergeant G. Quinn DFM. It was to be Edwards' 36th operational sortie. His planning for the raid envisaged the whole bombing force holding close formation up to the target area, after which the Blenheims would separate into a loose line abreast about 100-200 yards apart and select individual targets of opportunity over Bremen. And, despite the wording of Edward's VC citation later, it was never intended to withdraw and return in formation.

At precisely 0521 hours on 4 July, Edwards took off from Swanton Morley at the head of his squadron's nine Blenheims, and was soon joined by the six 107 Squadron bombers, but three of the latter soon abandoned the raid for various reasons. The remaining dozen bombers, in good formation, roared across the North Sea at a height between 50 and 100 feet and eventually crossed in to Germany a few miles south of Cuxhaven, then turned south to Bremen. Their trip across the sea had been in the glare of a cloudless summer sky, though on reaching Germany they saw patchy clouds – too thin for cover – at about 5-7,000 feet above them.

Visibility over Germany was excellent – a mixed 'blessing' for the bomber crews who could see for miles ahead, but could equally be seen by German ground defences, which began to put up a veritable wall of tracer and black bursts of shellfire in depth as the Blenheims made their final approach to Bremen.

Leading his men right up to the outer ring of these defences, which included a host of cable-tethered balloons close-hauled at 500 feet height right around the city; Edwards ordered the 'spread' formation – after which it was every man for himself. By that time the flak in front of

Edwards was (in his words), 'terrific and frightening' – bursting mainly at the aircraft height of 50-100 feet and permeating the sky to the extent that Edwards and his crew could smell cordite.

Jinking his way through flak, balloon cables, and a host of telephone and telegraph overhead wires, Edwards plunged through the heart of the flak and released his bombs over the centre of the dock area, then flew as low as possible over the heart of Bremen until he reached the outer suburban area before banking left and circling the city at some 50 feet. In all he was under heavy and continuous fire for about ten minutes, and his aircraft was hit nearly twenty times, mainly underneath the rear fuselage, though one shell burst in the rear cockpit and wounded Quinn in the knee.

Behind Edwards the remaining Blenheims, spread across a mile-wide frontage, thundered at rooftop height across the city, bombing and running the gauntlet of open-sighted ground gunners. Sergeant MacKillop, in Z7426, received a direct hit and crashed in flames; while Flying Officer Lambert, in Z7486, was also hit and set afire, and was last seen heading inland. All the others suffered varying degrees of damage; in the case of Sergeant Jackson of 105 Squadron, destroying his hydraulic system and forcing Jackson to belly-land when he finally regained base at Swanton Morley. Two of 107 Squadron's trio were also lost, including the squadron commander Wing Commander L. V. E. Petley who crashed in flames onto a factory. The survivors twisted and turned their ways out of the deadly clouds of flak, with several trailing telegraph wires around wings and tailplanes, and began to make their individual runs for home.

Edwards, after circling Bremen, headed towards Bremerhaven and Wilhelmshaven and then spotted what appeared to be good cloud cover high ahead. Climbing quickly for this sanctuary he soon realised that the cloud was too sparse and, fearing radar-vectored Luftwaffe fighters at such an altitude, he promptly dived again to sea level and came out heading towards Heligoland. Skirting the latter he flew out to sea for nearly 100 miles north of the Friesians and then, finally, turned west for England. When he eventually landed back at base, just before noon, he was the last to return.

On 22 July Edwards was awarded a Victoria Cross for having, in the words of its citation, '. . . displayed the highest possible standard of gallantry and determination'; while his crew members Ramsay and Quinn received a DFC and a Bar to the DFM respectively.

Continuing on operations, Edwards next led 105 Squadron to Malta, arriving at Luqa airfield on 28 July, to play a part in the beleaguered island's epic campaign against Axis shipping in the Mediterranean theatre of operations. Three days after arrival he led six Blenheims in an attack on an escorted ship convoy 200 miles north-east of Pantellaria. The Malta detachment was relatively short and in October 1941, after 105's return to England, Edwards left the squadron to participate in a lecture tour of the USA, along with other outstanding pilots such as 'Sailor' Malan, Roland Tuck, Harry Broadhurst, Whitworth and the ex-Schneider Trophy winner, Boothman.

On his return he was posted as chief flying instructor at Wellesbourne Mountford in January 1942, and in the same month married Cherry, the widow of Flight Lieutenant H. R. A. Beresford. His tour of instructional duties ended when, on 3 August 1942 he returned to 105 Squadron as its latest commander. 105 had become the first RAF squadron (though not the first unit) to operate the now-legendary De Havilland Mosquito bomber; flying its first Mosquito operations on 31 May 1942. The squadron, when Edwards rejoined it, was based at Marham, Norfolk and well-versed in operating its 'Wooden Wonders' (the universal soubriquet for the wood-construction Mosquitos).

Edwards' return to operations brought him another close brush with death when returning from a daylight sortie on 29 August in Mosquito DK323. He ran head-on into a formation of 12 Focke-Wulf Fw 190's and sustained a hit in an engine coolant pipe. Outpacing the Fw 190's over the sea, he was forced to shut down the port engine, and eventually belly-landed at Lympne airfield. Undeterred, he continued to lead many of the squadron's low-level daylight bombing sorties into Germany. By the end of November a high priority target for No 2 Group's day offensive was the Philips radio and electrical components factory at Eindhoven, Holland. Situated in the heart of a 'friendly' city, the factory presented many problems to potential bombers, requiring high precision in bombing if civilian casualties were to be kept to an absolute minimum.

Operation Oyster – the attack on this factory - was eventually mounted on 6 December 1942. Taking part were Bostons, Mitchells, Venturas and Blenheims from 107, 226, 88, 21 and 464 Squadrons, accompanied by ten Mosquitos from 105 and 139 Squadrons led by Hughie Edwards.

Taking off in Mosquito DZ365 at 11.22 am, Edwards' Mosquito formation linked up with the Boston element near the Dutch coast and, despite attacks by Luftwaffe fighters on the route to target, bombed accurately. German flak and fighter opposition to the raid was heavy and of the 93 aircraft which participated, four Bostons, nine Venturas and a Mosquito were lost, and a further 23 returned with varying degrees of damage. The damage to the factory complex was heavy too, and after the war it was learned that Dutch civilian casualties had amounted to 25 killed.

For this, and his many other personally-led squadron sorties in 105's Mosquitos, Edwards was awarded a Distinguished Service Order on 5 January 1943; and on February 2nd he was promoted to Group Captain in command of RAF station Binbrook, with nearby Grimsby and Wickenby within his aegis of operational responsibility.

Although necessarily restricted by the chiefly administrative aspects of his latest appointment, Edwards still undertook occasional bombing operations over Germany; usually in the van of Binbrook-based 460 Squadron's Lancasters, on at least 15 missions during 1943-44. Then, in December 1944 he was posted to the Far East, becoming Group Captain Bombing Operations at Ceylon HQ, Kandy. In the following month he was re-appointed to headquarters South-East Asia Command (SEAC) as Senior Administration Staff Officer (SASO); and in the following two years held various senior staff appointments in Malaya and Batavia, resulting in the award of the OBE in February 1947. Deciding to remain in the RAF, he returned to England and attended the Bracknell Staff College, and in 1948-49 became SPSO at 21 Group HQ, Flying Training Command. In 1950 he returned to flying duties as OC Flying Wing at Brize Norton, and from 1951 to 1953 in a similar post at RAF stations Wyton and Benson consecutively.

With promotion again to Group Captain, Edwards became station commander at RAF Wattisham in 1953-56; before moving to Iraq as commanding officer at RAF Habbaniya until 1958. Promoted to Air Commodore on 1 January 1958, Edwards was appointed Commandant of the Central Fighter Establishment (CFE) at West Raynham, and exactly a year later received a CB in the 1959 New Year's Honours. In March 1960 he was made an ADC to HM Queen Elizabeth, and in January 1962 became Director of Establishments, RAF at Air Ministry. Finally, on 30 September 1963, Hughie Edwards retired from the Royal Air Force.

Returning to Australia, he took up a successful career in business, and in 1974 was knighted as a KCMG, and became Governor of West Australia, a post he was later forced to resign, due to ill-health, on 2 April 1975. Today, in semi-retirement Sir Hughie Edwards VC KCMG CB DSO OBE DFC, continues his connections with his business interests and former comrades in the RAF and RAAF.

Edwards died at his home at Darling Point, New South Wales, Australia on 5 August 1982.

27. James Allen Ward

The son of English parents who had emigrated from Coventry, James Allen – 'Jimmy' – Ward was born on 14 June 1919 at Wanganui, New Zealand, the Dominion's fifth city. Growing up to a lush backdrop of rolling green pastures and thickly-wooded hills and mountains, young Jimmy quickly grew to love his homeland; becoming fascinated with the history and legends of old New Zealand, and later learning something of the Maori tongue and the tribal chants and songs. Naturally attracted to any form of outdoor activity, Ward soon excelled in various sports, including Rugby, tennis and swimming; while his formative years were influenced strongly by the staunch Baptist faith of his parents, thereby being inculcated with a strong sense of responsibility and duty to those around him. As a boy he also developed a keen interest in aero-modelling; a hobby which he pursued throughout adolescence, in addition to a growing interest in forestry.

Educated initially at Wanganui Technical College, Ward decided on an academic career and entered the teachers' training college at Wellington, where a fellow pupil was Edgar Kain, later to achieve fame as 'Cobber' Kain, the RAF's first fighter 'ace' of World War Two. Completing his education at Victoria University College, Jimmy Ward commenced his teaching career at Castle Cliff School, Wanganui in 1939, but the outbreak of war in Europe soon changed his mind and he volunteered to join the Royal New Zealand Air Force that same year.

Accepted for training as a pilot, Ward enlisted on 1 July 1940, on which date he commenced his training at the Levin Initial Training Wing; and on 29 July reported to No 1 Elementary Flying Training School (EFTS) at Taieri, then completed his advanced instruction at Wigram. On 18 January 1941 Jimmy Ward was awarded his pilot's 'wings' and promoted to Sergeant; given a brief spell of embarkation leave, and on 30 January boarded the *Aorangi* to sail to Canada.

Reaching England in early March, Ward was posted to 20 Operational Training Unit at Lossiemouth, Scotland, where he received his final training for operations and was 'crewed' up, prior to joining his first operational unit, 75 Squadron, at Feltwell in Norfolk. Arriving at Feltwell on 13 June 1941, the following night – his 22nd birthday – saw him

257

detailed as second pilot of a Wellington bomber crew raiding Dusseldorf as his 'baptism' of operations.

During the following five weeks Ward participated in five more operational sorties over Germany. In each case he flew as second pilot to Squadron Leader R. P. Widdowson, a freckle-faced Canadian veteran of bombing operations in Wellingtons; learning his 'trade' swiftly before being given his own crew and aircraft to command. Ward's sixth operational sortie with Widdowson was on the night of 3 July in Wellington 1457, a raid on Essen; but four days later Ward and his crew were allotted a new aircraft, Wellington 1c, L7818, coded AA-R, on 7 July. A brief 15-minutes night flying test in the new 'Wimpy' was all the crew could manage, before the ground crews took it over again to prepare for that night's operations.

The target for No 3 Group's Wellingtons on the night of 7/8 July 1941 was Munster, and a total of 41 Wellingtons were detailed for the raid. Of these 75 Squadron was to contribute ten aircraft, including L7818, skippered by Widdowson, with Jimmy Ward as second pilot. The remaining crew of Wimpy 'R' were two fellow 'Kiwis', Sergeant L. A. Lawton, the navigator, and Sergeant A. J. R. Box, the rear air gunner. The wireless operator, Sergeant W. Mason hailed from Lincolnshire; while tucked into the minute front gun turret was Sergeant T. Evans, a Welshman.

At 11.10 pm Widdowson lifted the heavily-laden Wellington off Feltwell's runway and climbed steadily into the night, heading for the target and eventually arrived over Munster without incident. Having completed a successful bombing run, he swung the bomber out of the flak zone and turned for home across Holland – to all intents the operation had been a 'routine' job, successfully carried out, and all thoughts among the crew were directed to the 'home run' out of Europe and across the North Sea back to base. The night was bright and clear as the Wellington droned along at 13,000 feet above the silver-faced Zuider Zee, and Jimmy Ward, standing under the perspex bubble of the astro-dome, could see the Dutch coast fast approaching ahead.

Suddenly, savagely, the placid scene was disrupted as a hail of cannon shells ripped through the bomber from below. Unknowing, they had been stalked for some minutes by a Messerschmitt Bf 110 night fighter, which now began its onslaught by raking the belly of the Wellington. Its aim was deadly accurate, and shells ruptured the bomber's hydraulic lines, causing the bomb doors to flop open, and smashed through Mason's wireless set, and the crew's intercommunication lines.

In the rear turret, the 19-years old Box was hit in the foot by a sliver of shell, but was then startled by the sight of the twin-engined Messer-schmitt's belly directly in front of him as the night fighter banked away from its first attack. Instinctively Box fired all four of his machine guns at pointblank range, and saw the German fall away on its back, pluming smoke in the bright moonlight as it plunged to earth.

As the Wellington flew on, however, evidence of the German's accuracy became all too plain, as a split petrol feed pipe in the starboard engine gushed burning fuel in a five-feet long tongue of flame across the fabric-covered wing. Widdowson, seeing this, turned the bomber on a parallel course with the Dutch coastline below, then yelled for Ward.

Telling him to order the crew to don their parachutes, Widdowson then added, 'And see if you can put out that bloody fire.'

Making his way back into the middle fuselage, Ward passed on his skipper's orders to the other crew men, then with the help of Lawton and Mason, started ripping away the fuselage fabric on the starboard side near the burning engine. Through the gap created, Ward attempted to use a hand extinguisher, but to no avail as the slipstream whipped the liquid away.

Then, quietly and without fuss, Ward picked up a cockpit cover canvas and told Lawton, 'Think I'll hop out with this.'

Lawton immediately argued against the idea, but Ward insisted he was going 'outside', though he agreed at least to clip on a chest pack parachute. Tying a rope from the dinghy around Ward's waist, Lawton helped him remove the astro-dome cover, then assisted Ward as he edged himself through the 30-inch diameter hole in the top of the fuselage; the rope line 'anchored' around Lawton's chest.

As Ward emerged through the dome aperture, the howling 100 mph slipstream lashed against him, but Ward was studying the burning engine, figuring the best way to reach it. First he needed to climb down onto the wing root, three feet below; then he had to reach the engine, another three or four feet out along the wing. Gripping the edge of the astro-dome hole, he lifted one booted foot over the side and kicked a foothold in the fabric skin of the fuselage, and then repeated the process with his other boot. He was now onto the wing root, and lowered himself carefully to lie flat on the wing surface, the cockpit cover clutched firmly under him. His chest pack parachute baulked his attempt to flatten himself against the slipstream gale battering against him, and his only holds were further holes punched through the wing fabric.

Inch by inch, with the parachute hindering him, Ward pulled himself towards the gaping, flaming hole beside the starboard engine; then as the strain of hanging on with only his left hand began to send shafts of pain down his arm, he stuffed the cockpit cover into the flaming gap with his right hand, and held it there until sheer pain made him let go.

The rushing wind immediately began to pluck the cover free, so Ward again reached over and rammed it back into the gaping hole. Only seconds later the slipstream again pulled the cover free and the canvas sheet whisked away. Ward looked at the flames, now gushing out less forcibly. He could do no more, and almost on the point of exhaustion, he began to edge his way back to the fuselage.

With Lawton keeping his 'safety' rope taut, Ward gradually regained the astro-dome aperture and, after great difficulty, managed to get inside the bomber's fuselage again, where he sat dazed and physically exhausted. After the last few minutes of facing into the teeth of a gale-force wind, the utter stillness and relative quiet inside the aircraft were like a tomb.

Lawton went forward and reported to Widdowson, who then turned the bomber's nose out to sea and headed for England. On the way back the engine fire erupted briefly once more, but by now there was little danger of the wing catching fire as most of the surrounding fabric had been burned or torn away. Finally, just after 4.30 am on 8 July, Widdowson set the Wellington down on the airfield at Newmarket. Without flaps or brakes due to the ruptured hydraulics, the bomber settled on the runway and then ran the full length of the airfield before being halted by a boundary hedge, reinforced by a wire fence. Such was the damage to the Wellington that it was categorised as a 'write-off' and never flew again. Widdowson and his crew returned to Feltwell by road, where they told their stories to the Intelligence Officer and then went thankfully to rest and sleep.

As they slept, the squadron commander, Wing Commander C. E. Kay DFC, wrote up his official summary of the night's operations. In a column headed 'Awards recommended' Kay entered Widdowson's name for a DFC; Box's name for a DFM; and under Jimmy Ward's name he wrote 'Victoria Cross.'

Kay's recommendations were fully approved, and on 5 August 1941, the *London Gazette* announced the award of a VC to the shy young New Zealander. At Feltwell the news was received with huge enthusiasm, and the whole station personnel gathered at a special dinner in honour of the popular young 'Kiwi'. Typically, when finally persuaded to make a 'speech', Jimmy Ward confined his remarks to a sincere tribute to the work of the seldom-publicised ground crews of the squadron.

Ward, now skipper of his own crew, flew three more operations over Germany; his tenth sortie being to Brest on the night of 13 September, when he was forced to land back at Honington due to flak damage. Returning to Feltwell on the 14th, Ward was again detailed for operations on 15 September for a raid on Hamburg; one of 12 Wellingtons from 75 Squadron participating.

Leaving Feltwell at 7.45 pm, Ward was at the controls of Wellington 1c, X3205, with an all-NCO crew. High over Hamburg Ward's aircraft was hit repeatedly by accurate flak and burst into flames. Only the observer, Sergeant L. E. Peterson, and the wireless operator, Sergeant H. Watson managed to escape by parachute.

Jimmy Ward, with Sergeants Sloman, Toller and Toothill, died in the flames of their doomed aircraft. Only weeks later did news filter through the channels of the International Red Cross organisation that Jimmy Ward vc and his three friends had been buried in Ohlsdorf Cemetery, Hamburg.

28. Arthur Stewart King Scarf

The lone Blenheim was by all standards of common logic a doomed aircraft. It was beset by a dozen Japanese fighters deep into enemy-occupied territory; its only defence a single hand-operated Lewis machine gun and the skill of its pilot, and he with one arm shattered and mortal wounds in his back. Stubbornly refusing to abandon his mission, and utterly determined to bring his crew back, the pilot eventually succeeded in bringing his bomber to safety and, in near-impossible circumstances, landed without injury to his crew, only to succumb to his dreadful injuries within a few hours. Yet it was to be a further five years before the pilot's superb courage and devotion to his duty was fittingly recognised by the award of a Victoria Cross.

He was Arthur Stewart King Scarf, the 'unknown' VC of the Far East war of 1941. In a period when tales of individual heroism and dogged refusal to surrender to the invading enemy forces were myriad, Scarf's example of utter devotion to duty and intense determination to fight to the very end stands clear as a supreme act of valour.

Arthur Scarf, known to his family as 'John', and to his many friends and acquaintances later as 'Pongo', was born in Wimbledon on 14 June 1913. Educated principally at Kings College, Wimbledon, he gained little distinction academically, though his lack of bookish interest was in no way due to lack of intelligence. A cheerful, gregarious boy who delighted in the sheer joy of living, he channelled most of his energy into physical activities – playing rugby for the school XV with a verve and determination that marked him out as well above average – and a seemingly endless stream of pranks against established authority. The latter 'outlet' for his abundant energy and lively imagination, combined with his complete disinterest in pure academics, led on one occasion to his near-expulsion from the college. On leaving Kings College in 1930, he took up employment in an insurance office, but the cloistered atmosphere soon 'suffocated him' (to use his own expression), and he applied for enlistment in the Royal Navy – an extension of his abiding interest in sailing and 'messing about in boats' generally. Here his patent lack of academic qualifications served to frustrate his naval ambitions and he was rejected. Instead, in January 1936, he applied to join the RAF for pilot training, and was accepted by a discerning interview board whose decision was based mainly on the youngster's obvious potential rather than mere paper qualifications.

For his first three months Scarf underwent initial flying instruction at the AST, Hamble on Avro Cadet biplanes; then progressed to 9 Flying Training School, Thornaby, flying Hawker Hart trainers under the skilled guidance of veteran fliers Squadron Leader D'Arcy Grieg DFC AFC and Flight Lieutenant John Grandy (in later years, Chief of Air Staff, RAF).

His progress under instruction was unspectacular, but steadily improving throughout the course, and he eventually emerged as a competent, reliable pilot possessing a keen intelligent approach to all matters concerned with his job. To cover his fundamentally serious regard for the professional aspects of his 'trade', Scarf often adopted a 'pose' of being slightly baffled by technicalities, and requiring an instructor to repeat any points of instruction – a somewhat mischievous ploy which fooled none of his close friends, but provided much innocent amusement amongst his fellow pupils. Such mild prankishness was never based on malice or bad intentions; but was simply an extension of his naturally buoyant cheerfulness.

On graduation as a pilot on 11 October 1936, Scarf was posted to 9 Squadron at Scampton, Lincolnshire to fly the lumbering Handley Page Heyford bombers with which the unit was then equipped. His stay with 9 Squadron was brief and, after a short detachment to 206(GR) Squadron flying the new monoplane Avro Anson, he moved to 61 Squadron at Hemswell on 20 March 1937, flying Hawker Hind bombers. Just four weeks later, on 18 April, he was one of several pilots posted to Abingdon, Berkshire to form a new unit, 62 Squadron, flying Hinds, which eventually moved base to Cranfield in June 1937. Promoted to Flying Officer, Scarf was immediately detached to Manston in the summer of 1937 for a short navigation course, then rejoined A Flight, 62 Squadron at Cranfield.

With the quickening expansion of the RAF, 62 Squadron soon converted to more modern aircraft, Bristol Blenheim I bombers; the unit's first two examples arrived on 9 February 1938, to the delight of the crews who took quickly to the faster, heavier twin-engined monoplanes and soon became fully operational on the type. As the possibilities of a European war became imminent in the early months of 1939, 62 Squadron was ordered abroad, and in August the squadron left England bound for Singapore via India, with Scarf flying Blenheim I, L1258, JO-B as his 'personal' machine.

Arriving eventually at Tengah airfield, Singapore, 62 Squadron, though technically on 'active service', saw no warlike operations for the first two years of the war, its routine comprising exercises and practice flights simulating war conditions. Scarf took a full part in such 'manoeuvres'; revelling in the mock dogfights and bombing sorties, and indulging his natural prowess and skill in piloting his Blenheim. In February 1941, 62 Squadron changed bases and moved north to Alor Star in the Kedah Province, close to the neutral Siam border. With the Allies' increasing apprehension of Japan's intentions towards Malaya, it was considered highly probable that any Japanese invasion of the Malay Peninsula would come through Siam; thus 62 Squadron was poised as part of the RAF's first-line defences directly in the path of any such incursion.

Then, in December 1941, Japan struck. During the early hours of 8 December (local dateline) Japanese invasion troops beached at Kota Bahru on the eastern coast and, as scattered reports of this assault filtered through to Air Headquarters, five RAF squadrons were detailed for a first-light dawn attack on the invaders. 62 Squadron's Blenheim crews, unable to locate the Japanese in the prevailing rainstorm, flew to Patani and bombed a horde of Japanese invasion barges and landing craft.

The Kota Bahru 'invasion' had been in the nature of a feint attack designed to draw off air opposition from the main landing area centred around Singora and Patani, Siam, where Japanese infantry came ashore 'in parade ground order' without initial opposition. And it should be noted that these operations took place one hour and twenty minutes *before* the infamous air attack on the American naval base at Pearl Harbor.

By noon on 8 December Siam's army had surrendered to the Japanese, and the airfields at Singora and Patani were quickly inhabited by a host of Japanese fighters and bombers for frontline support of the land forces.

At Alor Star 62's Blenheims were in the process of being refuelled and re-armed after their dawn sortie when a formation of about 30 Japanese bombers suddenly appeared and proceeded to bomb the air strip, wrecking many of the squadron's aircraft and leaving only two Blenheims immediately serviceable. It was one of a series of simultaneous raids on RAF bases at Sungei Patani and Butterworth and Penang, and reduced RAF strength by half within thirty minutes of intense and accurate bombing and strafing; though by using impact fragmentation bombs mainly, the Japanese hoped to prevent serious damage to airfield surfaces and thus preserve them for future use.

Working through the day and night nonstop, 62's ground crews managed to patch up a number of the damaged Blenheims to flyable state, and the following day the squadron was ordered to move 45 miles south to Butterworth. With confirmation of Japanese occupation of Singora and Patani airfields, AHQ issued orders for raids on these objectives by 62 Squadron from Butterworth and 34 Squadron from Tengah. The first such attack was undertaken by six aircraft from 34 Squadron (three of their Blenheims being crewed by 60 Squadron personnel) just after noon. Promised an escort of Brewster Buffalo fighters, the Blenheim crews never saw their 'escort' and bombed alone. Three Blenheims were lost and the remaining trio landed at Butterworth. A second raid was detailed for take-off at 5 pm, comprised of 62's remaining Blenheims and the 34 Squadron survivors. It never materialised.

Bombed up and ready for take-off, the first aircraft, Blenheim I, L1134, PT-F, piloted by 'John' Scarf, taxied across the strip and then got airborne and began circuiting the air strip to wait for the other bombers to take to the air. Almost immediately a high-level formation of Japanese bombers swept over Butterworth and its bombs decimated the earthbound Blenheims, caught in the open and totally unprotected.

Helpless to intervene, Scarf could only watch and wait with a slender hope that some surviving aircraft might still join him in the air. There were none left to do so as the Japanese left the scene. In such circumstances Scarf would have been fully justified in abandoning the projected sortie, but his anger and frustration as he witnessed the destruction of his friends and their aircraft solidified into a grim determination to complete his allotted task, whatever the odds.

Accordingly, he set course for the Siam border, heading for Singora airfield some 30 miles into enemy-occupied territory. Flying low along the plain, Scarf skilfully evaded several attacks by roving Japanese fighters; his mid-upper air gunner, Flight Sergeant Cyril Rich, wielding his solitary Lewis machine gun effectively enough to prevent any close assault. As the Blenheim crossed the Siam border the fighters withdrew, probably due to emptying fuel tanks, and Scarf was able to approach his objective without further interference.

As he neared Singora, however, fresh Japanese fighters swept in to attack the lone bomber. Ignoring these, Scarf flew the Blenheim in one steady run across Singora, releasing his bombs, while Rich fired point-blank into the clustered rows of Japanese aircraft, parked (in his words) 'like a row of taxis'. As Scarf completed his bombing run and began to turn for home, two formations of six Japanese fighters each appeared and bore in for a kill.

Flying almost through the treetops and huge limestone outcrops, Scarf jinked the Blenheim from side to side, using every ounce of his considerable skill to evade each fighter onslaught. In the upper turret Rich used a total of 17 drums of ammunition in crisp, accurate bursts to fend off his tormentors. Struck repeatedly by machine gun and cannon fire from ranges of 200 to 1,000 yards, the Blenheim became riddled with hits.

Scarf, strapped immobile in his unarmoured seat, was soon grievously wounded. One burst of fire shattered his left arm (he was left-handed), while other bullets penetrated his seat and smashed into his back. As he slumped forward over the controls with the impact and shock of the bullets, his navigator, Flight Sergeant Freddie 'Paddy' Calder, yelled to Rich to leave his turret and come forward to help. Rich passed an arm around Scarf's chest and held him back in his shattered seat while the still-conscious pilot continued to guide his crippled aircraft south. Finally the fighters left the seemingly doomed bomber to its own fate and flew away north.

Minutes later Scarf saw below him the Alor Star air strip and decided to put down there. It is only conjecture now, but it was highly possible that Scarf realised that his only hope of help lay in the Alor Star hospital, next to the airfield; a thought intensified by the knowledge that his young wife, 'Sally' Lunn was a nurse there.

Married in Penang in April 1941, Elizabeth Scarf had been a regular Army Sister in the QAIMNS who originally arrived in Singapore in September 1940, and soon after her marriage to Scarf she had volunteered for duty at Alor Star as a member (then) of the Colonial Nursing Service, to be near her husband.

Rounding out in preparation for a landing, Scarf, with Rich still supporting him in his seat, and Calder leaning over the pilot to help in holding the control column, the Blenheim came in at 300 feet and lowered flaps and undercarriage alternately, then retracted the wheels – possibly as an indication to those below that there was a wounded man aboard. Gently turning until it was heading north, the bomber began to settle; skimming steadily across the many mud-surround 'walls' of the flooded rice paddy-fields, and finally ploughing through two feet of water-soaked rice and slithering to a stop about 100 yards from the hospital building.

Rich and Calder then tenderly lifted Scarf from his cockpit onto the wing and, oblivious of their petrol-soaked aircraft, all three lit up cigarettes and calmly waited for the hospital personnel now rushing to their aid. An RAF medical officer, Flight Lieutenant Peach, had Scarf transferred to a stretcher and taken immediately into the hospital, accompanied by Rich and Calder. Scarf had received a shot of morphia to ease his pain, but remained fully conscious and, typically, very cheerful. He had lost a great deal of blood and his pulse was feeble and rapid, but as he drank copiously of glucose, the nursing staff managed to steady the pulse and stop the bleeding. The doctors wanted to operate immediately but had doubts whether they could save his smashed left arm, and arranged for an immediate blood transfusion as the first step.

Scarf's wife Sally's blood was found to be compatible and she contributed two pints in the operating theatre. As Scarf was wheeled into the theatre he continued to be cheerful, even exchanging jokes with the nursing staff. Then as Sally left the theatre Scarf squeezed her hand and said, 'Keep smiling, Sal'. No sooner had Scarf's wife gone out than he collapsed and died – due mainly to massive secondary shock and his terribly weakened condition.

In the ensuing chaos and tragedies of the disastrous Malayan campaign most records of the period were either lost or deliberately destroyed, and it was not until 1946 that the full story of Scarf's superb valour was brought to the notice of the RAF authorities. He was immediately recommended for the posthumous award of a Victoria Cross, and this was approved and then gazetted on 21 June 1946; his widow reeciving the award at an investiture on 30 July that year.

Shortly after Scarf's parents contributed a sum of £800 to the RAF to create the Scarf Trophy. Comprising a silver kris, mounted on a wood carving of the outline of the Malay Peninsula, the trophy was for annual award to the Far East Air Force squadron considered most proficient in weaponry.

How many other deeds of individual valour and intense devotion to duty during the dark days of 1941-42 in Malaysia remain unheralded is now impossible to compute or record. Perhaps 'John' Scarf's superlative gallantry and courage may stand not only as a worthy individual example, but as a form of memorial to those unknown men and women of the 'Forgotten War'.

Arthur Stewart King Scarf

[270]   Eugene Esmonde

29. Eugene Esmonde

'I can think of no greater honour, nor a better way of passing into Eternity than in the cause for which the Allies are fighting this war.' Thus wrote Eugene Esmonde in 1940, in a letter to his home in Ireland. It was a simple, deeply sincere expression of the spirit of utter dedication which motivated Esmonde throughout his Service career; the very essence of 'Devotion to duty' which Esmonde epitomised to his last breath. Less than two years after writing those words, Esmonde died in an action still regarded by many as possibly the outstanding example of raw courage and superlative pursuance of duty of the Second World War.

Esmonde's dedicated spirit was bred from generations stretching back into the mists of time to his Norman forbears; a blood line in which was firmly embedded an unwavering allegiance to Roman Catholicism with its indivisible inherited sense of duty and honour, and an inherited Irish tradition of consigning all things English to perdition in the continuing crusade to remain independently Irish. If such a background seems paradoxical in a man willingly undertaking regular service in England's aerial forces, it is merely one of many thousands of examples of truly heroic Irishmen whose independent views on political differences did not prevent them staking their lives in Britain's cause over several centuries.

The son of Doctor John and Eily Esmonde, Eugene Esmonde was born on 1 March 1909, and grew up at Drominagh, the imposing family home above Lough Derg, Tipperary. One of his earliest recollections of Drominagh was the portrait of a great-uncle adorning the drawing room wall, Colonel Thomas Esmonde, who had won a Victoria Cross in the Crimean War. His childhood was spent as one of a large family of children; his father's first marriage having produced three boys and three girls, while his second, to Eily, added another girl and six more boys, one of whom was Eugene, twin brother to James Esmonde.

Educated initially at Wimbledon College and Clongowes Wood, Ireland, Eugene next attended St Peter's College, Freshfield where his suitability for a missionary priesthood was adjudged and, in the event, declined. Still determined to pursue a career which would allow him to travel and broaden his horizons, Esmonde applied for a Short Service Commission (SSC) in the Royal Air Force, and was enlisted on a five years' engagement on 28 December 1928 for pilot training and a commission.

During the five years of his RAF engagement Esmonde served for a period as a fighter pilot with 43 Squadron, and also served for several months with the embryo Fleet Air Arm; but on 28 December 1933 his SSC ended, and Esmonde was transferred to the RAF Reserve for a stipulated four-years' period. At that time Imperial Airways, forerunner to BOAC and the present British Airways, was in the process of expanding its global routes; consequently Esmonde applied for a pilot's post and was quickly accepted into civil aviation.

For the following five years Esmonde flew many of the British Empire air routes, ferrying passengers, mail, and other pay loads to India, Australia and the Far East; piloting both land and sea planes, including Class G flying boats from Hythe and on the Hong Kong-Malaya routes. By 1938 he had accumulated relatively wide experience as a pilot, and had come to be recognised particularly for his highly responsible attitude to his various responsibilities. As such, for example, in July 1938 he was entrusted with delivering the first all-up air mail from Alexandria, Egypt to Brisbane, Australia. In January 1939, however, he received a letter from the Admiralty, offering him a chance to rejoin the Fleet Air Arm ' . . . in a position of responsibility'. It meant a choice between his existing well-paid appointment with Imperial Airways and a problematical future in the FAA. A further communication offered him specifically a commission as a Lieutenant-Commander, FAA with a guarantee of 15 years' regular service and the probability of further engagement thereafter.

Privately happy to return to Service surroundings, Esmonde accepted this offer and re-enlisted on 14 April 1939. By then he had a total of some 6,500 hours flying to his credit. After a few weeks' refresher flying on FAA aircraft and techniques, Esmonde was appointed commander of 754 Squadron, FAA at Lee-on-Solent on 8 May, and on the last day of May was re-appointed in command of 825 Squadron, FAA, on HMS *Kestrel*.

No 825 Squadron had been the first unit to be fully equipped with Fairey Swordfish torpedo aircraft, having exchanged their previous Fairey Seals for the 'Stringbag' (as the Swordfish was universally nicknamed) in July 1936. Of biplane configuration, the Swordfish was an extremely manoeuvrable design, possessing a superlative low-range performance. In the event and despite its antiquity the Swordfish was flown operationally throughout 1939-45 with great distinction. Yet no one could deny the design's utter lack of speed or effective range; its maximum speed with a full war load barely topped 130 mph. The handling qualities in control at such low speeds made the Swordfish ideal for its designated purpose as a carrier-borne torpedo and reconnaissance bomber, but in an aerial conflict where fighter opposition alone could outpace it by a factor of three, the 'Stringbag' was overtly out-dated. In attempting to wage war in an aircraft with 1918 characteristics, the 1939-45 Swordfish air crews of the Fleet Air Arm never failed to display a superb blend of courage and determination far above the ruck, and established a record of solid achievements on a par with the finest deeds of any other similar air crew 'community'.

On taking command of 825 Squadron, Eugene Esmonde quickly set to work to weld his crews into a disciplined, efficient unit. Though small in stature, Esmonde's commanding personality soon inculcated his juniors with a respect seldom accorded to most men. Always immaculate in appearance, Esmonde pervaded an air of constant proficiency and re- sourcefulness, thereby creating complete confidence in any man who followed him; one of the rare men whom men would follow under any circumstances without query.

On 11 July 1940 the squadron was transferred to the aircraft carrier *Furious*, by which time Esmonde had acquired the nickname 'Winkle', though the origin of this soubriquet is still something of a minor mystery. The antithesis of anything flamboyant, Esmonde had, nevertheless, adopted a personal insigne for his own Swordfish – a Crusader's head – alongside the aircraft nose; a symbol of his private dedication to the cause for which he was now fighting. For the next twelve months Esmonde and his crews saw plentiful action at sea, and by the spring of 1941 were part of the air complement of the carrier *Victorious*.

On 23 May Esmonde led his Swordfish crews off the carrier to hunt for the German Atlantic raider *Bismarck*, and just after midnight located his target and attacked. Running a gauntlet of heavy flak, he made the first torpedo drop, and then continued making dummy attacks to help draw the flak away from his crews as each bore into release their 'fish'. One torpedo scored a hit amidships on the *Bismarck*, flooding its main boiler room and causing the loss of 1,000 tons of fuel and oil. Gathering his men behind him, Esmonde then led them back to the carrier through atrocious weather conditions and achieved a safe landing aboard *Victorious*. His skill and courage on this operation were recognised by the award of a Distinguished Service Order on 16 September 1941.*

On 14 June 825 Squadron was transferred to another aircraft carrier,

---

* In the same action, two of Esmonde's brothers, Witham and Esmonde's twin brother James, were aboard separate ships involved in the *Bismarck* episode.

the *Ark Royal*, and was still aboard the *Ark* on 13 November 1941 when the carrier was crippled and finally sank. Esmonde's cool actions that day in ensuring his squadron survived and reached safety led to his being subsequently Mentioned in Despatches; the *London Gazette* citation of 20 January 1942 mentioning particularly Esmonde's 'Courage and devotion to duty.'

At Lee-on-Solent naval air station Esmonde 're-formed' his faithful 825 Squadron as best he could. By 1 January 1942 he commanded a total of six three-man crews and a seventh pilot, to operate a total of six Swordfish. Four of the crews had been with Esmonde on *Ark Royal*, and he was tasked with preparing the unit for further service in northern waters; indeed by the end of January an advance party of personnel had already been sent ahead to Scotland. Then, on 3 February Esmonde was asked if he wished to participate in an Admiralty contingency plan to prevent the break-out from Brest of the German capital ships *Scharnhorst* and *Gneisenau*. Accumulated naval intelligence clearly indicated that these ships were about to move through the English Channel to Baltic ports, where they could then provide a major threat to Allied shipping in the north Atlantic. It was anticipated by the Admiralty that such an 'escape' bid would be undertaken at the next no-moon period – only a week or so away.

Esmonde was well aware that his squadron was well under strength and by no means fully fit for operations as yet, but the proposed plan for a night attack by the Swordfish would at least provide a modicum of relative safety for the antiquated Swordfish in any such sortie. Accordingly Esmonde volunteered 825 Squadron for the mission – code-named Operation Fuller – and on 4 February led his handful of aircraft to the forward airfield at Manston, Kent to stand by for the eventual signal to attack. At Manston he was welcomed by the RAF station commander, Wing Commander Tom Gleave, and for the next few days, despite the snow and ice weather conditions, flew for a few patrols around the southeast coast line to familiarise himself and his crews with the area. On 11 February Esmonde travelled to London to attend an investiture at Buckingham Palace, where he received his DSO award, and then quickly returned to Manston to resume his readiness state for Operation Fuller.

The early morning of 12 February 1942 started as yet another 'routine' stand-by exercise, with Esmonde busy with minor details of equipment for his under-strength unit, and one Swordfish crew taking off mid-morning for a practice flight in the local area. Then Esmonde was called to the telephone in Manston's operations room – to be told that the German ships were already sailing to the mouth of the English Channel –

in broad daylight! Esmonde's plan for an attack under the cover of darkness was now void – it would mean leading his six out-dated biplanes on a sortie in full view of the formidable German defences of heavy guns, flak and a considerable array of Luftwaffe fighter protection.

Having volunteered for the original plan, Esmonde could honourably have withdrawn from such a suicidal mission at this point – no jot of blame or disgrace would have attended such a decision in view of the vastly changed circumstances he would now face. The agony of decision was reflected plainly on Esmonde's face – witnesses in the same room have testified to the greyness which coloured the little man's features as he mentally balanced the lives of his men against the fearful odds of survival.

Then the telephone spoke again; a call from No 11 Fighter Group, promising Esmonde an escort of five fighter squadrons for his mission. The time was noon. This offer swayed Esmonde into deciding to carry out his attack, and he accepted the escort offer, emphasising the need for these fighters to be on time. Then, passing the news to his crews quickly, Esmonde made his way to his aircraft.

His own crew, Lieutenant W. H. Williams (observer) and Leading Airman W. J. Clinton (air gunner) were already aboard Swordfish W5984, 'H' when he reached dispersal; and the other five crews were soon aboard and ready to go. Taxying out to the end of the runway, Esmonde gave one final look at the sky for his still-missing fighter escort, saw none, then waved an arm to the other crews and began his take-off run. It was now 12.25 pm.

Esmonde's hasty revised plan was to attack from 50 feet height, in two sections. In the lead, Esmonde spearheaded three Swordfish in line astern formation; with Sub-Lieutenant B. W. Rose piloting W5983, 'G' as his No 2, followed by Sub-Lieutenant C. M. Kingsmill in W5907, 'L'. The second trio flew in a Vic formation 1,000 yards behind Kingsmill, led by Lieutenant J. C. Thompson in W4523, 'F', with Sub-Lieutenant C. R. Wood in W5985, 'K', and Acting Sub-Lieutenant P. Bligh in W5978, 'M' on either beam.

Each was carrying a single torpedo, and each aircraft's defence against the expected cannon-armed Focke-Wulf and Messerschmitt fighters was a single, hand-operated Lewis machine gun in the rear cockpit. Fully loaded, each Swordfish could only attain a speed of perhaps 85-90 knots – sitting targets for any trained gunner or fighter pilot.

Orbiting Manston for a few minutes, Esmonde scanned the air anxiously, looking for the promised fighter escorts – these were already five minutes late in rendezvous. Overhead a giant black cumulus cloud was forming, as the weather conditions began to deteriorate quickly. Esmonde

led his men to Ramsgate and orbited once more, still waiting for the
tardy fighters; then to his relief, ten Spitfires hove into sight and closed
with the circling Swordfish. Within a minute Esmonde realised that these
were the only fighters around him; less than a quarter of the promised
number. There was now no time to wait any longer, and Esmonde set
course for his objectives, some 23 miles away out in the Channel; about
15 minutes' flying time.

Just ten miles east of Ramsgate the Swordfish met their first opposition
as two flights of Messerschmitt fighters appeared and made a slashing
attack along the line of biplanes.* These were immediately engaged by the
Spitfires and driven north, but were immediately followed by another
20-plus Luftwaffe fighters who bore in from the rear of Esmonde's front
flight and raked the fabric-covered Swordfish with a hail of cannon
shells. Twisting and evading this onslaught, Esmonde's flight refused to
be diverted from their path and continued to head towards the open
Channel area, still determined to reach the main targets.

Then, at 12.50 pm Esmonde sighted the enemy fleet ahead – an awesome array of naval might, with long lines of destroyers screening the
huge battle cruisers, and under an air 'umbrella' of literally hundreds of
Luftwaffe fighters scouring the sky above their naval charges.

Already the German gunners had spotted Esmonde's puny formation
coming in, and opened fire with their long range guns at the oncoming
biplanes, creating a huge splash barrier curtain in front of the aircraft.
Still under close and heavy attack by dozens of German fighters,
Esmonde's front three aircraft continued their attack run, with Esmonde
selecting the second battle cruiser, the *Scharnhorst*, as his target.

In the second Swordfish, its observer, Sub-Lieutenant Edgar Lee saw
Esmonde's aircraft sustain a direct hit from one of the myriad of shells
pouring towards him; the shell ripping away Esmonde's port lower
mainplane outboard of the interplane struts, and at the same moment
saw smoke and flames begin to plume from the Swordfish. Yet Esmonde
still continued his run-in towards the *Scharnhorst*, and at 3,000 yards
range – further than normal torpedo dropping range – the leader was
seen to be preparing to drop his torpedo. Lee watched Esmonde's weapon
slide into the water – then watched horrified as Esmonde's aircraft
enveloped in flames, and still under fighter attack, curved downwards
steeply and crashed into the sea.

Passing over the spot where Esmonde crashed, Rose was hit in the
spine by flak shrapnel. In agony, Rose continued his dropping run against
the *Scharnhorst*, feebly evading the continuing murderously close attacks

* For full details see *Eugene Esmonde, VC, DSO,* by C. Bowyer, W. Kimber, 1983.

by German fighters, released the torpedo, then turned away and eventually ditched his blazing aircraft clear of the German escort screen. The aircraft sank within a minute, but Lee and Rose managed to get into a dinghy, their companion, Leading Airman A. L. Johnson being dead already and sinking with the Swordfish. Nearly two hours later both men were rescued from the sea by a British vessel.

The third aircraft of Esmonde's flight, piloted by Kingsmill, also plunged through the holocaust of bursting shells and fighter assaults. All three crew members were wounded and the Swordfish was ablaze after a hit by a shell which ripped out two cylinders from its engine. Penetrating the outer German screen, Kingsmill got within 1500 yards of the *Scharnhorst*, released his torpedo, swayed out of the attack run and eventually ditched his flaming aircraft in the sea. All three crew men were soon retrieved by a British launch. The fate of the rear Vic formation of Swordfish, led by Thompson, remains unknown to this day.

As the wounded Rose summoned his last dregs of energy to ditch his crippled Swordfish in the Channel, Edgar Lee watched Thompson's flight go overhead, heading through a rain of shells and fighter assaults above the inner screen of destroyers, still on track for their torpedo runs. All three literally disappeared from Lee's sight as they merged with the dense spray clouds of the German heavy guns' splash barrage curtain. None of these three gallant crew was seen again.

Back at Manston that same evening, Edgar Lee, the only unwounded of the five survivors, walked into the Mess in a hushed silence from the many RAF men gathered there. And Manston's commander, Tom Gleave, retired to his office, where he made out a report to his Group commander, Air Vice-Marshal Leigh-Mallory. Gleave completed his report with the words, 'I am of the opinion that Lieutenant-Commander Esmonde is well worthy of the posthumous award of the Victoria Cross'. The five survivors of the epic attack were awarded four DSO's and a CGM; while Gleave's heartfelt recommendation on behalf of Eugene Esmonde was officially approved – a unique decision of a naval officer receiving a posthumous VC on the recommendation of an RAF officer. The investiture took place on St Patrick's Day, 17 March 1942, when Esmonde's mother attended Buckingham Palace in company with two of Eugene's brothers and received the cross from the King.

At the end of April the body of Eugene Esmonde VC DSO, part-supported by a semi-inflated life-jacket, was washed ashore at the mouth of the river Medway, and was taken to Chatham. From neck to waist were a line of bullet holes down his back. He was then buried with full naval honours in Gillingham Cemetery.

Perhaps his finest epitaph was the note in the German War Diary for that fateful day in February 1942 : '. . . the mothball attack of a handful of ancient planes, piloted by men whose bravery surpasses any other action by either side that day.' Or perhaps the personal tribute which Group Captain Tom Gleave paid, 'Those Swordfish crews were courage personified. . .'

30. John Dering Nettleton

In 1919 the former Royal Navy cruiser HMS *Thames* was offered up for private sale, and a South African master mariner, Captain T. B. F. Davis, bought the ship and immediately presented it as a gift to the South African Navy, in memory of his son Howard Leopold Davis who had been killed in the 1914-18 war. After a stormy trip the *Thames* eventually reached Cape Town on 26 March 1921, and on 1 April that same year was re-commissioned as the South African Training Ship (SATS) *General Botha* and permanently anchored in Simon's Bay.

From that date until 13 May 1947, when the *Botha* was towed out of anchorage into the bay and then sunk by the Simonstown's coastal guns, the ship was a training ground for some 2,400 sea cadets. Most of these went on to make long careers in merchant and service navies, but some opted to join the other fighting services. During 1939-45 a total of 83 ex-cadets died in action, while 63 received one or more decorations for gallantry. One such ex-*Botha* boy was Adolph Gysbert 'Sailor' Malan DSO DFC, one of the RAF's greatest fighter pilots of World War Two; while heading the honours list was John Dering Nettleton, RAF bomber pilot and holder of a Victoria Cross.

Born on 28 June 1917 at Nongoma, Natal in South Africa, Nettleton was the grandson of Admiral A. T. D. Nettleton, Paymaster-in-Chief, Royal Navy. Following the family tradition, Nettleton decided his future would be in the navy and, after leaving school he sat the entrance examination for the RN College at Dartmouth, only to fail to gain a pass mark. He then joined the *Botha* as a cadet in 1930 and, on graduation three years later, became 3rd Officer of the merchant *Mattawin* of the Elder Dempster Canadian-South Africa line. After some eighteen months' sea-going experience he returned to Cape Town where he became an apprentice civil engineer to the city's divisional council.

Travelling to England in the autumn of 1938 with his mother for a holiday, Nettleton decided to join the Royal Air Force, and on 6 October began elementary pilot training at No 8 E and RFTS, Reading. Accepted by the RAF for a Short Service Commission, Nettleton was commissioned on 14 December 1938 on the same day as he reported to No 12 FTS, Grantham, and two weeks later transferred to 11 FTS, Shawbury. Graduating as a pilot on 22 July 1939, his first active posting was to

207 Squadron at Cottesmore; followed by another move, to 98 Squadron at Hucknall, on 30 September. At the end of November he joined 185 Squadron at Cottesmore, then an operational training unit for Hampden bomber crews, and continued to serve on instructional units until 26 June 1941, on which date he joined an operational bomber unit, 44 Squadron at Waddington, flying Hampdens over Germany. On 17 July he was promoted to Squadron Leader and for the following five months participated in various bombing sorties over Europe, by day and by night, and being mentioned in despatches in December 1941.

No 44 Squadron – 25 per cent of its crews being men from Rhodesia and South Africa – was selected as the first unit to be equipped with a new, four-engined bomber destined to become the mainstay of Bomber Command in the latter years of the war, the Avro Lancaster; its first three examples arrived on Christmas Eve, 1941. Despite severe snow and icy conditions, 44 Squadron's crews managed to get some practice in with the new bombers, but it was not until 3 March 1942 that the unit flew its first Lancaster war operations – a mining 'drop' in the Heligoland Bight, led by Nettleton in Lancaster L7546, which passed off without incident.

During the following weeks a few isolated bombing sorties were undertaken; meanwhile a second unit converted to Lancasters, 97 Squadron. On 14 April Nettleton flew Lancaster L7578, KM-B on two separate one-hour daylight formation practices, and rumours were circulating at Waddington that 44 Squadron was working up for 'something special'. On 15 April, flying L7578 again, Nettleton led his men on a 'round-Britain' low-level tour which lasted almost 5½ hours – giving further credence to the rumours. Unknown to the 44 Squadron crews, seven Lancasters of 97 Squadron were also practising tight, low-level formation flying.

Finally, on the morning of 17 April 1942, and after Nettleton had given a new Lancaster allocated to him, R5508, KM-B, a brief air test; the Lancaster crews at Waddington were called to the briefing room for an operational sortie. The target was the M.A.N.* diesel engine factory at Augsburg in southern Germany – some 1000 miles across France and Germany, and in broad daylight !

Out on the airfield the ground crews were completing fuelling and arming eight Lancasters of 44 Squadron (one aircraft being simply a reserve standby machine); filling the petrol tanks to their maximum capacity of 2,154 gallons, and hoisting four 1,000lb GP high explosive bombs, fitted with 11-seconds delay detonators, into each aircraft bomb bay. Take-off for the raid was set for mid-afternoon.

* M.A,N. – Maschinenfabrik Augsburg Nürnberg A.G.

At 3.12 pm John Nettleton lifted Lancaster R5508, 'B' off the Waddington runway, followed by six other Lancasters from 44 Squadron. Once all were airborne and beginning to close up in tight formations, the last Lancaster to leave circled and returned to base, being simply a reserve machine to slot into any gap at the start of the sortie. The remaining six aircraft settled into two Vics of three as they drummed low across Lincolnshire heading southwards. In front Nettleton had Warrant Officer G. T. Rhodes in Lanc, L7536 'H' to his left, and Flying Officer J. Garwell DFC DFM in R5510, 'A' to starboard. The second Vic close behind was led by Flight Lieutenant N. Sandford in R5506, 'P', with Warrant Officer J. E. Beckett in L7565, 'V' to port, and Warrant Officer H. V. Crum in L7548, 'T' to starboard.

The six bombers were soon linked up with six more Lancasters from 97 Squadron, based at Woodhall Spa, and led in similar two-Vics formations by Squadron Leader J. S. Sherwood DFC in Lancaster L7573, OF-K.

The rendezvous came over Selsey Bill and all twelve dropped to a mere 50 feet as they thundered across the English Channel. Ahead of them a force of 30 Boston bombers and almost 800 fighters were variously busy bombing and strafing targets away from the bombers' planned route, in the hope of drawing off any Luftwaffe fighters and thereby provide the Lancasters with a safe run across Europe. As the bombers hugged the waves towards the French coast line, Nettleton's front two sections began to draw ahead of Sherwood's formation, flying slightly north of the intended flight path. Sherwood made no attempt to catch up; the briefing had allowed for separate attacks if circumstances decreed such, and Sherwood was highly conscious of the need to preserve fuel on such an extended sortie. Still keeping as low as possible to keep under any radar defences, the twelve aircraft roared across the French coast and headed deep into Germany.

For much of the initial journey across enemy-occupied territory the bombers met no serious opposition from ground defences and none from the Luftwaffe, but as Nettleton's six aircraft – now well ahead of the 97 Squadron formation – skirted the boundary of Beaumont le Roger airfield they ran out of luck. As the bombers appeared a gaggle of Messerschmitt Bf 109's and Focke-Wulf Fw 190's of II Gruppe/Jagdgeschwader 2 'Richthofen' were in various stages of landing after an engagement in the Cherbourg area with some of the diversionary RAF raids. For a moment the Lancaster crews thought they hadn't been spotted, but then several German fighters were seen to snap up their undercarriages and turn quickly in their direction.

Unescorted, at tree-top height, and in broad daylight, the ensuing onslaught could have only one conclusion for the Lancasters. The rear Vic of Nettleton's formation was first to be attacked, and the first Lancaster to go was Beckett's; hit by a hail of cannon shells from Hauptmann Heine Greisert and diving into a clump of trees like a roaring furnace of flames. Next to go was Sandford who was attacked by Feldwebel Bosseckert and had all four engines set afire before exploding in a giant fireball. Then Crum was jumped by Unteroffizier Pohl in his Bf 109, 'Black 7' and had his port wing erupt in flames. Jettisoning his bomb load immediately Crum promptly put the crippled Lancaster down on the ground, as per the pre-agreed briefing instructions. Unbeknown to Crum his crash was recorded in the *Jagdgeschwader*'s 'Game Book' as its 1,000th claimed victory of the war.

The fighters now started attacks on Nettleton's front Vic of three Lancasters. By then they had been joined by Major Oesau, a 100-victory 'ace' officially forbidden to fly more operations, but who had jumped into a fighter and taken off on first sight of the Lancasters, followed by his wing man Oberfeldwebel Edelmann. Oesau selected Rhodes for his victim and closed to within 10 metres (sic) firing all guns and cannon in a withering hail of fire. The Lancaster's port engines both erupted in flames which spread instantly to the starboard motors. The bomber reared abruptly – 'as if in agony' (sic) – stalled harshly, plunged straight down; passing between Nettleton and Garwell in a vertical dive and missing both by mere inches.

By now most of the fighters were forced to withdraw due to lack of fuel, and the two surviving Lancasters, though damaged, continued their journey. Finally reaching the objective both flew straight across the target factory in close formation, released their bombs, and began the run-out. At that moment Garwell's aircraft was hit badly by the alerted ground defences and, pluming smoke and flames, dropped towards the ground as Garwell put the Lancaster down quickly, finally slithering to a halt and saving the lives of all but three of his crew.

Nettleton, now alone, pulled away from the scene and set course for the return journey. By then the evening darkness was closing in, providing a form of protection for the lone bomber as it retraced its path across Germany and France. Behind him Sherwood's six Lancasters were now approaching the target, now well marked by smoke from the initial attack. Going in at rooftop level, virtually in line astern, the first Vic bombed, then *dropped* to street level to get under the flak curtain, and ran out. Sherwood's aircraft was hit and burst into flames; flew straight into the ground and exploded.*

* Astonishingly, Sherwood survived, being shot through his canopy on impact. The rest of his crew perished.

In the second trio, two Lancs were hit on the run-in and both burst into flames. Warrant Officer Mycock DFC in Lancaster, R5513, 'P' – despite his aircraft being 'a ball of fire' (sic) – continued his bombing run but then exploded in the air. The other burning bomber, skippered by Flying Officer E. A. Deverill, completed its bombing run and pulled away, still trailing flames from one engine. The other four, after running the terrifying gauntlet of ground fire, bombed and turned for home, riddled with flak damage but safe. Later, Deverill's Lancaster, the fire extinguished but bearing a ten-foot gash along its fuselage flanks, formated with another 97 Squadron aircraft and came back to base. Of the 12 aircraft which set out seven failed to return; of the 85 men, 49 were 'missing'.

Nettleton eventually landed at Squire's Gate aerodrome, near Blackpool just before 1 am, and telephoned Waddington to report on the mission and ask about the survivors. On 28 April the *London Gazette* announced the award of a Victoria Cross to John Nettleton, and a flock of DFCs, DFMs and a DSO to the other survivors of the raid. Much press propaganda was expounded on the 'vast damage' achieved at Augsburg; though post-war examination of German records show that only 17 of the 1,000lb bombs actually hit part of the engine factory, five of which failed to explode, causing only three per cent of the machine tools in the whole plant to be put out of action. Nettleton was then sent on a six-weeks' tour of the USA, lecturing and inspecting American industrial complexes, and returned to Waddington in June.

On 17 July 1942 he married Section Officer Betty Havelock, WAAF in Lincoln, and was then posted 'internally' to No 44 Conversion Flight at Waddington. In November 1942 Nettleton was detached to 1661 Heavy Conversion Unit, but on 4 January 1943 he was promoted to Wing Commander (acting) as commander of 44 Squadron, and returned to operations.

On the night of 12/13 July 1943, Nettleton was skipper of Lancaster ED331, 'Z' of 44 Squadron, one of 14 aircraft from the unit which set out to raid Turin. Taking off at 10.23 pm Nettleton's Lancaster failed to return. His death was not officially presumed until an announcement made on 23 February 1944 – ironically, on the same day that another notice announced the birth (on 19 February) of the son he never saw, John Dering Nettleton.

31. Leslie Thomas Manser

On the night of 30/31 May 1942, the commander of RAF Bomber Command, Arthur Harris, implemented his long-considered 'Thousand Plan' – despatching at least 1,000 bombers to concentrate their bombing on a single target, the ancient cathedral city of Cologne. In doing so Harris sought to prove to his political masters and the other two Services that his command could undertake the only effective offensive against Hitler's Germanic empire at that period of the war. Apart from the obvious effect on German morale, such an operation, if completed successfully, would (Harris hoped) end the many months of inter-Service wrangling over the capability of his bomber crews to provide a significant contribution to Britain's war effort, and thus nullify the constant 'milking' of Bomber Command's aircraft and crews by other RAF commands.

That night a total of 1,046 bombers, supported on fringe sorties by a further 88 'intruder' aircraft, were initially despatched to Cologne. By dawn on 31 May, 41 bombers had failed to return from the main force; seven more had crashed on return killing most of their crews; and three of the 'intruders' had been lost. One of the 'missing' bomber captains was a slim, handsome youngster who had celebrated his 20th birthday only three weeks before the Cologne raid – Leslie Thomas Manser.

Though young in years, Manser's selfless sacrifice that night displayed a mature sense of responsibility normally associated with the actions of a veteran. And in deliberately forfeiting his own young life in order to save his crew, Manser perpetuated a tradition among all bomber skippers.

The son of T. J. S. Manser, a civil engineer in Post and Telegraphs, Leslie Manser was born on 11 May 1922 in New Delhi, India, and on the family's return to England, attended St Faith's School, Cambridge and Cox's House, Aldenham, Hertfordshire, when his family took up residence in Radlett, Hertfordshire. On leaving school Manser applied to enlist in the Army but was rejected. He next attempted to join the Royal Navy, only to be turned down again. Determined to 'join the war', Manser then applied to join the Royal Air Force and, to his delight, he was enlisted as a potential pilot on 14 August 1940.

Completing his initial training, he was commissioned as a Pilot Officer on 6 May 1941, and six days later went to the No 2 School of Air Navigation, Cranage; then joined No 14 OTU, Cottesmore for final operational training and crewing-up, flying Handley Page Hampden bombers. On 27 August he joined his first operational unit, 50 Squadron, flying Hampdens from Swinderby, and two nights later undertook his first operational sortie as second pilot to Pilot Officer Ford on a bombing raid against Frankfurt.

Flying six more sorties in the following eight weeks, all in Hampdens, Manser was sent to 25 OTU, Finningley on 7 November 1941 for a month; then posted back to 14 OTU, Cottesmore on 9 December as an instructor. Impatient to return to the operational scene, Manser applied to rejoin his squadron but, on 21 March 1942 was sent instead to 420 Squadron at Waddington – a Canadian unit operating Hampdens. His stay with the Canadians was brief, however, and on 3 April he finally rejoined 50 Squadron, now based at Skellingthorpe, Lincolnshire and in the throes of exchanging their obsolescent Hampdens for the new Avro Manchester twin-engined 'heavy' bombers.

Fifty Squadron's first operation with Manchesters was flown on the night of 8 April; a *Nickel* sortie to Paris, dropping a load of propaganda leaflets in place of bombs, in which Manser piloted his first Manchester. He flew a further five sorties during April and May but, like most Manchester captains, had his 'share' of technical troubles with the design's recalcitrant Vulture engines and a host of other mechanical faults and failures which dogged the operational career of the Manchester bomber.

On 6 May Manser was promoted to Flying Officer, by which time he was becoming recognised as a skilful pilot and extremely competent captain. On first acquaintance, Manser's slender figure and 'too-handsome' features tended to give the impression of a 'soft' adolescent, but once airborne Manser's crew quickly realised that this was a completely false impression. As skipper, Manser was quietly-spoken but completely in control; issuing necessary orders and instructions in a firm voice which brooked no argument. Added to his obvious competence in handling a bomber, Manser's qualities quickly established confidence amongst his crew – the first pre-requisite for successful teamwork in the air and, perhaps, eventual survival.

At Skellingthorpe, during the last week of May 1942, rumours were already rife of a forthcoming 'special' operation, though its objective and scope were still guesswork. By the morning of 30 May, fifteen crews from 50 Squadron had been detailed on the night's operations order, but these did not include Manser's crew. Instead, Manser and another squadron pilot were detailed to go to Coningsby and bring back two Manchesters to Skellingthorpe, and then prepare to stand by in readiness for possible last-minute inclusion in the night's task. Manser brought back Manchester

L7301, 'D', an ex-106 Squadron aircraft, and the subsequent air test showed that it was not a particularly good machine. Nevertheless, it was airworthy and therefore included in the night's operational strength.

That evening the Manchester's capacious bomb bay was filled with 1,260 four-pound incendiary bombs, and at one minute after 11 pm Leslie Manser got airborne from Skellingthorpe at the start of his 14th operational sortie. Attempting to climb to the bomber's nominal service ceiling of perhaps 18,000 feet, Manser soon found that 'D-Dog' was aptly named – beyond 7,000 feet with a full bomb load the Manchester's Vulture engines began to overheat.

Accepting the inevitable, Manser might with good conscience have returned to base and abandoned the sortie. Instead he chose to complete his mission, reflecting philosophically that at this much lower height he might well avoid the main flak belt which would be concentrating mainly on the bulk of the bomber force thousands of feet higher up.

As he approached Cologne an hour later, however, the Manchester was picked up by roving searchlights and immediately became the focal point for several flak guns. Manser refused to take evasive action on this crucial stage of his bombing run-in, and held the bomber straight and level as it ran up to the target. Ignoring the increasingly accurate shell fire, Manser continued to hold a rock-steady course until his bomb aimer, Flying Officer Richard Barnes, yelled, 'Bombs gone'.

About to turn away and climb for safety height, Manser almost at once had the controls torn from his hands as a direct hit from the flak punched the Manchester from below, slicing away the rear half of the bomb bay doors and jolting the bomber viciously, peppering the fuselage and wings with a hail of shrapnel slivers.

Instinctively grabbing his control column, Manser pushed it hard forward, diving to get away from the flak and searchlights, and flew through a trelliswork of 20mm cannon tracer shells before finally levelling out in darkness at 800 feet. The fuselage was filled with smoke and flames, and on the intercomm Manser heard his rear gunner, Sergeant B. W. Naylor report that he was wounded. Sergeant Baveystock, the co-pilot, and Pilot Officer Norman Horsley (wireless operator) went aft and checked that the bomb bay was free of its former incendiary load.

Climbing with difficulty to 2,000 feet again, the Manchester wallowed dangerously, hardly controllable, but Manser continued to keep it flying. Then the port engine exploded into a gusher of flames which enveloped the width of the wing, threatening to explode a main petrol tank inside the wing. Coolly, Manser ordered Baveystock to feather the port propeller and operate the internal fire extinguisher. This the second pilot did, but

Leslie Thomas Manser

John Dering Nettleton

Rawdon Hume Middleton

Hugh Gordon Malcolm

the flames seemed just as strong. Still Manser waited calmly for the fire to diminish – and, incredibly, it did.

Setting course hopefully for the emergency forward airfield at Manston, Kent, Manser gave orders to the crew to jettison everything loose or removable – above all things, he had to have height if they were to reach Manston.

Even as the crew began pushing everything loose down through the flare chute, Manser realised that his hope to regain England was remote. The crippled bomber was steadily losing height and he could do little to prevent the slow descent. He therefore gave the order to don parachutes and prepare to abandon aircraft. The front gunner Sergeant A. Mills released the forward escape hatch; while Horsley assisted the wounded Naylor back to the main fuselage side door.

By now the speed of the Manchester was hovering near the stalling point and Manser gave the order to his crew to bale out immediately. Each member obeyed without hesitation, leaving only Baveystock with Manser in the front cockpit. Clipping on his own parachute pack, Baveystock unclipped Manser's pack and tried to clip it onto his skipper's chest harness, but Manser, only too aware that it could only be a matter of seconds before the aircraft would be beyond his control, waved Baveystock away, yelling, 'For God's sake, get out.'

The bomber was now vibrating alarmingly as Baveystock dropped into the nose and dropped through the open front hatch. His parachute had no time to deploy and seconds later the co-pilot plunged straight into about five feet of dyke water.* Overhead the Manchester ploughed into the earth some yards beyond the edge of the dyke and erupted in flames.

By remaining at his failing controls those extra few seconds Leslie Manser had preserved the lives of his crew, but sacrificed his only slim chance of personal survival. The Manchester had crashed three miles east of Bree, a tiny Belgian village close to the Dutch border.

With the exception of the navigator, Barnes, who injured himself when he came to earth and was therefore captured, all other crew members were quickly secreted by the local villagers and two days later were in hiding in Liege. Within the next few weeks these were passed through the 'Comet' underground escapers' system, through Brussels, Paris, St Jean de Luz, over the Pyrenees, and eventually to Gibraltar; from where all were flown back to England. After their interrogation in England, the full story of Leslie Manser's last endeavours to save his crew led to the posthumous award of a Victoria Cross on 20 October 1942.

The little bronze cross was presented to Manser's family at an investi-

* Later, Flight Lieutenant L. Baveystock DSO DFC DFM.

ture on 3 March 1943; but on 31 May 1965, in a small ceremony at RAF
Waddington, attended by most of Manser's crew on that fateful night in
1942; Cyril Manser, Leslie's brother, formally presented the cross on loan
to Wing Commander W. J. Stacey of 50 Squadron – the first occasion on
which the Royal Air Force had been invited to act as custodian for a
Victoria Cross.

32. Rawdon Hume Middleton

Few, if any, of the many thousands of men who fought in the air during the 1939-45 war found anything 'romantic' or 'glorious' in their daily and nightly tasks of killing and destroying; nor did they ever feel 'heroic' about seeing close friends killed or terribly maimed. Yet they returned to the battle because they felt a strong sense of duty, which had to be discharged faithfully and with all the courage at their disposal. To the air crews their foremost duty was to their brother fliers, and this was especially true of the bomber crews. Irrespective of his rank, the first pilot was the captain or 'skipper' of the bomber, and his crew looked to him for the final decision on any matter. He in turn assumed full responsibility for the aircraft and the lives of his crew – a responsibility which weighed heavily upon the shoulders of the many youthful bomber captains, and on many occasions was literally a decision between preserving their own lives or those of their crews. Such a decision had to be made by a young Australian bomber pilot high in the night skies of Italy in the winter of 1942. Unhesitating, he chose to try to save his crew.

Born on 22 July 1916 at Waverley, New South Wales, Rawdon Hume Middleton could trace his ancestors back almost 100 years in Australia to the Reverend G. A. Middleton MA who left Cambridge, England in 1820 and settled in the vast, raw continent; while one member of his family 'tree' was the noted explorer Hamilton Hume, a great-uncle. His father, Francis Rawdon Hume Middleton, was a sheep farmer, and young Middleton and his younger brother Osman grew up in the open ranges of the outback; receiving their academic education at various schools, but mainly at Gilgandra and Dubbo High School. When his father became manager of a sheep farm and grazing property at Leewang, Yarrabandai, near Brogan Gate, 'Ron' Middleton became a jackeroo, working with his father riding the range and shepherding the stock; a tall (nearly six feet), rangy boy with deep brown eyes who seldom indulged in the normal extrovert activities of most youths, but excelled in any form of outdoor sport, particularly cricket and tennis.

On the outbreak of war in Europe Middleton decided he wanted to join the fight against Nazi Germany and eventually achieved this ambition by enlisting in the Royal Australian Air Force (RAAF) on 14 October 1940 at No 2 ITS, Bradfield Park, earmarked for pilot training. Undergoing his initial training at 5 EFTS, Narromine, he completed his instruction in Canada; leaving his homeland on 22 February 1941 and gaining his 'wings' as a Sergeant pilot on 6 June 1941. On 15 September he arrived in Britain and was sent to 23 OTU on 7 October for the final phase of operational training; being promoted to Flight Sergeant on 6 December 1941. Three weeks later, on 1 January 1942, Ron Middleton joined his first operational unit, 7 Squadron RAF, based at Oakington, Cambridgeshire, flying the giant Short Stirling heavy bombers; the first squadron of the RAF to operate Stirlings.

Middleton's initial stay with 7 Squadron was brief and he was soon detached to RAF Waterbeach for a month, from where he was posted to 149 Squadron on 26 February; another Stirling unit, based at Lakenheath, Suffolk. Here Middleton finally commenced his operational flying, gaining early experience as a second pilot on sorties over Germany. At first Middleton, though a painstakingly thorough pilot if unspectacular, appeared a rather sombre character to his fellow crew members, almost melancholic in nature.

This generally gloomy outlook changed significantly after one particular sortie on the night of 6/7 April. Still second pilot, Middleton was detailed to attack Essen, and during the mission the Stirling was attacked by a Messerschmitt Bf 110 night fighter. The German's onslaught did considerable damage to the bomber's starboard wing, rendered one engine useless, and ruptured the hydraulic system; resulting in the undercarriage collapsing as the bomber landed back at base. Surviving this ordeal without injury, Middleton seemed to accept it as his real 'blooding' on operations, and thereafter became more cheerful and sociable.

His eleventh operation on the last night of July, to Dusseldorf, saw him as captain of his own crew for the first time, flying Stirling W7566, 'C-Charlie' as his regular aircraft with 149 Squadron.

On 25 August Middleton and his crew were posted to 7 Squadron, one of the four 'founder-member' units of the newly-created Path Finder Force, and three nights later made Middleton's sixteenth operational sortie, ostensibly to Nuremburg. In the event the mission proved to be something of a fiasco. Bad navigation brought Middleton 100 miles astray from his designated objective and he found himself over Munich instead. Going down to a mere few hundred feet over the city, the Stirling's gunners proceeded to strafe the streets – unaware that the German Führer, Adolf Hitler, was passing through Munich at that moment.

Returning to England, Middleton had an anxious time coping with a bare minimum of fuel, due to the 'diversion' to Munich, and on approaching the English coastline with petrol tanks almost dry, he put the Stirling down immediately at the forward airfield at Manston, Kent. As the giant bomber settled onto the runway all four engines cut – starved of fuel. With no power control it ploughed its way horrendously through a gaggle of Spitfires parked around the runway and finally crashed through the station armoury; losing both wings in the process, before grinding to a halt.

Next day Wing Commander 'Hamish' Mahaddie from 7 Squadron fetched Middleton and his crew back to Oakington, where he gave the Australian a straight choice; if he would exchange his navigator, the crew could stay with the PFF, otherwise it meant the crew would be posted out of PFF. Middleton refused point blank to split up his crew, and consequently on 2 September he returned to 149 Squadron to resume operations with the main bomber force.

His next operation came on 14 September, a bombing sortie to Wilhelmshaven, but due to engine troubles he was forced to return early. By the close of that month he had flown four more sorties; two of them on 'Gardening' missions, sowing sea mines in the Bay of Biscay area. His twenty-third sortie, on 13 October was to Kiel in Stirling W7619, and flak damage forced him to make the return trip with two engines fully feathered. And on 23 October Middleton made his first sortie across the Alps to attack Italy; bombing Genoa in Stirling BF392, and eventually landing back at Manston with only three engines giving power and his petrol tanks almost empty. He returned to Genoa on the night of 7 November; had a 'Gardening' sortie on 10 November; then retraced his path over the Alps to Turin on 20 November – his twenty-eighth operational trip.

By now Middleton's air gunners had already completed their tours of operations (at least thirty sorties), but volunteered to stay with Middleton for the final two trips needed to complete the pilot's tour. On 28 November 1942 Middleton and his crew were briefed for their next sortie – yet another long slog across Europe and over the towering Alps to bomb the Fiat factories at Turin, Italy; just one of 182 bombers to be despatched against this vital objective.

For this operation Middleton was detailed to skipper Stirling BF372, OJ-H, an aircraft he had flown only once before. His crew comprised seven other men. Second pilot was Flight Sergeant Leslie Hyder, an ex-Glasgow student on his fifth operation, and his navigator by now was Flying Officer George Royde. The wireless operator was Pilot Officer Norman Skinner, 31 years old and a former journalist from Scarborough; whilst the flight engineer was a 19 years old ex-Halton aircraft apprentice, Sergeant James Jeffery from Dorset.

The trio of air gunners were all operational veterans. In the front turret was Sergeant John Mackie, a tough Scot hailing from Clackmannanshire, for whom this was to be his 31st sortie; and in the mid-upper turret sat Douglas Cameron, another Scot – ex-gamekeeper and vastly experienced in bomber operations. In the rear turret was Sergeant Harold Gough, an ex-garage mechanic and, like Skinner, from Scarborough; now about to undertake his 33rd operational trip.

Their particular aircraft, 'H-Harry', was by means the best Stirling on the squadron, having already given its ground crew several headaches in the context of maintenance. Now, with a full 8,000lb bomb load, maximum petrol capacity, and the long haul over the Alps to Italy facing him, 'Ron' Middleton knew he would need all his skill and experience, and maybe the usual 'ration' of good luck to accomplish this mission successfully.

At 6.14 pm that evening he lifted the overladen Stirling from Lakenheath's long runway and began coaxing the aircraft to its highest possible ceiling for the journey across Europe. Within an hour it became apparent that H-Harry was living up to its reputation as a 'dog'; eating up precious petrol excessively, its automatic pilot 'George' inoperative, and unable to climb higher than 12,000 feet. Checking fuel states with Jeffery, Middleton was told that they could still make the round trip but with only a minimal margin for safety. The skipper decided to 'press on', at the same time warning Royde that he would need to navigate *through* the Alps which reached 15,000 feet on some peaks and ridges.

There was no moonlight that night and as Middleton entered the French Alpine range he could only steer through the menacing peaks and ridges by spotting snow-covered tips and rifts on either side. The fuel state was still marginal due to unforecast head winds en route, but Middleton was now fully occupied with avoiding disaster by collision as he threaded his path through the mountains.

Tension amongst the crew was momentarily relieved when Mackie in the nose turret quipped drily to Gough in the rear, 'I hope I see the next mountain before you'.

Then Mackie yelled to the pilot, 'Mountain dead ahead.'

Middleton said in frustration, 'We're coming to a dead end', then ordered the bomb doors opened in readiness to jettison the bomb load.

Before he could release the bombs however, Mackie called again, 'It's there. Look. To starboard.'

Through a gap in the mountains he could see the lights of Turin, with pyrotechnic flares from preceding Lancasters already illuminating the target.

'How's the fuel, Jeff?' Middleton asked the flight engineer.

'OK skipper,' came the reply.

'Right, we're going down,' said Middleton, and began weaving gently down towards the city below.

As the Stirling emerged from the mountain range it was immediately engaged by the Italian ground defences, whose guns punched a hole through the Stirling's port wing and splashed shrapnel along the aircraft. Continuing his dive, Middleton levelled out at about 2,000 feet above the city and began his run, at the same time telling Hyder to help him with the controls.

Almost immediately the Stirling was hit again – a direct hit in front of the pilot's windscreen, between Middleton's and Hyder's seats. Hyder received shrapnel in both legs and the side of his head, while Norman Skinner further back was hit in one leg. The windscreen was blasted apart, exposing the pilots to a roaring icy slipstream which created havoc in the cockpit.

In the captain's seat Middleton was injured grievously. A sliver of shrapnel tore through the right side of his face, taking out the eye and leaving the bones of his right temple and cheek exposed. At the same instant other shards of red-hot metal punctured his side, chest and legs. Saying, 'I'm hit', Middleton doubled up under the impact shock and fell forward over the controls. The Stirling dropped its nose and began to dive headlong, continuing to be hit by bullets and shrapnel as it plunged into the flak bursts. Hyder, dazed and in pain, instinctively hauled back on the stiffening controls and finally recovered from the dive at a mere 800 feet.

As he began to pull the aircraft into a climb, Middleton regained consciousness and yelled hoarsely to Hyder, 'Hang on.' Reaching 1500 feet again, the bomb load was released, and then Middleton ordered Hyder back into the fuselage to have his wounds dressed on the rest bunk. Skinner meanwhile remained at his radio, not mentioning his own leg wound; while Gough continued to fire his guns until further flak rendered his turret hydraulics unserviceable.

Mackie came out of his front turret and stood by Middleton, helping to set a compass course away from the fires and flak; noticing as he did so two parachutists floating down below into the pink-red glow of the city. Cameron helped Hyder dress his leg wounds but then Hyder insisted on returning to the cockpit to help Middleton; groping his way forward with his flying suit stained with blood, and more blood bubbling from the outer fringe of his leather oxygen face mask.

Back in the cockpit a 150 mph gale was howling through the shattered windscreen, playing in full force on the huddled figure of Middleton, but the Australian remained conscious and began to organise the return trip. The odds facing him were daunting; at least four hours' flying before reaching the English coast if nothing else happened to the crippled bomber. He considered the alternatives. Rather than face the gaunt Alps again he could set course for North Africa, but the prospect of the extended flight across the Mediterranean did not appeal to the crew. He could also fly to neutral Switzerland, where the crew would be interned in comfort and his wounds could be treated reasonably quickly. He rejected these thoughts, telling his crew, 'I'm going to try to make our coast.'

Getting a course for home from Royde, Middleton then set the rear crew members to lightening the wallowing bomber, and Royde, Jeffery, Skinner, Cameron and Gough began chopping away any part of the internal sections they could shift and dumping the useless weight overboard. Ammunition belts, oxygen bottles, flares, camera, seats, bunk, fire extinguishers – even the sextant was thrown out. By now the moon had risen and the Alps could be clearly seen, bathed in blue-white light.

Royde plugged into the intercomm at one point and asked Middleton, 'Shall we jettison the guns, skipper?'

The crew heard the pilot reply, in noticeably weak tone, 'OK, George. Carry on. But try not to talk to me. It hurts too much when I answer.'

Refusing the offer of a drink of coffee, Middleton remained in his seat, not moving, staring with his remaining eye through the broken windscreen at the moon-bathed mountain peaks around him, edging the Stirling gently northwards. Beside him stood Mackie, helping, comforting; while in the right-hand seat sat Hyder, fighting off recurring bouts of faintness and surging pain.

Finally leaving the mountains behind them the crew settled down for the trip across France, droning on over the sleeping countryside below, with Middleton still immobile in his seat guiding his aircraft steadily despite the agony of his shattered body and the constant loss of blood from his awful wounds. Over southern France the bomber was suddenly coned by several searchlights and, gathering strength from some unplumbed depths, Middleton threw the Stirling into quick evasive manoeuvres and managed to escape from the probing lights. Growing weaker by the minute from blood loss, unending pain, and the waves of secondary shock, and almost blind sitting in the icy blast of the slipstream playing through his windscreen, Middleton remained silent – his mind filled with just one purpose, to get his crew back home safely.

As he finally reached the Channel coastline of France the bomber was yet again under fire from some coastal defences. Middleton once more took evasive action until, through a mist of pain, he could vaguely see the English Channel slipping away beneath him. The only question remaining now was the critical fuel state, and Middleton asked Jeffery for a check. 'No more than five minutes flying, skipper,' came the answer.

The crew began to prepare for ditching in the Channel, but Middleton was still determined to give his crew every possible chance of survival, and pulled the aircraft up to 2,500 feet and headed over Dymchurch village to a point two miles inland, where he turned the Stirling into a parallel course with the coastline and then ordered his crew to bale out.

Hyder, by then semi-conscious and suffering badly from his wounds and exposure, was helped to the escape hatch by Mackie, who put the pilot's hand on his parachute ripcord 'D' handle and then pushed him out.

Royde, Cameron and Gough followed suit through the hatch, then came Skinner, twice wounded in the leg, leaving his radio and clipping on his parachute as Middleton began to head the Stirling's nose out to sea again, rather than risk injury to civilian houses below in any crash-landing.

As Skinner dropped away from the bomber he looked back and saw no more parachutes come out of the bomber as it vanished southwards over the Channel. Minutes later Skinner crashed through the roof of a disused hut, near a farm cottage; safely brought to earth. It is mere conjecture now to describe the final moments of the three men still aboard the Stirling as it nosed seawards.

Both Mackie and Jeffery took to their parachutes shortly after Skinner's exit, and their bodies were recovered the following afternoon by a naval rescue launch. There was no sign of the Stirling or its captain, Ron Middleton; both had dived into the sea at approximately 3 am on 29 November, a few miles off Dymchurch in the English Channel.

On 13 January 1943 the *London Gazette* announced the posthumous award of a Victoria Cross to Middleton; while, unknown to the gallant Australian, official notification was received at RAF Lakenheath of Middleton's promotion to Pilot Officer, effective from 14 November 1942 – just two weeks before his ultimate flight. The surviving members of his crew were each awarded a DFC or DFM according to rank, these being gazetted on 27 January.

Then, on 1 February 1943, the shattered body of Ron Middleton was discovered, washed ashore on Shakespeare Beach, Dover, whence the Channel tides had eventually carried it. The RAF gave him a warrior's funeral. Taken to Mildenhall, Middleton's body lay on a catafalque in the tiny airfield chapel overnight with fellow air crew senior NCO's mounting an all-night vigil. The following morning, 5 February, Rawdon Hume Middleton VC RAAF was buried with full military honours in St John Church cemetery, Beck Row, Mildenhall.

The VC citation compiled by officialdom was unusually lengthy and detailed, but possibly the summary of Middleton's self-sacrifice was best described by an anonymous 'RAF Spokesman' who said of him :

It does not seem possible that even death could have had the heart to seek out and destroy such tenacious, valiant and enduring courage. No man will ever know what force uplifted that tortured body in its last struggle for the lives and liberty of a faithful crew.

Or perhaps his most fitting epitaph is expressed in an extract from Chapter 15 of St John's Gospel, 'Greater love hath no man than this, that he lay down his life for his friends'. . . .

33. Hugh Gordon Malcolm

When the 1919 Trenchard-Churchill Memorandum for the post-1918 permanent Royal Air Force 'created' a school at Halton for the training of aircraft apprentices as the future skilled tradesmen of the Third Service, it also provided for an establishment from which would emerge the future permanently-commissioned officers of the RAF – the RAF College at Cranwell in Lincolnshire; the world's first air academy.

Cranwell, originally a Royal Naval Air Service station titled HMS *Daedalus* which came into being in December 1915, was selected as the site for this new air college, and the first cadet course commenced on 5 February 1920 – a date still commemorated annually as 'Founder's Day'. By September 1939 and the outbreak of World War Two, more than 1,000 cadets had successfully graduated from the RAF College and passed into the Service. During the years 1939-45 a total of 931 ex-Cranwell graduates saw service with the RAF, of whom 326 lost their lives. Overall, ex-cadets were awarded more than 600 decorations for gallantry and superb devotion to duty, including three George Crosses, 82 Distinguished Service Orders, 269 Distinguished Flying Crosses – and one posthumous award of a Victoria Cross to Wing Commander Hugh Gordon Malcolm.

Born at Broughton Ferry, Dundee, Scotland on 2 May 1917, Hugh Malcolm received his early education at Craigflower Preparatory School, Dunfermline and then entered Trinity College, Glenalmond in Perthshire. Deciding to make the Royal Air Force his future career, Malcolm entered Cranwell as a cadet on 9 January 1936, and eventually graduated as a commissioned pilot in December 1937. On 18 December he joined his first unit, 26 Squadron at RAF Catterick, and was immediately detached to the School of Army Co-operation at Old Sarum, Wiltshire for a short course of instruction on his future duties. Rejoining his squadron, he then settled down to the peacetime routine of flying the unit's Westland Lysander aircraft on a variety of air exercises and general training in liaison with nearby army formations.

On 20 May 1939, however, Malcolm's promising career was almost abruptly ended when, while piloting a Lysander in practice for a forthcoming Empire Air Day display at Manchester, he crashed, receiving severe injuries including a fractured skull. For nearly four months

Malcolm became a patient in the Princess Mary Hospital, Halton, where one of his nurses later became his wife Helen. Declared fit for flying again, Malcolm returned to 26 Squadron on 26 September 1939. On 12 July 1940 Malcolm was posted to another Lysander unit, 4 Squadron, based at Linton-on-Ouse; and on 21 September the same year, with promotion to Flight Lieutenant, he moved to Scotland to join 241 Squadron at Inverness, still piloting Lysanders. Yet another posting came on 3 March 1941 when he was sent to join 225 Squadron at Tilshead (later in the year, Thruxton) as B Flight commander and continued flying Lysanders.

In December 1941 Hugh Malcolm was further promoted to Squadron Leader, and in the following month was posted to 17 OTU, but quickly returned to more active service when he joined 18 Squadron at Wattisham as a Flight commander on 13 April. Equipped with Blenheim IV bombers, 18 Squadron was a veteran unit of No 2 Group, RAF, employed in (mainly) constant daylight operations over occupied Europe. Soon after Malcolm joined the squadron the Blenheims came increasingly to be used for night 'intruder' sorties in support of main bombing force raids. An example of such a role was the night 30/31 May 1942 when the first '1,000-bomber' raid, against Cologne, was mounted by Bomber Command. That night 18 Blenheims from 18 Squadron flew intruder sorties against three Luftwaffe air bases, with Malcolm leading seven of these against St Trond airfield. The Blenheim IV aircraft by then, however, was in urgent need of replacement by a more modern design, and on the night of 17/18 August a Blenheim of 18 Squadron completed the ultimate Blenheim sortie within RAF Bomber Command.

A week later the squadron was stood down from operations in order to re-equip and prepare for overseas service, being one of several light bomber units already ear-marked for aerial support of the forthcoming Allied invasion of North Africa – Operation Torch.

Moving from Wattisham to West Raynham on 24 August, 18 Squadron began to receive its 'new' designs, Blenheim V's. The unit also 'received' a new commander, when Hugh Malcolm was promoted to Wing Commander in September and succeeded to the appointment. Leaving 2 Group in October, 18 Squadron then joined three other Blenheim V-equipped units, 13, 114 and 614 Squadrons, in forming 326 Wing, and in early November moved to North Africa, becoming based initially at Blida airfield in Algeria.

The unsuitability of the Blenheim V was amply illustrated on 18 Squadron's first operational sortie in North Africa on 17 November. Leading his squadron, Malcolm attacked Bizerta airfield at low-level, in clear daylight and without fighter escort. After bombing and strafing the target,

Malcolm's formation ran into bad weather conditions and Luftwaffe fighters on the return flight, losing two bombers in an air collision and two others to the German fighters. Returning to Bizerta on 28 November, Malcolm again led his men through a fury of anti-aircraft fire to bomb, then despite the wall of flak being thrown up by ground defences, deliberately led the Blenheims back across the airfield several times to gun-strafe parked aircraft and installations.

On 4 December eleven Blenheim V's of 326 Wing were flown to a forward landing ground at Souk-el-Arba for close support tactical bombing in aid of the army formations in the battle area. At 9.15 am that day six Blenheims, led by Malcolm, took off to search for German troop concentrations or other suitable targets in the Chougui area, and finally located a Luftwaffe landing strip some ten miles north of Chougui. Bombing and strafing this objective, Malcolm led his formation back and landed at Canrobert at noon to refuel before eventually returning to Souk-el-Arba.

Within an hour of landing, Malcolm received a message from the forward Army battle zone, requesting an air operation against the same area he had just attacked. It would mean a daylight attack, over a fiercely contested battle zone, without the benefit of specific fighter cover – the latter could not be organised in the limited time available to Malcolm. Knowing these hazards well, he decided to fly the sortie. The 1st Army had requested the raid, and Malcolm's over-riding priority was his duty to support the hard-pressed infantry.

All eleven Blenheims were detailed for the sortie – a mixed bag from each of the three squadrons of 326 Wing. At 3.15 pm Malcolm led off in Blenheim V, BA875, 'W' of 18 Squadron, with his crew of two, Pilot Officers J. Robb (navigator) and James Grant DFC (wireless operator/air gunner). Behind Malcolm a Blenheim burst its tail wheel and slewed off the dusty strip, out of commission; but the remaining nine became airborne and began to close into tight formation – their only defence if they met any Luftwaffe fighters. Two fighter sweeps of Spitfires from Souk-el-Arba and a third from Bone were airborne ten minutes before the bombers, ostensibly to patrol the Chougui area but the bomber crews were, for all practical purposes, on their own.

Only 20 minutes after leaving a Blenheim of 614 Squadron (BA825, 'J') skippered by Pilot Officer G. W. Sims, developed serious engine trouble and went down to a crash-landing 15 miles east of Souk-el-Arba, though its three-man crew survived the landing without serious injury.

Malcolm now had just eight Blenheims behind him – four from 614 Squadron, and four from 13 Squadron. As the bombers reached the forward fighting zone, German observers signalled their approach to the nearest Luftwaffe airfield, where Gruppen I and II of Jagdgeschwader 2 were alerted and despatched to deal with the bombers. Reaching the target the Blenheims circled to identify their objective, then started to bomb – only to set upon by a horde of Messerschmitt Bf 109 fighters from JG2.

The ensuing five minutes of frantic combat became a massacre of the Blenheims. Oberleutnant Julius Meimberg, who claimed three Blenheims in flames, later described the action thus :

In the afternoon we hear that 12 Bostons* are on their way to Mateur. We sighted these and chased them; the bombers were flying at very low level. All the Bf 109's attacked immediately and one Boston was on the ground in flames already before I had a chance of opening fire. I attack one and it starts to burn at once, losing height and crashing. I then attacked one on the left and, as I am flying in a curve, I can see five already shot down. Several Bf 109's at this time are in quite a crowd behind the Yankees (sic). I then shoot down a third which goes down burning and crashes. I can only fire a little at the fourth I attack as all my ammunition is then gone. The battle only lasted about five minutes.

The massive German fighter opposition – at least 50 fighters – afterwards claimed a total of 12 Allied bombers destroyed but three Blenheims survived the first onslaught and eventually crash-landed within the Allied lines; two of these still with bombs aboard due to the lightning attack above the objective preventing them completing their bombing runs. Of these three crews, four crew members were injured and all three aircraft wrecked, but each crew was salvaged by Allied troops.

One of the last to be shot down (from the scanty evidence available) was Hugh Malcolm's Blenheim, which was seen to crash and erupt in flames some 15 miles west of the target. An infantry officer and two other men arrived at the scene of the crash only minutes later and, despite the intense heat and detonating ammunition, were successful in retrieving the body of James Robb. By then the burning aircraft made it impossible for the gallant soldiers to even attempt to extract Malcolm or Grant.

Hugh Malcolm's cool determination to complete this ill-fated sortie, against all the odds but in his constant endeavour to fulfil his duties, was the culmination of a flying career in which his qualities of courage and

* Meimberg was unfamiliar with Blenheim aircraft, hence the mistaken identity reference here.

leadership had been manifest. Fittingly, he was awarded a posthumous Victoria Cross on 27 April 1943.

Several months later, when Lady Tedder, wife of the Middle East Air Commander-in-Chief, came to open the first of a chain of Service rest and leisure recreation centres in North Africa, she named it the Malcolm Club; a title thereafter applied to the remainder of such clubs throughout the Middle East.

34. William Ellis Newton

The fourth Australian-born airman to be awarded a Victoria Cross, William ('Bill') Newton was nevertheless the only member of the Royal Australian Air Force in an RAAF unit, under RAAF control, to be thus honoured. And it was originally recommended not for a particular act of supreme valour, but for sustained gallantry and devotion to duty over a long period of operational flying.

It is a tragic coincidence that, even as the recommendation for Newton's VC award was about to be forwarded through the normal administrative 'channels', he died in action, still exemplifying the superb courage and determination for which he had come to be renowned amongst his immediate contemporaries. Even the manner of his eventual death, in a 'ceremony' barbaric to occidental minds, was in keeping with the calm courage Newton had always displayed in life – unwavering to the very end.

Born on 8 June 1919 at St Kilda, Victoria, Australia, Newton was the only son of Mrs Minnie Newton, second wife of a dental surgeon, Charles Ellis Newton; though he grew up in the company of two half-brothers, John and Lindsay, and a half-sister Phyllis, the children of his father's first marriage. Educated finally at Melbourne Grammar School, Bill Newton grew into a tall, handsome boy, who revelled in all forms of sport or athletic pursuit and variously represented his school in cricket, football and swimming, apart from becoming a senior prefect and a sergeant in the school's cadet corps. On leaving school his sporting activities continued; he was selected as a member of the Victoria 2nd XI cricket team, but his immediate ambition was to join the RAAF and learn to fly. Deferring to his mother's wishes, however, he first entered employment as a materials warehouseman with a cotton and silk merchant firm in Melbourne, and was soon 'marked' for future executive promotion such was his diligence in his work.

On 5 February 1940 Newton was called for military service in the RAAF and sent to No 1 EFTS, Parafield, Victoria for elementary aircrew ground instruction; and on 6 May posted to 21 Squadron, Laverton, Victoria for basic flying instruction. Commissioned as a Pilot Officer on 28 June 1940, Newton completed his advanced training at No 1 SFTS, Point Cook, Victoria by 9 September, on which date – to his personal

William Ellis Newton

Leonard Henry Trent

dismay – he was posted to CFS, Camden, New South Wales for further training as a flying instructor, such had been his obvious skill as a pilot. On 10 December 1940, accordingly, Newton reported to No 2 SFTS, Wagga, New South Wales to commence a tour of duty as an instructor, teaching novitiate pilots, and on 28 December was promoted to Flying Officer.

For the following ten months Newton continued his instructional duties conscientiously, but his single purpose was to join a front line squadron for operations, and he forwarded several applications to this effect – all without success. On 5 November 1941 he was posted to No 5 SFTS, Uranquinty, NSW – again as an instructor – and began to despair of ever seeing operational service. Then his hopes were raised when, on 4 February 1942, he was sent on a navigation and reconnaissance course at GRS, Laverton, Victoria; and then moved to an Operational Training Unit (OTU) for a conversion course to Lockhead Hudson bombers on 13 March. His further promotion to Flight Lieutenant came on 1 April; then, on 9 May 1942, he finally achieved his ambition when he was posted to an operational unit, 22 Squadron RAAF. The squadron then was still based in Australia, in the process of working up on new aircraft; Douglas Boston attack bombers originally intended for the Dutch Air Service but diverted to the RAAF and sent to 22 Squadron to replace their out-dated Wirraway aircraft.

With the arrival of the Bostons, the squadron was virtually re-established in personnel too, and Newton was but one of several pilots posted in from non-operational posts to bring the unit up to operational strength. The first Bostons to arrive posed many problems for their Australian air and ground crews – all maintenance and flying hand books were printed in Dutch only; while tools and spare parts were non-existent. Nevertheless, the crews were delighted with the Boston and, on the simple principle that problems were merely things to overcome, proceeded to familiarise themselves by dint of sheer practical experience – literally flying by 'the seat of their pants'. The common task soon welded the air and ground crews into a fighting team, dedicated to the cause of efficiency and effectiveness. Newton, displaying his normal meticulous approach to any task undertaken, soon mastered the Boston, and quickly showed his proficency in handling the bomber.

In early November 1942, the Bostons flew northwards from the mainland to Port Moresby, New Guinea; there to join the RAAF's No 9 Operational Group, and becoming based at Ward's Field which they shared with 30 Squadron RAAF's Beaufighters. 22's role was defined as 'intruder' – the RAAF interpretation of ground attack bombing and strafing – but early on the squadron suffered the loss of nine aircrew in three separate Boston sorties – all caused by the detonation of the aircraft's bomb loads in the air – an inauspicious beginning. The early operations for 22 Squadron were mainly concerned with attempting to prevent the Japanese establishing a beach-head in the Buna-Gona area of Oro Bay, New Guinea. It was a period in Allied fortunes when air supremacy was inexorably being wrested from the Japanese, but in which the Nipponese naval strength was still in a very strong position in the South Pacific region.

By December 1942 the Japanese land forces were concentrated along the northern coastline of Papua, fiercely resisting all Allied attempts to dislodge them. 22 Squadron, along with its fellow Australian and USAF units, was almost continuously engaged in bombing and strafing raids in the zone; always meeting heavy and accurate opposition from well-sited Japanese anti-aircraft batteries, and having to run the gauntlet of fire each time they set out.

In the event, by late January 1943, the only main Japanese positions still held in any strength lay along the coastline of the Huon Gulf, notably at Lae. This foothold in New Guinea the Japanese were determined to retain and in late February assembled a large convoy of seaborne troops and material, intent on reinforcing Lae. Allied intelligence soon learned of this and, when the 16-ship convoy, carrying almost 9,000 men, finally left Rabaul for Lae in the early hours of 1 March, the Allied air units were preparing to meet it.

At dawn on 2 March, six Bostons from 22 Squadron, including Newton, swept across Lae airfield, strafing, bombing, and putting the strip out of action temporarily, thus preventing its Japanese aircraft operating in defence of the approaching convoy. The convoy was soon bombed and devastated by Australian and American aircraft, losing 12 ships and approximately a third of the 9,000 personnel aboard; an action thereafter-titled the Battle of the Bismarck Sea.

Immediately following this Allied triumph, 22's Bostons became heavily engaged in attacking the Japanese remaining bases in New Guinea, particularly Lae and Salamaua. In these sorties, flown at tree-top height through veritable curtains of highly accurate ground fire, the Boston crews bombed and gunned every suitable target they could find; paying a penalty of shell-tattered aircraft on almost every sortie.

Bill Newton, usually wearing a soft-top cricket hat, took part in most of these hazardous operations, and became well-known for his refusal to be deterred by ground fire; always going straight for any designated objective irrespective of the opposition being thrown up at him. By 16

March Newton had accumulated an operational tally of 50 sorties during his service with 22 Squadron; and his 51st on that date brought him close to death.

Taking off in Boston A28-15, with Flight Sergeant John Lyon and Sergeant B. G. Eastwood as crew, Newton attacked along the Salamaua isthmus; his bombs and guns setting fire to his target. Jinking through the wall of ground-fire on the run-out the Boston was riddled by shells, damaging both wings, puncturing fuel tanks, and seriously damaging one engine. Newton could easily have flown to a forward landing strip at Dobodura, less than forty miles away and occasionally used for refuelling by the Allied bombers, rather than face a 180-miles flight in a crippled aircraft back to base. Newton, however, knew that the squadron needed his aircraft – any mishap in landing at Dobodura might mean the complete loss to the squadron of a valuable machine. Accordingly, he struggled back to Ward's Field and accomplished a safe landing.

The damage to the Boston was so widespread that it necessitated changing both wings, both engines, both propellers, new fuel tanks, myriad minor repairs and almost 100 temporary patches to the airframe. On climbing out of the Boston, Newton, with a wide grin, remarked to his Sergeant fitter, 'You blokes like problems, so here's a beaut for you.' This sortie particularly, in addition to his previous 50 operational sorties, led his squadron commander to make out a recommendation to higher authority that Newton should be awarded a VC.

At this period 22 Squadron possessed only a dozen Boston aircraft, at least three of which were usually 'non-operational' at any given time; hence the unit had devised a system whereby all available aircraft were flown on alternate days by each of the two flights. Thus it was not until 18 March that Newton's name again appeared on the operations list. Allotted Boston A28-3, DU-Y, with his usual crew of Lyon and Eastwood, he was detailed to repeat the raid of 16 March by again attacking Salamaua.

Sweeping in at less than 50 feet height, Newton bombed a single building, only yards away from an anti-aircraft battery, but as he lifted over the target the ground defences scored several hits on his Boston, setting fire to one engine and raking its fuselage and wings. The following aircraft saw Newton turn away and head for the shore line, where it flew parallel to the beach and finally ditched in the sea – clearly Newton was attempting to provide himself and especially his two crew members with the best available chance of survival. Only two men were seen to leave the sinking Boston and swim towards the beach. These were, in fact, Newton and Lyon; Eastwood presumably drowned or was already dead. The two survivors reached the shore but were soon captured by troops of the Japanese No 5 'Sasebo' Special Naval Landing Force, and both were transported to Lae for intensive interrogation.

For the next ten days Newton and Lyon suffered in their interrogators' hands and then, on 29 March, John Lyon was summarily executed by being bayonetted in the back.* Newton was taken back to Salamaua where he was handed over as a 'prize' to his original captors, and on 29 March 1943, as dusk was falling, Newton, his hands bound, was led to the perimeter of a large bomb crater at Kila Point. Here, Naval Sub-Lieutenant Komai drew his favourite Osamune sword and, with one stroke, beheaded his prisoner. The Japanese guards then buried Newton's body in the crater.

On the day that William Newton died the RAAF, unknowing of his true fate, posted him as 'Missing, believed dead'; based partly on the evidence reported by other Boston crews accompanying Newton on 18 March, who said that the shot-down Boston's pilot escape hatch was not jettisoned and there was no sign of a dinghy. From this it had been deduced that Newton had died in the aircraft. The details of Newton's final flight were added to the existing recommendation for a Victoria Cross, and on 19 October 1943 the *London Gazette* announced the posthumous award of a VC to Bill Newton.

On 30 November 1945, Newton's mother received his cross from the hands of HRH The Duke of Gloucester in a ceremony at Melbourne; and eventually presented her son's awards to the Australian War Memorial in Canberra.

Evidence of the manner of Newton's execution was later discovered amongst captured Japanese documents; in particular the personal diary of one Japanese soldier who was a witness. After the war an official investigation into all war crimes committed by the Japanese reported the discovery and identification of Newton's crater grave, and the body was re-interred in Salamaua Military Cemetery. Newton's executioner, Komai, was killed in action in the Philippines area later in the war; while Rear Admiral Fujita, Japanese naval commander in the Lae-Salauma area who authorised Newton's killing, committed suicide by cutting his own throat at the close of hostilities rather than stand trial for war crimes.

* Lyon, though an Australian citizen, was originally born in Glasgow, Scotland.

35. Leonard Henry Trent

Second of three New Zealand airmen to be awarded a Victoria Cross*, Leonard('Len') Trent was born at Nelson, New Zealand on 14 April 1915. Educated principally at Nelson College, he matriculated in 1933 and began employment in commerce. In January 1937, however, he joined the Royal New Zealand Air Force, a Service which though bearing this title since 1934, only became a separate entity from Army administration and control on 1 April 1937. Thus Trent was amongst the first batch of future pilots for the RNZAF; trained at Wigram – one of only two air stations then existing – on Vickers Vildebeest biplane bombers.

The first Chief of Air Staff for the new Service was an RAF officer 'on loan', Group Captain Ralph Cochrane, later to achieve fame as commander of RAF Bomber Command's 5 Group during World War Two; and his appointment reflected the close liaison between the two air Services. Exemplifying this liaison was the implementation of a scheme originally proposed and agreed in 1926 during the Imperial Conference whereby RAF and RNZAF officers were attached to each other's Service for extended training and experience; and under this 'exchange' arrangement Trent was attached to the RAF in England in July 1938.

By the outbreak of war Trent was serving with 15 Squadron, flying Fairey Battle bombers, and on 2 September 1939 was one of the pilots who flew to France under Operation Panther – the transfer of the Advanced Air Striking Force (AASF) intended as a deterrent to German air assault on France.

Based initially at Bethenville, 15 Squadron flew its first mission, a reconnaissance, on 6 September, and five days later took up 'residence' at Vraux, near Chalons. Trent flew just one sortie in France – an armed reconnaissance of the Siegfried Line of fortifications from 20,000 feet – during which he and his crew became anoxic through lack of oxygen and eventually had to abandon the sortie. By 10 December 1939 the squadron had returned to England where, based at Wyton, it exchanged its out-dated Battles for Bristol Blenheim IV bombers and commenced conversion training. By May 1940, when German forces invaded the Low Countries and instigated their *blitzkrieg* advance through Belgium,

* Second in the context of action date; though third in terms of actual award date.

Holland and France, the squadron was on permanent standby for bombing operations over the Continent.

During the following two months the Blenheim crews, including
Leonard Trent, played their full part in the hopeless attempts to stem
the German advance, losing most of their existing aircraft and crews and
some of the replacements hastily sent to the unit. By late June, and the
collapse of France, 15 Squadron began a series of raids against German-
occupied airfields and strategic targets in Germany; but Trent left the
squadron on 1 July with an appointment as a flying instructor at 17 OTU,
Upwood. Here his ostensible 'rest' tour from operational flying included
routine 'circuits and bumps' instruction of embryo crews in Avro Ansons
and Blenheims; but once, during take-off in a Douglas Boston for a
familiarisation flight, Trent saw his starboard engine burst into flames as
he became airborne. Making a quick circuit of the airfield, he brought the
Boston in again, its wing a mass of flames, and achieved a safe landing.
His skill on this occasion brought him a Commendation from his Air
Officer Commanding; while later in July he was awarded a DFC for
his tour of operations with 15 squadron.

Completing his tour as an instructor, Trent was promoted to Squadron
Leader and, on 9 March 1942, posted to Headquarters, No 2 Group,
Bomber Command as Operations Officer; but his wish to return to actual
operational flying was granted five months later when, on 20 August, he
joined 487 Squadron at Feltwell, Norfolk with the appointment as B
Flight commander. 487 was designated as a New Zealand squadron, with
a large proportion of its crews of 'Kiwi' origin, and had been officially
formed on 15 August as one of three units to operate the new Lockheed
Ventura bombers. On 16 September the squadron received its first three
Venturas and by 8 October had nine on strength.

Its first major operation came on 6 December 1942, when the squadron's Venturas formed part of nearly 100 Venturas, Bostons and
Mosquitos sent to bomb the Philips Radio factory at Eindhoven. The
complete formation for this low-level attack – Operation Oyster – was
led by Wing Commander J. E. Pelly-Fry of 88 Squadron, behind whom
came two Mosquito formations led by Wing Commander Hughie
Edwards vc dfc, and, in a rear formation, 487 Squadron's Venturas,
including Trent. In terms of accurate bombing and destruction, the
operation was most successful, but the intensive opposition from ground-
fire and other causes led to four Bostons, one Mosquito and nine Venturas
being lost, while another 20 aircraft (mostly Venturas) suffered varying
degrees of damage.

For the following three weeks bad weather conditions nullified operations, and it was not until 22 January 1943 that 487 Squadron re-commenced bombing sorties over Europe. By the beginning of May Trent had completed a total of 23 operational sorties, and had been offered the chance of attending a Staff College course; a necessary pre-requisite to further promotion for any regular-serving officer. Trent declined the offer, preferring to remain on operations and being aware that he might soon succeed to the command of 487 Squadron. At the beginning of April the squadron had moved base to Methwold, some three miles from Feltwell; settling in to its new quarters quickly and resuming bombing operations on 4 April.

A bombing raid against the Royal Dutch Steel Works at Ijmuiden on 2 May by 487's sister Ventura squadron, 464, had achieved only modest success, and it was decided by 2 Group headquarters to repeat the attack the following day, 3 May 1943, using just six Douglas Boston IIIa's of 107 Squadron in a low-level attack aimed at the heart of the steel works. In conjunction with this sortie, and as part-diversion for the expected stiff Luftwaffe resistance, 14 crews of 487 Squadron were briefed for a near-simultaneous attack on Amsterdam power station; heavily escorted in three groups by nine squadrons of Spitfires and Mustang fighters.

The New Zealand bomber crews assembled for briefing just after midday and were told that the strike against Amsterdam was also intended as encouragement for the Dutch Resistance underground movement, and Dutch workers generally who at this time were organising labour strikes in defiance of their Nazi overlords. The day was a perfect summer's day of sunshine and blue skies – perfect flying weather. The 487 crews had originally been briefed in the early morning for a raid on Flushing docks and, indeed, had been on the point of clambering into their fully loaded aircraft when this operation was suddenly cancelled and the crews sent back for early lunch and a new briefing for the fresh target, Amsterdam.

In the event 12 Venturas were detailed for the new target, in two formations of six aircraft, led by Trent, who had tossed a coin with the squadron commander, Wing Commander G. J. Grindell, for the privilege of leading the operation. Piloting Ventura AJ209, EG-V, with Flight Lieutenant V. Phillips as navigator, Flying Officer Roy D. C. Thomas as wireless operator and Sergeant W. Trenery as mid-upper gunner; Trent led the first six Venturas off Methwold's runway just after 4.30 pm, but as the aircraft formed into two formations, Sergeant Barker in Ventura 'Q' had his escape hatch blown away and was forced to abort the mission.

From Coltishall the close support Spitfire squadrons soon joined Trent's men, stationing themselves a few hundred yards away on each beam, and the whole formation set course for Holland, flying at sea-level to keep

under the German radar warning network. Unbeknown to the bomber
crews, two events had already sealed their fate. Two Spitfire squadrons,
122 and 453, had set off earlier to create a diversion and 'draw the teeth'
of the Luftwaffe away from the bomber route, but these units, instead of
approaching the Continent at sea level, had climbed high at the beginning
and consequently alerted the Luftwaffe fighter defences.

The second event could not have been foreseen. On this same day the
German Governor of Holland had decided to visit Haarlem, a town only
five miles from the bombers' flight path, and a large force of German
fighters had already assembled to provide wide air cover over the Haarlem
area. The early warning provided by 122 and 453 Squadrons of an
impending Allied air raid merely intensified German apprehension of an
attack against Haarlem, resulting in yet more fighters being alerted and
airborne by the time Trent's Venturas were within striking range of the
Dutch coast. In all, some 70 Focke-Wulf Fw 190's and Messerschmitt Bf
109's were, in effect, lying in ambush for the approaching bombers and
their escorts.

Meanwhile Trent's eleven Venturas spotted the Dutch coast ahead and
began their pre-planned climb to bombing height at 12,000 feet. Trent,
as was his practice, donned a steel helmet over his flying helmet – a
custom which though regarded on the squadron as a mild eccentricity on
Trent's part was based on the New Zealander's past experience in France
in 1940. The Spitfire escorts moved out to positions 500 feet above and
500 yards out on each quarter as pre-arranged.

Theoretically, Trent, whose Ventura had been specially fitted with a
VHF radio set for voice liaison with the escort, should have been warned
of any Luftwaffe interceptors; but the VHF reception was blanked out
by the surrounding bombers. Thus, Trent's first warning of German
fighters came from Roy Thomas, in the astro-dome, who shouted, 'Here's
a whole shower of fighters coming down out of the sun – they may be
Spitfires . . . Hell's teeth, they're 190's and 109's! Watch 'em, Tren (to
the gunner in the mid-upper turret).'

Ordering the following Venturas to close up into one formation, Trent
doggedly carried on towards his objective Amsterdam, only ten minutes
flying time away. The Focke-Wulfs set upon the Spitfire escorts, separat-
ing these from the bombers, and a sprawling, wheeling dogfight ensued;
meanwhile some 30 Messerschmitt Bf 109's bore in at the rear and flanks
of the Venturas.

One of the first victims was Ventura AE916, 'C', piloted by Flight
Lieutenant A. V. Duffill, deputy leader of the bombers. With both engines
on fire, gun turret smashed, hydraulics ruptured, and two wounded crew

men, Duffill was given no alternative but to turn for home. Two other Venturas turned to follow him, but were quickly shot down.

By the time Trent was approaching Haarlem, twisting and evading every onslaught from the Messerschmitts but always returning to his bombing course, a further three Venturas were shot out of the formation one by one. Two more soon fell away, shattered by the hail of cannon shells, leaving Trent and two others to run-in to Amsterdam. As the fighters bore in yet again, this time from Trent's starboard beam, one Bf 109 made a fatal mistake by pulling round fully in front of Trent, banked in front of the Ventura's nose at merely 100 yards' range.

Trent immediately pressed his firing button for the pilot's nose battery of two .303 and two .50 machine guns; the Messerschmitt rocked its wings, then fell away upside down and eventually dived into the earth at full bore. A minute later Trent's No 3 pulled out of formation, its port engine pluming flames as it headed downwards, leaving Trent and one other Ventura to complete the final bombing run as the power house target came into the bomb aimers' view.

Concentrating solely on his instrument panel, listening to Phillips' instructions for the last seconds of his bombing run, Trent ordered Thomas to stop giving him evasive action instructions; then as Phillips yelled, 'Bombs gone', looked up from his panel and realised that the remaining Ventura had also disappeared.

Reaching for the bomb doors lever to close these, Trent had decided to go down low as his only slender hope of survival; but at that moment an explosion in the aircraft blasted the flying controls out of Trent's hands. Waggling the control column and kicking the rudder bars, Trent realised that all control had gone, though both engines were still operating smoothly.

Shouting to the crew to abandon the aircraft, Trent tried his controls just once more as the navigator came past him and disappeared into the rear fuselage. Then the uncontrollable Ventura reared up violently, stalled, fell off upside down and began to spin rapidly. Jettisoning his escape hatch above his head, Trent fought against the centrifugal forces trying to pin him to his seat, and then the aircraft blew up; ejecting Trent into space at 7,000 feet.

Tumbling down with his hand on the parachute ripcord D-ring, Trent deliberately delayed operating his parachute until he reached some 3,000 feet. As he floated down a mini-rain of jagged metal portions of his aircraft fell past him* and he finally landed heavily in a ploughed field on

* Trent's Ventura crashed at Kometen Polder, near the Fokker Works, at 6 pm, just north-west of his target.

the outskirts of Amsterdam's suburban area. Within minutes Trent was captured by German soldiers, and after cursory first aid treatment for a minor scalp wound, was about to be driven away when he was greeted by his navigator – the only other survivor of his crew.

After several weeks of interrogation, including two weeks of solitary confinement, Trent was eventually transferred to a regular officers' prisoner of war camp; going to Stalag Luft III, a camp for aircrew prisoners. Not content to 'sit out the war' as an unbidden 'guest' of Germany, Trent soon joined the prisoners' master organisation for escaping, and when, under the determined leadership of Roger Bushell*, plans were laid well in advance for a mass escape from Stalag Luft III by tunnels under the outer perimeter wire fences, Trent became one of the helpers and took responsibility for all security matters.

Then, on the night of 24 March 1944, the mass escape commenced. Just before 5 am the following morning Trent emerged from the tunnel exit hole, crawled clear of the hole and was about to dash for the nearby shelter of trees, when a German sentry on his patrol beat appeared. Lying still in the snow, Trent had the nerve-racking experience of having the sentry actually step over him, then stop when he spotted another escaper. The mass escape was thus discovered, and Trent was taken back into custody. Ironically, his discovery may well have saved his life, because of the 76 men who had escaped that night, all but three were soon re-captured and, of these, 50 were deliberately murdered by the Germans on a direct order from Hitler.

Officially transferred back to the RNZAF in June 1944, Trent was eventually repatriated to England after the German surrender in May 1945. Only then did the full story of the disastrous Ventura bombing raid of May 1943 become known, and on 1 March 1946, Leonard Trent was awarded a Victoria Cross for his determined leadership and devotion to duty.

Granted a permanent commission in the postwar Royal Air Force, Trent pursued a normal career series of postings and appointments; being Chief Flying Instructor at Oakington in the early 1950's, and becoming commander of the re-formed 214 Squadron at Marham in March 1956, flying Vickers Valiant V-bombers, which participated in the Suez Crisis operations later that year. On 1/2 September 1956, Trent piloted a Valiant non-stop from Lowring Base, USAF, Maine to RAF Marham – the first non-stop Atlantic flight by a V-bomber. On 1 July 1959, with promotion to Group Captain, Trent became station commander of RAF

* Squadron Leader R. Bushell, former 601 Squadron, AAF and OC 92 Squadron when originally captured in May 1940.

Wittering; was appointed ADC to HM The Queen in 1962; and during the next three years was attached to the British Defence Staff in the USA, and the British Embassy in Washington, USA. Finally, in April 1965, Leonard Trent retired from the RAF and returned to his native New Zealand.

Trent died in the North Shore Hospital, Auckland, New Zealand on 19 May 1986.

36. Guy Penrose Gibson

With the possible exception of Leonard Cheshire, no air VC is probably better known by name to the public than Guy Gibson. Books, films, feature articles and a myriad of references have appeared over the past 35 years to the exploit which brought Gibson the supreme award so deservedly. Yet little, relatively, has been published of his long operational career before May 1943 – a fighting record in which he served as a bomber and fighter pilot, and was awarded four gallantry medals for his outstanding prowess.

At the time of his death in action Guy Gibson had flown an overall total of 177 operational sorties; 76 of these as a bomber pilot and the remainder in fighters. Few, if any, operational pilots of the RAF during 1939-45 could match such an extended tally of missions. Even with such a prodigious number of operational flights, Gibson was never content with his various non-operational postings and duties, and constantly sought to return to the 'sharp end' of the war; a quest which eventually led to his death.

Born on 12 August 1918 at Simla, India, Gibson was the son of Nora and A. J. Gibson, and whilst still a baby was brought to England to live in Folkestone, Kent. Here he attended the St George's Preparatory School before becoming a pupil at St Edward's School at Oxford. Although no more than average in academics, young Guy was best remembered at school for his sporting activities and, particularly his 'very determined character'. On leaving school he decided he wanted to learn to fly and, in 1935, applied to Vickers Aviation for a job as a test pilot, but was tactfully advised to join the RAF to gain some experience first. Thus when Gibson finally joined the RAF it was simply a move to be given flying instruction and experience prior to a flying career in civilian industry.

Commencing training at the Yatesbury civil school on 16 November 1936, Gibson was commissioned on 31 January 1937, and moved to No 6 FTS on 6 February for advanced instruction. Graduating on 4 September 1937, he was then posted to 83 Squadron at Scampton, to fly the unit's Hawker Hind biplane bombers. The unit was still flying Hinds at the time of the Munich Crisis of September 1938, but in the same month received a few Bristol Blenheim I monoplane bombers to begin

conversion training of its crews for their imminent re-equipment with
Handley Page Hampden bombers. 83 Squadron's first example of the
Hampden, L4048, arrived at Scampton on 31 October 1938, and by
9 January the following year the squadron was up to its full 12-aircraft
establishment with the new design.

As war with Nazi Germany became a distinct possibility in the summer
of 1939, 83 Squadron (as in the case of all other bomber units) received
orders on 26 August to standby at two hours' readiness to leave Scampton
under the Bomber Command 'Scatter' dispersal plan; and on 1 September
six Hampdens were fully bombed up for immediate standby for possible
operations. Finally, on 3 September nine Hampdens of 83 Squadron were
put on immediate standby, fully armed, for the unit's first war sorties; and
at 6.15 pm six of these left Scampton with orders to bomb German naval
units, led by Squadron Leader L. S. Snaith AFC, and including Guy
Gibson flying Hampden L4070, 'C'. In the event the bombers found
no targets and returned to base, jettisoning their bomb loads into the
North Sea en route.

For the following seven months 83 Squadron flew no war sorties, apart
from a few sea patrols during a brief detachment to Lossiemouth, Scotland in February-March 1940. Thus Gibson's second operational sortie
was not flown until 11 April 1940 – a mining trip in L4070. From then
until September 1940, Gibson flew a further 27 operational sorties over
Germany, and in the interim was awarded a DFC on 8 July. On 26
September he was taken off operations for a 'rest' at 14 OTU; was then
posted to 16 OTU on 11 October, where he agitated for a return to
operations, and was finally sent to 29 Squadron at Digby on 13 November
as a Flight Lieutenant to command the unit's A Flight.

Twenty-Nine Squadron was a night fighter unit, recently equipped with
Bristol Beaufighters, and after a spell at Wellingore in training, the squadron became based at West Malling from 29 April 1941 and continued
night defence operations with their new aircraft.

Gibson flew his first Beaufighter operational patrol on 10 December
1940, but had no success until the night of 12 March 1941, when with
Sergeant R. H. James as his observer, in Beaufighter R2246, he destroyed
a German bomber near Skegness. Two nights later he claimed a Heinkel
111. On 8 April, when returning from an uneventful night search,
Gibson's Beaufighter was attacked by an intruder Junkers 88 as it was
landing, and crashed through a hedge. Though his observer, Bell, was
wounded, Gibson survived without injury. He and James, again in
R2250, only managed to damage a German bomber on 23 April, but on
7 May Gibson blasted another bomber with his cannons and the German

aircraft exploded in mid-air. Three nights later Gibson's cannons would not function correctly and he could only spray a German bomber with the wing machine guns; but on 6 July he caught a Heinkel 111 over Sheerness and blew it apart. The final claims by the Gibson/James duo came on 21 October when Gibson tackled two Junkers 87's off Dover and damaged both. His last Beaufighter patrol with 29 Squadron was flown on 15 December 1941.

During his extended tour with the unit he was promoted to squadron leader on 29 June; awarded a Bar to his DFC on 10 September; and completed a total of 99 operational sorties in Beaufighters. His victory tally was three destroyed, one probably destroyed, and four damaged.*

After a short spell as Chief Flying Instructor at 51 OTU, Cranfield, Gibson once more returned to the operational scene on 13 April 1942 when he joined 106 Squadron at Coningsby to fly bomber operations again in Avro Manchesters and Lancasters. For the following eleven months Gibson remained with 106 Squadron and – as squadron commander – participated in most major raids flown during that period; including targets in Germany and Italy, and such spectacular operations as the massed bomber raid against Le Creusot on 17 October 1942. His final sortie with 106 was flown on 15 March 1943; a raid on Stuttgart in which one engine of his Lancaster became defunct on the outward leg, but did not deter Gibson from successfully completing his mission.

Due to commence leave the following day, Gibson was dismayed to find that his leave was cancelled and he was ordered to report to Group Headquarters. By then he had been awarded a DSO (gazetted 6 November 1942) and a Bar to the DSO followed on 30 March 1943. At 5 Group HQ, he was asked to fly one more 'special' operation, and was then given a free hand to literally form a new squadron especially for this sortie. The result was the official formation of 617 Squadron on 21 March 1943, with Wing Commander G. P. Gibson DSO DFC as its first commander.

The 'special operation' for which 617 Squadron was formed was an attack on six huge dams in Germany – those at Möhne, Eder, Sorpe, Ennepe, Lister and Schwelme – several of which supplied hydro-electric power for the vast industrial Ruhr complex. A force of 20 Avro Lancasters, specially modified, was mooted for the attack, each Lancaster carrying a unique weapon designed solely for the breaching of the dams. This weapon, a single cylindrical 'mine' weighing 9,250lb, of which 6,600lb was explosive content, was designed to be back-spun prior to release and then 'skip' along the surface of the dam lake until it met the

* To which should be added one Dornier destroyed on August 24/25 1940, when with 83 Squadron on a bombing sortie over Germany.

dam wall, when it would roll down the wall and finally explode 30 feet below the water level.

To be wholly effective however the 'mine' *had* to be dropped under precise conditions – at exactly 60 feet height above the water surface, 400-450 yards from the dam wall, at a speed not exceeding 250 mph . . . and at night. Such precision had never been attempted (or required) before of RAF bombers; thus Gibson and his crews had to invent their own mode of attack, the prime consideration being an ability to fly dangerously low over water at night. For six weeks the air crews practised low-level flying around Britain at near-suicidal heights, and gradually solved the various complexities of actually bombing within the predetermined parameters of height, speed and distance for final release of the 'mine'.

Then, starting at 9.30 pm on the evening of 16 May 1943, a total of 19 Lancasters, in three separate formations, began to take off from Scampton on Operation Chastise. Leading a formation of nine Lancasters was Guy Gibson in ED932/G, AJ-G, who was to mastermind the complete operation in the air, and whose primary target was the Möhne Dam. A second formation of five Lancasters was sent to the Sorpe Dam; while five more aircraft became a form of flying 'reserve'; ready to be directed in individually by Gibson to back up any particular failure of weapon or aircraft on any of the targets.

The events of the actual raid are now well recorded by Gibson's own account in his book *Enemy Coast Ahead*, and a host of official and other published accounts. Sufficient for the purpose of this narrative is to record the aftermath of the raid. Of the 19 Lancasters despatched initially, eight failed to return while three others failed to complete the sortie. The Möhne Dam was breached spectacularly, releasing a 36 feet-high tidal wave which drowned 1,294 people and 6,500 cattle, apart from destroying or damaging 125 factories and 46 bridges, and ruining 3,000 hectares of land. Other German reports state that 140-million cubic metres of water were released at Möhne, and that the tidal wave was still 18 feet high when it reached Schwerte, some 24 miles away from the dam. The Sorpe Dam was also breached, creating lesser but still significant damage to the surrounding countryside.

Of the eight crews who actually attacked and then returned, 33 received gallantry awards; while Guy Gibson who had formed and led the raid was awarded a Victoria Cross in the *London Gazette* issue of 28 May 1943. The mass investiture of the 'Dam-busters' (as they became dubbed) took place on 22 June by Her Majesty, Queen Elizabeth.

Guy Penrose Gibson

Lloyd Allan Trigg

Immediately after the raid, 617 Squadron was officially stood down from operations temporarily, but Gibson managed to fly one 'spare' sortie on the night of 2 August, before leaving England the following day as one of Winston Churchill's entourage visiting Canada for the Quebec Conference, and the USA. In America on 13 October, Gibson was invested with the American Legion of Merit by General 'Hap' Arnold, USAF, and Gibson finally returned to Britain in December 1943, with a posting to a desk job in Air Ministry in the Directorate of Accidents. A posting to RAF Uxbridge followed in March 1944, and he attended the brief wartime course at the Staff College, Bulstrode Park, before returning to a semi-operational post as a staff officer at HQ, 55 Base, East Kirkby on 12 June. Whilst here he 'scrounged' another operational sortie by piloting a 630 Squadron Lancaster to Thiverny in daylight on 19 July; but on 2 August he moved to HQ 54 Base, Coningsby – still officially non-operational. At this period Gibson was offered the chance to resign from the Service to become a prospective Parliamentary candidate for Macclesfield, but Gibson declined the invitation to enter politics while the war was still in progress.

From Coningsby he managed to fly three more individual operational missions – two in a Lightning during August, and a Mosquito sortie on 10 September to Le Havre – but his persistent requests for a full return to the operational scene were firmly refused by higher authority. Finally, the AOC-in-C, Bomber Command, Arthur Harris, 'relented' by sanctioning 'just one more sortie' for Gibson, though Harris insisted that it must be a 'soft target'. The sortie selected was a reasonably large attack by 220 Lancasters and 10 Mosquitos against railway and industrial centres at Rheydt and Munchen Gladbach on the night of 19 September 1944.

Detailed as Master Bomber for the whole operation, Gibson piloted Mosquito B.XX KB267, 'E' of 627 Squadron, with Squadron Leader James B. Warwick DFC as his navigator. The main force of bombers eventually released 652 tons of high explosives and incendiaries onto the targets, and lost just four Lancasters and one Mosquito – the latter being Gibson's 'E-Easy'. His voice was heard by other crews at a few minutes before 10 pm saying, 'Nice work chaps, now beat it home.' Forty-five minutes later his Mosquito was seen by a ground witness curving over Steenbergen, its engines 'spluttering' to a stop. It then became 'an arc of flames curving to earth' and exploded into the ground, throwing its unrecognisable crew out of the wreckage.

Next morning the owner of the farmland on which Gibson crashed discovered the pilot's wallet and secreted it from the German authorities who, on the basis of the sole identifiable item, a letter in Warwick's battle dress pocket, buried both remains in a single grave in the local cemetery at Steenbergen, Holland.

After the war the Imperial War Graves Commission identified Gibson as the second man, and replaced the single white cross with two official headstones, inscribed separately, on the single grave.

37. Lloyd Allan Trigg

Third of three New Zealand-born airmen to be awarded a Victoria Cross, Lloyd Trigg was almost unique in that the recommendation for his supreme honour was based solely on evidence supplied by his enemies; the only witnesses to his final act of superb courage. The son of a farmer, Trigg was born on 5 June 1914 at Houhora, North Auckland, and received his secondary education at Whangarei High School. Here he proved to be an excellent sportsman, playing rugby for the school first XV, and rose to the rank of Company Sergeant-major in the school cadet unit. Gaining entrance to the Auckland University College, he later returned to farming and became a non-commissioned officer in the North Auckland Rifles Regiment, a territorial force. In the following years Trigg travelled the Northland extensively, part of the time as a sales representative for a firm of agricultural machinery manufacturers.

Since boyhood he had been deeply interested in flying, and had occasionally toyed with the idea of joining the New Zealand air force; but in January 1938 he married Nola McGarvey and settled in the Victoria Valley in North Auckland, becoming the father of two sons, John and Wayne, born in April 1939 and July 1940 respectively. The outbreak of war in Europe had an immediate impact on the people of New Zealand, at that period still closely linked with Britain and the global empire. And, in common with many hundreds of other young 'Kiwis', Lloyd Trigg applied for enlistment in his country's air service.

Joining on 15 June 1941, Trigg was first sent to the Initial Training Wing at Levin, then on 27 July was posted to No 3 EFTS, Harewood to commence pilot training. On 22 September, under the Empire Training Scheme, Trigg left New Zealand bound for Canada, where, on 11 October, he began his final novitiate training at 12 SFTS, Brandon in Manitoba. Graduating on 16 January 1942, Trigg was awarded his pilot 'wings' and commissioned as a Pilot Officer the same day; and in the following month sent to No 31 General Reconnaissance School, Charlottestown on Prince Edward Island for conversion training to Lockheed Hudson bombers. After this course, Trigg gathered together the individual members of his future crew; was promoted to Flying Officer on 1 October 1942; and sailed to England for posting disposal.

His stay in the Mother Country was short and at the end of November he proceeded overseas to West Africa; joining 200 Squadron on the first day of 1943. Equipped with Hudsons, 200 Squadron at this time was based at Yundum airfield, some four miles inland from the mouth of the Gambia River, near Bathurst, roughly 100 miles south of Dakar. This single-runway air strip was situated in the centre of an area long known as the 'White Man's Grave' – renowned for its oppressive heat and humidity during the six-monthly rainy 'season', and ultra-heated desert-like dryness in the remaining half-year; conditions to which were added a constant exposure to malaria and blackwater fever for all personnel.

Nearby was another RAF unit, 95 Squadron (Short Sunderlands) based at Bathurst, at Half Die Camp (the curious name of the latter referring to an earlier cholera epidemic which killed half of the local native population. . . !) Between them the two squadrons were tasked with air protection of West African coastal waters, covering the vital merchant and naval convoy routes along the eastern Atlantic seaboard.

Lloyd Trigg quickly adapted to his surroundings and his designated duties. Tall (5 feet 10 inches), sporting a small but neat moustache, Trigg said very little and remained reserved, seldom visiting the Mess except for necessities. A fellow pilot summed Trigg by saying, 'He seldom spoke, but had a fantastic determination. He hated the Germans and his sole interest was in getting the war won so that he could return to his family.'

Just ten days after joining 200 Squadron, Trigg flew his first operational sortie, a five and a half hours' anti-submarine patrol in Hudson 'A-Apple' with a three-man crew. By the end of February he completed a further eight sorties on convoy protection and submarine hunts. Continuing his convoy escort and shipping reconnaissance patrols throughout March, Trigg had his first tastes of direct offensive action when, while scouting the fringe areas of one convoy, he sighted a U-boat and immediately swung into an attack pattern; straddling the submarine's track with a spaced 'stick' of depth charges, though without visible result.

Two days later his keen eyes spotted another U-boat and without hesitation made a bow attack; one of his depth charges being seen to explode on the submarine's bow. Trigg's constant keenness to fly and his dedication to his tasks, exemplified by his actions during those early months, led to the award of a Distinguished Flying Cross which was gazetted on 16 June 1943.*

In May the squadron was notified that it was soon to exchange its Hudsons for long-range American Liberators, and three complete crews, including Trigg's, were detached to the newly-formed Liberator OTU at

* The news of this award did not reach 200 Squadron until shortly after Trigg's death.

Nassau in the Bahamas for conversion training, and at the same time to 'pick up' the necessary 'extra' crew members – a second pilot and three wireless-operator/air gunners – to fill a Liberator crew establishment. On completion of the OTU course the three enlarged crews were sent to Dorval, Quebec, to take over the specific Liberators earmarked for 200 Squadron, and then set out on the long journey back to Yundum; flying across the Atlantic to Prestwick, and then flying south via Ras-el-Ma, North Africa, across the Bay of Biscay; finally going through the Atlas Mountains and over the vast stretches of the Sahara Desert, to reach Yundum on 18 July 1943.

With their arrival, at the height of the rain season, the huge Liberators immediately presented the squadron with a host of operating problems. Yundum's sole runway of perforated metal plates, 2,000 yards in length, had become a sea of mud with lush green grass growing through the perforations. A fully loaded Liberator on take-off created a bow wave of water and liquid mud ahead of its main wheels, producing a noticeable de-celeration; while landing was equally hazardous because the abundant grass sheared off at the edges of the metal plates when brakes were applied, resulting in horrendous skids akin to attempting to land on thick ice. With no alternative the squadron moved its Liberators to the USAAF base at Rufisque, near Dakar, 100 miles further north for the working-up period; returning to Yundum only after the rains had abated.

Trigg's Liberator crew was a typical 'mixed' team of nationalities. His second pilot, Flying Officer G. N. Goodwin was a Canadian, while the two navigators, Flying Officer Ivan Marinovitch and Flying Officer J. J. S. Townsend, hailed from Auckland, New Zealand and Stroud, Gloucestershire respectively. Three of the wireless operator/air gunners, Flight Sergeants T. J. Soper, A. G. Bennett, and L. J. Frost were all New Zealanders; whilst the fourth Wop/AG was another Englishman, Pilot Officer A. R. Bonnick from Hendon, London. Of these, Marinovitch and Bennett had crewed with Trigg from his first operational sortie with 200 Squadron in January 1943.

The change from Hudsons to the cumbersome Liberator brought with it a change in operational technique for anti-submarine attacks. With the increasing tendency for U-boat commanders to remain surfaced and rely on their flak gun batteries for protection, speed and manoeuvrability were essentials for any aircraft captain. Though a highly reliable machine, the Liberator lacked manoeuvrability in this context, requiring half a mile radius even for a turn. Normally cruising at 160 mph at heights between three and 6,000 feet, the squadron's Liberators' 1,500 feet per minute descent rate to a 50 feet attacking height took up to four long minutes; a sitting target for the U-boat flak gunners with their 20mm cannons.

Normally 200 Squadron's aircraft carried a bomb load of 16 depth charges (each 660lb USA type) and used these in two attacks of eight DC's each, with a pre-set interval of 60 feet spacing between each depth charge. The skipper released the depth charges by means of a press-button on his control column wheel; but the salvo jettison lever, by which a complete bomb load could be dropped in one release, was located between the two pilots, low on the pedestal face.

In the early hours of 11 August 1943, two Liberator crews prepared to take-off on the unit's first sorties in their new aircraft, skippered respectively by Trigg and Warrant Officer 'Rikki' Johnson. Trigg was at the controls of Liberator BZ832, 'D', and became airborne at 0729 hours. It was to be a routine shipping patrol, keeping a weather eye open for any signs of German U-boats; a prospect in view of 12 long hours 'watching water' as the Liberator flew out over the monotonous vista of the Atlantic Ocean. Then, at 0945 hours Trigg spotted a surfaced U-boat in position 12° 20′ N., 20° 07′ W.; some 240 miles south-west of Dakar, and approximately 6,000 yards away. It was the *U-468*, a 500-ton submarine commanded by Oberleutnant zur See Clemens Schamong; his first command.

On only its third war patrol, the *U-468* had sailed from La Pallice on 7 July 1943, in company with *U-373*, and hugged the French and Spanish coasts until well clear of the notorious Bay of Biscay before moving on to its designated operational area off the west coast of Africa. The U-boat's patrol proved to be uneventful, with no attacks delivered or sustained, and after the failure of its refuelling ship, *U-462*, to make a rendezvous (*U-462* had been sunk en route) Schamong was returning to base when he first spotted Trigg's Liberator.

As the Liberator began its long run-in for attack, the U-boat's two 20mm cannons were swung into action and soon scored direct hits on the aircraft, setting it afire. The crippling damage to his aircraft did not deter Lloyd Trigg who continued his bombing run-in, not deviating from his course or attempting to evade the deadly accurate fire of the German cannons.

Coming in from the submarine's port quarter, the Liberator roared over the *U-468* at 50 feet height, releasing six depth charges; two of which exploded within six feet of the submarine's hull. Then, still descending, with a raging fire in its centre section, the Liberator hit the sea some 300 yards beyond its prey – and the neoprene-lined, leather fuel tanks erupted on impact with a massive explosion. Damage to the *U-468* was catastrophic and it began to settle immediately with water pouring into its innards in several places. Engines, motors, transformers and bilge pumps were torn from their beds; a 65-gallon fuel tank crashed and ruptured; the after torpedo tube ruptured and a two-inch jet of water poured in, while other water ingress entered the battery compartment and within minutes the U-boat filled with choking clouds of chlorine gas, suffocating several crew men.

In the ensuing panic some 20 crew members managed to reach the upper deck and jumped overboard; many of these being injured and swiftly killed by sharks and barracuda. The submarine sank on an even keel within 10 minutes. Schamong, two other officers, and four ratings were the only survivors.

The seven survivors continued to swim around, keeping predatory fish off by submerging their heads and 'roaring' below the sea surface; then one of the ratings discovered the Liberator's rubber dinghy. Normally located in stowages on each side of the aircraft fuselage near the wing leading edge, the impact of the crash had sprung the stowage cover plates and flung the dinghy clear. Inflating the dinghy from an air bottle, the rating and two others scrambled into it, and an hour later the remaining four Germans succeeded in reaching the large dinghy and also climbed aboard.

Next day Sunderland 'H' of 204 Squadron located the drifting dinghy, dropped supply bags and then radio-guided HMS *Clarkia* to the spot, which retrieved the Germans. The surviving U-boat crew men were eventually sent to England for interrogation, arriving there on 10 September, and although adamant in refusing to divulge any technical details about the *U-468* or other naval matters, both Schamong and his First Lieutenant, Leutnant zur See Alfons Heimannsberg, were unreserved in their outspoken admiration of the courage and performance of the Liberator's crew.

From their detailed descriptions of Trigg's last gallant and determined sortie, the interrogating authorities pieced together the full story, and on this first-hand evidence a recommendation was forwarded that Lloyd Trigg should be considered for the award of a posthumous Victoria Cross. The recommendation was approved without delay and the VC award promulgated on 2 November 1943.

38. Arthur Louis Aaron

'In my opinion, never even in the annals of the RAF, has the VC been awarded for skill, determination and courage in the face of the enemy of a higher order than that displayed by your son on his last flight.' Thus wrote Sir Arthur Harris, commander-in-chief of RAF Bomber Command to the parents of Flight Sergeant Arthur Louis Aaron DFM in November 1943.

Though of small consolation for the loss of a beloved son, Harris's sincere tribute was heart-felt, and shared by all who had witnessed Arthur Aaron's superlative courage. Grievously injured, Aaron's single-minded determination to preserve the lives of his crew over-rode all other considerations in his last hours; exemplifying the close bond of comradeship amongst the bomber crews, and epitomising the heavy responsibility borne by so many youthful bomber captains.

Born in Leeds on 5 March 1922, Arthur Aaron was the son of an Englishman, Benjamin Aaron, who had married a girl originally from Switzerland but who had come to Scotland before the first world war to the family of the Rector of Aberdeen University, Adam-Smith. From his earliest years young Arthur became fascinated by two things, mountains and flying – a tragically prophetic combination of interests. His absorption with mountains – possibly inherited from his mother's background – found expression in many rock-climbing expeditions; while the boy's first ecstatic taste of the pure joy of flying came with a short flight with one of Alan Cobham's travelling aerial 'circuses' near Penrith.

Educated at Roundhay Secondary School, Aaron won an art scholarship in 1939 and entered the Leeds College of Architecture as the start of his intended career. Still keen on flying, he joined the Leeds University Squadron of the Air Defence Cadet Corps (later retitled Air Training Corps), and eventually enlisted in the RAF for pilot training on 15 September 1941. In early December he was sent to the USA and commenced flying instruction at No 1 (British) FTS, Terrell in Texas; graduating as a Sergeant pilot on 19 June 1942.

Returning to England, Aaron underwent further advanced instruction at No 6(P) AFU and No 26 OTU, before being sent to No 1657 Heavy Conversion Unit (HCU) to acquire experience in handling the giant four-engined Short Stirling bomber. Finally, on 17 April 1943, Aaron joined his first operational unit, 218 '*Gold Coast*' Squadron based at Downham Market in East Anglia.

From his first operational sortie – a 'soft' trip dropping mines in the Bay of Biscay – Aaron, quiet and mild-mannered on the ground, exercised a firm discipline over his crew in the air. His constant aim was efficiency in the bombing role, and towards this end he insisted that each crew member gained some experience of other members' jobs. It meant improved understanding and co-operation; knitted each member into a cohesive whole as a team, ready to cope instinctively with any untoward situation which might arise. Promoted to Flight Sergeant on 1 May 1943, nevertheless Aaron's authority over his crew was not by his rank but by his status as the crew skipper; age or rank seniority held little meaning to an operational crew when actually flying.

During the following three months Aaron and his crew completed 20 sorties over Europe, bombing a wide variety of targets in Germany and enemy-occupied territory. An early indication of the young pilot's streak of determination came on the night his Stirling was partly crippled by flak on his approach to the target. Undeterred by the damage, which had left his aircraft only marginally controllable Aaron continued his sortie, bombed the objective, and then brought the Stirling home again safely. His action that night brought him the award of a Distinguished Flying Medal (DFM)*.

In the afternoon of 12 August 1943 Aaron and his crew were briefed for their 21st operational sortie. The target was Turin – their first trip to Italy. Piloting Stirling EF452, HA-O, Aaron took off from Downham Market into the lowering sun of a warm summer evening, lifting the nose of the bomber which, like some winged dinosaur, laboured upwards, struggling to gain precious height with full petrol tanks and a maximum bomb load. Inside its fuselage the crew automatically busied themselves, preparing for the long haul across France to Italy; by now an experienced crew whose teamwork worked like silk. Navigating was Sergeant Bill Brennan, a Canadian, while the bomb aimer, another Canuck, was Flight Sergeant Allan Larden. At the wireless set sat Sergeant T. 'Jimmy' Guy, and nearby the flight engineer Sergeant Malcolm Mitchem. In the mid-upper gun turret Sergeant J. Richmond, having tested his guns and turret, was settling down to the constant vigil he would need to maintain for many hours to come; as was Sergeant Thomas McCabe, a Manchester man, seated in the cramped, lonely rear gun turret.

All had been well briefed and were pleased with the target – a combined attack wherein the Stirlings were to bomb Turin, while Halifaxes

* Gazetted 19 October 1943.

of 6 Group were attacking Milan. Crossing the French coast near Caen at 10,000 feet, Aaron continued to coax the overburdened Stirling upwards, gaining height steadily in the brilliant moonlight. Reaching a comfortable 14,000 feet ceiling, Aaron levelled out and continued southwards, passing Le Creusot and eventually approaching the Alps. He was well used to the Stirling's lack of a safe ceiling by now, but he was not particularly worried; the sheer beauty of the Alps bathed in clear moonlight to port capturing his and his crew's admiration. To Aaron, fascinated with mountains since childhood, the grandeur of the scene was breathtaking. Pointing to Mont Blanc, he remarked, 'Boy, would I like to climb that.'

Then the crew's attention was brought back to the job in hand – Turin had loomed into view ahead and below.

Aaron called for the bomb doors to be opened; Allan Larden slithered down into the nose position to prepare for dropping the bomb load; Mitchem climbed into Larden's vacated seat, his fingers poised over the bombing panel switches – smooth, trained movements, carried out instinctively without fuss.

Richmond's voice from the mid-upper turret crackled over the intercomm, 'Watch that bloke up front, Art.'

Aaron leaned to his right and saw on the starboard side another Stirling of the main stream, slightly below and wallowing rather too close for comfort. 'OK, Ritch,' replied Aaron.

Hardly were the words out of his mouth than Richmond's voice came back, yelling, 'Christ, he's firing at us !' Below their starboard wing tip the rear gunner of the other Stirling had opened fire, and at about 250 yards range was raking Aaron's aircraft from starboard wing to port and back again.

'Fire back at him, Ritchie'.

'I can't, the wing tip's in the way.' The time was 1.20 am on Friday, 13 August. Lying in the nose, Larden was startled to see half a dozen fingerholes suddenly appear in the fuselage two feet from his face to the right. Back inside the fuselage Brennan collapsed in a cascade of maps, pencils and instruments as one bullet went clean through his heart and he died instantly.

Larden was then stung into action by the voice of Mitchem shouting, 'My God, fellows, look at Art. Oh, poor Art. Give me a hand, Allan.'

Swinging up into the cockpit Larden saw Aaron hunched over to his left and covered in blood from a gaping wound in the face, his right arm dangling useless and limp, held on by only a few tendons. The instrument panel was a shambles of blood-flecked glass and torn metal, while the pilot's side of the front windscreen was blown apart. Both inboard engine throttle levers were smashed and bent; and by now the Stirling was in a powered 250 mph dive, with Mitchem in the right-hand pilot's seat fighting the controls to straighten the plunging bomber, and throwing agonised glances at his grievously injured skipper in the other seat.

As Mitchem slid out of the co-pilot's seat, Larden took his place – an instinctive trained movement, needing no conscious thought – and the Canadian gradually regained control of the diving Stirling and levelled out between the menacing Alpine peaks at about 4,000 feet. Meanwhile Mitchem and two others gave Aaron morphia injections and bundled him amidships between the spars. Before accepting this rough first aid treatment however, Aaron – still, astonishingly, conscious – insisted on knowing Larden's intentions for getting the bomber to safety.

Unable to speak, he scratched a message with his left hand on the back of the dead navigator's log, telling Larden to head for England. Larden gave him an OK sign, and only then did Aaron permit medical aid to be given.

In point of fact Larden had no choice for the moment but to continue flying southwards through the surrounding mountain peaks, having to constantly fight for control of the crippled bomber. The automatic pilot was inoperable, cables for the trimming tabs dangling broken from the roof, hydraulic lines ruptured thus rendering the rear turret useless and slopping oil in the fuselage mid-section. Added to all this the starboard inner engine was threatening to overheat, and there was still a full bomb load aboard. Taking stock of all these items, Larden began to head eastwards over the lower mountains towards Austria, but then, as he cleared these lower peaks, he turned through south to head westward, hoping to reach British-occupied territory in Sicily. Baling out amongst the snow-covered peaks was considered briefly and rejected – apart from almost certain death by freezing in the mountains, the crew would not risk Aaron to further injury.

At his wireless set, Jimmy Guy continued to transmit to base but the response was virtually inaudible. It meant that the crew were ostensibly alone in the sky, without a position fix or accurate course to fly, and having little idea of their precise location.

After what seemed an age the Stirling crossed the Italian coast at Spezia where Larden promptly jettisoned the bomb load into the harbour area. Mitchem now checked the state of the engines and fuel, and then relieved Larden at the controls while the latter went aft. Moving Brennan's body from the gangway, he told the other crew members to check their parachutes and the aircraft dinghies for damage, and then get them ready for use. This done, Richmond went forward to take a spell at piloting the bomber, relieving Mitchem, and Larden had a brief 'conference' to decide what to do on arrival in Sicily.

Guy informed him that Group in England had finally faded out of range, then sent out a plain language distress call to Bone airfield in North Africa; an emergency call which paid off when he received a reply telling him not to land in Sicily but to try to make Bone across the Mediterranean.

By this time Larden and Mitchem had realised that they had both had narrow escapes from the original 'attack' by the unknown Stirling's rear gunner. Larden had two bullets in his right buttock, while Mitchem's right flying boot had been cut in two at the ankle by three bullets; two of which had scraped the bone. Telling McCabe to sit facing the flight engineer's instrument panels, Mitchem told the rear gunner to yell out when the first warning indicator came on; then with Larden returned to the front cockpit and took over the two pilot seats, while Richmond went back to stay with Aaron.

Desperately weak from loss of blood and the waves of shock, Aaron rallied sufficiently to scratch out a question, 'How navigate?' Guy and Richmond reassured their skipper that they were on course for Bone airfield, and had a map bearing to get them there. Aaron lay back again, exhausted even from this brief effort to ensure his crew's safety.

For nearly four hours the Stirling droned on across the moon-dappled surface of the Mediterranean with Larden, under Mitchem's skilled guidance, alternating engine power and carefully extracting the last drop of precious petrol from each tank in turn. Then Larden saw ahead two searchlight beams forming an inverted 'V', which were then joined by a third, forming a marker tripod of light. Still unable to contact Bone by R/T, the Canadian was not sure if the lights indicated friend or foe, but homed right over the beams and let Guy obtain a reciprocal. Two miles out to sea Larden turned again and came back over the airfield. Below him the strip was lighted but there were mountains at the back of the aerodrome, making any landing hazardous for a novice pilot.

Yawing round in a jerky right-hand circuit, Larden prepared to land, only to finally receive a message from the aerodrome warning him of a crashed Wellington bomber at the end of the main runway. Larden decided to make a wheels-up landing alongside the runway, but at that moment fate stepped in.

Aaron regained consciousness as the effect of the morphia wore off and, alerted instinctively by the (to him) crude manoeuvring of the aircraft, asked Guy what was happening. Guy told him they were about to land.

With a face practically shot in two and black with caked blood, and his right arm dangling by the tenuous support of a few tendons, Aaron immediately started to crawl forward to take command of the landing. As Larden remarked later, 'Who could deny such an indomitable spirit?'

As the two gunners helped their skipper into his seat, Larden slid into the co-pilot's seat, and Mitchem went back to his instrument panel.

Aaron had only his left arm to operate controls and, being unable to talk, could only indicate his wishes by nodding his head. Unaware of the wrecked Wellington at the far end of the main runway, Aaron automatically lined up the Stirling for a normal landing approach, ignoring Larden's shouts (if indeed he heard him). It could only have been sheer experienced instinct which made Aaron aware that the let-down was wrongly placed, and he nodded to Larden to open throttles and go round again.

On his second approach Aaron was again dissatisfied and signalled to Larden to open up and circuit. Automatically obeying his skipper's unspoken order Larden advanced the throttles – to the dismay of Mitchem, who yelled that they would have to land this time; the petrol was virtually gone.

The Stirling made its third approach but, at only 500 feet above the runway edge, Aaron indicated to Larden to go round yet again. Larden shouted that there was no fuel for another circuit – they *must* land. Aaron, his mind possibly impaired by his awful pain, seemed unable to comprehend this and began to pull on the throttles. In sheer desperation Larden swung his arm and thumped Aaron across the chest to make him release the controls – and Aaron collapsed completely, only his eyes glaring at his co-pilot in an unforgettable reproach.

With the bomber at stalling point and the port wing beginning to drop, Larden pushed the control column hard forward and held tight as the desert sand rushed up towards him; then heaved back sharply. The aircraft tobogganed in for a belly-landing, scooping earth and sand in a monstrous tidal wave as it careered to an eventual halt. They were down. The time was 6 am.

As the dust settled, Arthur Aaron was quickly removed and taken to the base hospital, where surgeons operated to remove bullets from the pilot's right chest cavity (probably those which had near-severed his arm). The rest of the crew were medically checked over and treated for their various minor wounds.

It was only after this that they learned that the Stirling's bomb bay still contained one of their bombs, which failed to reelase over Spezia; while Larden was presented with the safety buckle of his Sutton parachute harness. Two bullets had struck this, jamming the mechanism in the 'released' position. Had he decided to bale out he would have fallen straight through the harness. . . .'

All through the day the survivors prayed silently for their skipper and indeed at first he appeared to be responding well. Then, in the early evening, they learned that he had finally succumbed to his appalling injuries at approximately 3 pm. He was buried with full military honours in Bone military cemetery.

On 3 November 1943 the *London Gazette* published the official citation for the award of a posthumous Victoria Cross to Arthur Louis Aaron; its narrative discreetly attributing the attack on the Stirling to 'an enemy nightfighter'. For their own parts in this epic of courage, Allan Larden was awarded a Conspicuous Gallantry Medal (CGM), and Mitchem and Guy each received a Distinguished Flying Medal (DFM). On 25 February 1944, Aaron's parents received their son's awards at a Buckingham Palace investiture and shortly afterwards Benjamin Aaron was present at a mass parade of ATC cadets in Wellington Barracks, London, where the ATC Commandant, Air Marshal Sir Leslie Gossage read out the VC citation of their most distinguished ex-cadet.

Two years later, in August 1946, the parents' house was burgled and all Aaron's medals stolen, but after a police appeal the medals were returned through the mail anonymously. In December 1953 Aaron's father presented his son's medals to the Leeds City Museum for permanent public display.

39. William Reid

The relatively high number of air crews during 1939-45 who originally hailed from Scotland is seldom publicised. The reputation of the dour, fighting Scot is based firmly on centuries of splendid examples of rugged determination – some might call it stubbornness – unsurpassed raw courage and, not least, a strain of the legendary Celtic devotion to any worthy cause. In the RAF, particularly amongst the bomber crews, any Scot was usually welcomed because of his dependability in all circumstances, utterly reliable attention to vital details, and – no less – his normally marked abhorrence of extrovert praise or 'blather'. It is perhaps no coincidence that of the 32 air VCs awarded in World War Two, six went to men born and bred in Scotland.

William ('Bill') Reid VC, would be the first to deny that he 'typified' his race, especially in terms of outstanding courage; a denial sincerely based on a genuine modesty. Yet in circumstances which might justifiably have deterred most men – wounded twice, struggling to control a crippled aircraft with dead and wounded crew members aboard, and only part way to his designated objective – Bill Reid said nothing of his injuries to his crew, completed his mission, and then brought his comrades back to England and safety. Reid explains his action as 'just common sense', but his VC citation prefers to interpret his superb courage as, '. . . tenacity and devotion to duty beyond praise.'

The son of a blacksmith, Reid was born at Baillieston, Glasgow on 21 December 1921. Receiving his main education at the Coatbridge Secondary School, he studied metallurgy for a brief period but then applied to join the RAF. Officially accepted into the RAFVR on 28 April 1941, he was given deferred service until August that same year, and then reported to the Initial Training Wing at Newquay, Cornwall to commence pilot training. In November he was drafted to Monckton, Canada to complete his instruction, and on 3 December was posted to No 2 BFTS Lancaster in California, USA for his advanced course. On 19 June 1942 Reid received his 'wings' and a commission, and set sail for England where, on 4 August, he reported to No 6 APU, Little Rissington for training on twin-engined Airspeed Oxfords – the usual pre-requisite for future bomber pilots. On 15 September 1942 Reid moved on to 29 OTU, North Luffenham, expecting here to be crewed up prior to an

William Reid

Arthur Louis Aaron

operational posting, but his skill as a pilot led to him being 'screened' to an instructor, flying obsolete Wellington bombers; albeit with a promise of an eventual posting to a Lancaster unit for a tour of operations.

The promised posting did not materialise until July 1943, when he was sent to 1654 Conversion Unit, Wigsley near Newark to accustom himself to Avro Lancasters briefly, and then, on 6 September, was posted to 61 Squadron at Syerston, Newark to commence Lancaster bombing operations. In fact, his first operational mission had been flown as second pilot in a Lancaster of 9 Squadron on 30 August – a raid on Munchen-Gladbach with a 15,000lb bomb load.

On 22 September, in Lancaster LM360, 'O', Reid set out to bomb Hannover, but finding he was unable to climb above 14,000 feet with a full bomb and fuel load, he jettisoned the 4,000lb 'Cookie' bomb near the Dutch coast and then completed his mission successfully. Three more sorties were flown that month – to Mannheim, Hannover and Bochum; followed by three more trips (Munich, Kassel and Stuttgart) during the first week of October. By now Reid had been promoted to Flight Lieutenant and was already gaining something of a reputation on his squadron for quiet determination and dependability as a bomber captain. On 22 October, again in Lancaster LM360, 'O', he raided Kassel, though on return he had to land away from base, at Swinderby. His next operation came on the evening of 3 November 1943. A force of 600 bombers were detailed to raid Dusseldorf, including Reid as captain of Lancaster LM360, 'O'.

For this trip Reid had a six-man crew. As navigator he had Flight Sergeant J. A. Jefferies, an Australian; Flight Sergeant Les Rolton as bomb aimer; Flight Sergeant J. W. Norris as flight engineer; and Flight Sergeant J. J. Mann as wireless operator. In the mid-upper gun turret was Flight Sergeant D. Baldwin DFM, an experienced gunner hailing from Nelson, Lancashire; while another veteran gunner, on his second operational tour, Flight Sergeant A. F. 'Joe' Emerson, occupied the lonely rear gun turret. At one minute before 5 pm Reid became airborne from Syerston and steadily climbed towards the coastline, heading towards Holland; the start of his tenth operational sortie.

Crossing the Dutch coast at 21,000 feet, Reid's windscreen suddenly exploded in a blinding flash, and he felt as if his head had been blown off. A Messerschmitt Bf 110 night fighter had attacked from dead astern, its cannon shells damaging both gun turrets of the Lancaster and shattering Reid's cockpit. Hit in the head and shoulder by stray slivers of shell, Reid was also struck in the body and face by a myriad of jagged perspex fragments from the windscreen. Fortunately none had penetrated his eyes, though his eyelids were scratched and torn.

Half-dazed by the impact, Reid managed to get his goggles over his eyes to protect them from the howling icy slipstream battering him through the broken perspex canopy. Blood was flowing freely from his face and shoulder and Reid could taste it in his mouth, but the slipstream quickly coagulated the flow. The Lancaster, badly hit, nosed downwards for 2,000 feet before Reid managed to regain control. The port elevator was badly hit, several instruments (including the compass) out of commission, and the hydraulics partly damaged.

He heard Alan Jefferies yell, asking Reid if he was OK. Reid, though feeling 'half-dead' (sic) replied, 'Yes, I feel all right' – he could see no purpose in worrying the crew about his injuries. He then checked that the other crew members were unharmed, and calmly decided to continue his mission to Dusseldorf. It was a decision with no 'heroic' overtones; simply a logical (to Reid) move. To turn back would have meant running head-on through the following main stream of bombers, and that would undoubtedly be dangerous to both Reid's aircraft and the main force. It was 'common sense' in Reid's way of thinking to continue the sortie.

Jamming on hard left rudder constantly to counteract the tendency of his aircraft to yaw because of the elevator damage, Reid had hardly begun to settle down before a Focke Wulf Fw 190 bore in from the port beam and raked the whole length of the bomber's fuselage with a murderously accurate hail of cannon shells. The navigator, Jefferies, died instantly and crumpled to the floor of the fuselage; while Mann, the wireless operator, fell on top of Jefferies, seriously wounded. Norris too was hit in his left arm, and Reid was also hit. Other shells ruptured the aircraft's oxygen and hydraulic systems, and further damaged the two gun turrets.

Despite his own wounds, Norris clipped an emergency oxygen bottle onto Reid's supply tube and then helped the pilot in holding the control column steady, as the stricken bomber slowly levelled out again at 17,000 feet. Still conscious Reid again calmly continued his sortie, still determined to reach Dusseldorf. Without the use of his compass now, Reid looked for the Pole Star and flew on that until he recognised Cologne on the starboard side, and began his final approach to his target; reaching the objective nearly an hour after the second night fighter attack.

With both arms folded around the control column to hold it rock steady, Reid flew across the centre of the target, and Rolton released the bomb load accurately. Then, as Reid steered slightly northwards to clear the flak zone, Rolton and the wounded Norris stood by Reid, ready to help in controlling the heavily damaged bomber for the long return trip. Navigating as best he could by the stars, Reid was steadily getting weaker now. The constant physical effort in keeping on hard left rudder, and holding the control column with both arms, fingers linked, was sapping his remaining strength.

Near the Dutch coast he ran into a heavy flak barrage, but managed to get through without further damge or injury until the Lancaster was well out over the North Sea. Then, without warning, all four engines spluttered and cut, and the bomber wallowed into a flat spin. Reid, by then without oxygen as the emergency supply petered out, was light-headed and slow in reaction. Norris, also light-headed from his own wounds, had forgotten to change over the petrol cocks to a full tank; but instinctive training told him what was wrong and he swiftly rectified the fault. All engines resumed their former full power and the Lancaster levelled out to continue its flight home.

As he approached the English coast Reid, aware of the low petrol state of his aircraft, and the ruptured hydraulics (the bomb doors had remained open after bombing and could not be retracted), decided to try to land at Wittering, where the extra length of available runway offered possible safety.

Then he spotted a cone of searchlights, indicating an airfield below. Having no precise idea of his location, Reid circled the lights and flashed his landing lights to indicate his distressed aircraft condition; then prepared to land. With the hydraulics useless, he had to use an emergency pressure bottle to handpump the undercarriage down, and this exertion in addition to the descent into warmer levels re-opened his wounds. His head wound began bleeding freely again, threatening to obscure Reid's vision.

Les Rolton positioned himself behind his skipper, ready to pull him out if he lost consciousness or control; while Reid ordered his remaining crew to prepare for a crash landing. As the Lancaster touched down, the undercarriage collapsed, shot through, and the bomber scraped along the concrete runway for perhaps 60 yards before finally halting. Reid had landed at Shipdham, base for the 44th Bombardment Group, USAF; the time was one minute after 10 pm.

As the crew were evacuated from the Lancaster Reid discovered for the first time that Jefferies was dead – a bullet through his head – and that Norris and Mann were wounded. All were taken immediately to the station's medical centre for treatment, but Mann died of his injuries the following day.

In hospital Reid was visited by his Group commander, Air Vice-

Marshal Cochrane, who finally extracted the full story of the raid from all the crew's reports and promptly recommended the survivors for gallantry awards. Norris, for his gallant part, was later awarded a Conspicuous Gallantry Medal (CGM), and 'Joe' Emerson received a Distinguished Flying Medal (DFM). To his personal astonishment, Bill Reid was notified by Cochrane that he was to receive a Victoria Cross.*

On being discharged from hospital Reid was given a month's convalescent leave, then told to report to Cochrane, who informed him that he was to join 617 Squadron – the famed 'Dam-Busters' unit. Privately delighted with this 'compliment', Reid asked permission to take with him Les Rolton from his old crew, whom Reid had known since OTU days; also Flying Officer Luker, a wireless operator and friend of Reid's.† Cochrane readily agreed to this request, and on 13 January 1944 Reid reported to his new unit at Woodhall Spa and was allotted to C Flight of 617 Squadron.

Allotted Lancaster ME557, 'S' as his 'personal' aircraft, Reid underwent several weeks of specialised training in 617's bombing techniques; then on 18 April flew his first sortie with the squadron, bombing the Juvisy marshalling yards near Paris. Two days later he returned to Paris and released a dozen 1,000lb bombs on the La Chappelle railway complex. Only two more sorties were flown that month, to Brunswick and Munich – the latter sortie being routed via the Alps and Milan.

By early June 617 Squadron's Lancasters were modified to carry a new weapon – the 12,000lb high explosive DP (Deep Penetration) bomb, nicknamed 'Tallboy'. Intended for specially selected 'Thick Skin' (i.e. heavily protected) targets, the 'Tallboy' required meticulous skill in accurate release.

Reid's first 'Tallboy' sortie came on 8 June in the squadron attack on the Saumur rail tunnel, led by the squadron commander, Wing Commander G. L. Cheshire DSO DFC (later VC). The result was complete destruction of the tunnel, preventing a German panzer division from being rushed to the Allied invasion beach-head established precariously only two days previously.

On 14 June he carried another 'Tallboy' to Le Havre, home of the notorious E-boats. Spearheading a 400-bomber force, 617's crews blasted the pens and harbour with their DP bombs.

Next day a similar force set out to destroy the U-boat pens at Boulogne,

---

* Gazetted 14 December 1943.

† Of his former crew; Norris was taken off operations, Baldwin returned to 61 Squadron and completed his tour, while Emerson also returned to operations but was killed in action later.

but heavy clouds over the target precluded accurate bombing, and Reid was one of several pilots forced to return with his 'Tallboy' still on board (jettisoning was not permitted except in dire emergency). By then Hitler had launched his terror campaign of V1 robot flying bombs against England, and 617 became one of many units concentrating on destruction of the flying bombs' sites and storage depots.

On 19 and 20 June Reid flew daylight sorties to V1 sites at Pas de Calais; dropped a 'Tallboy' on Wizernes rocket site on 24 June; followed next day by another daylight sortie to release a 'Tallboy' onto Siracourt V1 site; again led by Cheshire. On his first run-in Reid had his bomb 'hang-up', but circled and came in again for a successful release on target. After a brief leave, Reid flew to the Wizernes rocket site again on 20 July but was unable to complete his sortie due to thick cloud conditions over the objective. Five days later the target was another V site, Watten, in the Pas de Calais area, onto which Reid dropped another 'Tallboy'.

On the last day of July 1944, 617 Squadron was linked with 9 Squadron for a 'Tallboy' attack on a V-weapon storage dump in a railway tunnel at Rilly La Montagne, near Rheims. Over the target Reid released his bomb from 12,000 feet, when he felt his aircraft (ME557, 'S') shudder under the impact of a 1,000lb bomb, dropped from another Lancaster 6,000 feet higher. The bomb ploughed through Reid's aircraft in mid-fuselage, severing all control cables and fatally weakening the structure. Reid felt his control column go sloppy, realised what had happened, and gave the order to bale out. As the rest of the crew came forward to abandon the Lancaster, the bomber slid into a dive, pinning Reid in his seat with pressure forces.

Reaching overhead he managed to release the escape hatch panel, and struggled to get out. Just as he emerged the Lancaster broke in two and Reid tumbled down, accompanied by a hail of metal fragments from his aircraft. Landing safely, Reid was captured within the hour by German troops, and later met his wireless operator, Luker, also a prisoner.

The two gunners had died in the rear part of the fuselage; while Les Rolton and the remaining two crew members perished in the forward section of the Lancaster. Reid was imprisoned in Stalagluft III, Sagan initially, and was later moved to Stalag IV, Belleria; before being finally repatriated to England in May 1945 on Operation Exodus – the Bomber Command air retrieval of prisoners of war from Europe.

Leaving the RAF in January 1946, Bill Reid began studies at Glasgow University and, later, the West of Scotland Agricultural College; eventually earning a B Sc (Agric) in 1949. Today he is employed by an international firm producing agricultural products, based in London.

40. Cyril Joe Barton

Courage is defined in most dictionaries as fearlessness. Yet true courage is generally recognised as the ability to overcome a deeply-felt, instinctive fear of certain circumstances or situations, and deliberately face those circumstances again. And when the result may well be certain death the deliberate decision to face it must constitute supreme courage. Such a decision faced every member of the bomber crews each time they prepared to fly against the enemy opposition awaiting them over any designated target throughout the years 1939-45. The odds against individual survival were always slim, and this was well recognised by the crews even before they commenced operational flying. It speaks volumes for the courage of those crews that they continued to carry out their duties, night after night or in the harsh light of day, despite such dreadful odds. Let it be remembered too that every single aircrew member was a volunteer – Bomber Command (indeed, all Commands of the RAF) had no 'pressed men' in its ranks of operational fliers.

Inevitably, as with any section of the human race facing a common peril communally, individual bomber crews became close-knit 'brotherhoods'; bound in comradeship by duty and an interdependence on which their ultimate survival might hang. Leading a crew, in every sense, the bomber captain, or 'skipper', needed qualities of character in which his crew could have trust and faith; in his strong hands, so often, lay their lives.

Cyril Joe Barton was one such bomber skipper. Young, on the brink of manhood, and devoted to his crew, Barton – 'Cy' to his crew – possessed another quality which sustained and gave meaning to his life, and his attitude to his fellows; a deep, sincerely-held Christian faith in his God. His faith was exemplified in his last hours as he fought to the end, attempting to save the lives of his fellow men.

Born at Elveden, Suffolk on 5 June 1921, Cyril Barton was raised in Surrey, and after attending studies at the Kingston-upon-Thames Technical College, became apprenticed as a draughtsman in an aircraft factory at Tolworth. Even in his earliest years he openly acknowledged his deep Christian beliefs, attending various bible classes and, on occasion, giving talks and lectures on those Christian principles in which he wholeheartedly believed. In doing so he never once attempted to impose his own beliefs on others in any 'missionary' context; instead he preferred to 'lead' by the example of his own life and attitudes. A teetotaller and non-smoker himself, nevertheless he was no prude, and his natural sheer joy of life found expression in any company.

Volunteering for aircrew duties with the RAF, Barton was eventually enlisted on 16 April 1941 and, after basic training, he was promoted to Leading Aircraftman (LAC) on 1 November, and then sailed to the United States of America to commence pilot instruction. Arriving at Darr Aero Technical School, Albany, Georgia on 17 January 1942, he made his first-ever flight two days later in a PT17 trainer, and flew 'solo' for the first time on 20 February. Completing his preliminary training at Darr Aero on 4 July, Barton moved to Cochran Field, Macon for basic instruction until 7 September; on which date he again moved, to Napier Field, Duthan, Alabama, for advanced training.

Graduating as a Sergeant pilot on 10 November 1942, Cy Barton returned to England, and was posted to No 6(P) AFU, Chipping Norton on 15 March 1943, before joining No 19 OTU, Kinloss in Morayshire on 4 May. At Kinloss Barton began to select the members of his future bomber crew. As navigator he chose Sergeant J. L. 'Len' Lambert, and then 'recruited' Pilot Officer Jack Kay as wireless operator, and Flying Officer Wally Crate, a Canadian, as bomb aimer. The fourth member to be chosen was an air gunner, Sergeant Freddie Brice, from Devon.

The embryo crew first flew together, in a Whitley, on 1 June, and for the next four weeks began to get used to each other, both in the air and on the ground. Leaving Kinloss on 3 July for a 14-days' leave, Barton and his crew next reported to No 1663 Heavy Conversion Unit (HCU), Rufforth in Yorkshire on 17 July, and quickly completed the crew establishment by persuading Sergeant Maurice Trousdale, flight engineer, and Sergeant Harry Wood, air gunner, to join them.

Whilst at Rufforth, Cy Barton undertook his first two operational sorties over Germany, without his as yet untested crew. On 24 July he became second pilot to the crew of a 76 Squadron Halifax, DK203, 'A' for an attack on Hamburg; and three nights later, again as second pilot, in Halifax DK241, 'Q', returned to Hamburg. This 'blooding' of operations stood Barton in good stead for his future duties, and on 1 August he made his first conversion flight in a Halifax with his complete crew – still as second pilot – and then settled down as skipper to train his crew to operational standard.

From the start Barton's constant goal was efficiency – he had no place for slackers in his crew. In the air he imposed just one strict rule, no swearing; but once on the ground again he left the crew to their own devices and amusements, and when accompanying his crew to the nearest town in off-duty hours would be the first to buy them a round of drinks in the local public house before slipping away, usually with his navigator, to visit the nearest cinema. In the communal billet he shared with the other non-commissioned crew members, Barton joined in their pastimes, but was never afraid to kneel by his bedside in their presence to say his nightly prayer before retiring to sleep.

Throughout August Barton and his crew completed their conversion training on Halifax bombers, practising and sharpening their individual and collective skills, and on 5 September moved on to Breighton airfield to join their first operational unit, 78 Squadron; with Barton being promoted to Flight Sergeant on the same day, and commissioned as Pilot Officer on 26 September.

After a week's day and night flying practice, Barton and his crew undertook their first collective operational sortie; a bombing raid on Montlucon in Halifax 'U', on 15/16 September. Within the following two weeks they had flown four more sorties, against Hannover, Mannheim and Bochum, all in Halifax 'Y'. On 11 November, during a raid on Leverkusen, Barton's aircraft received hits from predicted flak, injuring the navigator and bomb aimer, but Barton brought the Halifax back and made an emergency landing at Woodbridge.

With his full crew again, Barton resumed operations on 22 November with a raid on Berlin; then bombed Frankfurt on 25 November, Stuttgart on the next night, and completed his operations with 78 Squadron on 29/30 December by returning to bomb Germany's capital city, Berlin. On 15 January 1944 Barton and his crew were posted to Snaith airfield, where a new squadron, 578, was officially formed the same day from C Flight of 51 Squadron. Here Barton managed to fly a further sortie on 30 January – his third trip to Berlin – before 578 Squadron moved to its own airfield at Burn on 6 February. His first sortie from Burn – an $8\frac{1}{4}$-hours round trip to Stuttgart – was flown in a new Halifax, LK797, 'E', in which Barton was to fly his remaining sorties. Three nights later, in a raid on Frankfurt, however, 'E's' bomb doors failed to open during the attack and Barton was eventually forced to jettison the bombs in one salvo near Darmstadt and then return to base with the doors still gaping open. The experience did not deter Barton from piloting 'E' again four nights later, when he returned to Frankfurt and bombed the objective successfully.

On 24 March he made his fourth raid on Berlin, without incident, and two nights later bombed Essen. Unknown to Barton when he took off that night, 26 March, his promotion to Flying Officer had been officially pro-

mulgated and was wending its way through the administrative channels
to Burn. Having come to regard Halifax LK797, 'E' as their 'personal'
machine, Barton and his crew decided to emblazon the aircraft with its
own individual insigne – a sword, named Excalibur, emerging downwards
through a cloud, and pointing at a swastika surrounded by flames. The
'Excalibur' insigne was drawn on the side of the Halifax's nose in chalk,
preparatory to a more permanent painting job, during the last days of
March.

Late in the morning of 30 March 1944, Cy Barton and the other crew
captains were called to a preliminary briefing. A major raid – a 'maximum
effort' – was to be flown that night by Bomber Command; a mass raid
against the city of Nuremburg, flying more than 600 miles deep into
Germany. Halifax LK797, 'Excalibur' was loaded with a full complement
of incendiary bombs and the crew prepared for a late evening take-off.
The prospects weren't good – a half-moon of full brilliance and almost
complete lack of cloud cover at height promised a night ideally suited for
the Luftwaffe's night fighter defences. It was to be Cy Barton's 19th
operational trip – and his last.

At precisely 9.16 pm the first of 782 bombers despatched on the raid
left its base airfield, and within the following 98 minutes the remaining
bombers had become airborne. At Burn, Barton took off at the mid-way
point of the bomber stream – at 10.12 pm – and began his run down the
English coastline heading for Europe, gaining height steadily. His crew,
in accordance with their skipper's normal orders, used the intercommunication system minimally – Barton abhorred 'idle chatter' once in
the air – and busied themselves in preparation for the long run to
Nuremburg.

Climbing above the sparse cloud, the Halifax continued in the full
silver brilliance of moonlight – 'almost as light as day', in the words of
Freddie Brice, Barton's rear gunner – and by the time it reached the
enemy coast the crew could plainly see other bombers in the stream
around them, each heading south-east towards Ghent. As they crossed
the Dutch coast some light flak appeared from various coastal batteries
but did not particularly worry the bombers.

In the luminous moonlight, the chief danger would be night fighters,
and Barton periodically reminded his crew, particularly Brice in the rear
and Wood in the mid-upper turrets, to keep their eyes peeled. Turning
due east onto the second long leg of the planned route, Barton flew south
of Liege and Bonn for just over an hour, then began to turn southwards
for the final 70-odd miles run-up to the target.

So far Barton had been fortunate in escaping the attention of the

German defences. Halfway along the 'long leg' two searchlights had suddenly snapped on ahead of him, pointing vertically and not moving. Flying between these 'markers', he next saw ahead of him the first fighter flares – pale red parachute flares dropped above the bombers' route by high-flying Junkers 88's to signal their presence to the roving night fighter packs already airborne. As the hovering flares settled into a slow descent the bombers found themselves flying through a double lane of lights, almost like an illuminated runway, their flight path sky-marked with precision. Out of the clear sky came the night fighters, probing and hacking at the bomber stream, and in Barton's Halifax the bomb aimer reported seeing several other aircraft being attacked and shot down ahead. Unknown to Barton's crew, more than 50 of their fellow crews had become fighter victims before 'Excalibur' turned for its final run south to the target. But at that moment their luck ran out.

As Barton banked to start the last leg of his course, two German fighters appeared in front of him, attacking nose-on, their cannons pushing long dotted lines of white tracer at the bomber. The fuselage of the Halifax shuddered as the shells raked along its flanks, puncturing two fuel tanks, knocking out the radio and the rear turret controls, setting the starboard inner engine afire, and cutting the crew's intercomm lines.

In the tail, Brice felt the thuds in the fuselage and then had a fleeting glimpse of a Junkers 88 flashing past him overhead. Barton instinctively threw the aircraft into a violent weaving pattern. Seconds later Brice saw the Junkers closing in again from the starboard quarter. With no intercomm available to warn Barton, Brice reached for his emergency light button, waited, then as the German bore in, sent a series of dashes on the button to Barton to indicate evasive action to starboard, at the same time swinging his guns to bear on the oncoming fighter. Barton responded by throwing the bomber to starboard immediately; Brice pressed his gun button – and nothing happened. His gun firing system was 'out'.

The Junkers, foiled by Barton's swift evasive move, broke off his attack without firing and turned away. The Halifax continued its corkscrewing evasion and Brice, seeing no sign of the fighter, pressed his call button again, sending a series of Morse 'R's' (Dot-dash-Dot); the signal to resume course.

Hardly had Barton straightened out when the Junkers appeared again, on the starboard quarter. Brice flashed a series of dashes – evasive action – and as Barton again commenced corkscrewing another hail of bullets and shells ripped into the Halifax, which began vibrating, while the burning engine trailed a long plume of sparks past the tail until its propeller flew off and dropped away.

The fighter wheeled away again and Brice signalled a series of ''R's to resume course; only to be immediately corrected by Harry Wood in the mid-upper turret who could now see the Junkers coming in from the port beam, and accordingly called for evasive action to port with a series of dots on the call light. Frustrated again, the Junkers switched to an attack from below, scoring more hits, and then (apparently) disappeared.

After a few seconds Barton resumed his course to target again. Brice now realised that the trail of sparks from the burning engine had ceased, the vibration had died down, and they seemed to be flying normally. Then the persistent Junkers made its final onslaught, racing in from above and almost dead astern. Brice flashed a series of dashes for evasion to starboard, and as the Halifax heeled over, the German began to break away; hastened by a well-placed burst of tracer from Wood in the mid-upper turret. Brice could see the tracer heading for the dead centre of the Junkers' fuselage, but then it was lost to his vision as the bomber continued its corkscrewing manoeuvres.

The German never returned, and as the crew realised this Barton took stock of the damage. The first shock for him was to discover that his navigator, bomb aimer, and wireless operator were no longer in the aircraft. During the furious exchanges of messages on the emergency call light, one or all of these had mistaken the Morse 'R' (Dot-dash-Dot) for 'P' (Dot-dash-dash-Dot) – the latter being the signal for 'Parachute'; in other words, 'Bale out'. Accordingly all three, knowing seconds were usually vital in such an emergency, had jettisoned the floor hatch panel in the nose compartment and abandoned the aircraft.

Barton checked the physical damage to the aircraft with Maurice Trousdale – there was obviously a lot of fuel gone from the two ruptured tanks (some 400 gallons it was later estimated); one engine was useless; the radio and intercomm systems and the rear turret were out of commission; and he was now without navigational or wireless guidance.

If Barton had now decided to bale out the rest of his crew and himself; or at least jettison the incendiary bomb load and abort the mission, no one could have blamed him. He took neither decision, preferring to 'press on' to the target and complete his duty.

As a result of the violent evasive manoeuvres taken to escape the several night fighter attacks, Barton had little precise notion of his actual location at that moment. Nevertheless he continued on what he presumed was his planned course, reached a city and personally released the bomb load.* Then, guided by the Pole Star, and the tiny pilot's flight map

* Available evidence, though fragmentary, suggests strongly that in fact Barton bombed Schweinfurt, north-west of Nuremburg – an understandable error in identification in the circumstances.

strapped to his knee, Cy Barton started the long journey home to England.

As the Halifax droned across the coastline again, Brice – still maintaining his lonely vigil in the useless rear gun turret – heard a knock on his turret doors; opened these, and found the flight engineer, Trousdale standing there. He relayed Barton's message to Brice to leave the turret and come forward; to Brice's relief at being able to speak to someone again. Making his way to the front cockpit, Brice tapped Barton on the shoulder, and received a happy smile and a thumbs-up from the pilot, who told the gunner that with a bit of luck they'd soon hit the English coast. Barton had already asked Trousdale and Wood whether they wanted to try to reach home, or take the shorter route to Switzerland and be interned. Both had voted to try for home.

Droning northwards over apparently endless stretches of the North Sea, Barton continued sending out MAY DAY calls on the radio, which though apparently defunct might have been transmitting though not receiving. The actual course flown by Barton cannot now be resolved, but it seems likely that he must have flown virtually parallel to the east coast of England out of sight of land, using up precious fuel and time in his untutored bid to navigate accurately. At one point the crew's morale leapt as a Beaufighter hove into view, and they used a torch to flash SOS distress signals at the 'friendly' aircraft; but the Beaufighter flew on, apparently unaware of their signals.

Shortly before dawn Barton, conscious of the desperate fuel state, sent Trousdale back to be ready to switch tanks the moment any engine failed, but seconds later he spotted a light shining below. The moonlight had now gone, so he made for the light and confirmed that they were over land at last. Cruising in over the coastline, Barton, with Brice standing beside him, was grinning again and once more gave his habitual thumbs-up sign. His joy was short-lived as he realised the engines were beginning to die, starved of petrol. He yelled to Trousdale to switch tanks which was promptly done. Then, knowing there were only minutes to go, he ordered the three remaining crew members to take up crash positions. All three sat behind the rear spar on the floor, their hands behind their heads, and waited. Barton, alone now in the cockpit, desperately guiding an engine-less bomber in a flat glide, had little control.

Out of the dawn haze in front of him loomed a twin row of terraced houses, and he pulled hard to jump the obstacle. A wing demolished most of the chimney pots along the north side of the street, dipped and destroyed the end house, swept on through some gardens and greenhouses, and finally demolished a footbridge across a deep railway cutting; breaking off the rear fuselage (containing the three crew men) which fell into the cutting; while the wings, engine and forward section of the Halifax scattered widely in a rain of hurtling metal.

Cy Barton had come to earth in Ryhope village colliery, County Durham; some 200 miles north of his squadron base airfield. The only civilian casualty was a local miner walking to work to the west of the footbridge, who was overtaken by the careening aircraft and killed. The time was minutes before 6 am on 31 March.

The dazed crew members in the rear portion of fuselage were soon rescued by other miners, given rough first aid on the spot, and then taken to Cherry Knowle Hospital for expert medical care. They were told that Cy Barton had already been taken away to hospital, but the following morning learned that their gallant pilot had died on reaching the hospital.

On 6 April 1944 they buried Cyril Barton in Kingston cemetery, but on 27 June, came the posthumous award of a Victoria Cross. The closing lines of the citation read : 'In gallantly completing his last mission in the face of almost impossible odds, this officer displayed unsurpassed courage and devotion to duty.' Yet, in the heartfelt tribute paid to Barton by one of his surviving crew, Freddie Brice, 'How can words portray a true picture of such a man as Cy?'

41. Norman Cyril Jackson

On the initial introduction of four-engined heavy bombers into RAF Bomber Command in late 1940, a new category of air crew was mooted – flight engineer. The obvious need for an 'extra' crew member to relieve pilots of the chores of constantly checking fuel states, engine temperatures and a hundred other facets of coping with a multi-engined aircraft resulted in an Air Ministry Order, No A190/41 in March 1941, defining the duties and conditions of service for the fresh air crew role. Basically, would-be flight engineers had to be trained ground tradesmen in the Group 1 trade of Fitter IIE (Engines), who were physically fit for flying duties, and who volunteered. Appropriate rank and privileges would be granted to those volunteers who successfully completed a brief course in air gunnery and flying procedures; though it was understood from the start that such men would eventually revert to their basic ground trade on completion of their aircrew operational tours of duty. Despite the 'temporary' nature of the new crew category, there was no lack of volunteers from amongst the ground maintenance staff. Eventually, as Bomber Command became predominantly a heavy bomber force, the flight engineers became a permanent integral part of operational air crews. Heading the long list of awards and decorations made to flight engineers is Norman Cyril Jackson VC.

Born in Ealing on 8 April 1919, Jackson was adopted by the Gunter family as a small child, and on leaving school entered engineering; eventually qualifying as a fitter and turner. At the outbreak of war Jackson, though married by then and in an occupation which could have exempted him from military service, volunteered to join the RAF, and was enlisted on 20 October 1939. After various training courses at Halton and Hednesford, he became classified as a Fitter IIE (engines) – a Group 1 tradesman, and posted overseas. His first unit was 95 Squadron, to which he reported on 2 January 1941; a Short Sunderland flying boat squadron based on the West African coast near Freetown.

For the following eighteen months Jackson continued to serve as an engine fitter on flying boats and marine craft, but the opportunity to remuster to flying duties as a flight engineer attracted him and he accordingly applied for training. As a result he returned to England in September 1942, and after six months at 27 OTU, moved to RAF St Athan at the end of March 1943 to complete instruction. Finally, with promotion to Sergeant, he was remustered as a flight engineer on 14 June, and posted to No 1645 HCU. On 28 July he joined his first squadron, 106, based at Syerston and flying Avro Lancasters.

With Sergeant (later, Flying Officer) Fred Mifflin as skipper, Jackson and his fellow crew members were soon engaged in operations over Germany. Mifflin, a Newfoundlander, had flown his first operational sortie as co-pilot on another crew's last sortie of its tour; and had then been 'chosen' by Jackson and his other crew as their future captain, despite Mifflin's reputation for being 'heavy-handed' in control of a Lancaster. The crew soon settled down together, and by mid-November 1943 had completed 14 sorties against the German cities. In late November, 106 Squadron was moved to another base, Metheringham, and quickly resumed its part in the nightly air offensive.

On the night of 2 December, while bombing Berlin for the fifth time, Mifflin's Lancaster, JB612, was a victim of the flak. Turning out of the target area the bomber was then attacked by a night fighter. With one engine 'out' and despite the damage to the aircraft, Mufflin brought his crew back safely. He returned the 'compliment' by bombing Berlin five more times by mid-February. On 24 April Mifflin's crew flew its 29th mission, in Lancaster JB664 bombing Munich. For Jackson it was his 30th sortie, having flown an 'extra' operation with another crew when its flight engineer was indisposed, but he intended staying with his crew until they too were tour-expired. Already Mifflin's crew had volunteered to stay together after their 30th sortie and transfer to the Path Finder Force; thus on 26 April Jackson cheerfully agreed to do one more sortie to stay with his friends, 'just for luck.'

The target on 26 April was Schweinfurt, 50 miles north-west of Nuremburg, entailing a 1,000-mile round trip deep into Germany. Mifflin and his crew were in good humour that evening, particularly Norman Jackson, who had earlier received a telegram informing him that his wife Alma had just given birth to their first son, Ian.

For this trip Mifflin was allocated a fresh Lancaster, ME669, ZN-O, but his crew remained as always. As navigator he had Flying Officer F. L. Higgins, while his bomb-aimer was Flight Sergeant Maurice Toft. Handling the wireless set was Flight Sergeant E. Sandelands. In the mid-upper gun turret sat Sergeant W. Smith, and 'Arse-end Charlie' (the rear gunner) was Flight Sergeant Johnson. At the flight engineer's panel array of instruments, as usual, stood Norman Jackson.

Taking off a few minutes after 9.30 pm, Mifflin set course southwards and soon ran into an unforecast head wind which impeded progress but

Cyril Joe Barton

Norman Cyril Jackson

caused him no undue worry. By the time he reached the target, however, he seemed to be alone; the last Lancaster of his particular formation to attack the objective. Holding the bomber rock-steady as he made his approach run, Mifflin felt the bomb load release and swung away from the city to begin the run for home. Flak opposition had been virtually nil – it had been 'a piece of cake', in RAF parlance. Then the voice of Sandelands came through Mifflin's earphones, telling the skipper that there was a blip on the 'Fishpond' radar set – another aircraft in the vicinity. It came from astern, so Mifflin warned Johnson in the rear turret to keep a sharp lookout. Again Sandelands' voice warned the pilot that the blip was closing range – too rapidly to be anything other than a fighter.

The Newfoundlander immediately began to corkscrew the Lancaster to evade, and the gunners opened fire as they glimpsed a fighter hurtling towards them from below and behind. At the same moment a hail of cannon shells, raked along the Lancaster's fuselage, the combined impact jolting the bomber and throwing Jackson to the floor. Scrambling to a blister window, he saw a Focke-Wulf Fw 190 banking swiftly away, and then saw the starboard inner engine of the Lancaster erupt in flames.

In an instinctive, trained reaction, Jackson pushed a button of his panel to operate the engine's internal extinguisher and saw the flames diminish; but seconds later the fire burst out again in even greater intensity. Jackson immediately realised the danger of the fire igniting the adjacent wing petrol tanks. If that happened the wing would explode. The solution seemed simple to Jackson. He had several times discussed the possibility of climbing onto a Lancaster wing in flight with Toft, and here was an opportunity to turn theory into practice.

'I think I can deal with it, Fred,' he said to the pilot.

'How?' replied Mifflin.

'I'll climb out on the wing with an extinguisher. That'll fix it.'

Mifflin, struggling to retain control of his damaged aircraft, accepted this incredible suggestion without comment, nodded assent, then yelled for the crew to prepare for baling out if necessary. Jackson's plan was to don his parachute, release the canopy inside the fuselage, and have Toft and Higgins hang on to the cords of the parachute, paying these out steadily as Jackson climbed out. In the event of being unable to return, Jackson could at least be released under some sort of control and float to earth.

Stuffing a hand extinguisher inside his battle dress blouse, Jackson climbed onto the navigator's table, pulled the ripcord of his parachute pack, and waited for Higgins to sort out the support lines. Toft soon joined them and helped Higgins. Releasing the upper escape hatch, Jackson started to squeeze himself through the opening.

As his head and shoulders emerged the freezing 200 mph slip-stream took his breath away, but with a firm grasp of the coaming of the hatch Jackson edged the rest of his body out and lay flat along the top of the fuselage. Then, never relaxing for a second his grip on the hatch opening, he slowly lowered his body until his feet were on the wing root below him. The engine was still burning fiercely and Jackson looked around for a hand-hold on the wing; then saw the leading edge air intake ahead of him.

Flinging himself hard forward into the teeth of the slipstream, Jackson managed to clamp his fingers into the intake and hold. His head was now in line with the wing leading edge, within arm's reach of the burning engine. Relaxing the grip of his right hand, he eased the extinguisher out of his battle dress blouse, gave the nozzle a sharp rap on the wing, and thrust the hissing jet into an opening in the engine cowling. With the full weight of his body now held only by his left hand grip on the air intake, he continued to hold the extinguisher in place, and was elated to see the flames begin to die down. His thoughts turned next to the much greater problem of how to regain the fuselage. Once he let go the air intake he would have no hold. Before he could ponder further, he felt the wing beneath him lift as the Lancaster went into a bank to port.

Almost immediately he heard the tearing sound of cannon fire, and felt sharp pains in his legs and back. The German fighter had returned. The shock loosened his grip on the extinguisher which was swept away, and the engine again erupted in a gout of searing flames which swept over Jackson's body. He felt his left hand grip relax involuntarily but could do nothing about it, and the howling slipstream lifted him from the wing and flung him backwards.

As the Lancaster tail flashed by, Jackson was abruptly pulled to a halt, only yards behind the rear gun turret. Like a fish on a line, Jackson was now dragged behind the twisting, falling bomber, held by the rigging lines of his parachute. These lines, already smouldering from the burst of flames from the engine before Jackson was torn from the wing, were being frantically played out by Toft and Higgins inside the fuselage before they too could bale out of the doomed bomber.

Suddenly Jackson was free of the aircraft and was dropping through the air alone. The fire had spread to the canopy of his parachute, which now held him as he twisted downwards. Taking stock of this new danger, Jackson began gripping the rigging lines with his bare hands to extinguish the smouldering cords. Above him the main canopy was slashed and torn, with burn holes riddling the silk. Continuing his rapid descent, Jackson could now feel the agony of his back and leg wounds, but his hands, shrivelled and contracted by the flames, were still numb.

The black earth came up with a rush and Jackson hit it hard, crumpling both ankles and plunging into a mass of bushes. As he slowly regained a modicum of consciousness, he vaguely checked himself for his injuries. Both ankles seemed broken, his legs ached abominably from shell splinters and shrapnel; his back was one dull ache. Both hands were severely burned, as was his face, with his right eye completely closed up.

At daybreak, Jackson, in pitiable condition, started his bid to find help – escape or evasion was his last concern now. Crawling painfully on knees and elbows, he slowly made his way across the edge of the forest he had landed in until many hours later (or so it seemed) he came to a cottage. Knocking the door of this with an elbow, he finally got response from a middle-aged German – who immediately spat insults at him – 'Churchill gangster', 'Terror *Flieger*' – before two young girls took Jackson inside the cottage gently and tried to comfort him.

Soon the cottage owner entered again, accompanied by local police officials and Jackson was made to *walk* to the nearest town, despite his terrible condition, with only the shoulder support of a village policeman to ease his pain. After crude first aid treatment had been given at the local hospital, Jackson was paraded through the town where the local populace kept up a barrage of jeers and insults, and even stoned him. By that time Jackson's condition was such that he was virtually immune to the treatment being meted out to him. For the next ten months Jackson slowly recuperated in a German hospital, though his burned hands never fully recovered.

Of Jackson's crew, Toft, Higgins, Sandelands and Smith escaped by parachute and became prisoners of war; but Fred Mifflin and his great friend Hugh Johnson both died in the aircraft. A little later the award of a DFC to Mifflin, recommended previously, was promulgated. When the surviving crew members were repatriated at the end of the European war the full story of Jackson's incredible action was disclosed, and on 26 October 1945 he was awarded a Victoria Cross.

His investiture with the bronze cross took place at Buckingham Palace on 13 November 1945; alongside another air VC, Group Captain Geoffrey L. Cheshire VC DSO DFC.

42. Andrew Charles Mynarski

The first of three Canadian airmen to be awarded a Victoria Cross during 1939-45 aerial operations, Andrew Charles Mynarski was the son of Polish/Canadian parents, born at Winnipeg, Manitoba on 14 October 1916. Educated successively at King Edward, Isaac Newton, and St John's Technical schools; in May 1936 Mynarski began a career in the fur trade as a furrier and chamois cutter, remaining in that profession until his eventual enlistment in the Royal Canadian Air Force. Although he saw brief uniformed service with the Royal Winnipeg Rifles (NPAM), a militia unit, in November-December 1940; it was not until 29 September 1941 that he finally joined the RCAF at the Winnipeg recruiting centre and, after initial recruit training, began his training for aircrew as a Wireless Air Gunner 'S' (WAG) at No 2 Wireless School, Calgary on 28 March 1942.

On 12 September he was posted to No 3 Bombing & Gunnery School at MacDonald, Manitoba where, on 18 December 1942 he was promoted to Sergeant and received his WAG brevet. Sailing from New York on 5 January 1943, Mynarski reached England a week later, and on 2 March joined 16 Operational Training Unit (OTU) for further training and crewing-up. Moving to 1661 Heavy Conversion Unit (HCU) on 10 June, he was then posted to 9 Squadron RAF on 31 October, an Avro Lancaster unit based then at Bardney, Lincolnshire; having in the meantime been promoted to Flight Sergeant.* After just one month with 9 Squadron, Mynarski was again posted, this time to 1668 HCU on 1 December, and further promoted to Warrant Officer II on 18 December 1943.

On 10 April 1944 Mynarski joined 419 Squadron RCAF at Middleton St George in County Durham. The third RCAF bomber squadron to be formed overseas, 419 had originally formed on 15 December 1941 under the command of the Canadian Wing Commander John 'Moose' Fulton DSO DFC AFC, and from him the unit gained its nickname as the 'Moose' Squadron; eventually incorporating the motif of an aggressive moose as its official squadron badge.

By April 1944 the squadron was part of the all-Canadian No 6 Bomber Group, and was equipped with Handley Page Halifaxes. Mynarski's first operational sortie came on the night of 22/23 April in Halifax III,

* With effect from 18 June 1943.

HR925, 'D' in a midnight raid against Laon but five nights later the squadron flew its ultimate Halifax sorties and then operated only Canadian-built Avro Lancaster X's. After necessary local conversion training on the Lancaster, Mynarski's crew made their next sortie on 1/2 May in Lancaster KB718, 'J' against St Ghislain. In mid-month Mynarski's crew flew on three successive nights – 10, 11 and 12 May – in three different Lancasters KB712, 'L'; KB719, 'T'; KB718, 'J' against Ghent, Boulogne and Louvain respectively; and were then 'rested' until 24/25 May, on which night, in KB736, 'M', they attacked Aachen. Two more operations during May were flown in KB736; bombing Bourg-Leopold on 27/28 May and Mont Couple on the last night of the month, their eighth operational sortie together as a crew.

By now the crew had become well accustomed to each other and were rapidly becoming an experienced team. Their pilot, Flying Officer Arthur ('Art') de Breyne, hailing from St Lambert, PQ, had flown two sorties as a second pilot before becoming skipper of this, his own crew. In the navigator's seat sat Flying Officer Robert Body; while the air bomber was Sergeant Jack Friday, and the wireless set operator Warrant Officer II Jimmy Kelly. The vital post of flight engineer was more than adequately filled by the only Englishman in an otherwise all-Canadian team, Sergeant Roy Vigars. Providing defence for their aircraft were two gunners; Flying Officer George Patrick Brophy from Port Arthur, Ontario, in the lonely rear gun turret, and in the mid-upper turret Andrew Mynarski. Individually skilled, all seven welded together as a disciplined, operational 'whole' once airborne; and in the first days of June 1944 they were allotted their 'own' Lancaster X, KB726, 'A-Apple' – the fighting 'team' was now complete.

Like most operational squadrons of the RAF at this time, the prime effort was being made to soften or destroy German defences and communications in occupied France – a vital pre-requisite to the impending Allied invasion of Europe. On the night of 5/6 June – the eve of D-Day – Art Breyne and his crew in 'A-Apple' bombed communication targets at Longues; and on the next two consecutive nights attacked Coutances and Acheres. Then, on the night of Monday, 12 June 1944, sixteen Lancasters from 419 Squadron were detailed to participate in a bombing raid on the marshalling yards at Cambrai. It was to be a low-level attack, bombing from a height of only 2,000 feet – something of a rare novelty for the Lancaster crews.

At the controls of KB726, A-Apple, Art Breyne got airborne from Middleton St George at 9.44 pm. In the Lancaster's bomb bay were sixteen 500lb GP bombs and two 500lb GP Long-Delay bombs – 9,000lb of high explosive. The weather conditions were favourable, promising a good visibility above the objective and therefore a clear bombing run. Although unaware of it at the time, Andrew Mynarski's commission as a pilot officer had been made effective from the previous day. Crossing the French coast, Breyne began his approach to Cambrai. Around the target the flak defences were highly active, flinging a veritable barrage of shells and tracers at the oncoming bombers. Before reaching the objective, however, a Junkers 88 night fighter appeared suddenly on Breyne's port beam boring in with cannons firing in a lightning attack, and then sweeping up from below and astern, continuing to rake the Lancaster.

Immediately both port engines of the bomber failed and a raging fire broke out in the rear fuselage, just behind Mynarski's mid-upper turret, spreading quickly along the port wing. George Brophy, in the rear turret, had borne part of the brunt of the hail of cannon shells; having his turret's hydraulic lines shattered and leaving him with only manual operation to rotate the gun 'egg'. Operating this, Brophy broke the winding handle – he was now trapped, unable to get out unaided. Breyne swiftly checked his controls and realised his hydraulics were gone; then, calculating the fire damage to both port engines and the blazing port wing, ordered his crew to abandon ship.

Obeying his skipper's order, Mynarski climbed down from his mid-upper turret into the smoke and heat inside the fuselage and was about to make his way forward to the escape hatchway, when he glanced backwards at the raging fire in the rear and realised Brophy was still in the rear turret. Mynarski could simply have considered that Brophy's fate was already sealed in the inferno, and therefore continue to make his own escape. Instead he immediately scrambled through the burning fuselage until he reached the rear turret where, having no other means, he tried as best he could with his hands to rotate the jammed turret to let Brophy out.

Within seconds the lower half of Mynarski's flying clothing was soaked in burning hydraulic oil, but he continued to hammer and beat against the solid turret, trying to obtain some movement in it. Inside the turret Brophy could see Mynarski's flaming clothing and frustrated attempts to save him, and knowing how near to the ground the aircraft was, yelled to Mynarski to leave him and get out before it was too late.

Reluctantly, Mynarski left him and went to the escape hatch, but before diving through he straightened up and saluted Brophy – a sincere gesture of farewell to a comrade. He then plunged through the hatch and hurtled down – his clothing and parachute a mass of flames. Falling to earth at speed, like a human torch, Mynarski hit the ground hard, and though some local Frenchmen soon discovered him he was so badly burned that he died soon after from his horrifying injuries.

The stricken Lancaster meanwhile, its wing now fully alight, stalled and crashed; exploding on impact and scattering sections in every direction. By some near-miracle Brophy's turret was flung clear of the burning wreckage and he survived; as did the remaining members of the crew. Mynarski's deliberate delay of his own escape from the doomed bomber in order to go to a comrade's assistance had cost the gunner his life. His supreme sacrifice was not forgotten, and at the end of the war when the rest of the crew were repatriated from the prisoner-of-war camps, they told higher authority of Mynarski's last moments. As a result, on 11 October 1946 Andrew Mynarski was awarded a posthumous Victoria Cross. He had been buried in Meharicourt Cemetery, France, but in Canada his name soon came to be honoured in various ways. In Winnipeg the Junior High School in Machray Avenue was renamed Andrew Mynarski; and an almost unique honour was accorded to him when a group of lakes at Latitude 56° 10', Longitude 99° 12' were collectively titled Mynarski Lakes in his permanent memory.

Within the postwar RCAF they created the Mynarski Trophy – presented to the RCAF by members of the RCAF Association who were formerly members of the World War Two Polish Air Force. This trophy – a handsome silver bowl on its own pedestal base – is awarded annually to the RCAF Station whose married quarters community council makes the most effective use of its resources in developing a youth recreation programme suited to the community's needs.

43. David Ernest Hornell

The tasks of RAF Coastal Command crews in the years 1939-45 were many and varied, but their prime role was the constant protection of the vital Allied merchant shipping supplying the United Kingdom. Such protection involved them in seemingly interminable hours of mainly rewardless patrols over the oceans, seeking an elusive, cunning prey – the wolves of the sea, U-boats. But submarines were by no means the only enemies. Apart from the ever-present danger from marauding Luftwaffe interceptors, the greatest opponents to any lone Coastal crew were the elements. Endless miles of friendless sea allied to pitiless winds, blistering heat by day or cruel sub-zero temperatures by night, were collectively responsible for killing more crews than anything perpetrated by the 'enemy'.

Any aircraft crew brought down in the sea – if they survived the impact – faced almost certain death if they were not rescued within a reasonable time. Apart from any physical injuries sustained before or during the 'ditching', crews faced a daunting prospect of being entirely at the mercy of raw nature in its most powerful guise; while their sole life support was usually a fragile dinghy – a few square feet of highly vulnerable gum elastic. Even if they withstood the debilitating exposure to wind, sun and bitter cold, the chances of being retrieved quickly were hair-thin – a yellow micro-dot upon thousands of square miles of grey water and helpless passengers of unknown winds and currents.

Such was the fate of a 34 years-old Canadian pilot, David Ernest Hornell. Shot into the ocean by the U-boat he had just destroyed, he and his crew spent nearly 21 hours clinging tenuously to a single dinghy and Hornell, blinded and dying, devoted his last hours to succouring his crew – a selfless action which cost him his life.

Born on 26 January 1910 at Mimico, Ontario, Canada, David Hornell was the son of Harry Alexander Hornell. On the birth of his younger sister Emily, Hornell's mother died and the two children were raised by an aunt until the father re-married. Educated at Mimico High School and the Western Technical School, Toronto, David Hornell proved to be an all-round athlete and sportsman at school, playing rugby, tennis and other sports with great enthusiasm, and showing particular prowess in

371

track events. Although he won a scholarship in his last year at school, with the opportunity to enter a university for advanced education and academic qualifications, Hornell chose instead to take up employment with the Goodyear Tire & Rubber Company in Toronto, working in the firm's research laboratories. By the outbreak of war in 1939 Hornell seemed set for a successful career with this company but the urge to enlist and serve his country in the armed forces eventually proved too strong to resist.

On 8 January 1941, just three weeks before his 31st birthday (when he would have been deferred from uniformed service due to the existing age limits), Hornell enlisted voluntarily in the RCAF at No 1 Manning Depot, Toronto; and on 4 February began training at No 1 Wireless School, Montreal. On 22 April he reported to No 3 Initial Training School, Victoriaville, Quebec, to commence pilot instruction and two months later, on 27 May, moved to 12 EFTS, Goderich, Ontario for basic flying training. His final advanced instruction commenced on 15 July 1941 at 5 SFTS, Brantford, Ontario, and he received his 'wings' and a commission as Pilot Officer on 25 September.

After a short course at 31 GR School, Charlottestown, Prince Edward Island in October-November 1941, Hornell was posted to 120 Squadron RCAF and attached to the RCAF station Coal Harbour, Nova Scotia on 23 December; flying his first operational patrol of the coastal waters on 26 December. On 30 January 1942 he made his first flight in a Supermarine Stranraer biplane flying boat, and thereafter flew many patrols in Stranraers along Canada's eastern seaboard, though without any direct contact with an enemy submarine. For the following two years Hornell remained based in Nova Scotia, during which period he was promoted to Flying Officer (25 September 1942) and Flight Lieutenant (15 April 1943). On 26 January 1943 he married Genevieve Noecker, a former music teacher and friend of Hornell's sister Emily; while in April 1943 he was 'loaned' to the Boeing Aircraft Company as a test pilot on various Boeing aircraft being built for the RCAF.

On 22 September 1943 Hornell was posted to Eastern Air Command headquarters at Halifax, and soon after arrival finally got his wish to be with a front-line operational unit when, on 9 October, he joined 162 Squadron RCAF – a Canso-equipped unit which had just moved from Yarmouth to Dartmouth in Nova Scotia. On 7 December, 162 Squadron received preliminary warning of an impending move out of Canadian waters for an active post in the Battle of the Atlantic, and on the last day of December David Hornell, among others, was sent ahead of the aircraft to the squadron's new base at Reykjavik, Iceland.

On 6 January 1944 the first squadron Cansos flew in to Reykjavik, and on 25 January the squadron made its first operational patrol. The Consolidated Canso, as equipping 162 Squadron, though rugged and reliable, was by no means an ideal machine for 162's prime task. With only two 1,050 hp engines, external wing-racked radar and bomb loads, and merely two manually-operated .303 Browning machine guns in the nose turret (other Brownings were hand-operated from the side fuselage blisters); the Canso was painfully slow in performance and ill-armed to combat the batteries of 20mm and 37mm cannons then fitted to all sea-going U-boats, whose policy was still to stay on the ocean surface and fight it out with any attacking aircraft.

From Reykjavik Hornell continued his operational flying on Cansos by flying initially as second pilot to various flying boat captains, chiefly 162's commanding officer Wing Commander C. G. W. Chapman, but on 1 May 1944 he flew his first patrol as a Canso captain with his own crew. It was a period of mounting preparation by the Allies for the imminent invasion of Europe, and in anticipation of an increase in U-boat depredations, 162 Squadron arranged for a 'permanent' detachment of three Cansos and their crew to Wick in northern Scotland; the first trio being sent to Wick on 24 May, and being relieved on a regular basis by other unit aircraft and crews. Hornell's first spell at Wick came from 2 June to 12 June 1944, during which time he flew two sorties without incident. He then returned to Wick on 18 June, and flew two more sorties, on 20 and 23 June; the latter being his 60th operational sortie since December 1941.

On 24 June he and his crew prepared for their third sortie of this particular detachment. Their aircraft was Canso 9754, coded 'P'; and as his seven-man crew Hornell had Flying Officer Bernard C. Denomy as second pilot, and Flying Officer S. E. 'Ed' Matheson as navigator. His three wireless operator/air gunners (WAG's) were Flying Officer Graham Campbell, Flight Sergeants Israel Joseph ('Joe') Bodnoff and Sydney Cole; while the two flight engineers were Sergeants D. S. Scott and Fernand St Laurent. All were Canadians, relatively well experienced, and thoroughly trained as a skilled team. At 9.30 am Hornell became airborne from Wick and headed northwards.

At 7 pm, after nearly ten hours of fruitless searching, Hornell was approximately 120' North of the Shetlands beginning his return flight to base, when Bodnoff and Cole in the port side gun blister spotted a submarine some five miles away off their port quarter, fully surfaced. Informing Hornell on the intercomm, Cole then collected the aircraft camera and relieved Campbell at the radio set; while Campbell went forward to the nose guns – a crew drill for any attack. Hornell meanwhile sounded the aircraft Klaxon horn, calling all crew to 'Action Stations', and promptly swung the Canso into an attack pattern.

At four miles from the U-boat the Canso came under the opening fire of the submarine's flak guns, and Hornell took evasive action, though without deviating from his attack heading. The first shell damage was to the radio aerials, cutting off all transmission signals from Cole, still sending out routine signals to base. During the two minutes' run-in Hornell's aircraft suffered a hail of further flak damage; with chunks of the starboard wing being torn out and, as the Canso closed the range, riddling the fuselage and exploding inside the body of the flying boat.

One accurate burst shattered the starboard engine which erupted in flames and burned the adjacent wing section from leading to trailing edges. Denomy in the co-pilot's seat, struggled to feather the propeller of the burning motor, while Hornell continued to use every ounce of his considerable strength and skill to keep the bucketing Canso on its attack course. At 1200 yards' range the aircraft's gunners began firing, splashing the U-boat's conning tower, but one of the nose guns almost immediately jammed. The side blister guns joined in the firing with difficulty as the Canso vibrated violently with each successive hit by the flak.

At 800 yards range the Canso was plunging through a veritable curtain of shells, when the firing from the German gunners suddenly ceased as the submarine commander (Oberleutnant zur See Ernst Sauersery) swung his ship to port, broadside on to the Canso's attack course, a standard tactic to reduce the chances of being hit by the expected stick of depth charges from the air. Hornell roared over the U-boat at a mere 50 feet and released his depth charges in a perfect straddle. The U-boat's bows were lifted clean out of the sea by the explosion and fell back into a mountainous plume of spray.

Having released his depth charges Hornell pulled back hard on the controls trying to gain height. The starboard engine still aflame fell away from its bearings completely, and gushing oil and petrol increased the fire in the starboard wing. Inside the fuselage smoke was filling every compartment. Reaching a height of 250 feet, Hornell already knew he would have to ditch on the sea, and while he still had a semblance of control, he edged the Canso's nose into the prevailing wind and prepared to land on the water.

Skimming the 12-foot waves, the Canso touched, bounced to 150 feet, touched again, bounced to 50 feet, then finally 'stuck' and came to a halt; the whole starboard wing and fuselage side a roaring mass of flames. Hornell and Denomy immediately climbed through their cockpit escape hatches and the rest of the crew began to evacuate the already-sinking

Canso through the port blister opening. St Laurent tossed one of the air-craft's pair of rubber dinghies out; then dived after it, while Bodnoff and Scott launched the second dinghy. Cole meanwhile was busy grabbing emergency ration boxes and water bottles, and was the last member of the crew to leave the aircraft; by which time the fuselage was half-filled with water. The whole crew evacuation had taken less than five minutes.

Pulling away from the burning aircraft because of the risk of explosion, the crew saw the Canso slide under the waves about 10 minutes later. Seven of the crew were then in or hanging on to the second dinghy, when they spotted St Laurent about 100 feet away struggling to right his overturned dinghy. Making their way to him, Campbell and Matheson managed to get the dinghy upright and clambered in, but as they were helping St Laurent into it the dinghy blew up, ejecting all three into the icy cold sea again.

All eight men now had just one four-man dinghy for support. Hornell, on seeing St Laurent's original struggle with the dinghy had stripped off his uniform trousers and dived into the sea to assist him; and now, instead of putting the trousers back on for protection he tied knots in each leg and used them for baling water out of the remaining dinghy. At first the crew split into two 'shifts' whereby four men sat in the dinghy while the other four clung to the sides, immersed in water up to their necks; but after an hour it was decided to try to get everyone in or onto the dinghy as the best hope of eventual survival. In this they succeeded except for Scott, whose legs still trailed in the sea.

As the night wore on the surface of the sea was whipped by 50 knot winds into a 40 feet swell, and the tiny dinghy was tossed like a cork. Just before midnight a Catalina from 333 Squadron, piloted by a Norwegian, Lieutenant Johannsen, was sighted and Campbell fired three of the two-star red distress cartridges provided in the dinghy. Johannsen, who was merely returning from a routine patrol and therefore passed over the dinghy by sheer coincidence, spotted the third cartridge and immediately located the survivors – not only Hornell's crew but, some distance away, a cluster of dinghies filled with survivors of the U-boat. Dropping sea markers and flame floats to mark their position, Johannsen radioed their location to base, requesting immediate air-sea rescue services, and then circled the area attempting to find any more survivors. After 30 minutes he returned to Hornell's crew and flashed down by Aldis lamp the mess-age, 'Courage – HSL (High Speed Launch) on way – help coming.'

Then, after another circuit, he flashed down, 'U-boat killed'.* For the

* *U-1225* was sunk 6300N/0050W, 120' North of the Shetlands.

next 14 hours the Catalina continued to circle, replenishing the flame
floats, and continuing to keep track of the tiny dinghy; but by then St
Laurent succumbed to the bitter cold and died. After attempting resuscita-
tion, the crew reluctantly put his body over the side. By now the dinghy
had been capsized several times by the mountainous waves, and the crew
were weakening rapidly.

After some 16 hours in the dinghy, the crew were heartened by the
arrival of an ASR Warwick aircraft which flew low over the dinghy and
dropped a lifeboat by parachute. Unfortunately the lifeboat's parachute
release gear failed to function properly and it eventually fell some 500
yards away from Hornell's men. By then Hornell's condition was almost
pitiful. Blind, and terribly weak from exposure and cold, his thoughts
were still concerned with saving his crew as he started to attempt to swim
through the heaving sea to the lifeboat in the hope of retrieving it.
Knowing his physical condition, Denomy prevented Hornell from trying,
and helped as best he could to comfort his skipper. Then, some three hours
later, Scott, who had endured many hours of immersion in the water,
finally died, and once more the crew were forced to commit the body
of a close friend to the sea depths.

Denomy, Cole and Bodnoff, who seemed to regain strength from some
unplumbed depths at this stage, began intensive work to aid Hornell,
Campbell and Matheson as the latter three grew noticeably weaker still,
and were still comforting their comrades some two hours later when a
Short Sunderland appeared from nowhere, beating low over the sea
directly over them.

The flying boat was guiding a high speed ASR launch to the dinghy,
and soon after Cole spotted the launch heading at full speed towards
him. Their ordeal had lasted 20 hours and 35 minutes. Coming alongside
the dinghy, the launch crew immediately hauled Hornell, Campbell and
Matheson aboard, while Bodnoff, Cole and Denomy managed to climb
the rope ladders thrown over the side, assisted by several of the launch
crew.

David Hornell was now unconscious and the rescue crew worked un-
ceasingly for more than three hours attempting to revive him, but to no
avail. In the opinion of medical authorities later Hornell must have died
about 20 minutes after being brought aboard the rescue launch. While
the remaining crew were treated for exposure and shock, the launch sped
back to land, reaching Lerwick some 14 hours later.

David Hornell was then buried in the grounds of Lerwick Hospital,
while the other crew members were admitted to hospital for treatment
and rest. After another four to eight days the survivors left hospital and

returned via Iceland to Canada for 'Survivors' leave', now fully recovered from their nightmare sojourn on the ocean.

The story of David Hornell's outstanding courage in pressing home his attack on the U-boat with a crippled aircraft, in flames, and in the teeth of frightening flak opposition; followed by many hours of suffering in the sea, constantly keeping alive the spirits of his crew and attempting everything within his limited power to ensure their safety – added up to an epic of selfless bravery. That courage was recognised by the posthumous award of a Victoria Cross on 28 July 1944. For their individual parts in this epic, Denomy was awarded a DSO; Campbell and Matheson received a DFC each; and Cole and Bodnoff each received a DFM. The two dead crew members Scott and St Laurent could only be awarded a Mentioned in Despatches under the contemporary ruling in such matters.

On 12 December 1944, David Hornell's widow, Genevieve, received her husband's bronze cross from the hands of the Earl of Athlone, Governor-General of Canada at a special ceremony held in Government House, Ottawa, Canada.

44. John Alexander Cruickshank

As an island kingdom, Great Britain's literal lifelines for imported food, goods and materials stretch across the oceans of the world. The protection of her vital sea arteries has been the prime function of the Royal Navy for centuries, and with the advent of the aeroplane that stalwart defence extended its limits to hitherto undreamed parameters. Starting during the 1914-18 European war, seaplanes and flying boats steadily assumed a greater importance in the defence of Britain's coastal waters, until in 1936 a separate entity within the Royal Air Force aegis came into existence – Coastal Command. In constant close liaison with the Senior Service, RAF Coastal Command provided the 'long arm' of defence; aerial protection and vigilance over vast stretches of ocean hitherto denied to the Navy.

At the outbreak of war in September 1939 Coastal Command immediately swung into action, and never ceased its daily and nightly 'watch and ward' cover until many months after the eventual cessation of hostilities. It was a task little publicised, despite its prime importance in Britain's struggle, yet without the patient and dogged devotion to duty of the Coastal crews the final Allied victory would have been virtually impossible. During the years 1939-45 Coastal Command aircraft destroyed at least 212 enemy submarines and seriously damaged a further 120; while other shipping targets sunk or crippled amounted to millions of tons. Nevertheless, the Command's even greater contribution was the untold number of enemy vessels prevented from preying on Allied merchant shipping simply by the unceasing air cover provided by the Coastal crews. This aerial 'umbrella' seldom (relatively) provided the crews with any sustained high-key action against the declared enemy; indeed, the bulk of Coastal Command crews accumulated many hundreds of operational flying hours without ever sighting a U-boat or coming into direct conflict with opposing forces. Instead they spent a majority of patrols simply 'watching water' – hour upon monotonous hour searching and sweeping over a featureless vista of grey-green tossing waves stretching from horizon to horizon. The need for an exhausting, never-ceasing vigilance throughout eight, ten, twelve or more hours of every patrol was paramount, and when this patient searching was on occasion

John Alexander Cruickshank   [379]

Andrew Charles Mynarski

David Ernest Hornell

Ian Willoughby Bazalgette

'rewarded' by the sight of the arch-enemy a crew swung immediately into action, forgetting all fatigue and pressing home attack after attack with utter determination whatever the odds against them. Just four Coastal men were awarded a Victoria Cross – three of these posthumously. The fourth was an Aberdonian ex-bank clerk, John Alexander Cruickshank.

Born on 20 May 1920 in Aberdeen, Cruickshank was a pupil of Aberdeen Grammar School and, later, Daniel Stewart's College, in Edinburgh; during which time he became a Boy Scout patrol leader in the 4th Edinburgh Troop. In 1938 he entered the Commercial Bank of Scotland as the start of a banking career, but on 10 May 1939, a few days before his nineteenth birthday, Cruickshank enlisted in the Royal Regiment of Artillery, Territorial Army as a gunner. On the outbreak of war he was called for service and continued to serve with the Royal Artillery until early 1941, when he applied for transfer to the RAF for training as aircrew. On 30 June he officially transferred from the 129th Field Regiment, RA, to the RAF's aircrew reception centre, and on 19 July 1941 began basic training at No 11 Initial Training Wing; being promoted to Leading Aircraftman on 1 September. Posted to Toronto, Canada on 15 September, Cruickshank underwent elementary pilot training and later commenced his advanced instruction on 10 December 1941 at the US Naval flying base at Pensacola, USA. Completing his instruction, he was awarded pilot 'wings' on 9 July 1942, and the following day was commissioned as a Pilot Officer, RAFVR. Arriving in England in early October, Cruickshank was next posted to No 4 (Coastal) OTU at Invergordon for operational training and crewing; where, on 10 January 1943, he was promoted to Flying Officer. Finally, fully-qualified as a flying boat pilot and with his crew, Cruickshank joined his first operational unit, 210 Squadron, on 25 March 1943.

Flying the squadron's Consolidated Catalina flying boats, Cruickshank soon adapted to the unit's routine of operations, and on 10 July 1944 was further promoted to Flight Lieutenant. By then Cruickshank had completed 47 full operational sorties, apart from many other 'non-operational' flights, but – in common with many of his fellow 'boat' skippers – had seen little excitement or direct offensive action against the enemy. He was by now one of the more experienced aircraft captains on his squadron; recognised as an utterly dependable pilot, skilled in his duties.

During the morning of 17 July 1944, John Cruickshank began his usual preparations for what was to be his 48th operational patrol. His aircraft was Catalina JV928, DA-Y, and for this trip he was taking a ten-man crew, including himself as captain. His second pilot was Flight Sergeant Jack Garnett, while a third pilot, Sergeant S. I. Fidler, was fresh to the operational scene and included to gain experience. Navigation was in the capable hands of Flying Officer J. C. Dickson, though most Coastal Command pilots were necessarily skilled navigators in their own right; and the aircraft's flight engineer was another experienced man, Flight Sergeant S. B. Harbison. Two other experienced men were the wireless operators Warrant Officer W. C. Jenkins and Flight Sergeant H. Gershenson. Two air gunners, both qualified wireless operators, were Flight Sergeant J. Appleton and Sergeant R. S. C. Proctor; and as was a custom on 210 Squadron, the crew included a skilled rigger, Flight Sergeant A. I. Cregan. It was a highly competent crew, well salted with men who had already flown hundreds of hours over the ocean, and skippered by a pilot in whom all placed their trust – and their lives – with utmost confidence.

At 1.45 pm Cruickshank got airborne from the Sullom Voe base to start a patrol calculated to last at least 14 hours. For the next eight hours the Catalina swept its patrol area, seeing little of importance, and its crew were reaching the point of thinking ahead to the return to base as the end of yet another monotonous sortie.

Then, at 9.45 pm the radar screen showed a contact at 6821N, 0556E – a surface vessel some 43 miles dead ahead. The flying boat at that moment was flying at 2000 feet above the ocean and Cruickshank's immediate reaction to the sighting report was to approach the unidentified 'contact'. Further on he suddenly saw the vessel – a submarine, doing approximately 14 knots on the surface. At first the crew thought it must be a 'friendly' sub, but Cruickshank ordered a recognition cartridge to be fired and the code letter of the day to be flashed to the submarine to ensure identification. His answer was an immediate heavy box barrage of flak – it was a German U-boat.

Cruickshank's response was to pull the Catalina into a complete circuit around the U-boat and begin his first run-in, descending from 1,000 feet to 50 feet as he nosed towards his target. At 1,000 yards' range the Catalina's front gunner commenced firing to make the German gunners take cover, and his tracers splashed around the submarine's conning tower and ricocheted away in crazy parabolas; then the waist blister guns joined in the attack.

Roaring over the U-boat the Catalina's depth charges failed to release, so Cruickshank turned to port, climbing to 800 feet and continuing his turn to begin a second attack. Shouting to his crew, 'Everybody ready?', Cruickshank paused to hear the responses, then yelled, 'In we go again.' The U-boat was now nearly stationary, giving its gunners a more stable platform as they prepared for the Catalina's second attack.

Flak shells began to slash along the flanks of the flying boat as it bore in; then as the U-boat came directly under Cruickshank's vision, one shell exploded inside the Catalina, creating havoc. The navigator, Dickson, was killed instantly, Appleton was hit in the head by shrapnel, Harbison wounded in both legs. In front of Garnett's second pilot seat his windscreen shattered, and further inside a fire broke out.

Cruickshank received wounds in both legs and his chest, but gave no indication of his injuries, intent as he was on completing his attack. From 50 feet above the U-boat Cruickshank personally released a stick of six depth charges in a perfect straddle of the submarine, then pulled up into the clouds of sea fog ahead of him.

The aircraft crew saw no more of their target, but behind them the *U-347*, commanded by Oberleutnant zur See Johnann de Bugr, was rapidly sinking – Cruickshank's aim had been true. *U-347* had been one of an Arctic flotilla, and this was only her second war patrol. In the Catalina the crew took stock of the damage and crew injuries. The hull was riddled with flak damage, with a foot-long gash along the water line. The aircraft radar set was out of commission, and one of the main petrol lines was leaking fuel steadily. The latter was particularly worrying; in their immediate location, 190-degrees west of the Lofoten Isles, northwest of Norway, the crew realised that it was at least five hours' flying time to base at Sullom Voe.

The various holes in the main hull were stuffed with various canvas engine covers and 'Mae West' preserver life-jackets by various crew members; while up front Garnett took over the controls from Cruickshank and told Appleton to come and tend to the skipper's wounds. Appleton began to cut away the legs of Cruickshank's uniform trousers to staunch the obvious flow of blood, and then Cruickshank's face went white and he fainted. Garnett and Appleton managed to lower the unconscious pilot from his seat and carried him aft to the only remaining unburned rest bunk; then Garnett returned to his forward seat.

Appleton began to dress Cruickshank's leg wounds and only then discovered the several chest wounds suffered by his captain – Cruickshank had not said anything about these. As the pilot regained consciousness soon after, he immediately made a move to go forward to his seat at the controls, being anxious about the fuel state, but Appleton restrained him gently, explaining that Garnett had everything under control there.

Cruickshank's next thought was for his navigator, but from the look on Appleton's face, realised that Dickson must be dead already; indeed, he must have unconsciously known this after the explosion in the aircraft during the second attack run, and had instinctively taken over the release of the depth charges.

During the five and a half hours' journey back to Scotland, Cruickshank refused morphia in case it fuddled his brain, and several times he lapsed into unconsciousness due to the continuing loss of blood weakening him. Each time, as he regained his senses, his first thoughts were for the safety of the crew and the state of the aircraft. Garnett was still in the captain's seat in front, in spite of his own wounds, and remained there until the Catalina finally reached Sullom Voe.

It was still dark then and when Appleton went aft to tell his skipper they were over the base, Cruickshank insisted on being helped forward to the front cockpit where, propped up in the second pilot's seat, he took over command again. Only able to breathe with difficulty and in great pain, Cruickshank ordered that they must continue circling base until first light to ensure a safe landing.

For the next hour the Catalina droned in large circles over Sullom Voe, while its crew jettisoned guns and other equipment to lighten ship in preparation for the landing; then between them Garnett and Cruickshank brought the flying boat down onto the sea. No sooner had the hull begun to settle than the fuselage became part-flooded with sea water pouring in through the myriad of shell holes. In a final bid to save the crew and machine the throttles were opened fully and the Catalina flown right up onto the beach.

The waiting medical officer climbed aboard and found Cruickshank, who collapsed and had to be given an immediate blood transfusion before he could be removed from the aircraft. Then, strapped on a stretcher, he was taken directly to hospital, where a thorough examination revealed that John Cruickshank had received a staggering total of 72 individual wounds; the most serious being those in his chest and legs.

On 1 September 1944 the *London Gazette* announced the award of a Victoria Cross to John Cruickshank, and a Distinguished Flying Medal to Jack Garnett for his splendid part in the whole action; and on 21 September both men attended an investiture at Holyrood House to receive their awards from the hands of King George VI.

Cruickshank did not return to operational flying, being posted to Headquarters Coastal Command at Northwood in Middlesex on 14 December 1944; and he eventually left the RAF on 13 September 1946 to resume his 'interrupted' banking career. In early 1977, after a successful career in international finance, 'Jock' Cruickshank came home to Edinburgh to retire from business.

45. Ian Willoughby Bazalgette

From 3 September 1939 to 8 May 1945, RAF Bomber Command lost a total of 8,325 aircraft on operations in Europe; a figure which does not include the many other aircraft which returned tattered and torn from flak and fighter damage and were later repaired and returned to front-line service by the unremitting labours of Service and civilian maintenance staffs. In human terms this overall loss total represented 47,268 individual aircrew members killed in action; young vibrant men, many of whom failed to reach their majority before their young lives were cut off abruptly and savagely in the skies over Europe.

Faced with the prospect of an initial tour of operations comprising a nominal 30 sorties before being temporarily 'rested', the life expectancy of any member of a bomber crew was slim; particularly during the heavy bombing offensive of 1942-45. Even if he survived such a first tour of operations, he could be recalled later for a second tour; after which any further operations could only be flown on an entirely individual volunteer basis.

Yet, such was the unique comradeship, community spirit, and (in certain cases) the magnetic 'appeal' of operational life on the bomber squadrons, that many bomber men willingly volunteered to remain on operations rather than 'rest' in a relatively safe occupation elsewhere. In doing so they knew only too well the escalating odds against survival on every additional sortie – and many paid the price of death for tempting fate so courageously. Many such 'bomber barons' – the esoteric RAF term for veteran bomber men – eagerly volunteered for the elite Path Finder Force; No 8 Group, Bomber Command; a specially-formed group of experienced crews whose prime task was to locate and mark bombing objectives ahead of the main bomber streams in the unceasing struggle for higher precision in aerial destruction of Nazi Germany. Three men of the Path Finder Force were awarded the Victoria Cross – all three posthumously – and the first of these was Squadron Leader Ian Willoughby Bazalgette. DFC.

Born of English parents in Calgary, Alberta, Canada on 19 October 1918, Ian Bazalgette attended the Toronto Balmy Beach School as a child before being brought to England in 1927, when he continued his education at Rokeby, Wimbledown and, later, with a private tutor. On

16 July 1939 Bazalgette enlisted in the Royal Artillery and was eventually commissioned as a Second Lieutenant on 7 September 1940; serving initially with the Searchlight Section, RA and later, in Scotland, as an instructor. The mundane duties offered little hope of active fighting duties and Bazalgette applied for transfer to the RAF Volunteer Reserve. Accepted on probation for pilot training, he was sent to Cranwell on 13 September 1941 and had his first solo flight a week later. On completion of the *ab initio* stage of training at Cranwell, Bazalgette was officially promulgated as Pilot Officer, RAFVR with effect from 24 January 1942, and posted to 25 OTU, Finningley to complete his instruction. Finally, on 15 September 1942, Bazalgette became fully qualified and next day joined his first operational unit, 115 Squadron at Mildenhall, Suffolk, to fly Wellington bombers.

His first sortie, a mine-laying trip, was flown on 30 September. By the end of November he had undertaken a total of 12 operations, including two to Turin, Italy; though his eighth – a daylight bombing sortie to Essen – had to be aborted due to clouds obscuring the target, and he jettisoned his bomb load before returning to base.

At the end of November 1942, 115 Squadron moved to nearby East Wretham airfield to begin conversion from their obsolete Wellingtons to new four-engined Avro Lancasters; standing down from operations temporarily until new crews and aircraft had been received and trained. Bazalgette's first Lancaster sortie took place on 22 March 1943 when he set out in DS615, 'N' to bomb St Nazaire – only to be recalled part way.

His next trip, on 26 March, in the same Lancaster was a night raid on Duisburg, but flak damage to the aircraft hydraulics caused him to belly-land on return and he hit a tree on the perimeter of the airfield; fortunately without injury to himself or his crew.

The following night, in Lancaster DS622, 'T', he made his first raid on the German capital, Berlin, and returned to the 'Big City' two nights later. On 3 April, in DS617, 'N', Bazalgette made his second attack on Essen – only to be recalled before reaching his target. That same day he was awarded a DFC (gazetted 9 July 1943) for his previous record of determination and skill on operations.

During the remaining weeks of April Bazalgette flew four more sorties, against Kiel, Duisburg (twice) and Stettin; then on 1 May he made a third attempt to raid Essen, his 'bogie' objective. Yet again he was unable to complete the sortie, having to abort the trip due to severe icing locking his control surfaces. Three more trips over Germany were flown in May, and on 12 June he received promotion to acting Squadron Leader.

During the next eight weeks he successfully completed five more operations over Germany; the final operation being against Milan in Lancaster DS664, 'X' on the night of 12 August 1943. He was then deemed to have completed his first operational tour (though in a private letter to Group Captain T. G. Mahaddie DSO DFC AFC he wrote '3 Group finished me after completing 29th trip . . .'), and was sent on post-operational leave, pending posting to an instructional job.

The thought of a Flight commander's routine task at an Operational Training Unit dismayed Bazalgette. Remembering a visit by the Path Finder Force's famed 'Hamish' Mahaddie to 115 Squadron, when Mahaddie had lectured on PFF technique and suggested Bazalgette might be able to join PFF on completion of his first tour of 'ops', he applied for transfer to 8 Group. His application was quietly 'squashed' by higher authority, in order to exchange-post Bazalgette with an OTU instructor who wanted to join 115 Squadron for operations, and on 1 September Bazalgette was posted to Lossiemouth, Scotland where he became C Flight commander on 20 OTU.

Here he first came to know Flying Officer Douglas Cameron DFM who was the OTU's Gunnery Leader. Cameron had won his DFM when an NCO air gunner with 149 Squadron, and had been one of the crew of Pilot Officer R. H. Middleton VC's last operational sortie. When Bazalgette finally left Lossiemouth on 20 April 1944 to return to operations, he took Douglas Cameron with him as the first of his new crew, and Cameron became Bazalgette's regular rear gunner for all his remaining operational sorties, including his last.

Bazalgette's return to the operational scene was to 635 Squadron at Downham Market, one of the PFF's units, and in the last week of April he attended the PFF Conversion course at Warboys. His first sortie with the Path Finders came on 6 May, in Lancaster ND895, when he dropped a dozen 1,000lb HE bombs on a marshalling yard at Mantes Gassicourt. Four more attacks during May were against similar communications targets; part of Bomber Command's prelude to the imminent 'D-Day' invasion of Europe by the Allied armies.

On the invasion day, 6 June, flying ND950, Bazalgette attacked some shore batteries at Longues as his personal contribution to smothering the German defences, and the next day dropped 7,500lb of high explosive on an ammunition dump in the Foret de Cerisy. Two days later, flying ND811, 'T', Bazalgette's objective was the Luftwaffe base at Rennes, where his eighteen 500lb bombs stitched a line of craters across the main runway. For a raid against the Cambrai railway yards on 12 June, Bazalgette, piloting ND821, was selected as deputy master bomber; one of the first marker aircraft, and ready to take over complete direction of the main force raid in the event of the master bomber suffering any casualty or mechanical fault. Three days later, this time at the controls of his 'personal' Lancaster, ND950, 'M', Bazalgette was again selected as deputy master bomber for an attack on the Lens railway complex.

On 12 June 1944, England had suffered its first attack by VI robot flying bombs, and as this fresh menace began to escalate into a daily onslaught, Bomber Command was tasked with the destruction of the VI base launching sites along the French coastal areas. On 23 and 24 June, Bazalgette was one of the force despatched to bomb the VI sites at Coubronnes and Le Grand Rossignolle respectively; acting as one of the marking formation over the latter target.

In the first two weeks of July, Bazalgette flew six more sorties, against VI sites, railway yards, and German troop concentrations; three of which saw him either marking or illuminating the target. Then, on the 20th he was chosen as Master bomber for a daylight attack on the VI site at L'Hey. On 23, 24, 25 and 28 July, he returned to the vital role of marking targets, at Kiel, Stuttgart and Hamburg; then on the 30th was again Master bomber, for a daylight tactical support bombing raid in support of the Allied beach-head invasion forces. His 54th operational sortie was a daylight raid on Chappel Notre Dame on 1 August, on which he was yet again selected as deputy to the Master bomber.

On Friday, 4 August, the PFF mounted a daylight raid of 61 Lancasters to attack another VI storage depot at Trossy St Maximin, close to Leu d'Esserent; a target which had already received heavy consecutive attacks on 2 and 3 August. Of the total force, 14 crews from 635 Squadron were detailed, including Ian Bazalgette who was to be one of the marking formation spearhead. The whole raid was to be under the direction of Wing Commander D. W. S. Clark as Master bomber, and his deputy Flight Lieutenant R. W. Beveridge DFC of 635 Squadron.*

For this sortie Bazalgette was flying Lancaster ND811, 'F2-T', with six men as crew. His navigator was Flight Lieutenant Geoff Goddard; bomb aimer, Flight Lieutenant I. A. Hibberd; and wireless operator Flight Lieutenant C. R. 'Chuck' Godfrey DFC – all three of whom had crewed up with Bazalgette at Lossiemouth and joined 635 Squadron together; along with the rear gunner, Doug Cameron DFM. The flight engineer, Sergeant George Turner, had joined the crew on the squadron; while the remaining member, an air gunner, was Flight Sergeant V. V. Leeder, RAAF,

---

* Bazalgette's VC citation incorrectly credited him with being the master bomber on this sortie.

'loaned' to Bazalgette for this particular sortie in place of the regular mid-upper gunner.

At the target and its approaches the German defences were well alerted by the previous two days' raids, and as the *OBOE* Mosquitos swept across the depot, the flak crews prepared to meet the incoming main force of bombers. As the master bomber made his first run-in, he had his Lancaster's starboard elevator damaged and the length of the fuselage raked with flak.

Behind him came his deputy, Beveridge, running across the target to assess the Mosquitos' markers for accuracy. His Lancaster received direct hits, erupted in flames, and dived into the ground at full bore. The sky above the rocket depot was by then a veritable wall of bursting flak.

Starting his run-in through the barrage came Bazalgette, intent on dropping his markers accurately. His Lancaster was soon hit in several places; both starboard engines being put out of action and the starboard wing and part of the fuselage bursting into flames. Inside the fuselage Hibberd was grievously wounded, having his arm and part of his shoulder torn away; while smoke and fumes filled the fuselage and temporarily overcame Leeder in the mid-upper turret. Hibberd was carried back to the rest bunk bed and given morphia, but his state was critical.

The rest of the crew attempted to quell the raging fire, while Cameron in the rear turret, realising his intercomm was not working, swung his turret to beam and saw that the starboard wing was already burnt down to its framework. Inside he also noticed several inches of petrol slopping along the fuselage floor towards him.

Bazalgette regained control of the plunging Lancaster and continued his marking run, but as he released the markers the aircraft fell away in a slow spin; its burning wing blazing even more intensely. Struggling with the controls Bazalgette finally achieved a modicum of guidance over the crippled Lancaster as it continued to lose height, and maintained control for perhaps 30 miles.

Then, after consultation with Turner, and knowing that he could not regain height, he ordered the crew to bale out. Reluctantly, because of the mortally wounded bomb aimer and the semi-suffocated Australian gunner, Godfrey, Goddard, Turner and Cameron obeyed their skipper, though by then the Lancaster was only 1,000 feet above the earth. Bazalgette could easily have baled out too, but being unable to ensure his two remaining crew could evacuate the aircraft safely, he chose to stay with them and attempt a landing. Approaching the village of Senantes, he was seen to turn away from the cluster of houses and farms and let

down into a nearby field. The Lancaster touched earth in a perfect landing – then exploded.

The four survivors of the crew were quickly hidden from the Germans
by local Maquis and Resistance patriots, and all four managed to evade
capture until the eventual liberation of the area by the advancing Allied
armies. The bodies of Leeder and Hibberd were recovered from the
wreckage and taken away by the Germans, but local civilians managed to
secrete Bazalgette's remains until the arrival of the liberation forces. Then,
on 8 October 1944, in a ceremony attended by Bazalgette's sister, Ethel,
the mortal remains of Ian Willoughby Bazalgette were formally dedicated
and interred near Senantes.

After the close of the European war, and the return of the survivors of
Bazalgette's last crew to England, the full story of the pilot's last sortie
were pieced together, and he was immediately recommended for the
award of a posthumous Victoria Cross; which was later gazetted on 17
August 1945. His cross and other decorations were handed to Bazalgette's
mother at an investiture on 18 December that year.

If an epitaph was needed for Ian Bazalgette, no better tribute could
be made than the opinions of two members of his crew – men who probably knew him better than anyone. Doug Cameron, a veteran of four
tours of operations, has described Bazalgette as, '. . . a magnificent pilot
and a born leader, adored by all his crew'; while Geoff Goddard said of
his late skipper, ' . . . an excellent pilot, cool, efficient, with the capacity
to inspire confidence in all who flew with him . . . popular with both
ground and air crews.'

The depth of sincerity in both men's tributes may be judged by the
simple lasting accolades of Cameron, who named his only daughter,
Margaret Middleton Bazalgette Cameron*; while Geoff Goddard named
his son Ian in memory of a courageous pilot.

---

* 'Middleton' for Pilot Officer R. H. Middleton vc raaf with whom Cameron flew
on the Australian's final, gallant operational sortie – see Chapter 32.

46. Geoffrey Leonard Cheshire

Courage is an indefinable quality. Its myriad of facets include the quiet, uncomplaining courage of the cruelly disabled, the wholly unconscious courage of men more concerned with other people's lives than their own, and the lip-biting courage of men who fear what they are about to do . . . but do it. Perhaps true courage is just that – overcoming a natural, instinctive fear and deliberately attempting to complete a given task. Nevertheless, there can be no yardstick for courage It can be summoned from one unsuspected unplumbed depth for one split second of time, or it may extend over many hours, days, even years of sustained yet controlled fear. Of the 51 men ever awarded a Victoria Cross for aerial operations, just five received the bronze cross for an extended period of operational flying and outstanding prowess, rather than a specific act of supreme valour.

Of these men, four served during the 1914-18 conflict, but the sole such recipient during 1939-45 was Geoffrey Leonard Cheshire. Serving in the RAF throughout the Second World War, Cheshire completed a total of 103 operational bombing sorties; a bald figure which, apart from its sheer numerical connotation, gives little hint of the contribution made by Cheshire both as an individual and as a leader of men.

Born in Chester on 7 September 1917, Cheshire was the son of Dr Cheshire, Professor of Law, and bursar at Exeter College, Oxford. Educated at Dragon School, Oxford and Stowe before joining Merton College, Oxford University to study for a degree in law, with a secondary interest in languages. Even when still at Chatham House, Stowe, Cheshire seemed to attract friends of a kindred spirit, for three of his closest school chums were all later to gain great distinction for personal bravery – Jack Randle, who was to gain a posthumous VC in Assam; Jock Anderson, another posthumous VC while serving with the Argylls; and Peter Higgs who was killed in action with 111 Squadron RAF during the Battle of Britain.

Entering Oxford University in October 1936, Cheshire pursued the hedonistic pleasures of an undergraduate's life to the full – fast cars, drinking bouts, decorative blonde girl-friends, and any escapade which provided an element of forbidden danger. In this he was little different from any other healthy nineteen-years old boy – displaying an attitude with, in his own words*, '. . . little aim in life other than my own pleasure and profit, both of which I pursued with relentless determination.'

In 1937 a new interest entered his life – flying. The promise of a faster form of 'danger' appealed to his adolescent mind and he joined the University Air Squadron; having his first flight under the tutorship of Flight Lieutenant† John Whitworth at Abingdon on 5 February 1937 in an Avro Tutor, and finally going 'solo' on 8 June. Completing his training, he was commissioned in the RAF Volunteer Reserve on 16 November 1937 and resumed his studies.

Mobilised at the outbreak of war, Cheshire reported to No 9 FTS, Hullavington in October 1939 for further Service training and received his RAF 'wings' on 15 December. With promotion to Flying Officer on 7 April 1940, he underwent final operational training at 10 OTU, Abingdon and Jurby, and on 6 June 1940 arrived at Driffield, Yorkshire to join his first unit, 102 Squadron equipped with the ungainly Armstrong Whitworth Whitley bombers.

His first operational sortie was flown three nights later, as second pilot to the New Zealander, Pilot Officer P. H. Long DFC, and Cheshire soon realised how little he really knew about the serious responsibility he was about to assume as a bomber captain with his own crew. Comprehending that complete confidence in the 'skipper' was the first essential of any good crew, Cheshire set out to master his 'trade'. As he himself put it in his part-biography, 'You have got to be good, and they have got to know it, and they will only know it by results. For once you cannot bluff. . .'

Tackling his task methodically, Cheshire first got to know his aircraft by blindfolding himself and then wandering around it until he could identify any item he needed in the dark; then, after one sortie over the North Sea when his Whitley developed engine trouble, he enlisted the skill of his ground crew to teach him about the engines and airframe components.

For the next five months, flying from 102 Squadron's various bases at Driffield, Aldergrove and Linton-on-Ouse, Cheshire gained invaluable front-line experience in bombing Germany; raiding targets at Berlin, Kiel, Essen, Duisburg, Bremen and Cologne. It was this last objective that brought him his first real trial of courage and skill as a bomber captain.

On the night of 12/13 November 1940, piloting Whitley, P5005, 'N-Nuts', Cheshire's objective was an oil refinery at Wesseling, near Cologne. Over the target cloud obscured the refinery and, after circling

---

* *Bomber Pilot* by G. L. Cheshire; Hutchinson, Revised 1955 edit.
† Later Air Commodore J. N. Whitworth CB DSO DFC.

for 50 minutes, he decided to attack an alternative, the railway yards at Cologne. The barrage of flak which had been severe during his circuiting over Wesseling appeared to lessen as he made his bombing run-up to Cologne, with bomb doors open and about to release a flare. Then, in a gigantic explosion, shrapnel shredded the Whitley and one sliver detonated the flare still inside the bomber. A ten-foot chunk of the side fuselage was ripped open and the rear fuselage filled with flames and smoke as Cheshire fought to regain control of the aircraft. Continuing his run, he released his bomb load and took stock of the damage to aircraft and crew.

The wireless operator, Henry Davidson, had been blinded by the explosion but refused to leave his post; continuing to transmit signals to base. The rest of the crew fought the flames and eventually extinguished these, leaving Cheshire to guide the savaged bomber for the next five hours homewards in the teeth of an 80-mph nose wind.

Reaching base safely, Cheshire was awarded an immediate DSO for his coolness under fire, while Davidson received a Distinguished Flying Medal for his fortitude.

In January 1941 Cheshire completed his first tour of operations, but immediately volunteered for a second tour, and was posted to 35 Squadron at Linton-on-Ouse. 35 Squadron, newly re-formed in November 1940, was the first unit to operate Handley Page Halifax four-engined bombers, and commenced operations on 11/12 March 1941.

On 7 March 1941 Cheshire was further decorated, with a DFC; while in the following month he received a Bar to his DSO for 'outstanding leadership and skill on operations.' His promotion to Flight Lieutenant was promulgated on 7 April 1941, and shortly after he was detached for ferry work to the USA and Canada. Promoted to Squadron Leader on 15 October, Cheshire completed his second tour of operational flying, and on 22 January 1942 was posted to No 1652 Heavy Conversion Unit (HCU) at Marston Moor as an instructor. Despite the ostensible 'non-operational' nature of his duties with the HCU, Cheshire managed to fly four operational missions during the next four months, including the first of 'Butch' Harris's famous '1,000-bomber' raids.

Then, in August 1942 he returned to the operational scene for a third tour as commanding officer of 76 Squadron, another Halifax bomber unit, based at Linton-on-Ouse from mid-September 1942. By coincidence, 76 was the unit on which Cheshire's younger brother Christopher had been serving as a pilot when, on 12/13 August 1941 he had been shot down over Berlin and became a prisoner of war.

Having been awarded a second Bar to his DSO in April 1942, and now holding the acting rank of Wing Commander, Leonard Cheshire was by then one of the most decorated pilots in RAF Bomber Command. Yet, when on leave in Oxford that summer, wearing civilian clothes, he was accosted by a white-haired elderly lady who upbraided him in no uncertain terms; decrying the fact that '. . . a young, fit chap like him was not in uniform fighting for his country', and then presented Cheshire with a small white feather – the badge of cowardice! Cheshire, seldom at a loss for the *mot juste*, was left speechless. . . .

Continuing to lead and inspire the crews of 76 Squadron Cheshire finally left his squadron on being appointed as Station Commander of Marston Moor on 1 April 1943, with the rank of Group Captain – at 25, the youngest man in the RAF to hold such a responsible position.

His departure from 76 Squadron was noted in the unit diary by a tribute : 'It was under the character and personal supervision of Group Captain Cheshire that the squadron became what it is today – one of the best in Bomber Command.'

The new duties as commander of a complete RAF station left Cheshire – probably for the first time in his life – feeling like a fish out of water; floundering in the unfamiliar daily routines of pure administration and mundane, though vital, duties of a training establishment. His various schemes for improving aircraft maintenance and other aspects of the station's commitments were, to say the least, unorthodox if well-intentioned; but when the opportunity arose in September 1943 to return to operational flying, albeit with reversion to Wing Commander rank, Cheshire seized the chance eagerly.

His new command was 617 Squadron, a unit already overtly publicised for its initial bombing mission in May 1943 against the Mohne and Eder dams in Germany, led by Wing Commander Guy Gibson VC DSO DFC. Now, based at Woodhall Spa airfield, 617 was virtually a 'special' squadron, manned in the main by veteran air crews who had volunteered to continue operational flying beyond their 'required' two tours.

On taking up his appointment however Cheshire was dismayed to be ordered to train his squadron assiduously on high-level bombing techniques. Throughout his past operational career he had always preferred to attack a target at low level – indeed, he professed that heights terrified him – and thus was opposed to the contemporary policy of high-level bombing. For four months 617 continued its training, seeing no active operations and steadily lowering its morale. Then, on 8/9 February 1944 the squadron was sent to destroy the Gnome-Rhone factory at Limoges, France, with strict orders to hit the factory only and under no circumstances damage or harm nearby French workers' homes and lives.

Cheshire, piloting a Lancaster, decided to prove his theory of low-level bombing efficiency, and marked the target from a mere 200 feet height with perfect accuracy. The following bomber stream deposited their bombs with equal accuracy, resulting in the virtual destruction of the factory but causing no casualties amongst nearby French civilians.

In the face of such a practical demonstration, higher authority relented to Cheshire's demands for a smaller, faster aircraft for future low-level marking duties and supplied him with a De Havilland Mosquito for personal use. For the next two months 617 was detailed for a rapid succession of targets; Clermont-Ferrand's Michelin rubber factory, La Ricamarie, Angouleme, Bergerac, and the semi-disastrous attempt to bomb the Antheor viaduct in Italy. Using 12,000lb bombs 617 failed at Antheor and nearly lost several veteran crews.

The real vindication of Cheshire's penchant for low-level techniques came on the night of 24/25 April 1944, when 617 was given four Mosquitos to mark Munich for a force of 260 main force bombers. Munich, fourth largest city in Germany, and centre of the Nazi cult, was heavily defended – at least 200 flak guns – and involved very deep penetration into German territory; leaving the Mosquitos with virtually no margin in fuel endurance. Piloted by Cheshire, Dave Shannon, Gerry Fawkes, and Kearns, the Mosquitos could only count on a maximum of 15 minutes reserve of fuel for the whole mission, with no allowance for any untoward incidents. Six Lancasters of 617 carried out a feint attack on Milan, dropping target flares as if in preparation for a main raid; while eleven Mosquitos of 627 Squadron flew ahead to drop 'Window' foil over the target to nullify German radar defence screens.

Cheshire and his three companions left Manston on a direct route to Munich thereby flying over the heavily-defended Augsburg area and coming under heavy fire from that point on. On reaching Munich Cheshire was trapped in a searchlight cone as the high Lancasters started dropping illuminating flares to light up the target area. With his Mosquito illuminated from above and below, Cheshire put his aircraft into a screaming power-dive, flattening out at 700 feet and releasing his red spot-fire markers accurately over the aiming point at 0141 hours. The other three Mosquitos placed their markers with equal precision, followed by a wave of Lancasters reinforcing the illumined aiming point.

As the main force commenced bombing on the markers, Cheshire circled the city at 1,000 feet to confirm that all was going to plan; apparently oblivious of the fact that he was well within flak range, and directly in the path of the cascade of falling bombs from the Lancaster stream high above. His Mosquito was hit several times by shrapnel, but disengaging from the flak zone proved more difficult than Cheshire had

thought, and for a full 12 minutes he needed every ounce of his considerable skill to avoid disaster and eventually run out of the danger area.*
Arriving back at Manston with nearly dry petrol tanks, he was almost
the victim of a marauding German nightfighter 'intruder', but switched
off all lights and landed safely in the dark.

Reconnaissance evidence the following morning showed stark evidence
of the raid's success. Most of Munich's public buildings had been
destroyed; six large barracks demolished (the city was a principal garrison
centre), and several Nazi Party buildings gutted by fire including the
Gestapo headquarters at the Wittelbascher Palais. Cheshire's predilec-
tion for low-level marking was now unquestioned by his superiors.

Continuing to lead every squadron raid, Cheshire brought the 'art' of
initial target-marking and Master bomber directing (a technique originated by Guy Gibson vc of 617 Squadron) to a high peak of efficiency.
On 4/5 May 1944, for example, he and Dave Shannon put down the
aiming markers for a bombing assault on Mailly-le-Camp, home of the
21st Panzer Division and nearly 20,000 troops; resulting in almost complete annihilation of these 'crack' formations.

Three nights after D-Day (the Allied invasion of Europe on 6 June)
Cheshire personally led a mission designed to knock out the Saumur
railway tunnel and thus block Germany's main rail supply line from the
south to Normandy. He released his markers no more than 40 yards from
the south-western entrance to the tunnel, and the main force of 19
Lancasters from 617 (including one piloted by Flight Lieutenant William
Reid vc) dropped their 12,000lb 'Tallboy' DP bombs on target, totally
demolishing the vital rail link. On 14 June Cheshire again led 617 in a
daylight raid against E-boat pens at Le Havre, without benefit of cloud
cover. Hit by flak early in the attack, Cheshire's aircraft continued to fly
over the target area until he was satisfied with the bombing accuracy of
his crews.

From the end of June until September 1944, RAF Bomber Command
concentrated on destruction of a new menace – the V2 guided missile.
Bombing V2 sites as these were discovered, Cheshire often marked these
objectives while flying a single-seat Mustang fighter. His first flight in this
type of aircraft is perhaps typical of the character of the man. The target
was a V2 site at Siracourt. Cheshire had not flown a single-seat, single-
engined aircraft for some four years, and had *never* flown a Mustang;
yet he familiarised himself as best he could with the aircraft on the ground,

* Questioned later about this, Cheshire replied, 'I don't know why I wasn't
frightened at the time . . . too busy, I suppose. Makes it difficult to assess courage,
doesn't it? . . .'

Geoffrey Leonard Cheshire

David Samuel Anthony Lord

Robert Anthony Maurice Palmer

George Thompson

and then took off on his first flight in the type to mark for the main Lancaster force bombing Siracourt. Completing his task, Cheshire returned to base and landed his unfamiliar aircraft in the dark.

On 6 July 1944, Leonard Cheshire flew his 100th operational sortie of the war – an attack on a missile site at Marquise – and immediately afterwards his Air Officer Commanding, 5 Group, Ralph Cochrane, sent for him and told him he was to be finally rested from operations. Unknown to Cheshire, Cochrane also forwarded a recommendation for Cheshire to be awarded a Victoria Cross. This was quickly approved and the award announced in the *London Gazette* dated 8 September 1944.

Two days later Cheshire, now a Group Captain again, left England bound for India, on posting to the Eastern Air Command headquarters at Calcutta; but by the end of the year had been moved to the USA, where he joined the British Joint Staff Mission in Washington, ostensibly to study tactical developments. Here he was selected to act as a British observer for the second atom bomb raid by the USAF against Japan, and in late July was sent to Guam, then Tinian Island, base for the B-29 Boeing Superfortresses tasked with this historic mission.

On 9 August 1945, Cheshire was in the third B-29 to fly to Nagasaki, where he witnessed the effects of the second atom-bomb attack; and soon after returned to England to report privately on what he had seen to the new British Prime Minister, Clement Attlee. At the end of 1945 Cheshire attended an RAF medical board and was told that he was suffering from psycho-neurosis. At his own request Cheshire was discharged from the RAF in January 1946.

The next few years of civilian life in the 'peace' era were years of idealistic ventures and schemes, and of searching for the answers to imponderable questions by Leonard Cheshire. Still a young man, barely 30 years in age, he had spent his formative years, first in the totally irresponsible atmosphere of an undergraduate's existence, and then in complete and sudden contrast, in the swiftly-maturing company of death and destruction on a scale which outstripped logic and meaning – where total responsibility for other men's lives and futures had been thrust upon his youthful shoulders without preamble.

In 1948, after some unsuccessful ventures, Cheshire pioneered the first Cheshire Foundation Home for the incurably sick; an organisation which has since achieved world-wide recognition and international establishment. In August 1952 he entered Midhurst Sanatorium, having been diagnosed as a tuberculosis patient, but was discharged two and a half years later, and continued his life's dedication to the Foundation.

In the late 1950's Cheshire met Sue Ryder; a young woman of his own generation who had served in the Special Forces in Europe, and had since devoted her life to the cause of helping those members of Britain's former European allies left stranded and unwanted after Germany's defeat. They married and conjoined their individual and continuing self-appointed life's works of relieving the suffering of those in need, irrespective of class or race or creed.

In June 1981 Cheshire became a member of the exclusive Order of Merit, and in January 1991 was created a Peer.

47. David Samuel Anthony Lord

If an individual had to be selected to epitomise the dogged courage and splendid devotion to duty displayed by the many transport and supply aircraft captains of the RAF throughout the 1939-45 air war, then probably no finer pilot could be chosen than Flight Lieutenant David Lord. His flying career extended over five years of the conflict; a continuous record of operational flying stretching from cumbersome biplane Vickers Valentias to Douglas DC-2K's, DC-3's, and C-53's over India, Egypt, Libya, Burma and Germany. Although Lord would have been the first to deny such praise, his was a record of patience, cool resolution and utter determination in the face of a myriad hazards.

Genuinely modest, rather shy and self-effacing almost to the point of introspection, David Lord was highly respected and immensely popular with all whom he came into contact. With no conscious effort on his own part he inspired complete confidence in others by his calm acceptance of what he regarded as his clear duty, and, maintaining that private code of duty to the end, he died in a manner still regarded as one of the greatest acts of individual heroism of the war.

Born in Cork on 18 October 1913, David Lord's background had a military foundation for he was the son of a serving warrant officer in the Royal Welch Fusiliers. He received his first schooling at the Lucknow Convent School in India and, on returning to England, continued his academic education at St Mary's School, Wrexham. He next attended St Mary's College, Aberystwyth, from where he matriculated to the University of Wales. On leaving university Lord made a decision which might well have altered his future; he entered the English Ecclesiastical College at Valladolid, Spain, with the intention of studying philosophy and eventually becoming a priest. It was no casual decision but an extension of a childhood ambition. However, after two years he decided he had not found his vocation and therefore returned to Wrexham, where he took up temporary employment as assistant to a pharmaceutical chemist. In his spare time Lord tried his hand at writing, mainly short stories, and in 1936, encouraged by having several stories accepted for publication, he travelled to London to work as a freelance journalist.

Finally, on 6 August 1936 Lord enlisted as an airman in the RAF. Promotion to LAC in June 1937, and Corporal in August 1938 followed before his application for pilot training was eventually approved, and he commenced flying instruction at EFTS, Hamble on 6 October 1938. Continuing his training at 2 FTS, Brize Norton, he was awarded his 'wings' on 5 April 1939 and promoted to Sergeant on 8 August, with orders to join 31 Squadron at Lahore, India; arriving on his first unit on 7 October 1939. On 31 Squadron Lord was introduced to the Vickers Valentia – a trundling wood and fabric biplane design already obsolete. Despite their age 31's Valentias were needed for supply and transportation in support of units of the army and RAF still attempting to control the fighting tribes along India's North West Frontier Province (now, Pakistan), and it was not until June 1941 that the squadron first received modern replacements for their vintage aircraft. The new equipment was the Dougals DC-2 transport Dakota.

Lord, promoted to Flight Sergeant on 1 April 1941, and to Warrant Officer on 1 October in the same year, soon 'converted' to the new monoplane 'Daks', becoming a qualified DC-2K captain in December.

Meanwhile the war situation in North Africa necessitated reinforcement of the few supply squadrons already on operations there and, in October 1941, 31 Squadron detached eight Dakotas and their crews for support of the land operations in Egypt and Libya; one of the DC-2K skippers being David Lord. The detachment in the Middle East theatre lasted some four months but was not without incident. On 8 December, for one example, Lord was captain of DG475, 'X' on a routine supply sortie to Landing Ground (LG) 138, carrying some 1,500lb of stores and nine passengers. Ten miles north-east of their objective the Dakota was jumped by three yellow-nosed Messerschmitt Bf 109 fighters and, with Lord slightly wounded, was forced to land in the open desert. Gathering crew and passengers together, Lord led the ten-miles walk to LG 138, and next day was again airborne on yet another supply sortie.

Returning to India in February 1942, Lord continued the daily routine of supply and communication flying and on 28 April qualified as captain on DC-3's. On 12 May he was commissioned as a Pilot Officer, and in the following month added to his qualifications by becoming a captain of the C-53 Skytrooper transport design.

With the gradual return of the Allied armies in Burma to the offensive, Lord and his fellow crews soon found themselves in constant demand for air-drop supply of the various individual units of the army operating deep in Japanese-held territory well behind the so-termed 'front lines'. Implementing Orde Wingate's inspired decision to maintain such troops solely from the air – 'down the chimney', in the contemporary expression – the Dakotas and Skytroopers were called upon to deliver and collect almost every imaginable item of military and domestic equipment to the courageous Chindits and other guerilla fighters. The task called for spot accuracy in supply dropping, needle-sharp navigation, and no little courage to take a relatively slow, unarmed aircraft between the lush green-carpeted mountains and into dank steaming valleys of Burma. Yet every supply captain and crew member was only too conscious of his responsibility to the men on the jungle floor, and each discharged that responsibility faithfully and constantly.

Lord's personal prowess on these operations was recognised officially by an Air Officer's Commendation, and later he was mentioned in despatches. Finally on 16 July 1943 he was awarded a Distinguished Flying Cross.

In December 1943 Lord, known by then universally as 'Lummee' (his favourite expression), was sent home to England, having completed four years of continuous operational flying, and he arrived in England on 6 January 1944, with the acting rank of Flight Lieutenant.

After a brief disembarkation leave, Lord reported to 271 Squadron at Doncaster, another Dakota unit, and spent much of the following few weeks in training for the role of airborne equipment supply and airborne trooping. On 29 February the squadron moved base to Down Ampney where further intensive training was undertaken not only in airborne troop carriage but also in glider towing duties. With the near certainty of an imminent invasion of Europe by the Allied forces, 271's crews trained hard and well.

As his personal crew at this time Lord had Flying Officer Ager as second pilot, Flying Officer D. I. MacDonnell as navigator, and as wireless operator, Alexander – 'Alec' – Ballantyne, an ex-Warrant Officer now commissioned as Flying Officer.

On the eve of 'D-Day', 5/6 June 1944, Lord participated in Operation Neptune, dropping a load of paratroops six miles east-north-east of Caen, despite intense flak defences which holed the Dakota's rudder, elevators and hydraulic system. The next few weeks saw 271's crews engaged in a succession of supply and resupply drop sorties for Allied troops in the Normandy beach-head.

After two months of bitter and bloody fighting from June to August 1944, the Allied invasion armies finally broke out of the beach-head and thrust inland towards Germany. The headlong rush across Europe quickly liberated several major cities such as Paris and Brussels and by early September the supreme Allied commander, General Eisenhower, was considering the possibility of 'one final blow,' to demoralise the enemy and thus bring hostilities to a rapid conclusion.

Unable to strike such a blow, Eisenhower chose instead to attempt a bypassing of the heavily fortified Siegfried Line as its western end and thereby 'roll up' the German west flank; at the same time establishing a foothold on Germany's border from which to spring a final offensive into the heart of Hitler's Germanic empire.

The plan to outflank the Siegfried Line – originally submitted by General Bernard Montgomery – would if successful not only provide just such a springboard but would isolate German forces in Holland and, even more important, free the port of Antwerp and solve the increasingly difficult supply route to the advancing Allied armies. The plan for an airborne assault – Operation Market – entailed a triple attack at Arnhem, Nijmegen-Grave and Eindhoven with a primary objective of capturing bridges across the lower Rhine, Waal and Maas rivers respectively. Meanwhile 30 Corps of General Dempsey's 2nd Army was to penetrate from the south and link up with the paras – Operation Garden.

On 10 September the decision to implement Market-Garden was taken, and immediately encountered its first major snag. Ideally the whole airborne forces were to be carried over in a single day's operations – but there were insufficient transport aircraft available for such a huge operation. Instead it was decided to have three consecutive air drops on 17, 18 and 19 September – an arrangement which in the event was to prove a primary reason for the failure of Market-Garden.

On Sunday, 17 September the first mass air drop set out for Arnhem. From 271 Squadron 24 Dakotas were contributed to the air armada, one of these being piloted by David Lord. He was without two of his regular crew. MacDonnell had gone on leave to get married, while Ager's place had been taken over by 19-years old Pilot Officer Richard Medhurst, son of an Air Marshal and fresh to operational flying. To take over MacDonnell's duties, Lord asked Flying Officer Harry King if he would care to join the crew, and King, an experienced ex-policeman, agreed to fill the navigator's job. The day's operations went smoothly, meeting little serious opposition and achieving an estimated 98 per cent success.

The following day, 18 September, saw Lord acting as a tug pilot for an Airspeed Horsa glider crammed full with troops of the 1st Airborne Division, bound for Landing Zone (LZ) 'S', six miles from Arnhem and just north-west of Wolfhezen. German opposition had stiffened considerably since the previous day and Lord's Dakota came under a hail of flak, resulting in its rear fuselage and tail assembly being riddled with shrapnel. The reception did not deter Lord.

In the words of one member of the Horsa crew, Staff Sergeant J. Rye DFM, who later wrote to Lord's parents :

I flew in a glider behind your son to Arnhem on 18 September the day before he was shot down at Arnhem. . . . I guess I owe my life to his determination to 'press on regardless'. Through most of the journey a faulty starboard engine made the journey difficult. His words to me and my glider pilot through the intercomm were a great encouragement, and helped accomplish a very difficult trip.

Tuesday, 19 September, dawned bright and clear over the besieged 1st Airborne at Arnhem and the 'Red Berets' looked forward cheerfully to their promised resupply air drops scheduled for 10 am. In England, however, a thick mist of fog and low cloud forced a postponement of the planned early take-off. At Down Ampney 271's crews waited impatiently for the word to go. Lord was due to pilot Dakota III, KG374 on this sortie, and his crew comprised 'Dickie' Medhurst, Harry King, Alec Ballantyne, and four RASC despatchers; Corporal Philip E. Nixon, Private Leonard S. Harder, and Drivers Jimmy Ricketts and Arthur Rowbotham.

By mid-day the weather prospect seemed to have improved and at a little after 1 pm seventeen Dakotas of 271 Squadron began take-off. Each was loaded with ammunition panniers to be dropped on Dropping Zone (DZ) 'V' on the north-west outskirts of Arnhem – though unknown to the RAF this DZ was by then in German hands.

The outward trip was plagued by thick cloud initially but as the Dakota stream neared Holland this cloud gave way to irregular patches of dense haze. Due to an error in timing a planned fighter escort had already exhausted its fuel and was already returning to bases, but the transport stream received no interference from the Luftwaffe en route to Arnhem. Navigating by dead reckoning and *GEE*, Harry King gave Lord an estimated time of arrival over the DZ as 3 pm, and when less than 10 miles from target zone Lord began to let down through the swirling haze; breaking into clear skies at 1500 feet and immediately seeing the lower Rhine ahead.

Suddenly the Dakota was engaged by intense flak and hit in the starboard engine which trailed a slender streak of smoke and then burst into flames. Lord asked if anyone was hurt and on King's reply that all were OK, told Medhurst to punch the fire extinguisher button for the crippled engine.

He then asked King, 'How long to the DZ?'

'Three minutes' flying time, skipper,' came the reply, adding that the Rebecca set was out of commission.

Lord told him not to bother, he would drop the load visually now that they were so close, and added an order for the crew to be prepared to bale out because of the burning engine.

King picked up his parachute and walked to the rear of the fuselage and found the four despatchers starting to drop the ammunition panniers as Lord gave them a green light signal. The Dakota was then down to 900 feet tracking across the DZ; its starboard engine fire beginning to threaten the whole wing. When the despatchers received a red light to cease dropping two panniers still remained.

On learning this Lord edged the burning aircraft into a steep bank, turning for an immediate second dropping run and coming even lower to level out at 600 feet for the drop. By then the awesome spectacle of the blazing Dakota struggling to complete its appointed task had gripped the attention of both British and German ground troops, and there was an eerie lull in the savage fighting as all watched the air drama.

As soon as the remaining pair of panniers had been manhandled out, Lord gave an order for his crew to bale out, though he made no move to prepare himself for abandoning the doomed aircraft. Harry King donned his parachute and then helped the despatchers with theirs. He then turned towards the open doorway, noticing at the same time Medhurst making his way back from the cockpit.

The next few seconds were a blur. With a tearing blast of tortured metal the starboard wing fell away from its anchorage, and the sudden whip of the uncontrollable aircraft shot King clear into space. Watched breathlessly by men of the 10th and 156th Battalions of the Paratroop Brigade below, King plunged to earth and at the very last moment his parachute deployed sufficiently to part-brake his fall and he hit the earth on his back hard, but alive; some 400 yards north of the DZ near a farm with a tall water windmill. The time was exactly 3.16 pm.

Behind him the Dakota plummeted into oblivion, carrying David Lord, Medhurst, Ballantyne and the four army despatchers to their deaths. From the time the aircraft was first hit to the moment Harry King dazedly consulted his watch on the ground the whole episode had lasted nine minutes.

Joining forces with the complement of a glider which landed nearby, King eventually spent that night fighting alongside paratroops of the 10th Battalion, Parachute Regiment holding Wolfheze railway station, but at 9 am the following morning he and 61 others became prisoners of war. Repatriated to England eventually on 13 May 1945, King made a full report on his last operational sortie to the commander of 271 Squadron, who forwarded a recommendation for Lord to be awarded a posthumous VC. This was approved and the citation was announced on

13 November 1945; Lord's parents received their son's decorations at an investiture on 18 December.

Two years later, on 19 September 1947, a memorial to Lord was unveiled in Wrexham; while his family presented the Lord Trophy to the RAF as an annual award to the Transport Command squadron considered most proficient in the supply role. On 11 November 1968, at Brize Norton, David Lord's brother, Wing Commander F. E. Lord AFC, performed a ceremony of naming a VC10 aircraft of 10 Squadron (XR810) as DAVID LORD, VC, in token of all of the unit's aircraft which carried the names of other air vc's. In attendance were many VIP's, including Flight Lieutenants William Reid vc and Harry King.

48. Robert Anthony Maurice Palmer

Despite the energy, determination, and no little sacrifices made by the bomber crews of the RAF in the early years of World War Two, it would be historically true to say that it was not until 1942 that RAF Bomber Command began to give evidence of its true potential for its part in the aerial bombing offensive against Hitler's Germany. By the end of that year the command possessed its major weapons – four-engined, truly 'heavy' bomber aircraft, heavy bombs, and many of the vital radar bombing and navigational aids necessary for precision location and destruction of any target. It also possessed a considerable number of well experienced, veteran bomber crews; men who were well aware of the ineffectiveness generally of bomber operations prior to 1942, due to lack of adequate equipment and insufficient experience in the conduct of true strategic bombing operations.

One result of the bomber barons' urging was the formation in August 1942 of the Path Finder Force (PFF); a tiny nucleus of five squadrons of bombers tasked with the vital role of spearheading future major bombing raids by locating and 'marking' targets accurately. During the remaining three years of war, the PFF – titled No 8 (PFF) Group, Bomber Command – expanded to become, eventually, a force of 19 squadrons, manned almost exclusively by volunteer crews, and including many of the RAF's most experienced bomber men.

In its unceasing endeavours to improve precision and techniques in the bombing offensive, the PFF evolved a system of appointing a Master Bomber for many major raids from late 1943 – a task originated by Wing Commander Guy Gibson vc for his famous dam-busting raid with 617 Squadron in May 1943. The Master Bomber's role was literally that of 'Master of Ceremonies'; directing the bombing of the main force, ensuring that target markers were accurately placed, advising main force pilots of decoy markers, correcting ill-aimed bombing, and generally ensuring that a maximum concentration of bombs was dropped in the right place accurately. Although such men were of necessity highly experienced bomber captains, pure rank was not the criterion for selection as a master bomber; indeed many such men, individually directing perhaps a total of 7-8,000 men in a single raid, held rank no higher than the Army equivalent of captain or major. Such responsibility was a heavy one for men mostly in their early 20's, but none failed in their duty, which included remaining over the target for an extended period during the height of anti-aircraft gun and fighter opposition to ensure their task was carried out to the very best of their ability.

Three such men of the PFF, killed in the course of their duties, were awarded posthumous Victoria Crosses; Ian Bazalgette,* Edwin Swales,† and a 'man of Kent', Robert Anthony Maurice Palmer. The son of A. R. F. Palmer, an ex-Royal Corps pilot, Robert Palmer was born in Gillingham, Kent on 7 July 1920, and educated at Gravesend County School and Gordon School. His boyhood was part-coloured by the stories he extracted from his father about the vintage flying era of 1914-18, and his various hobbies soon became orientated to aviation. On leaving school Palmer was employed in the Borough Surveyor's Department at Gravesend, but on 22 August 1939 he enlisted in the RAF Volunteer Reserve and was promoted to Sergeant next day. Commencing pilot training at No 3 Initial Training Wing (ITW), Hastings on 25 September 1939, he moved to the Desford EFTS for elementary flying instruction, and then joined No 12 FTS, Grantham on 8 June 1940; graduating as a Sergeant pilot on 7 September, and being posted to No 15 OTU at Harwell. On 16 November 1940, Palmer reported to his first operational unit, 75 Squadron, flying Wellington bombers from Feltwell, Norfolk.

Palmer's stay with 75 Squadron lasted ten days, during which time he flew as second pilot to Pilot Officer Morton in Wellington 'R' for three operational sorties over Germany to gain experience; then on 26 November he was re-posted to 149 Squadron at Mildenhall, Suffolk to complete his first tour of operations on Wellingtons as skipper of his own crew. This was accomplished relatively quickly and on 13 February 1941 Palmer was taken off operations and posted to No 20 OTU, Lossiemouth in Scotland as an instructor. Here he was promoted to Flight Sergeant on 1 June 1941, and then commissioned as a Pilot Officer on 29 January 1942.

His prolonged stay on instructing duties had by then frustrated Palmer, who forwarded repeated applications for a return to operations, but all were rejected by higher authority. Nevertheless, when the first three '1,000-bomber' raids were mounted in early 1942, Sir Arthur Harris, commander of Bomber Command, was forced to include many aircraft and crews from the training stations in order to achieve his '1,000' figure, and Palmer managed to skipper a bomber on each such raid on 30 May, 1 June and 25 June 1942. Further promoted to Flying Officer on 1 October,

* See Chapter 45.
† See Chapter 50.

and Flight Lieutenant on 28 December 1942, Palmer continued to dun higher authorities for a return to operations, but remained unsuccessful in this bid for action. In 1943, still serving with C Flight of the OTU, Palmer came under the command of Squadron Leader Ian Bazalgette DFC, another ex-operational pilot trying to return to a squadron, who later gained a posthumous VC with the Path Finder Force. Sympathising whole-heartedly with Palmer's situation, Bazalgette added his recommendation to Palmer's latest application for more active service, pointing out that Palmer had by then been instructing for almost three years, and had accumulated nearly 1400 flying hours on such duty. Whether Bazalgette's words were in any way responsible is not known, but shortly after, on 9 November 1943, Palmer finally left Lossiemouth on posting to the Path Finder Force; going initially to the PFF Mosquito training unit at Warboys, and then joining 109 Squadron on 16 January 1944.

No 109 Squadron, equipped with De Havilland Mosquito all-wood bombers, and stationed then at Marham, Norfolk, had been the pioneer unit to use and develop the *OBOE* radar aid, and as such had been permanently 'attached' to the PFF from its original formation. Palmer settled back into a vastly different operational scene to that which he had left three years before, but quickly adapted to the Mosquito bomber, flying his first operational sortie in aircraft 'N-Nuts' (DK558) on 3 February, with Ray Esler as his navigator – delivering four 500lb bombs to Krefeld. On 1 April, 109 Squadron moved base to Little Staughton, near St Neots, Cambridgeshire which airfield it shared with another PFF unit, 582 Squadron (Avro Lancasters); by which time Palmer had almost completed his second tour of operations.

Awarded a Distinguished Flying Cross on 30 June 1944, he volunteered to continue on operations and on 8 December received a Bar to his DFC for having completed 100 operational sorties overall. Two days later he was promoted to Squadron Leader. Few bomber captains in the RAF ever achieved a total of 100 sorties, and Palmer could easily have opted to be taken off operations having survived such a prodigious tally. He chose instead to stay with his squadron.

In France the Allied armies received a serious set-back on 16 December when General von Rundstedt launched a determined offensive along a 22-miles front. Within a week his forward troops had penetrated the Allied lines to a depth of nearly 60 miles, and the Allied Supreme Commander, General Eisenhower asked for RAF Bomber Command support to disrupt the German lines of transportation and communication. Prime targets were the various railway marshalling yards and major junctions in order to cut possible reinforcement supply lines.

A bomber raid against the Gremburg marshalling yards at Cologne was due to be flown on 20 December by elements of the PFF, but was postponed due to cloud and fog conditions. The same raid was mounted again on 23 December as a daylight sortie, comprising a total of 27 Lancasters and three Mosquitos from 35, 105, 109 and 582 Squadrons based at Bourn, Gravely and Little Staughton – all Path Finder units. The raid was to be made in three formations, each led by an *OBOE* Lancaster, backed up by an *OBOE* Mosquito. All bombs were to be released in salvo on seeing the leading aircraft's bomb load drop – and chosen as Master Bomber and leader of the front formation was 'Bob' Palmer, making his 111th operational sortie.

Foregoing his usual Mosquito aircraft, Palmer 'borrowed' a 582 Squadron Lancaster for this sortie, PB371, coded 60-V, and apart from his personal navigator on 109, Flight Lieutenant George Russell DFC, he took along an experienced 582 Squadron crew. Second pilot was Flight Lieutenant Owen Milne DFC, and a second navigator was Squadron Leader Albert Carter DFC. The signals operator was Flight Sergeant Bert Nundy; the mid-upper turret gunner, Flying Officer William Dalgarno; and, in the rear turret, sat a Canadian, Warrant Officer Yeulatt. Deputy master bomber for the raid, close behind Palmer in the front formation, was Flight Lieutenant E. C. Carpenter DFC, flying an *OBOE* Mosquito.

Taking off from Little Staughton at 10.27 am, Palmer was first away, followed just two minutes later by Lancaster PB120, 'P' piloted by a Canadian of German extraction, Flight Lieutenant Walter Reif who, with his crew, was due to complete his operational tour with this trip. Once assembled the three formations set course for Germany but suffered the immediate loss of two Lancasters which collided above the Thames Estuary, killing both crews.*

The weather forecasters had promised 10/10ths clouds at 10,000 feet over Cologne, but 20 miles short of their objective Palmer's formation, flying at 17,000 feet, ran into open skies; clearly visible targets for the highly accurate predicted flak guns below. Starting his necessarily prolonged rock-steady run-in, Palmer ignored the fury of bursting flak surrounding him, refusing to take evasive action in order to ensure an accurate drop. The flak soon found its mark, setting two engines on fire, and filling the nose, fuselage and bomb bay with smoke and flames.

Knowing full well that the following bombers were awaiting the release of his bombs as their signal to jettison their loads simultaneously, Palmer continued his run-in in the blazing Lancaster until he received the radar release signal, and then pressed the bomb switches. Hardly had he done so

* Some crew members baled out into the sea but died of exposure.

than the doomed bomber fell away in a blazing spiral to earth where it crashed in flames; the only crew member to escape being the rear gunner Yeulatt who successfully parachuted down. Behind Palmer, Carpenter's Mosquito was attacked by a host of Luftwaffe fighters closing in on the leading formation, and was shot down, burning.

Next to suffer was Walter Reif. Only seconds after releasing his bombs, his Lancaster received a direct hit in the open bomb bay and erupted in flames; being simultaneously attacked by German fighters. Yelling to his crew to bale out, Reif stayed at his controls in the hope of steadying the crippled bomber whilst his crew took to their parachutes. The two air gunners obeyed Reif's order and abandoned the aircraft safely, but the Lancaster then dived straight into the heart of Cologne and exploded.

When the last battered bomber finally returned to England they totted up the cost of this urgently requested sortie. Of the 30 aircraft originally despatched, seven Lancasters and one Mosquito failed to return; while every other aircraft without exception had suffered varying degrees of heavy damage from flak and fighter cannons. One of the latter was the Lancaster piloted by the 582 Squadron South African, Edwin Swales, who with his crew fought off repeated attacks and returned safely, and was later awarded a DFC for his coolness that day. Just two months later Swales was to die performing a Master Bomber's duties, and was awarded a posthumous VC.

Just east of Cologne the bodies of Robert Palmer, Walter Reif and their crews were buried in a village cemetery at Hoffnungsthal; and on 23 March 1945 came the announcement of Palmer's posthumous award of a Victoria Cross. After the cessation of hostilities in Europe, the dead crews were re-interred in the British cemetery at Rheinberg; and on 18 December 1945, Robert Palmer's father attended an investiture to receive his eldest son's gallantry awards. As the closing lines of Palmer's VC citation described him, 'His record of prolonged and heroic endeavour is beyond praise.'

49. George Thompson

Throughout the annals of RAF Bomber Command during the years 1939-45 one factor stands supreme above all others – the unique bond of esoteric loyalty between individual members of each crew. Brought together almost arbitrarily prior to the start of operational flying, each crew swiftly became a team, interdependent on each other's skill, experience and devotion to their specific role. Such interdependence and trust was vital – each individual's life depended on it. Only by welding themselves into a silk-smooth, efficient working team could they hope to accomplish their designated duties and stand any chance of beating the terrifying odds against ultimate survival. In the common hazard, each bomber crew quickly became a tight-knit 'community'; coming to know their fellow crew members more intimately than blood relations as each successive mission was completed. It was an understanding which transcended man-made barriers of race, creed or colour, with the bulk of crews being composed of men from all walks of life and many different backgrounds; a true 'commonwealth' blending of personalities in which the only criterion was ability – and no little courage.

Heading each crew was the captain, or first pilot – the 'skipper' – to whom each crew member looked for final authority. In the air – and usually on the ground – his decisions were accepted as 'law', without question. Nevertheless, each crew man was expected, indeed, required to use his own initiative when circumstances demanded it. The operational history of the bomber crews is inundated with a myriad of examples of individual initiative by men who, without thought or concern for their own life, risked death to aid a fellow crew member. Almost without exception, such men acted instinctively with no conscious attempt at 'heroics'; simply reacting instantly to seeing a fellow crew member in jeopardy. Such selflessness, deliberate or unconscious, exemplified the depth of a crew's bond with each other. Epitomising that bond, George Thompson's unselfish concern for the safety of two fellow crew men saved the life of one, but cost him his own.

The son of a Scottish ploughman, George Thompson was born on 23 October 1920 at Borestone Cottage in the parish of Trinity Gask, Perthshire. His early education came from the Portmoak Public School and, later, Kinross Higher Grades School, a senior secondary school; and on leaving at the age of fifteen, he became apprenticed to a grocer in Kinross. Serving a four year apprenticeship, Thompson finally qualified as a certificated grocer, but by then war had been declared and Thompson's thoughts turned naturally to military service. His first move was to join the Argyll branch of the Local Defence Volunteers (LDV) – precursor of the national Home Guard – but in the summer of 1940 he applied to enlist in the RAF; only to be given deferred service.

With typical quiet determination, Thompson, not content to merely await officialdom's eventual decision, volunteered again in late 1940; this time for flying duties. He attended an aircrew selection board on 7 January 1941, but was not selected, and therefore enlisted as ground crew three days later. As a boy he had developed an interest in radio and wireless, and therefore opted for training in the RAF wireless trade. Completing his trade training in October 1941, he was posted briefly to RAF Coningsby before being sent overseas to Iraq on 11 February 1942.

For the following eighteen months Thompson quietly and efficiently carried out his duties in Iraq, but was increasingly bored by what he considered to be mundane, unexciting jobs. Accordingly he again applied for flying duties, was accepted, and arrived back in England in mid-August 1943 to commence training as an air wireless operator. Graduating from No 4 Radio School as a Sergeant Wop/Air on 29 November, he next attended a short air gunnery course, and completed his training at No 8 (B) AFU.

On 2 May 1944 he reported to No 14 Operational Training Unit (OTU), Market Harborough in order to join a bomber crew and then complete crew training prior to actual operations. At the OTU one pilot, Flying Officer Harry Denton, a farmer from New Zealand, had already 'enlisted' his future bomb aimer, Ron Goebel, and a navigator, Ted Kneebone; and it was Kneebone who suggested to Denton that he invite George Thompson to join the crew, Denton had already noticed Thompson, a tall, raw-boned, tough-looking NCO with an open face and pleasant Scots accent, and was favourably impressed. To fill the two air gunners' places, he then invited a pair of Welshmen to join the 'team'; Sergeant Haydn Price and Sergeant Ernest Potts.

All six men quickly settled down as a crew and, after some 80 hours practice flying in Wellington bombers, went on to a heavy conversion unit to fly Short Stirlings, near Lincoln, where they 'recruited' their future flight engineer, Wilf Hartshorn. Now a complete crew, Denton and his men underwent a short conversion course to Lancasters, and were posted on 29 September 1944 to 9 Squadron at Bardney, Lincolnshire to commence an operational tour.

Edwin Swales

Robert Hampton Gray

The first operational sortie was flown on 6 October when Denton piloted Lancaster LM548 to Bremen for a five-hours' round trip; and was soon followed by two more sorties that month, to Flushing and Nuremburg respectively on the 11th and 19th. A lull in operations for the squadron during November gave the crew little to do, but on 4 December, Denton flew Lancaster NG249 to bomb Heilbronn successfully. Meanwhile Thompson had been promoted to Flight Sergeant with effect from 30 November.

On New Year's Eve, the crew joined most of Bardney's station personnel in the traditional festive celebrations – Thompson, being fiercely proud of his Scottish ancestry, looking forward to suitable celebration of 'Hogmanay' – when the dance was interrupted by a Tannoy loudspeaker message, ordering ten of the Lancaster crews, Denton's included, to report to the briefing room. Here they were told that there was to be yet another attack on a prime target, the Dortmund-Ems Canal, at dawn the following day.

At 5 am on 1 January all 70 air crew were awakened and soon reported for final briefing. The weather was freezing cold, with buildings and aircraft coated in hoar frost as the crews finally climbed into their Lancasters. For this trip Harry Denton was allotted Lancaster PD377, 'U', with a bomb load of a dozen 1,000lb high explosive bombs tucked inside its belly. Detailed as first to go, Denton started his take-off run just before 7.45 am, taking up most of the runway before finally becoming airborne. Climbing laboriously to 500 feet he began a turn, and saw the Lancaster due to follow him career off the runway and erupt in a holocaust of flames; followed by the third bomber which also crashed, but from which the crew managed to escape without serious injury – a black start to the sortie.

Along with 100 other 5 Group bombers, Denton flew independently to a point over northern France, and then settled into various loose formations at 10,000 feet for the last leg to the objective. Visibility was good in clearing skies as they made the final approach to the Dortmund-Ems waterway, and Denton made a perfect run-in, with Goebel only needing to ask for slight corrections. As the first of the 12 thousand-pounders dropped away from 'U-Uncle's' bomb bay, the pilot started correcting the flying attitude of the Lancaster, compensating for the shift in load distribution, until the final bomb was released. Once Goebel had checked physically that the bomb bay was indeed empty, he would give Denton the customary 'Bombs gone' message, and the pilot could close the bomb bay doors, trim the aircraft and head for England.

Flak opposition had already claimed several Lancasters ahead of

Denton and he was poised to swing his bomber out of the immediate danger zone, when a deafening explosion right in front of him knocked him momentarily unconscious. An 88mm shell had found its mark, shattering the nose compartment where Goebel had been crouching, tearing the top off the pilot's perspex canopy, and setting the port inner engine on fire.

A split second before this hit, though unknown to Denton then, a second shell had torn a six feet square chunk out of the under-fuselage just below the mid-upper turret, slashed through the trimming controls and ruptured the hydraulic lines, thereby leaving the bomb doors gaping open. Inside the fuselage a raging fire immediately broke out, fed by the hydraulic oil slopping from the burst pipelines, and engulfed Ernie Potts seated in the dorsal gun turret, immediately above the point of impact of the shell.

Denton recovered his senses quickly, took stock of the burning engine, and punched the relevant extinguisher button which soon doused the danger there. The icy gale howling through his shattered canopy cleared the smoke of the explosion but fed force to the roaring flames in the rear fuselage. Having feathered the burning engine, Denton was left with an unevenly powered aircraft, and had to apply hard right rudder constantly while pushing the control column fully forward to prevent the aircraft's tendency to nose-up into a stall. By sheer chance Denton's instrument panel was still intact, but behind him Ted Kneebone's navigational charts and maps had gone – sucked out of the aircraft by the slipstream gale roaring through the fuselage. Goebel then appeared from his nose compartment, smoke-blackened but uninjured, carrying the torn remnants of his parachute pack.

In the rear fuselage George Thompson could see the havoc caused by the flak, and realised that with both turrets on fire, the gunners were in deadly peril. Working without gloves at his wireless set, and relatively lightly clad, the tall Scotsman instinctively moved aft to help the gunners.

While Denton set a rough course to get them away from Germany, Thompson, clinging by fingers and toes to the sides of the fuselage, eased himself past the gaping hole in the floor to Pott's dorsal turret just beyond. Then, slowly and deliberately, he extricated the unconscious gunner from his seat. Potts' flying clothing was already aflame, and Thompson's clothing began to burn in the furnace. Getting Potts clear of the turret, the Scot humped him across his shoulders and began the perilous journey forward, along the side of the fuselage and hovering over the jagged hole. One slip or loss of balance and both men – each without a parachute – would have fallen to earth. Immensely strong,

Thompson achieved the feat and bore Potts to a relatively safer place forward, where he proceeded to beat out the gunner's flaming clothing with his bare hands.

By then Thompson's own clothing was a shambles; his trousers having been almost completely burned away. Fire had also seared his bare hands and face, and the icy gale of slipstream must have caused him agony. But, having seen that Potts was being cared for, Thompson then turned his attention to Haydn Price, trapped in the rear turret in the centre of the furnace. Price, once he realised the aircraft was ablaze, and getting no response on the intercomm, had decided to bale out. Rotating the turret manually to the beam, he removed his flying helmet, disconnected the leads to his electrically heated flying suit, and flipped opened the turret doors behind him in order to fall backwards out of the aircraft.

As soon as he opened the doors he became engulfed in a fierce rush of flames which immediately singed off his hair and almost burned away his ears. Pulling the doors to promptly, Price rotated the turret back to its normal aft-facing position, where he heard someone knocking from inside the fuselage. Opening the doors, he saw Thompson, who told him to 'come on out, Taffy'. Burned and shocked, Price eased himself into the fuselage with Thompson's help, and was then assisted forward, past the gaping hole in the floor, until he found relative safety alongside the still-unconscious Potts.

Thompson by then was in a shocking state of burns and blackened, charred clothing; his face, hands and legs blistering and contracting in the still-howling slipstream. Yet he was still not content. Fearing that the pilot might order the crew to bale out, he made his way forward to Denton's cockpit to tell him about the two injured gunners. The pilot, his mind and hands full with the continuing struggle to control the shattered Lancaster, had no recollection afterwards of seeing Thompson at that time; though in the state that the young Scot was by now he was virtually unrecognisable, even to his friends.

With Hartshorn and Goebel helping alternatively, Denton was nearing the Rhine when Goebel pointed to some flak on the starboard side. As the pilot started to take evasive action the aircraft was hit in the starboard inner engine, which immediately ceased pulling and had to be feathered. By now the bomber was down to about 5,000 feet and steadily descending, when Denton received a fright as a flight of German fighters suddenly appeared, heading straight towards him. Luckily, these ignored the lame bomber, being fully intent on fleeing from a Canadian squadron of Spitfires right behind them.

The Spitfires on seeing the wallowing and obviously crippled Lancaster abandoned their prey and formated on the bomber, attempting to guide it to their own airfield. Soon the Lancaster was only a few feet above the earth, and Denton, on the point of exhaustion from his efforts, knew he had only minutes left in which to put the aircraft onto the ground. One attendant Spitfire suddenly shot in front of him and plainly indicated danger from some high tension cables looming up in front of the bomber. With a supreme effort Denton lifted the aircraft over these, and then spotted a village dead ahead. Avoiding the possibility of crashing here, he turned towards a pair of fields bisected by a long hedged ridge and set the Lancaster down diagonally across these.

Touching earth halfway across the first field, the bomber punched its way through the ridge and broke up in mid-fuselage the separate sections finally coming to a stop before reaching the far edge of the second field. Smashed petrol feed lines gushed raw fuel everywhere but there was no fire, and the crew managed to get out of the wreckage, including Potts who had temporarily recovered semi-consciousness.

The first person Denton saw afterwards was George Thompson and the sight shocked him. With face, hands and legs burned black, and only the tattered, charred remnants of his clothing left to cover him, Thompson still found the strength to remark, 'Jolly good landing, skipper.' Checking the others, Denton sent Goebel off to find help in the nearby village of Heesh, while he and Kneebone took Thompson to a cottage across the field. Hartshorn, himself part-burned, helped Price and Potts to the cottage; where all the crew received rough first aid from the friendly owners.

Meanwhile their 'escort' of Spitfires had radioed to base the location of the crashed bomber, and soon there appeared an ambulance containing two Service doctors. All were taken to the Eindhoven Catholic hospital except Goebel who was picked up by members of an Army unit and eventually transferred to Rauceby RAF Hospital in Lincolnshire, having lost the first joints of all his fingers due to severe frostbite.

The mid-upper gunner Ernie Potts lapsed back into unconsciousness soon after transfer to the hospital and never recovered, to die some 18 hours later; but Haydn Price, though badly burned around the head and having to spend many months undergoing plastic surgery to build up his ears and face again, finally made a full recovery; he owed his survival to the courage of George Thompson. Hartshorn was also sent home to Rauceby hospital for treatment to his burns but was able to leave the medical centre a few weeks later.

Thompson was initially tranferred to No 50 Military Field Hospital where a series of penicillin injections and other treatments appeared to put him on the slow road to recovery; and he remained a model patient, cheerful and without complaint, but his ordeal was heightened by the incursion of pneumonia and on 23 January 1945 he succumbed to his dreadful injuries and illness. Shortly after he was buried in the Brussels Cemetery of Evere-les-Brizelles.

On 20 February the *London Gazette* announced the award of a Victoria Cross to the gallant Scot; the citation for which underlined Thompson's self-sacrifice by stating :

When the aircraft was hit Flight Sergeant Thompson might have devoted his efforts to quelling the fire and so have contributed to his own safety. He preferred to go through the fire to succour his comrades. He knew that he would then be in no position to hear or heed any order which might be given to abandon aircraft. He hazarded his own life in order to save the lives of others. Young in years and experience, his actions were those of a veteran.

50. Edwin Swales

During the war years 1939-45, under South African law, no member of its armed services could be compelled to serve outside the Union of South Africa – in the 'Outer World', to quote a contemporary phrase – though any member was permitted to volunteer for such duty. In the tradition created during 1914-18 by thousands of young South Africans eager to serve alongside British and Empire forces in the struggle with Germany, Edwin Swales was but one of many more citizens of South Africa who fought on the Allied side against Hitler's vaunted Third Reich in World War Two. Born at Inanda, Natal on 3 July 1915, Edwin Swales was educated at the Durban High School and matriculated in 1934. Taking employment with a local branch of Barclays Bank, Swales was a keen sportsman, excelling in rugby, cricket and squash rackets; playing rugby for Natal, a provincial team loosely equivalent to a British county side. On 1 June 1935 he enlisted in the Natal Mounted Rifles (NMR), an active citizen force similar to the British Territorial Army, and by 31 May 1939 had completed his term of service, having risen to the rank of Warrant Officer II. Returnng briefly to his banking career, he was then mobilised for full-time service in the NMR on 15 September 1939, and served on routine duties until 9 June 1940; on which date he officially volunteered for more active service outside the Union.

In the same month the NMR was 'converted' for foreign service and came under the aegis of the 2nd South African Infantry Brigade and, after a final period of intensive training, was sent to Kenya which was under threat from the Italian army. A further move for 2nd Brigade to southern Abyssinia in February 1941 brought it into the front line of the armies which retrieved that area from Italian domination. The brigade was next sent to North Africa, where it fought gallantly through the *Crusader* offensive, Gazala battles and the fighting retreat by the Allies to Alamein. Finally, after serving through the successful counter-offensive from El Alamein, 2nd Brigade was withdrawn from the fighting and sent home to South Africa.

Swales, who had played a full part in every facet of the Brigade's fighting record, now volunteered on 17 January 1942 for a transfer to the South African Air Force (SAAF) and, on being accepted for pilot training, moved to No 75 Air School, Lyttleton, near Pretoria on 2 February to commence instruction. Completing the initial phase of training on 8 October, he next moved to No 4 Air School, Benoni, and made his first solo flight on 29 October in a DH Tiger Moth. In February 1943 he reported to No 21 Air School, Kimberley for advanced 'conversion' training on twin-engined Airspeed Oxford aircraft; finally being awarded his 'wings' on 26 June and being commissioned as a Second Lieutenant, SAAF on the same day.

In August 1943 Swales was offered a choice of duties. He could spend the following six months in South Africa as an instructor, or apply for secondment to the Royal Air Force for operational flying in the European theatre of war. Swales' decision was unhesitating, and on 21 August he was officially seconded to the RAF; sailing with 60 other volunteer pilots in the *Rangitata* and reaching England in November. On 1 December he commenced a three months' advanced course of training at 6 AFU, Little Rissington flying Ansons and Oxfords; being promoted to First Lieutenant on 26 December; then moved to 83 OTU, Peplow for conversion training on Wellington bombers. In June 1944 he completed his lengthy instructional period with a brief course at Warboys; the night training unit of the elite Path Finder Force of RAF Bomber Command, where Swales made his first acquaintance with the Avro Lancaster bomber.

In the first week of July 1944 Swales – known to his fellow crews as 'Ted' – joined 582 Squadron of the PFF, based at Little Staughton and equipped with Lancasters. Joining B Flight, Swales made his first practice flight on 6 July, and in the following week finally commenced operations.

His first sortie came on 12 July, a daylight raid in Lancaster PB149, 'D' against Thiverny, and this was quickly followed by two more day raids, both on 19 July against Mont Cordon and Cagny. In the early evening of 23 July he bombed the Foret du Crol, and later that evening took off again to 'deliver' six 2,000lb bombs to Kiel. On his return from Kiel he diverted to the Handley Page factory airfield and slightly misjudged his approach to the unfamiliar airfield and crashed; sustaining light concussion and facial injuries but without serious injury to his crew.

Five nights later he was sent to bomb Hamburg but, due to engine malfunction, was forced to abandon the sortie before reaching Germany. The daylight trips continued in August, with Swales bombing L'Isle Adam with 13,000lb of high explosive on 3 August.

Next day, in Lancaster PB963, 'J', he was one of a large formation detailed to destroy the missile launching site at Trossy St Maximin. Over the objective flak opposition was intense, destroying the deputy master bomber's aircraft, and crippling one of the marking 'backers' piloted by

Squadron Leader Ian Bazalgette DFC.* Swales' aircraft received its 'share' of flak damage but he bombed accurately and returned safely. During the rest of August he flew seven more operations, two of which were daylight sorties.

In September Swales was transferred from B to A Flight of 582 Squadron, and flew five sorties during the first two weeks of that month before having a short period of leave. Returning to operations in early October, he flew Lancaster PB149 on the night of 5 October as one of the sky-marking formation for a raid on Saarbrucken, and repeated this task on the night over Dortmund. A week later, on 14 October, in Lancaster PB963, 'J', he undertook a daylight raid on Duisburg but predicted flak very nearly brought an end to his career. With both port engines feathered, the starboard outer engine failing, and shattered hydraulic lines, Swales completed his bombing and eventually belly-landed near Brussels without the use of flaps or undercarriage, but without injury to himself or his crew. Flown back to Little Staughton by a 'hack' Anson, Swales flew his next operation the following night as a 'blind illuminator' for a main force bombing Wilhelmshaven. Another marking sortie over Stuttgart followed on 19 October; then on 4 November he received notification of his promotion to Captain, and rejoined B Flight. Throughout November Swales flew just three sorties – all as a marker in the spearhead of main bombing formations.

In early December Swales completed four more sorties; two of these as deputy master bomber, but his 33rd operational sortie on 23 December proved to be outstanding. Taking off from Little Staughton at 10.30 am, he was one of a formation undertaking a specially requested raid to knock out the marshalling yards at Cologne. Master bomber for the sortie was Squadron Leader R. A. M. Palmer DFC of 109 Squadron, a sister unit to 582 at Little Staughton, flying a 'borrowed' Lancaster from 582 Squadron. As the bombers approached their target flak became viciously intense and highly accurate; shooting down the deputy master bomber's aircraft and causing Palmer's Lancaster to erupt in flames. Nevertheless, Palmer completed his marker-bombing run before spiralling to earth in flames.† On seeing the release of Palmer's bomb load, Swales released his own bombs in salvo in accordance with the pre-sortie briefing, and then heaved his Lancaster out of the flak zone.

Almost immediately he was jumped by five German fighters prowling like vultures around the edge of the flak area. Coolly, Swales swung his lumbering bomber from side to side, giving his gunners every possible

* See Chapter 45.
† See Chapter 48.

chance to retaliate. Fighting off five separate attacks, his gunners claimed one fighter destroyed and two more damaged. For his coolness under fire that day, added to his previous prowess, Swales was awarded a Distinguished Flying Cross.*

Flying two more sorties in December, Swales started the new year with a raid on Dortmund on the night of 1 January 1945; and the following night was selected as master bomber for a heavy attack against Nuremberg. Flying Lancaster PB538, 'M', he flew for nearly seven hours, leaving the target area only when he was completely satisfied that the main force had bombed accurately. Four more operations followed against Frankfurt, Ludwigshaven, Bonn and Goch; then he was again appointed Master bomber for a raid on Chemnitz on the night of 14 February. Though unaware of it personally, Swales' promotion to Major was already wending its way through the administrative 'channels' but by now the South African's main thoughts concerned a forthcoming crew leave due to start on 24 February; for which Swales had arranged to stay at the home of his navigator, Dudley Archer.

Then on the night of 23 February he was chosen as Master bomber for a 374-aircraft raid on Pforzheim, a vital rail junction halfway between Karlsruhe and Stuttgart, and on the main German rail line leading to the American 7th Army front. Flying his usual Lancaster, PB538, 'M', Swales' crew were Squadron Leader D. P. D. Archer DSO DFC (navigator); Pilot Officer R. A. Wheaton RAAF (2nd navigator); Flight Lieutenant Clive Dodson DSO DFC RCAF (Bomb aimer); and Pilot Officer A. V. Goodacre RAAF (Wireless operator). The two air gunners were Flight Sergeant B. Leach (dorsal) and Pilot Officer N Bourne RCAF (Rear turret); while the flight engineer, Flight Sergeant George Bennington DFM had already completed 34 operational sorties with Swales. It was a highly experienced crew, comprised of men from four nations.

Take-off from Little Staughton was at 1636 hours and Swales made the outward journey without notable incident. Then, as he arrived over Pforzheim a Messerschmitt night fighter attacked, its fire hitting the Lancaster's starboard inner engine and holing the wing fuel tanks, and shattering Bourne's rear turret. Checking swiftly that no crew member was injured, Swales calmly feathered the stricken engine and continued his marking run-in over the target. Releasing his target indicators in a shimmering cascade, he circled the target area and began issuing his radio instructions to the backers-up and the first wave of main force bombers. Silhouetted against the glare of his own pyrotechnic TI's, with his radio signals pinpointing his position, Swales (like all master bombers)

* Gazetted 23 February 1945 – the day he died.

was a sitting target. Another night fighter suddenly bore in from his port beam, its cannon shells smashing a port engine and raking the Lancaster fuselage along its entire length. The bomber faltered under the fresh on-slaught and fell away to 4,000 feet height while Swales struggled to regain control and switched off the damaged port motor.

With only two engines giving full power, and ruptured fuel lines spew-ing oil and petrol, the South African still refused to abandon his task. Circuiting Pforzheim he continued to pass his instructions over the R/T, and only when he was convinced that the object of the raid had been accomplished did he turn to the problems of returning to base. (The operation was indeed a success, being one of the most concentrated attacks ever flown by RAF Bomber Command. For a loss of 12 bombers, a total of 1,551 tons of bombs was dropped and completely gutted some 350 acres of Pforzheim's built-up area.)

For Swales and his crew, the journey back was a flying nightmare. The crippled Lancaster was in sorry condition, and in the pilot's bucket seat Swales had no instruments or artificial horizon to help him in his bid to get his crew home safely. Gradually losing height and speed, he still hoped at first to reach the forward airfield at Manston, Kent; but after an hour's continuous fight with the groggy controls he found himself nosing into thin-layered cloud. Using every ounce of skill he possessed Swales managed to keep the wallowing Lancaster airborne until he knew he was at least over Allied-occupied territory, by which time his steadily descend-ing flight-path had brought the bomber down into turbulent cumulus clouds – conditions which made control of the aircraft virtually impossible.

Now the two remaining engines began to overheat, and Swales could feel the rudders becoming uncontrollable. Then, at about 3,00 feet, a control link sheared under the constant stress and the Lancaster skewed into a flat spin increasing to a semi-powered spin. Swales gave the order for the crew to abandon the aircraft but remained in his seat in a final attempt to hold the crazily veering bomber steady enough for his crew to bale out. The last crew member to go was Dudley Archer and only seconds later the night sky was lit by a brilliant explosion as the Lancaster hit some unseen high tension cables. At first light on the following day the crew inspected the wreckage of Lancaster 'M' strewn across two fields at Chappelle-aux-Bois on the outskirts of Valenciennes.

In the twisted metal ruin of the cockpit they found the body of their skipper, 'Ted' Swales; his strong hands still grasping the control column spectacle; while some yards away a booted foot still rested in a rudder bar stirrup. Determined to give his crew every chance of freedom and survival, Edwin Swales had remained at his controls until it was too late to save himself. His selfless sacrifice was fittingly recognised by the posthumous award of a Victoria Cross, gazetted on 24 April 1945; the ultimate sentence of its citation reading, '. . . he did his duty to the last, giving his life that his comrades might live'. Captain Edwin Swales vc DFC SAAF was the only member of the South African Air Force ever to receive the supreme award.

51. Robert Hampton Gray

The sixth Canadian airman to be awarded a Victoria Cross was also the last man so honoured. It was a posthumous award, made even more poignant by the fact that the action in which he died, and for which he was considered so eminently deserving of the supreme award, took place less than a week before the final day of the 1939-45 war. Robert Hampton Gray had survived five years of war, only to be killed within a few days of the ultimate Allied victory.

Born in Trail, British Columbia on 2 November 1917, Gray was the son of a jeweller, and was educated at Nelson; graduating from the High School in June 1936 and then undertaking four years' university studies for an arts degree in Alberta, Edmonton. On leaving university in early 1940 Gray immediately volunteered for service with the Royal Canadian Naval Volunteer Reserve; enlisting as an Ordinary Seaman at Calgary on 3 August 1940. Commencing pilot training at HMS *St Vincent*, Gosport on 3 December 1940, Gray completed his basic instruction on 5 October 1941, and next day was commissioned as a Sub-lieutenant and posted to HMS *Daedulus* (Lee-on-Solent) for further advanced training, and then moved to HMS *Heron* on 1 December for his final operational preparation. Then, on 10 March 1942 he joined his first squadron, 757, at HMS *Kestrel*.

Transferred to 789 Squadron, HMS *Afrikander* in May 1942, Gray remained with this unit on its various travels around South Africa and Kenya during the following year; and was promoted to Lieutenant on the last day of December 1942. On 1 April 1943, he was again transferred to a new unit, 877 Squadron at Korongo, Nairobi; continuing to add to his experience as a relatively senior fighter pilot with 877 for the next fifteen months of his service in Kenya. Of medium height, with straight blond hair and a fresh boyish complexion, Gray's slightly plump figure and unhurried manner in all things became a familiar and popular part of the squadron scene; earning him the nickname of 'Hammy' (a diminution of his second Christian name) wherever he went. Gray was proud of his Canadian birth and often regaled his companions with tales of home town life in Nelson, British Columbia – and was unmercifully ribbed about his 'hick town in the West' by the other pilots. Constantly cheerful and even-tempered, Gray accepted such leg-pulling with good humour; even playing a part of a 'dumb Colonial' as a form of near-British understatement when his work was praised or admired. Leaving Africa at the end of May 1944, Gray was sent to England and posted to 748 Squadron, HMS *Heron* on 18 June, but spent the next few weeks at home in Canada on leave. On his return to England he was appointed to HMS *Formidable* as replacement senior pilot – the equivalent of Second-in-Command – on 1841 Squadron, commanded then by Lieutenant Commander R. L. Bigg-Wither. He was to remain with 1841 until his death a year later.

HMS *Formidable*, an aircraft carrier with an armoured deck (one of the first three carriers with this feature) was then 'host' to four FAA Squadrons; 1841 and 1842 equipped with Corsair 'gull-winged' fighters, and 826 and 828 equipped with the ungainly Fairey Barracuda torpedo bombers. From July 1944 *Formidable* had participated in the large naval operations aimed at sinking the German surface raider *Tirpitz*, harboured at this period in Kaa Fiord, Norway, recovering from damage already inflicted by a particularly daring midget submarine attack in September 1943. During the last week of August 1944, under the aegis of Operation Goodwood, *Formidable*'s squadrons flew several strikes against the *Tirpitz* though cloud and fog conditions surrounding their objective prevented the Barracudas and Corsairs inflicting any significant damage. Although they met no Luftwaffe opposition, the naval aircraft crews faced a daunting barrage of flak each time, and in these strikes Hammy Gray set a splendid example of determination. Acting as a spearhead for the bombers, Gray led his men down to strafe German flak defences on each attack; on one occasion leading his section of Corsairs in a low-level strike against three enemy destroyers at anchor in the fiord. This last action was recorded on the aircraft cameras and on return to their carrier, the pilots ran the films through to judge results. Gray's own film showed that he had virtually flown 'right down the barrels' as he attacked one destroyer's bridge and guns. His name was mentioned in naval despatches soon after.

By April 1945 *Formidable* had joined the British Pacific Fleet in operations against Japan, south of Okinawa, and by July the naval actions had moved northwards. In the interim the carrier had participated in several engagements, and been subjected to various *Kamikaze* suicide-aircraft attacks, although her armoured deck absorbed much of the damage and permitted operations to be continued quickly. In July Gray participated in a variety of air strikes. On the 18th he led a strafing mission against enemy airfields; and on the 24th led a strike against shipping and airfields in the Inland Sea area. On 28 July he again led a strike to the Inland Sea zone, attacking a destroyer with his bombs and obtaining a direct hit (the ship was later reported sunk). These actions, added to an already established record of fine operational service, led to the award of a Distinguished Service Cross (DSC) for Robert Gray. On 30 July the Fleet withdrew for general replenishment for two days, but in the event remained out of action for nine days, due to a succession of typhoons in the operational area, and the imposed delay until the first atomic bomb was dropped on Hiroshima on 6 August. Intending to resume operations on 8 August, these were again postponed for 24 hours on receipt of a typhoon warning, but next day *Formidable*'s aircraft were able to return to their tasks. Prime targets were shipping south of Tokyo and off northern Honshu, with the object of maintaining pressure against Japan's dwindling naval forces and merchant shipping.

No 1841 Squadron was tasked with three RAMROD sorties for 9 August 1945 – fighter-bomber attacks aimed at destroying the Japanese Air Force's ability to take the offensive. The first RAMROD was led off at dawn by the squadron commander, Dick Bigg-Wither, at the head of a dozen Corsairs. The Captain of *Formidable* had asked Bigg-Wither to 'take it easy' and not take undesirable risks – with the release of the first-ever atomic bomb, the end of the war against Japan could only be a matter of days away, and unnecessary loss of lives was now to be guarded against. The briefing for all RAMROD operations that day specified a round of known Japanese airfields, making just one striking pass at each, to cause as much damage as possible, and to keep any Kamikaze aircraft grounded.

A few minutes after 8 am Hammy Gray led seven other Corsairs off the carrier's deck on the second RAMROD; his orders from Bigg-Wither being those which had applied already – airfields as priority targets, with 'worthwhile' targets as a matter of individual and circumstantial choice by formation leaders. Gray's eight Corsairs climbed to 10,000 feet and formed into two sections of four aircraft; Gray leading the first quartet in Corsair IV, FG-1D, KD658, '115'*, and the rear foursome led by his deputy, Sub-Lieutenant MacKinnon. Each Corsair was carrying a pair of 500lb high explosive bombs in addition to its usual battery of four .50 machine guns mounted in the wings. The intended landfall for Gray's mission was Kinkawsan Point, a tiny island some 30 miles north-east of the large town of Sendai.

After flying about 150 miles over the ocean the two sections eventually made landfall at the mouth of Onagawa Wan bay, and as Gray passed along the edge of the bay he spotted two Japanese destroyers, two

* Gray's usual Corsair, '119' was not available for operations that morning.

destroyer escorts and several other vessels all anchored in the western end of the bay. Mentally noting these as a possible alternate target, he continued inland, still searching for a primary airfield target as briefed.

On arrival over his intended objective Gray quickly realised that the target had already been raided by some other Allied aircraft, which had created considerable damage. Seeing no point in 'wasting' bombs on a crippled airfield, Gray radioed to the other Corsair pilots that he intended attacking the shipping they had seen in Onagawa Bay instead. Still at 10,000 feet, all eight Corsairs headed back to the bay; approaching from behind the cover of the hills virtually surrounding the inlet. Gray's instructions to his men were to dive from their present height on his signal, gathering high speed for the final attack from behind the hill-tops, and then run out of the bay at almost sea level eastwards to the open sea. As the diving Corsairs flashed over the hills in a 400 mph dive, a holocaust of anti-aircraft fire blossomed around and in front of them from dozens of sited guns in the hills and the naval ships at anchor ahead. Gray led in, released his bombs against a destroyer, the *Amakusa*, and began his run-out, skipping across the water at less than 40 feet height. The whole bombing attack took place in little more than 20 seconds of furious activity, and in those fleeting seconds Hammy Gray died as he left his target.

Sub-Lieutenant John Blade of MacKinnon's section, flying ahead of his section, released his bombs and emerged from the smoke and turmoil to find himself some 300 yards behind two other Corsairs. At that moment the Corsair to Blade's starboard (Gray's) erupted in flames at its port wing root, jerked into a steep starboard bank, then with wings ablaze rolled onto its back and plunged at full power into the waters of the bay. In Blade's opinion the aircraft must have dived straight to the sea bed because hardly a trace of oil was left on the sea surface to mark Gray's entry.

Jinking wildly through the flak, the remaining seven Corsairs flew out of the bay, re-formed under MacKinnon's leadership, and circuited the hills for a second attack on the shipping. As they roared into Onagawa Bay for the second time, they could see that Gray's victim, the *Amakusa*, had already sunk, and therefore concentrated on other vessels, leaving two of these badly damaged. On their return to the carrier, John Blade's Corsair with ruptured hydraulics was forced to belly-land, but he escaped injury; while the rest landed on safely.

Just six days later, on 15 August 1945, came the end of the war with Japan. Robert Gray's record of splendid leadership and personal example led to the posthumous award of a Victoria Cross on 12 November 1945.

In a letter to Gray's father shortly after Hammy's death, Captain P. Ruck-Keene paid sincere tribute to Gray's record and concluded his message of sympathy by describing Robert Gray as, '. . . the best and bravest fighter pilot in the ship and everybody loved him. The tragedy is all the worse coming so close to the end.' Yet perhaps a more succinct tribute to Hammy Gray's personality were the words of the newest pilot to join 1841 Squadron at that date, Sub-Lieutenant Albert Hughes, who wrote of him :

It was my first raid over Japan, but Lt Gray was so cheerful and inspired such confidence as a leader that my nervousness was allayed before we started. . . . He was liked and respected by all, and his death cast a shadow not only over the pilots but over the entire ship.

1939-1945

21. Gray, T.

3 Fairey Battles of 12 Squadron, RAF in France, late 1939.

4 German photo of Fairey Battle P3223 after the Maastricht bridges' raid, 12 May 1940. Its pilot, Norman Thomas, survived the crash.

[440]   5 12 Squadron officers at Guignicourt, France, early May 1940. Garland in centre figure in rear row.
        6 Donald Garland vc at far right of this informal group of 12 Squadron officers.

22. Learoyd

7 'Babe' Learoyd in flying helmet and Sidcot suit, 1939 when serving with 49 Squadron, RAF. [441]
8 Roderick Learoyd vc (far right) and Sergeant John Hannah vc at RAF Scampton on 22 March 1941 at the presentation of two Frank Salisbury oil paintings to the officers' mess. From left are Mr F. Handley Page, Group Captain Strang Graham MC GM (Station Commander), and Group Captain H. S. B. Walmsley OBE MC DFC.

9

10

9 Learoyd in uniform, 1940.

10 Wing Commander R. A. B. Learoyd vc (right) with the famed South African fighter pilot, Group Captain A. G. Malan dso dfc at a wartime charity function.

11 With the Miles Gemini, VR-GGG, in Malaya, immediately after leaving the RAF.

12 Learoyd poses with two members of a visiting ENSA concert party.

13 An ex-CO of 83 Squadron, Roderick Learoyd (right) attending a squadron reunion at RAF Scampton.

14 Wing Commander R. A. B. Learoyd vc (left) talking with HM the Queen Mother at a bi-annual reunion of VC and GC-award winners in London. At right is Brigadier the Rt Hon Sir John Smyth, Bt vc mc mp, Chairman of the VC Association then.

15 Nicolson in the cockpit of his 72 Squadron Gloster Gladiator, early 1939.

16 Standing on the wing of a 72 Squadron Spitfire, circa late 1939.

17 Hawker Hurricanes and pilots of 249 Squadron at North Weald in April 1941.

18 Nicolson convalescing from his injuries, November 1940 (2nd from right. At left of group is Flying Officer N. 'Fanny' Orton DFC, a veteran of the French campaign in May–June, 1940.

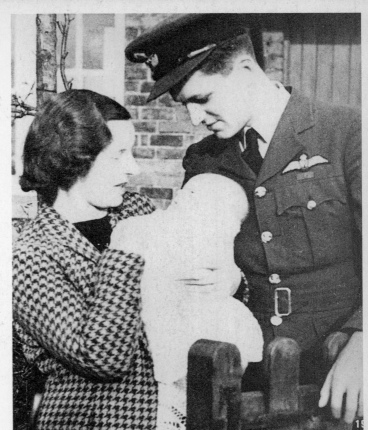

19 With his wife Muriel and their newly-born son, James Gavin Nicholson, October 1940.
20 Wing Commander E. J. B. Nicholson VC DFC (2nd from right) with Group Captain G. L. Cheshire VC DSO DFC (far right) at a Viceregal Garden Party at New Delhi, India, late 1944. Others, from left, are Naik Nand Singh VC, the Rajah of Faridkot, and General Auchinleck.

24. Hannah

21 John Hannah VC in the dorsal WOP/AG's turret of an 83 Squadron Hampden bomber, 1940.
22 and 23 Hannah, while convalescing from his burns at Rauceby RAF Hospital, Lincs, receives a telegram announcing his VC award.
24 Douglas A. E. Hayhurst, DFM.
25 George James and his wife Joyce, 6 April 1940, their wedding day.
26 The burned-out under-gunner's compartment of Hampden P1355 from which George James was lucky to escape alive.

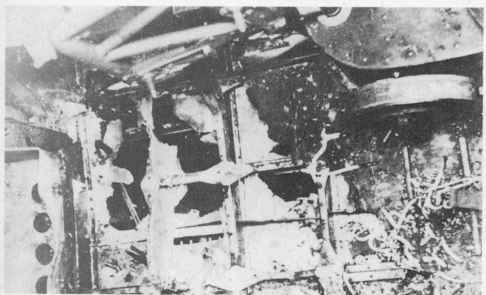

27 Sergeant John Hannah vc and Pilot Officer C. A. Connor dfc at a Buckingham Palace Investiture, 10 October 1940.
28 A section of John Hannah's charred compartment in Hampden P1355.

29 Scampton VCs — John [Ha]nnah VC shakes hands with [...]A. B. Learoyd VC at the airfield [wh]ich both flew from on their [aw]ard-winning sorties, 1940.
30 Mrs Janet Hannah (seat-[ed]) and her three daughters, [loo]king through 83 Squadron's [his]tory photo albums at RAF [Sc]ampton on 6 May 1967; the [dat]e on which Mrs Hannah pre-[sen]ted her late husband's bronze [cro]ss to his old unit.

29

30

31 Bristol Beaufort torpedo bomber, with its torpedo tucked under its belly.
32 Bristol Beauforts of 22 Squadron at dispersal.

26. Edwards

33 Wing Commander Hughie Idwal Edwards DFC, 1941.   [*453*]
34 Low-level view of a Bremen factory complex, taken during the attack of 4 July 1941.

35 Hughie Edwards (left) and his navigator, about to board a 105 Squadron DH Mosquito bomber, 1942.

36 Return from another mission. Edwards' Mosquito 'shuts down' after a bombing sortie.

37 Edwards (bare-headed, facing) and his navigator (left) discuss their recent sortie with Wing Commander Roy Ralston DSO AFC DFM (right) and another officer.

38 Edwards (left), now a Group Captain, with Group Captain W. D. David CBE DFC AFC at AHQ, Ceylon (Kandy) in late 1944.
39 Air Commodore Hughie Edwards at a Veterans Reunion in Australia, 1968.

40 'Jimmy' Ward vc as a child, with his mother.
41 Ward, aged 18, with one of his many aero-models, late 1937.

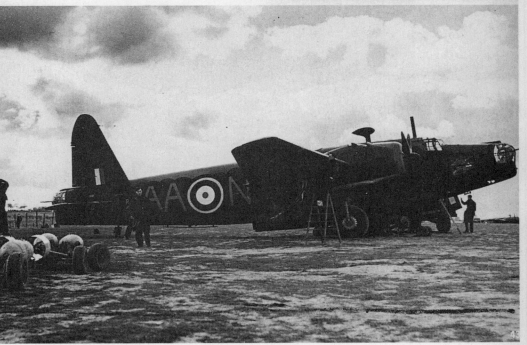

42 Sergeant J. A. Ward VC RNZAF.
43 Vickers Wellington of 75(NZ) Squadron at RAF Feltwell, early 1941.

44 View of Wellington, L7818, AA-R, of 75 (NZ) Squadron, showing the various holes in the skin fabric punched by Ward as he attempted to dowse an engine fire at 13,000 ft, 7/8 July 1941.

45 'Jimmy' Ward vc (centre figure) with his crew, 75 (NZ) Squadron, Feltwell, 1941.

46 Ward, in August 1941, broadcasting for the BBC radio in London.

28. Scarf

47 'John' Scarf (right) undergoing flying training at 9 FTS, Thornaby in July 1936.
48 Scarf (left) indulging one of his great loves, sailing, in an off-duty period, circa 1936.

49 Personnel of A Flight, 62 Squadron, at RAF Cranfield, 1938. Scarf is seated, third from right.
50 'John' Scarf tucked tightly in the nose of an Avro Anson of 206(GR) Squadron at Bircham Newton, 1937.

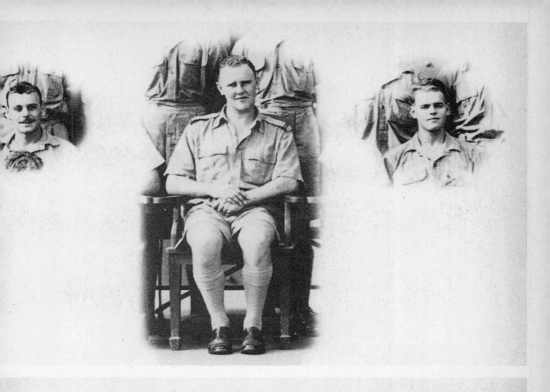

51 Scarf (centre) with Flight Sergeant 'Paddy' Calder (left) and Flight Sergeant Cyril Rich (right) : [461]
the crew of Blenheim L1134 on 9 December 1941. Photo taken at RAF Tengah, 1940.

52 Bristol Blenheim I, L1134, PT-F of 62 Squadron RAF, taxying towards take-off point at Tengah,
Singapore in February 1941 during the unit's move of base to Alor Star, Kedah Province, Malaya.
It was this aircraft in which 'John' Scarf VC made his ultimate flight.

53 Alor Star airfield, Kedah Province, Malaya, 1940, viewed from the south. Note surrounding jungle, swamp and rice paddy fields.

54 Singora airstrip, Malaya under Japanese occupation late 1941. Items 1 to 4 are various Japanese aircraft, wrecked or damaged; Item 5 is part of a tented accommodation area part-destroyed by Allied attacks.

55 Eugene Esmonde as a Flying Officer, RAF in the 1930 aerobatic team formed by 43 Squadron.

56 Eugene Esmonde in Imperial Airways uniform.

57 FAA aircrew of 825 Squadron decorated for their part in the *Bismarck* search. From left: Lieutenant P. D. Gick DSC; Lieutenant-Commander Eugene Esmonde DSO; Sub-Lieutenant V. K. Norfolk DSC; P. O. Johnson DSM. Behind them are Fairey Swordfish of HMS *Ark Royal*.

29. Esmonde

30. Nettleton

[464] 58 John Dering Nettleton vc as a first-year cadet on the South African training ship *General Botha*, 1931.

59 John Dering and his wife Betty (nee Havelock) after their wedding in Lincoln on 17 July 1942.

60 Avro Lancaster B1, L7578 in which Nettleton and his crew trained briefly for the Augsburg attack. Though marked KM-B, it was in another 'B-Baker' (R5508) that Nettleton actually flew the Augsburg mission.

The text on the memorial marker reads:

777646 SGT. B. D. MOSS. R.A.F
R64540 F/SGT. A. E. ROSS. R.C.A.F
918988 SGT. B. G. SEAGOE. R.A.F
1199025 SGT. J. H. HACKETT. R.A.F
1268146 SGT. R. L. TRUSTAM. R.A.F
42580 FL.T. R. R. SANDFORD. R.A.F
80067 P.O. H. A. P. PEALL. R.A.F
932122 SGT.G.W. J. HADGRAFT. R.A.F
777701 SGT. P. J. VERTNER. R.A.F
962127 SGT. R. E. WING. R.A.F
17. 4. 42

61 Nettleton's crew shortly after the Augsburg raid. Standing, left–right: L. H. Mutter, F. H. Harrison, C. S. C. McClure, D. N. Huntley. Seated left–right: P. A. Dorehill, J. D. Nettleton, D. O. Sands, C. F. Churchill.

62 The mass French grave for members of Sandford's and Beckett's crews. Crew members not mentioned on the marker include Beckett, Sergeant A. J. Harrison, Flying Officer Georie, and Flight Sergeant Law.

63 Some of the survivors. From left: Squadron Leader D. J. Penman DSO DFC, Sergeant D. N. Huntley DFM, Pilot Officer Desmond Sands DFC, Brendan Bracken (Minister of Information), Flight Lieutenant B. R. W. Hallows DFC, Sergeant R. P. Irons DFM and Squadron Leader J. D. Nettleton VC.

64 Nettleton VC (left) and Squadron Leader Whitehead DFC.
65 Wing Commander John Dering Nettleton VC.

31. Manser

66 Leslie Thomas Manser VC.
67 A rare, informal photo of Leslie Manser.

68 Avro Manchester 1 bomber.
69 Pilot's seat and controls in
an Avro Manchester.

70 Cyril Manser (brother of the VC) presenting Leslie Manser's cross to OC 50 Squadron, RAF at Waddington on 31 May 1965.
71 At the VC presentation ceremony on 31 May 1965 were members of Manser s crew, Wing Commander R. M. Horsley DFC AFC, Flight Lieutenant R. J. Barnes DFC, ex-Flight Lieutenants B. W. Naylor and A. Mills ; with (at far left) Leslie Randle, Manser's nephew and himself the son of Captain J. Randle VC.

72 'Ron' Middleton VC RAAF.

73 Short Stirling I bomber of 149 Squadron at Mildenhall, Suffolk, 1942.
74 Flight Sergeant Leslie Anderson Hyder DFM, second pilot to Ron Middleton on his last sortie.
75 Sergeant Harold Wray Gough DFM, rear air gunner in Middleton's crew.
76 George Reicher Royde (left) and Norman Skinner, navigator and wireless operator respectively in Middleton's crew.

74

75

76

[472] 77 The burial of Rawdon Hume Middleton, VC, RAAF in St John's Church, Beck Row, Mildenhall on 5 February 1943, with full ceremonial honours.
78 Middleton's body lying 'in state' at RAF Mildenhall on 4 February 1943, with fellow squadron air crews standing honour guard.

34. Newton

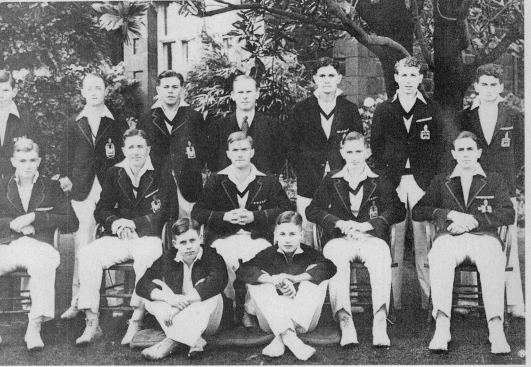

79 'Bill' Newton under training as a pilot, poses for the Press . . .
80 William Ellis Newton VC, RAAF (far right, centre row seated) in 1936 as a member of the Melbourne Grammar School Cricket XI.

81 W. E. Newton VC, RAAF with his step-brothers Captain Lindsay Newton, AIF and Surgeon-Lieutenant (D) J. E. Newton IRAN.
82 'Bill' Newton, when an instructor at No 2 SFTS, Wagga, NSW in 1941.
83 Newton, then a flying instructor at 2 SFTS, Wagga, NSW, studying an English publication.

84 and 85 Respectively, the starboard and port fuselage insignia of Douglas Boston III, A28-15, [475]
DU-Q of 22 Squadron, RAAF in which Newton flew many of his operational sorties.

86 Douglas Boston III, A28-3, DU-Y of 22 Squadron, RAAF in which Flight Lieutenant W. E.
Newton vc was shot down on his ultimate sortie.

35. Trent

[476] 87 Leonard Trent (centre) with Jack Edwards (left, later killed in action in France) and Roy Max, at their 'Wings' graduation at Wigram, NZ, 1938.

88 and 89 Trent as an operational pilot with 15 Squadron (Fairey Battles) in France, late 1939.

90 Lockheed Ventura, EG-J, *'Joybelle'* of 487 (NZ) Squadron.

91 Some of the 487 Squadron crews who participated in the Amsterdam raid of 3 May 1943. From left: Flying Officer O. Foster, G. W. Brewer, Squadron Leader L. H. Trent, Squadron Leader Turnbull, Wing Commander G. J. Grindell, AFC, Flight Lieutenant L. B. Taylor, Flying Officers Church, T. A. Penn, S. Cosha, S. Gabites. Behind them a squadron Ventura bomber, sporting a bomb log of 16 operational sorties completed.

36. Gibson

92 Pre-1939 group of 83 Squadron officers at Scampton, in Mess Dress. Gibson is seated, second from right, and immediately behind him, standing, is Squadron Leader (now MRAF Sir,) Dermot Boyle.
93 83 Squadron group, Scampton, early 1940. Standing, left–right: Harrison, Sylvester, Craig, Kernaghan, Guy Gibson, Johnson and Haydon. Seated: Mulligan, Pitcairn-Hill and Ross — these latter three later being skippers of three of the Hampdens which raided the Dortmund–Ems Canal on 12 August 1940, in which Flight Lieutenant R. A. B. Learoyd 'won' his VC.

94 William Rothenstein portrait of Guy Gibson DFC in August 1940.

95 Guy Gibson (centre front) with the crews of 106 Squadron in early 1942, Coningsby, Lincolnshire.
96 Gibson (in shirtsleeves) with his personal Lancaster crew on 106 Squadron, 1 September 1942
at Coningsby. From left: ?, Hutchinson, Gibson, Ruskell, Olwen and Jordan.

97 Guy Gibson (1) with Group Captain 'Gus' Walker DSO DFC.
98 Gibson and his crew climb into Lancaster AJ-G, ED932, 617 Squadron for the 'Dams Raid'.
From left: Trevor-Roper, Pulford, Deering, Spafford, Hutchinson, Gibson and Taerum.

99 HM King George VI examining photos of the damage to the Moehne and Eder dams, at   [483]
Scampton, 1943. At his elbow is Guy Gibson and Group Captain J. N. H. Whitworth DSO DFC.
  100 Gibson about to autograph a large photographic print of the shattered Moehne dam.
  101 and 103 Wing Commander Guy Penrose Gibson VC DSO DFC.
  102 A post-1945 view of Gibson's Lancaster, ED932, G-George at Scampton. The aircraft was
finally scrapped in July 1947.

37. Trigg

[484]   104 Lloyd Allan Trigg VC RNZAF as an aircrew cadet en route to Canada for pilot training in September 1941.
105 Trigg under training in Canada, 1941.
106 'Wings' – graduation photo on 16 January 1942 at 12 SFTS, Brandon, Manitoba. Lloyd Trigg is second from right, rear row (in peaked cap).

107 The 'undefeated' Anzac rugby team
31 GR School, Charlottetown, Prince
Edward Island, Canada in early 1942;
Trigg is at far left, rear row.
108 Flying Officer Lloyd Allan Trigg,
VC DFC RNZAF.

109 Trigg (second from left) with (left—right) Bennett, Marinovitch and Reynolds of his regular crew, 200 Squadron.
110 Liberator, 'L' of 200 Squadron at St Thomas Mount, India. It was in a similar aircraft that Trigg flew his ultimate sortie.

111 Arthur Louis Aaron vc DFM prior to enlisting in the RAF.   [487]
112 Aaron as an aircrew cadet, RAF.
113 Arthur Aaron under training, 1942 in the USA.
114 Aaron undergoing pilot training at No. 1 BFTS, Terrell, Texas, USA early 1942.

115 Short Stirling bomber of 218 (*Gold Coast*) Squadron, RAF.
116 Aaron's surviving crew at Bone, Algeria shortly after Aaron's death. From left: McCabe, Richmond, Allan Larden, Malcolm Mitchem, and 'Jimmy' Guy.

39. Reid

117 William Reid vc under flying instruction in the USA, early 1942.
118 'Bill Reid (3rd from left, standing) as a cadet pilot, USA, 1942.

[489]

119 Lancaster LM360, QR-O, crashed at Shipdham, displaying just part of its extensive flak damage.
120 Standing, left—right: Les Rolton and Frank Emerson: seated, Jim Norris, 'Bill' Reid vc and Cyril Baldwin – the surviving members of Reid's crew of Lancaster LM360, 61 Squadron.
121 Reid and Rolton.
122 William Reid vc (far left) with some of his 617 Squadron Lancaster crew.

123 Cyril Joe Barton VC as a cadet pilot in the USA, early 1942.

124 Leading Aircraftman C. J. Barton gives a cheerful thumbs-up on completing his first 'solo' flight on 20 February 1942 at Darr Aero Tech, Albany, Georgia, USA.

125 Sergeant C. J. Barton, on leave, 1943.
126 Putting up his crown – Cy Barton 'celebrates' his promotion to Flight Sergeant, 5 September 1943.

127 Newly-commissioned as a Pilot Officer, an ever-smiling Barton.

128 Cy Barton's crew. Left–right, standing: Sergeant J. Kay, Pilot Officer W. Crate RCAF, Cyril Barton, Sergeants L. Lambert and M. Trousdale. Kneeling: Sergeants F. Brice and H. Wood.

129 Barton's Halifax, LK797, LK-E after the crash at Ryhope — the rear fuselage section in which the three surviving crew members were huddled on impact.

41. Jackson

130 Norman Jackson as an AC2 at RAF Halton in March 1940. 3rd from right, second row from   [495]
rear.
131 Warrant Officer N. C. Jackson VC with Group Captain G. L. Cheshire, VC DSO DFC after a
Buckingham Palace investiture on 13 November 1945.

132 Andrew Mynarski shortly after
enlistment in the RCAF, 1941.

133 Mynarski after qualification as a WAG (Wireless Oper
Air Gunner), RCAF.

134 Flying Officer Art de Breyne RCAF, pilot of Mynarski's crew on 419 (Moose) Squadron.

135 Flying Officer George Brophy RCAF, rear air gunner of Mynarski's crew.

136 Mynarski's crew. From left: Flying Officer George Brophy, Pilot Officer William Kelly, Flight Sergeant Roy Vigars, Flying Officer Art de Breyne (skipper), Andrew Mynarski, Pilot Officer John Friday, and Flying Officer Arthur Body. 410 (Moose) Squadron, RCAF, Middleton St George, 1944.

[497]

43. Hornell

137 David Hornell as a cadet at 12 EFTS, Goderich, Ontario, 1941 in front of a Fleet Finch II trainer (No. 4581).

138 162 Squadron RCAF crew at Camp Maple Leaf, Reykjavik, Iceland on 14 June 1942. Left–right, front: Sergeants F. St Laurent, D. Scott, Flying Officer G. Campbell, Flight Sergeant I. J. Bodnoff. Rear, left–right: Flying Officers F. W. Lawrence, S. Metheson, Flight Lieutenant D. E. Hornell, Squadron Leader W. F. Poag.

139 Camp Maple Leaf, Reykjavik, Iceland, June 1944. From left: Donald Scott, B. C. Denomy,   [499]
S. R. Matheson, David Hornell, Graham Campbell.
140 and 141 Two views of Hornell's Canso, 9754 of 162 Squadron RCAF – taken at RCAF Station,
Yarmouth, Nova Scotia in mid-1943; the aircraft in which Hornell made his last patrol.

142 Retouched photo of the moment when Hornell and his surviving crew members were retrieved from their dinghy.

143 PB2B-2 Catalina, Serial JZ841, named in honour of David Hornell vc at its hand-over ceremony to the RAAF on 2 March 1945 at Boeing's Sea Island Plant, Vancouver. This aircraft saw service as A24-360 with 43 Squadron RAAF, but was finally disposed of in 1952.

44. Cruickshank

144 and 145 Flight Lieutenant J. A. Cruickshank VC RAF.   [501]

146 *U-347* under fire as Cruickshank attacked, 17 July 1944.
147 John Cruickshank signs his autograph.

45. Bazalgette

148 Ian Bazalgette (in Army uniform, seated 3rd from right) at Cranwell, September 1941, for pilot training and transfer to the RAF.

149 Ian Bazalgette (far left) and his crew on 635 Squadron, PFF. From left: Bazalgette, Goddard, Hibbert, Godfrey, unidentified air gunner (replaced on the final sortie by Flight Sergeant Leeder, RAAF), Cameron, and Turner. Doug Cameron had also been a member of Pilot Officer R. H. Middleton vc's last crew.

[503]

150 Summer camp for the Oxford University Air Squadron at Ford, 1938. Leonard Cheshire is 4th from left; centre is the chief instructor, Wing Commander F. L. B. Hibbert, with Squadron Leader P. Cracroft.   [505]

151 Cheshire signs the aircraft log, before a flight in the Hawker Hart trainer in background.

152 The fuselage of Whitley bomber, P5005, 'N-Nuts' of 102 Squadron, which Cheshire flew back from Cologne; thereby 'earning' his first DSO award.

153 Cheshire with his Halifax bomber crew on 35 Squadron, Linton-on-Ouse.

154 Cheshire as commander of 76 Squadron at Middleton St George. The extra 'ring' on his shoulder flaps was 'added' by a wartime press photographer, 'promoting' him to Group Captain . . .

155 Cheshire (right) with Group Captain P. C. Pickard DSO DFC (left) and Squadron Leader W. W. Blessing DSO DFC at a Palace investiture.

156 Flight Lieutenant Colin Keith Astbury DFC RAAF (left) toasts Cheshire on the award of the latter's Victoria Cross.

47. Lord

157 David Lord, as a newly-promoted Sergeant pilot, just after joining 31 Squadron at Lahore,   [507]
India in October 1939.
    158 David Lord (in tunic) on 12 May 1942 – the day he was commissioned as a Pilot Officer – on
31 Squadron.

159 Discussing the next air-drop. Lord (right) and the officer commanding 31 Squadron, Wing Commander W. H. Burbury DFC AFC (left) 1943.

160 Pilot Officer Richard Edward Medhurst, second pilot David Lord on 19 September 1944. He was just 19 years of age.

161 Flight Lieutenant Harry King, navigator on Lord's last sortie, and the only surviving crew member.

162 Flying Officer Alexander ('Alec') Forbes Ballantyne, Lord's wireless operator, seen here as a Warrant Officer prior to receiving his commission.

163 David Lord's parents, uncle, and brother Flight Lieutenant (later, Wing Commander) F. E. Lord AFC at the posthumous VC investiture, 18 December 1945.

48. Palmer

164 Squadron Leader Robert Anthony Maurice Palmer VC DFC RAF.
165 Avro Lancaster on its bomb run during a daylight sortie, 1944.

166 July 1970 — when surviving members of George Thompson's crew reunited to present a painting of their Lancaster to 9 Squadron, then at Akrotiri, Cyprus. From left: Wing Commander Dick (OC 9 Squadron), R. F. 'Harry' Denton, W. N. Hartshorn, H. 'Taffy' Price, E. 'Ted' Kneebone, and R. F. H. Goebel.

167 The parents of George Thompson VC, with Wing Commander R. L. Lamb RAF on 30 June 1972 at Kinross Secondary School, Scotland. The occasion was a presentation to the school of a model VC 10 (donated by 10 Squadron, RAF) as the George Thompson VC Dux Award Trophy, and to unveil the plaque in background.

50. Swales

[512] 168 'Ted' Swales and his crew on the morning of 23 February 1945. Swales (top figure), Dodson (in front of Swales) ; left–right, standing : Dudley Archer, Bennington, Wheaton. Front, left–right : Leach, Bourne, Goodacre.

169 Target view of Volkel airfield on 3 September 1944, from Lancaster PB120, 'P', 582 Squadron, PFF, piloted by Lieutenant E. Swales.

170 The scene over Pforzheim on the night of 23/24 February 1945, viewed from 12,500 feet.

171 Robert Hampton Gray with his sister Phyllis and their parents.   [513]
172 First leave, with his mother, 1941.
173 R. H. Gray, VC DSC RCNVR.
174 Informal view of Robert Gray, believed when serving with 789 Squadron, FAA, 1942.

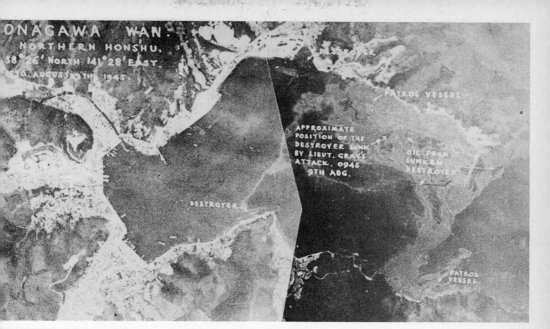

ONAGAWA WAN.
NORTHERN HONSHU.
38°26' NORTH 141°28'EAST.
AUGUST 9TH 1945.

PATROL VESSEL

APPROXIMATE
POSITION OF THE
DESTROYER SUNK
BY LIEUT. GRAY'S
ATTACK. 0945
9TH ABG.

OIL FROM
SUNKEN
DESTROYER

DESTROYER

PATROL
VESSEL

RMI 8J14. 10 Aug 45. 0640(9) K20.163mm. ONANAGAWA WAN.

175 Group of FAA pilots. R. H. Gray is third from left, standing. [515]
176 R. H. Gray (centre foreground, with peaked cap) in June 1943, when 877 Squadron, FAA
were 'working up' at Port Reitz.
177 877 Squadron group in Nairobi, May 1943. Gray is centre left, smiling at camera.
178 Overlap mosaic photograph of Onagawa Wan on 9 August 1945.
179 Scene at Onagawa Wan on the morning following Robert Gray's ultimate sortie, when aircraft
from HMS *Formidable* returned to 'finish the job'. View is from the north-east approach.

180 REUNION. Five surviving air VCs gather at the Dorchester Hotel, London on 11 February 1953 to attend the following day's premiere of the film *Appointment in London*. From left: Wing Commander R. A. B. Learoyd VC, Group Captain L. H. Trent VC DFC, Air Commodore H. I. Edwards VC DSO DFC, Flight Lieutenant W. Reid VC, and Warrant Officer N. C. Jackson VC. Here all were listening to a tape recorded by Group Captain G. L. Cheshire VC DSO DFC, at that date a patient in the Midhurst Sanatorium.

BIBLIOGRAPHY

Bibliography

The number of literary references, large and small, to airmen awarded the Victoria Cross published in the past sixty years is a daunting paper mountain facing the avid air historian. Much of such reference has been brief, inaccurate in varying degrees, or simply written for sensational effect. In the course of virtually a life-time's research into aviation history I have read and consulted thousands of books, articles, features and pure reference works, but the following list represents – in my view – the most essential 'short list' for any historian seeking background knowledge on the subject of this volume. Not all are entirely accurate in factual data – indeed, what author, myself included, can truly claim to produce a book of 100 per cent accuracy? It would be a brave, or entirely conceited man or woman who made any such claim. Nevertheless, sheer experience of the overall subject leads me to suggest that these are the more important reference sources to be necessarily consulted by those seeking in-depth and broader accounts of the air VC's, their deeds, and their contemporary scene. The discerning student will quickly note that of these titles only eight were actually written by VC-winners; the remainder were compiled by latter-day historians and authors.

BIOGRAPHIES

VCs of the Air	J. F. Turner; Harrap, 1960
The Air VCs	W. E. Johns; J. Hamilton, 1935
Winged Warfare	W. A. Bishop VC; Doran NY, 1918
Courage of the early morning	W. A. Bishop, Jr; Heinemann, 1966
Five Years in the RFC	J. T. B. McCudden VC; Aeroplane & General, 1918
McCudden VC	C. C. H. Cole; W. Kimber, 1967
Captain Ball VC	W. A. Briscoe & B. R. Stannard; H. Jenkins, 1918
The Boy Hero	W. A. Briscoe; Milford, 1920
Captain Albert Ball VC DSO	R. H. Kiernan, J. Hamilton, 1933
Albert Ball VC	C. Bowyer; W. Kimber, 1977

King of Air Fighters	J. I. T. Jones; Nicholson & Watson, 1934
Ace with One Eye	F. Oughton & V. Smythe; Spearman 1963
Mannock vc	F. Oughton; Spearman, 1966
Hawker vc	T. M. Hawker; Mitre Press, 1965
Sailor in the Air	R. Bell-Davies vc; P. Davies, 1967
Winged Diplomat	P. R. Reid; Chatto & Windus, 1962
Fighting in the Air	L. W. B. Rees vc; 1917
Kaleidoscope	L. Rhodes Moorhouse; A. Barker, 1960
Canada's Fighting Airmen	G. A. Drew; MacLean, 1930
Enemy Coast Ahead	G. P. Gibson vc; M. Joseph, 1946
Bomber Pilot	G. L. Cheshire vc; Hutchinson, 1943
Cheshire vc	R. Braddon; Evans Bros, 1954
No Passing Glory	A. Boyle; J. Collins, 1955
The Face of Victory	G. L. Cheshire vc; Hutchinson, 1961
Eugene Esmonde, VC, DSO	C. Bowyer; W. Kimber, 1983
Warneford, vc	M. Gibson; FAA Museum, 1979
Mick – Maj E. Mannock	J. Dudgeon; Hale, 1981
Venturer Courageous – Trent, vc	J. Sanderson; Hutchinson, 1983
A Formidable Hero – Lt R. H. Gray	S. Howard; Canav Books, 1987
Seven VCs of Stonyhurst College	Kirby/Walsh; THCL Books, 1987
Register of the Victoria Cross	THIS ENGLAND, 1988
Against the Odds – L. W. B. Rees	W. Williams; Bridge Books, 1989
The Airship VC – W. L. Robinson	R. Rimell; Aston Pubns, 1989
A Medal for Life	L. Bills; Spellmount Ltd, 1990
Nicolson, vc	P. Mason; Geerings, 1991
Middleton, vc	S. Bill; S. Bill, 1991

ASSOCIATED TITLES

The Bronze Cross	F. Gordon Roe; Gawthorn, 1945
For Valour	K. Hare-Scott; P. Garnett, 1949
For Valour	E. Leyland; Ward, 1960
The Victoria Cross, 1856-1964	Sir J. Smyth vc; Muller, 1965
VC Battles of the Second World War	C. E. Lucas-Phillips; Heinemann, 1973
The VC and the DSO	Sir O'Moore Creagh & E. M. Humphris; Standard Book Co., 1924

Official Catalogue of the RUSM	Lt-Col Sir A. Leetham, 1924
The Victoria Cross	Lt-Col R. Stewart; Hutchinson, 1928
VC heroes of the War	G. A. Leask; Harrap, 1917
War in the Air, 6 Vols, Maps, Apps	W. Raleigh & H. A. Jones; OUP, 1923-1934
Official History of Australia in the War, 1914-18, Vol VIII	F. M. Cutlack; Angus & Robertson, 1923
German Air Raids on Great Britain, 1914-18	Capt J. Morris; Sampson Low, 1925
Raiders Approach	H. T. Sutton; Gale & Polden, 1956
Zeppelins over England	K. Poolman; Evans Bros, 1960
Sixty Squadron	D. W. Warne & W. Young; Eurasia, 1966
Tiger Squadron	J. I. T. Jones; R. H. Allen, 1954
Air Fighter's Scrapbook	J. I. T. Jones; Nicholson & Watson, 1938
Fighter Pilot	'McScotch' (W. McLanachan); Newnes, 1935
Sagittarius Rising	C. Lewis; P. Davies, 1936
Scarlet & Khaki	T. B. Mason; J. Cape, 1930
From Sea to Sky	Sir A. Longmore; G. Bles, 1946
In the Side-Shows	W. Wedgewood Benn; Hodder & Stoughton, 1919
Fights and Flights	C. R. Samson; E. Benn, 1930
Offensive Patrol	N. Macmillan; Jarrolds, 1973
The Red Air Fighter	M. von Richthofen; Aeroplane, 1918
Royal Air Force 1939-45, 3 Vols	H. St G. Richards & D. Richards, HMSO, 1952-54
RAAF Official History, 4 Vols	Australian War Memorial, 1954
RNZAF Official History, 3 Vols	War History Branch NZ, 1953
The RCAF Overseas, 3 Vols	Oxford Press, 1944-45
The Dam Busters	P. Brickhill; Evans Bros, 1951
Channel Dash	T. Robertson; Evans Bros, 1958
The Fire was Bright	L. Kark; Macmillan, 1943
Bomber Squadrons of the RAF	P. J. R. Moyes; Macdonald, 1964
Strike Hard, Strike Sure	R. Barker; Chatto & Windus, 1963
Thousand Plan	R. Barker; Chatto & Windus, 1965
The Ship-Busters	R. Barker; Chatto & Windus, 1957
The Restless Sky	C. E. Kay; G. Harrap, 1964
New Zealanders in the Air War	A. W. Mitchell; G. Harrap, 1945

No 5 Bomber Group .... W. J. Lawrence; Faber & Faber, 1951

Tail Gunner .... R. C. Rivaz; Jarrolds, 1944

So Few .... D. Masters; Eyre & Spottiswoode, 1941 (Revised 1945)

Wings over the Somme .... G. H. Lewis; W. Kimber, 1976

For Valour .... Southdown Press, Melbourne, 1976

Log Book of   *After the Battle* Magazine, 1976
   Wg Cdr G. P. Gibson vc .... (Crown Copyright)

Bomber Group at War (5 Grp) .... C. Bowyer; Ian Allan, 1981

Operation Chastise .... J. Sweetman; Jane's, 1982

The Men Who Breached the Dam .... A. Cooper; Wm Kimber, 1982

Torpedo Airmen .... R. Nesbit; Wm Kimber, 1983

The VCs of Wales & Welsh Regiments . W. Williams; Bridge Books, 1984

Bristol Blenheim .... C. Bowyer; Ian Allan, 1984

Fighter Pilots of the RAF, 1939-45 ...... C. Bowyer; Wm Kimber, 1984

Tales from the Bombers .... C. Bowyer; Wm Kimber, 1985

Bomber Barons .... C. Bowyer; Wm Kimber, 1983

Men of Coastal Command, 1939-45 ..... C. Bowyer; Wm Kimber, 1985

The Wellington Bomber .... C. Bowyer; Wm Kimber, 1986

The Augsburg Raid .... J. Currie; Goodall Pubns, 1987

JOURNALS, MAGAZINES, PERIODICALS

Royal Air Force Quarterly, 1930-50, Various
Flight, 1912-46, Various
Aeroplane, 1912-47, Various
Roundel (RCAF), Various
Cross & Cockade (USA) Society Journal, Various
Cross & Cockade (Gt Britain) Society Journal, Various
Canadian Aviation Historical Society Journal, Various
Popular Flying, Various 1932-39
Flying, Various 1937-39
Air Stories, Various 1934-40
Air Mail (RAFA Quarterley), Various
Aircraft Illustrated Extra, Various 1970-74

Photo Credits

PART ONE

523

(*Pages 165-212*)

10   Via D. Furze, Esq
11   Author
12   Late S. V. Sippe
13   Lt-Col T. M. Hawker, MC
14   Lt-Col T. M. Hawker, MC
15   Lt-Col T. M. Hawker, MC
16   Lt-Col T. M. Hawker, MC
17   Author
18   Lt-Col T. M. Hawker, MC
19   Lt-Col T. M. Hawker, MC
20   Lt-Col T. M. Hawker, MC
21   P. J. Liddell, Esq
22   P. J. Liddell, Esq
23   P. J. Liddell, Esq
24   P. J. Liddell, Esq
25   P. J. Liddell, Esq
26   P. J. Liddell, Esq
27   P. J. Liddell, Esq
28   P. J. Liddell, Esq
29   E. Read, Esq
30   Author
31   C. J. Chabot, Esq
32   Imperial War Museum/A. J. Insall, Esq
33   Ministry of Defence (Air)
34   C. J. Chabot, Esq
35   Author
36   Captain L. Bell-Davies, RN
37   Author
38   RCAF Official
39   Via author
40   Via B. Hansley, Esq
41   Captain L. Bell-Davies, RN
42   Author
43   Wg Cdr G. H. Lewis, DFC
44   Author
45   Author
46   RAF Cranwell
47   RAF Cranwell
48   C. Rust, Esq
49   Author

50	OC 39 Squadron, RAF
51	Author
52	Imperial War Museum
53	Lt-Col T. M. Hawker, MC
54	C. Rust, Esq
55	Author
56	S. Mottershead
57	AVM G. H. White, CBE
58	Author
59	OC RAF Finningley
60	P. McNamara, Esq
61	P. McNamara, Esq
62	P. McNamara, Esq
63	C. Schaedel, Esq
64	P. McNamara, Esq
65	RAAF Official
66	RAAF Official
67	P. McNamara, Esq
68	Public Archives of Canada
69	Public Archives of Canada
70	P. Rosie, Esq
71	P. Rosie, Esq
72	K. M. Molson Collection
73	Author
74	Public Archives of Canada
75	Mrs L. B. Anderson
76	Mrs L. B. Anderson
77	Late Capt E. L. Foote, MC
78	Mrs L. B. Anderson
79	Mrs L. B. Anderson
80	Mrs F. Thornhill
81	Author
82	Mrs F. Thornhill
83	Public Archives of Canada
84	RCAF Official
85	Public Archives of Canada
86	Author
87	Public Archives of Canada
88	Public Archives of Canada
89	Author

(Pages 165-212)

90 Author
91 S. St Martin Collection
92 F. Selinger, Esq
93 F. Selinger, Esq
94 F. Selinger, Esq
95 Ministry of Defence (Air)
96 Via C. C. H. Cole, Esq
97 Via C. C. H. Cole, Esq
98 Author
99 Ministry of Defence (Air)
100 Via C. C. H. Cole, Esq
101 P. Rosie, Esq
102 Via C. C. H. Cole, Esq
103 Via C. C. H. Cole, Esq
104 Late J. C. Rorison, Esq
105 Air Cdre F. M. F. West, VC, OBE, MC
106 Via G. Reath, Esq
107 Air Cdre F. M. F. West, VC, OBE, MC
108 Author
109 Author
110 Public Archives of Canada
111 Captain J. Brown, RN Ret'd
112 Public Archives of Canada
113 Via E. A. Harlin, Esq
114 Public Archives of Canada
115 Public Archives of Canada
116 K. M. Molson Collection
117 Public Archives of Canada
118 Public Archives of Canada
119 Public Archives of Canada
120 Via D. R. Neate, Esq
121 Via D. R. Neate, Esq
122 S. St Martin Collection
123 S. St Martin Collection
124 Via G. S. Leslie
125 Dr F. K. Mitchell
126 Dr F. K. Mitchell
127 Dr F. K. Mitchell
128 Dr F. K. Mitchell
129 Author

419 SAAF Official
420 Public Archives of Canada

(Pages 437-516)

No. 1 Flt Lt R. M. Gray, RAF Ret'd
2 Flt Lt R. M. Gray, RAF Ret'd
3 OC 12 Squadron, RAF
4 Author
5 Author
6 Grp Capt Jackson, RAF Ret'd
7 P.N.A. Ltd
8 Graphic Photo Union
9 British Official
10 Wg Cdr R. A. B. Learoyd, VC
11 Wg Cdr R. A. B. Learoyd, VC
12 Wg Cdr R. A. B. Learoyd, VC
13 RAF Scampton
14 Author
15 Author
16 British Official
17 Imperial War Museum
18 Imperial War Museum
19 Wg Cdr F. M. Smith, DFC
20 Imperial War Museum
21 Graphic Photo Union
22 Author
23 Author
24 D. A. E. Hayhurst, DFM
25 D. A. E. Hayhurst, DFM
26 RAF Scampton
27 Author
28 RAF Scampton
29 RAF Scampton
30 RAF Scampton
31 Author
32 Imperial War Museum
33 British Official
34 Imperial War Museum
35 Imperial War Museum
36 Imperial War Museum

37	Imperial War Museum
38	Imperial War Museum
39	Private copyright
40	W. H. Ward, Esq
41	W. H. Ward, Esq
42	W. H. Ward, Esq
43	Fox Photos
44	RNZAF Official
45	RNZAF Official
46	W. H. Ward, Esq
47	Mrs K. Hair
48	Mrs K. Hair
49	Mrs K. Hair
50	Mrs K. Hair
51	Mrs K. Hair
52	Imperial War Museum
53	Mrs K. Hair
54	Imperial War Museum
55	*Flight International*
56	Imperial Airways Ltd
57	P.N.A. Ltd
58	A. W. Hamilton, Esq
59	A. W. Hamilton, Esq
60	Hawker-Siddeley Aviation
61	Imperial War Museum
62	A. W. Hamilton, Esq
63	P.N.A. Ltd
64	A. W. Hamilton, Esq
65	Imperial War Museum
66	C. Manser, Esq
67	C. Manser, Esq
68	Author
69	Imperial War Museum
70	OC 50 Squadron
71	OC 50 Squadron
72	RAAF Official
73	Author
74	Imperial War Museum
75	Imperial War Museum
76	Imperial War Museum

(*Pages 437-516*)

77   D. Cameron, DFM
78   D. Cameron, DFM
79   RAAF Official
80   Melbourne Grammar School Records, Australia
81   Dr L. Newton
82   F. Folmer, Esq
83   F. Folmer, Esq
84   RAAF Official
85   RAAF Official
86   RAAF Official
87   Grp Capt L. H. Trent, VC, DFC
88   Grp Capt L. H. Trent, VC, DFC
89   Grp Capt L. H. Trent, VC, DFC
90   Central Press
91   Author
92   Author
93   Wg Cdr R. Anderson, DSO, DFC
94   Ministry of Defence (Air)
95   Author
96   Wg Cdr F. Ruskell, DFC
97   Author
98   Imperial War Museum
99   RAF Scampton
100 OC 617 Squadron
101 Imperial War Museum
102 Author
103 Imperial War Museum
104 Mrs N. Trigg
105 Mrs N. Trigg
106 Mrs N. Trigg
107 Mrs N. Trigg
108 Mrs N. Trigg
109 Mrs N. Trigg
110 J. A. Griffin, Esq
111 Dr F. E. Aaron
112 Dr F. E. Aaron
113 Dr F. E. Aaron
114 Dr F. E. Aaron
115 Imperial War Museum
116 Via R. Barker, Esq

117	W. Reid, VC
118	W. Reid, VC
119	W. Reid, VC
120	W. Reid, VC
121	W. Reid, VC
122	Mrs C. Maidment
123	Mrs C. Maidment
124	Mrs C. Maidment
125	Mrs C. Maidment
126	H. C. Wood, Esq
127	Mrs C. Maidment
128	F. C. Brice, DFM
129	H. C. Wood, Esq
130	Private copyright
131	P.N.A. Ltd
132	Public Archives of Canada
133	Public Archives of Canada
134	Public Archives of Canada
135	Public Archives of Canada
136	Public Archives of Canada
137	Public Archives of Canada
138	Public Archives of Canada
139	Public Archives of Canada
140	C. Vincent, Esq
141	C. Vincent, Esq
142	Public Archives of Canada
143	D. Vincent, Esq
144	Imperial War Museum
145	Author
146	Imperial War Museum
147	Imperial War Museum
148	Private copyright
149	D. Cameron, DFM
150	*Flight International*
151	*Flight International*
152	Imperial War Museum
153	Imperial War Museum
154	Author
155	Imperial War Museum
156	Author

(*Pages 437-516*)

157 Author
158 31 Squadron Association
159 31 Squadron Association
160 Flt Lt H. A. King
161 Flt Lt H. A. King
162 Flt Lt H. A. King
163 Keystone
164 British Official
165 Author
166 OC 50 Squadron
167 OC RAF Leuchars
168 D. P. D. Archer, DSO, DFC
169 Author
170 Author
171 Public Archives of Canada
172 Public Archives of Canada
173 Public Archives of Canada
174 Public Archives of Canada
175 Public Archives of Canada
176 Wg Cdr P. Markham
177 Wg Cdr P. Markham
178 Public Archives of Canada
179 Public Archives of Canada
180 L.N.A. Ltd.

Index

(Place names are indexed separately following the general index)

INDEX OF PLACE NAMES